THE HISPANO HOMELAND

THE HISPANO HOMELAND

by
Richard L. Nostrand

UNIVERSITY OF OKLAHOMA PRESS
NORMAN AND LONDON

By Richard L. Nostrand

Los Chicanos: Geografía Histórica Regional (México, D.F.., 1976)
(edited with Ellwyn R. Stoddard and Jonathan P. West) *Borderlands Sourcebook: A Guide to the Literature on Northern Mexico and the American Southwest* (Norman, 1983)
(edited with Sam B. Hilliard) *The American South* (Baton Rouge, 1988)
The Hispano Homeland (Norman, 1992)

For Mom and Dad
To Whom I Am Most Indebted

This book is published with the generous assistance of the Wallace C. Thompson Endowment Fund, University of Oklahoma Foundation.

Chapter 1 is based upon Richard L. Nostrand, "Hispano Cultural Distinctiveness: A Reply," *Annals of the Association of American Geographers* 74 (1984): 164–69. Chapters 4 and 8 are based on Richard L. Nostrand, "El Cerrito Revisited," *New Mexico Historical Review* 57 (1982): 109–22, and "The Century of Hispano Expansion," *New Mexico Historical Review* 62 (1987): 361–86.

Map 10.1 is by Alvar W. Carlson. All other maps and figures 9.2 and 10.3 are by Richard L. Nostrand.

Nostrand, Richard L. (Richard Lee), 1939–
    The Hispano homeland / by Richard L. Nostrand.
       p. cm.
    Includes bibliographical references (p.   ) and index.
    ISBN 0-8061-2414-8 (alk. paper)
      1. Mexican Americans—New Mexico—History. 2. Human geography—New Mexico. 3. New Mexico—Geography. 4. Pueblo Indians.
    I. Title.
    F805.M5N67   1992
    978.9'0046872073—dc20   91-50867
                                         CIP

Text and jacket design by Bill Cason.

CONTENTS

List of Illustrations vi

List of Maps vii

List of Tables ix

Preface xi

1. The Hispano 3
2. Formative Colonization 26
3. Indian Articulation 49
4. Contiguous Expansion 70
5. Anglo Intrusion 98
6. Peripheral Attraction 131
7. Mexican Immigration 156
8. Village Depopulation 169
9. Urbanization 192
10. The Homeland 213

Appendix, Spanish Ancestry Data in the 1980 Census 233

Bibliography 239

Index 263

ILLUSTRATIONS

1.1 Penitente crucifixion, San Mateo, 1888   12
1.2 Spanish American children, Questa, 1943   18
3.1 Acoma village, 1941   56
4.1 Sheep with a shepherd, Cabezon Peak, 1890s   90
5.1 Jewish merchants, Las Vegas plaza, about 1880   113
5.2 Chloride, Sierra County, 1890s   118
5.3 El Cerrito appearance, 1941 and 1980   125
6.1 McAlpine sawmill near Catskill, about 1893   142
6.2 Section gang workers in New Mexico, 1943   151
8.1 Illfeld warehouse, Las Vegas, 1904   173
8.2 El Cerrito villagers, 1941   174
8.3 Martínez family leaving Cordova, 1939   176
8.4 El Cerrito villagers, 1980   178
9.1 Goat Hill in Pueblo, Colorado, 1900   194
9.2 Hispano urban hierarchy, 1850–1980   204
10.1 Córdova gristmill near Vadito, 1967   221
10.2 Quintana horno, El Cerrito, 1980   222
10.3 Homeland-shaping processes and outcomes   230

MAPS

1.1 The Borderlands context   5
1.2 Census enumerators in the Homeland, 1900   21
2.1 Spain in the sixteenth century   28
2.2 New Spain in the sixteenth century   30
2.3 New Mexico in 1680   33
2.4 Stronghold in 1790   40
3.1 Pueblo Indians about 1600   51
3.2 Missions staffed with Franciscans, 1601–80   52
3.3 Pueblo villages in New Mexico, 1832   58
3.4 Pueblo Indians in New Mexico Territory, 1900   60
3.5 Nomad Indians in New Mexico Territory and
     southwestern Colorado, 1900   66
4.1 Hispano farm/stock occupations in the
     Homeland, 1900   74
4.2 Hispano expansion to the east, 1790s–1880s   78
4.3 Hispano expansion to the north, 1790s–1880s   83
4.4 Hispano expansion to the west, 1790s–1880s   89
4.5 Hispano expansion to the south, 1790s–1880s   94
5.1 New Mexico's trade linkages, 1821–46   102
5.2 The Inland (intruder zone), 1850   104
5.3 Roman Catholic clergymen in the Homeland,
     1850 and 1900   111
5.4 Anglo occupations in the Homeland, 1900   115
5.5 Anglo numbers in the Homeland, 1900   120
5.6 The Inland (intruder zone), 1900   121
5.7 Anglo and Indian numbers in the Homeland,
     1980   126
5.8 The Inland (intruder zone), 1980   128
6.1 Hispano connections before 1870   133

6.2	California-born Hispanos in the Homeland, 1900	138
6.3	Hispano "Anglo" occupations in the Homeland, 1900	141
6.4	The Outland, 1900	146
6.5	Hispano connections, 1900–30	149
6.6	Hispano proportions, 1980	152
7.1	"Mexican" numbers, 1900	160
7.2	"Mexican" numbers, 1980	166
8.1	El Cerrito setting, 1980	172
8.2	El Cerrito occupance, 1940 and 1980	180
8.3	Case study villages, 1980	182
9.1	Pueblo, Colorado, 1988	200
9.2	Hispano numbers, 1900	207
9.3	Hispano numbers, 1980	210
10.1	Long-lots in the lower Chama Valley, 1915	218
10.2	Hispano areal growth, 1680–1980	227
10.3	Hispano relative decline, 1850–1980	229
10.4	Hispano Homeland, 1900	231

TABLES

1.1	Distinctively Hispano surnames	9
1.2	Hispano cultural distinctiveness	14
1.3	Homeland population composition, 1850	20
1.4	Homeland population composition, 1900	22
1.5	Homeland population composition, 1980	23
3.1	Pueblo Indians in New Mexico Territory, 1900	61
3.2	Nomad Indians in New Mexico Territory and southwestern Colorado, 1900	67
5.1	Anglos in the Homeland, 1850	106
6.1	Hispanos in California, 1850	136
6.2	Old Town–New Town populations, New Mexico Territory, 1900	144
6.3	Hispano nativity in the Homeland, 1900	145
A.1	Responses to Spanish categories 200–12, New Mexico and Colorado, 1980	235
A.2	Spanish/Hispanic responses, fifteen states, 1980	236

PREFACE

FOR SOME twenty-five years two borderlands have held my attention, those between history and geography and those between the United States and Mexico. From the first of these areas of overlap evolved historical geography, my subdiscipline of special interest, and from the second sprang Americans of Spanish-Indian or Mexican descent, my major research focus. This study of the Hispano Homeland is rooted in both borderlands, for historical geography is my method of inquiry, and Spanish Americans or Hispanos are my subject matter.

My purpose in this book is to interpret the Hispanos' experience geographically. My thesis is that Hispanos, in interplay with Pueblo Indians, nomad Indians, Anglos, and Mexican Americans, shaped and reshaped a Homeland. I analyze how this happened through eight geographical processes which are identified in the titles to chapters 2 to 9. From that analysis are two outcomes: internal zones or a morphology into which the Hispano region is carved, and the idea that because Hispanos adjusted to their natural environment, stamped it with their cultural impress, and created from both their natural environment and their cultural landscape a sense of place, their region is much more than their locale—it is their Homeland.

For my general interest in Latin America I thank my father, who, as cultural attaché in the American embassy, moved his family to Lima, Perú, for two and one-half years after World War II. What focused my Latin American interest on the United States–Mexico Borderlands in part was Carey McWilliams's book, *North from Mexico*. For cultivating my interest in historical geography, especially the historical geography of the United States, I am indebted to Howard H. Martin (1892–1966), my undergraduate professor at the University of Washington who introduced me to historical geography; D. W. Meinig (1924–), my graduate mentor at Syracuse University whose brand of historical geography I so deeply appreciate; and J. E. Spencer (1907–84), my graduate advisor at UCLA who instilled in me an appreciation for the "Berkeley" approach to geography.

When I began my research on Hispanos in 1976, the most recent original census schedules available from the National Archives, because of a seventy-two year confidentiality policy of the Bureau of the Census, were for 1900. I spent much of the next three years reviewing on microfilm some one million names, sorting out Hispanos, Mexican Americans, Pueblo Indians, nomad Indians, and Anglos and reconstructing their geographical patterns in 1900. The 1850 manuscript census schedules were analyzed for a second cross-section, and, as discussed in the Appendix, I was able to buy from the Bureau of the Census hard copy of a special computer run of ancestry data for 1980, which is used for a third cross-section. In 1980 I lived for two months in the village of El Cerrito, New Mexico. Little did I know how much I would rely upon El Cerrito for examples as my knowledge about the village continued to increase during many subsequent visits. By 1980 the outline for this book had taken shape.

While undertaking this study I benefited from the help of many people. For critical comments on parts of the manuscript and for other supportive activities I am especially indebted to Alvar W. Carlson, Fray Angélico Chávez, Lawrence E. Estaville, Jr., Charles F. Gritzner, Thomas D. Hall, Clark S. Knowlton, D. W. Meinig, Frances Anne Nostrand, Howard L. Nostrand, David A. Sandoval, Marc Simmons, Henry J. Tobias, and David J. Weber. To the "regulars" on my annual field trips to El Cerrito, Timothy G. Anderson, Brock J. Brown, and J. Douglas Heffington, and to those who facilitated our stays, John Burns, Joe C. de Vaca, Heidi Lanstra, and Jack Lanstra, I am deeply appreciative. Archivists Kent Carter and Phillip E. Lothyan of the Federal Archives and Records Centers in Fort Worth and Seattle, respectively, extended me many courtesies, and I received expert guidance from J. Richard Salazar and Alvin E. Regensberg of the New Mexico State Records Center and Archives in Santa Fe. The University of Oklahoma Research

Council, Norman Campus, generously provided funds to purchase a special computer run of ancestry data for 1980 and to support other phases of the project. Amy Forwoodson and Valene Bartmess were my skillful typists. And, of course, I thank my wife, Susan Emily Nostrand, whose love has so enhanced my life and who doubled as my critic and field assistant.

Parts of three chapters have already been published. For permission to reproduce these in modified form I thank Stanley D. Brunn, editor of the *Annals* of the Association of American Geographers, for use of "Hispano Cultural Distinctiveness: A Reply," vol. 74 (1984): 164–69, in chapter 1; and Richard W. Etulain, acting editor of the *New Mexico Historical Review*, for use of "The Century of Hispano Expansion," vol. 62 (1987): 361–86, in chapter 4 and for use of "El Cerrito Revisited," vol. 57 (1982): 109–22, in chapter 8. Maps 10.2 and 10.3 appeared in a guest focus box in C. Langdon White, Edwin J. Foscue, and Tom L. McKnight, *Regional Geography of the United States and Canada*, seventh edition (Englewood Cliffs, N.J.: Prentice-Hall, 1992), vignette 3-21. Permission to reproduce figures was secured as follows: Southwest Museum, Los Angeles (Fig. 1.1); Library of Congress, Washington, D.C. (Figs. 1.2, 6.2); Maxwell Museum of Anthropology, University of New Mexico, Albuquerque (Fig. 3.1); Special Collections, General Library, University of New Mexico, Albuquerque (Fig. 4.1); Western History Department, Denver Public Library (Figs. 5.1, 9.1); Museum of New Mexico, Santa Fe (Figs. 5.2, 6.1, 8.1, 8.3); National Archives, Washington, D.C. (Figs. 5.3, 8.2); the Johns Hopkins University Press (Map 10.1); and the *Annals* of the Association of American Geographers (Fig. 10.1).

My treatment of Spanish-language words may seem inconsistent without some explanation of the guidelines that were followed. Spanish-language words have been italicized (*fresada*) and accents and tildes have been retained (*décima, rivajeños*). The surprisingly large number of Spanish-language words that, according to *Webster's Third New International Dictionary*, have been absorbed into English (from acequia to vega) have been treated as English words. In Spanish given names and surnames, all accents and tildes have been retained (Hernán Cortés, Juan de Oñate), even though many persons in the present century have dropped these diacritical marks (Luis

Aragón). In Spanish place-names, following conventional practice, accents have been dropped for places located in the modern-day United States (Belen, Santa Fe), yet they have been retained for places located in Mexico or Spain (Santa Bárbara, León). On the other hand, tildes on place-names found in the United States have been retained (Doña Ana, Española) because they usefully indicate pronunciation.

My use of the term "Hispano," without an explanation, may also seem strange and even downright anachronistic. "Hispano," over the last quarter century, has been increasingly used to refer to the New Mexico-centered "Spanish" or "Spanish American" people. To emphasize their evolution as a people and to underscore the continuity of their culture, I have used "Hispano" beginning with the reconquest of New Mexico in 1693. That "Hispano" suggests a Spanish ancestry, that "Spanish American" or "Spanish" came to prevail only relatively recently and for complicated reasons, that Hispanos were once "Mexicans," and that today, when speaking in Spanish, Hispanos refer to themselves as *mexicanos*, are all discussed in chapter 1.

If this book helps in some small way to clarify the Hispanos' geographical "roots" and, thereby, to increase their self-knowledge and heighten their awareness of their heritage, then I shall feel gratified.

RICHARD L. NOSTRAND

Norman, Oklahoma

THE HISPANO HOMELAND

CHAPTER 1

✤ ✤ ✤

THE HISPANO

ONE AUGUST afternoon in 1969, in the far West Texas town of Muleshoe, I stopped to visit with the Roman Catholic priest. The Muleshoe priest was on vacation, and the Reverend Robert Hammond from across the New Mexico state line in Tucumcari was filling in. As we talked, Father Hammond pointed to a front-page headline in the local newspaper. "Look at that," he exclaimed, "the Spanish-speaking people of Muleshoe are preparing to celebrate Mexican Independence Day. In my thirty-five years at Saint Anne's Church in Tucumcari never once have I even heard of the event."[1] For me, Father Hammond's unexpected observation forcefully reinforced the point that New Mexico–centered Spanish Americans or Hispanos are different from Mexican Americans who live elsewhere in the Southwest.

THE BORDERLANDS CONTEXT

Hispanos and other Americans of Spanish-Indian or Mexican descent are by and large products of the "Borderlands," that zone in the Western Hemisphere where the sharply contrasting Latin and Anglo cultures overlap. Initially, people possessing a basically Latin culture advanced into New Spain's distant northern frontier, not as the result of one grand march but through thrusts that were separated in time and space. Ancestors of the Hispanos led the way by settling New Mexico's upper Rio Grande basin late in the sixteenth century. In the

---

[1] The Reverend Robert Hammond, interview with author while temporarily at Immaculate Conception Church, Muleshoe, Texas, August 22, 1969. Tucumcari, which is partly Hispano, and Muleshoe, which is partly Mexican American, are only ninety miles apart.

eighteenth century other Latin people colonized present-day Arizona, Texas, and California (Map 1.1a). The four outpost clusters that came to exist were remote from Mexico's Central Plateau, and they were isolated from each other. Not surprisingly, subcultures developed, at least among the Hispanos, Tejanos, and Californios, yet greater numerical strength and a long head start enabled the Hispano subculture to develop most fully.[2]

Many of the earliest colonists going to New Mexico were Spaniards, a Mediterranean people who probably included Moorish and other admixtures and who were both *peninsulares* (born in Spain) and creoles (born in New Spain). Many were also mestizos, the products of Spanish and Indian miscegenation in New Spain. Some were Indians, and a few were mulattos. In New Mexico these various peoples and those who came later intermixed with the sedentary and peaceful Pueblo Indians, but in time they seem to have intermixed to an even greater degree with the warlike and nomadic Indians. Children from nomad Indian bands were used as servants in Hispano households, and they and their mixed descendants were assimilated into the Hispano population. In a racial sense, this nomad Indian strain to a degree differentiates Hispanos from Mexican Americans in the Borderlands.[3]

In 1821, newly independent Mexico opened her northern frontier to non-Mexicans, and in varying degrees the three colonial subcultures were encroached upon by westward-moving "Anglos," as non-Indians and non–Spanish/Mexican Americans are known in the Southwest. Large numbers of Anglos from the southern United States quickly overran Texas, and the small Tejano population was largely engulfed by 1836 (Map 1.1b). California lured only a small number of hide and tallow traders to its littoral in the Mexican period, but when gold was discovered in 1848, Anglos immediately inundated Californios in Northern California, and thirty years later a real estate "boom of the '80s" had the same result

---

[2] The existence of these subcultures, each nestled in its separate political entity, in part explains Herbert E. Bolton's plural use of the term *borderlands* in *The Spanish Borderlands: A Chronicle of Old Florida and the Southwest*, Chronicles of America Series, vol. 23: 120–295.

[3] Fray Angélico Chávez, "Rejoinder" [to Nostrand's "Hispano Cultural Distinctiveness: A Reply"], *Annals of the Association of American Geographers* 74 (1984): 170–71.

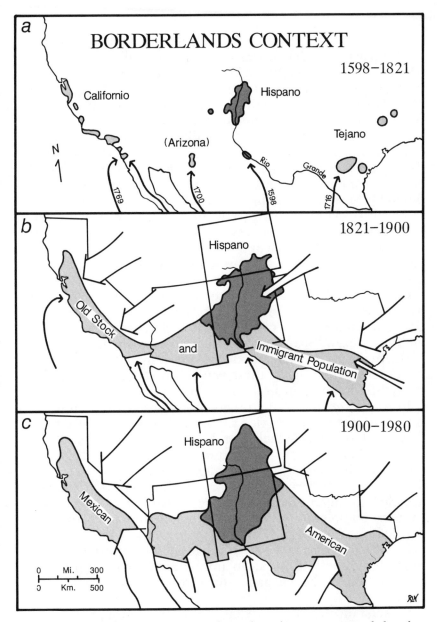

Map 1.1 The Borderlands context. These three frames are intended to be suggestive: widths of arrows and areas settled are approximations. Mexican immigration is relatively modest in the nineteenth century; Anglo intrusion continues in the twentieth century. Pueblo and nomad Indians have been omitted.

in Southern California. Lacking California's gold and Texas' position astride a dynamically expanding Anglo frontier, New Mexico in the nineteenth century attracted only modest numbers of Anglo trappers, traders, soldiers, and others, and by 1900 Hispanos still constituted two-thirds of the population of their New Mexico–centered Homeland.[4]

Mexico paid a heavy price for allowing Anglos to overlap into her northern frontier. In 1836, Anglo Texans and some Tejano allies revolted and created an independent Texas. Texas was then annexed to the United States in 1845, the first event whereby Mexicans became Mexican Americans. The annexation of Texas in part triggered the Mexican War, which resulted in Mexico ceding New Mexico and California to the United States. Mexicans in those two areas thus became Mexican Americans in 1848. The present-day political geography of the Borderlands was completed in 1853 with the Gadsden Purchase, the final event to make Mexican Americans of those Mexicans resident in the northern frontier. Altogether, then, through annexation, conquest, and purchase, more than eighty-thousand Spanish-speaking frontiersmen, most of them New Mexicans, became Mexican Americans.[5] And as a result of contact with Anglos, these people by midcentury were already becoming bicultural and bilingual.

In the latter half of the nineteenth century the number of migrants going from Mexico to this politically realigned territory was but a trickle each year. Following the Mexican Revolution of 1910, however, their numbers grew to floodlike proportions. The major immigrant destinations in the twentieth century were Texas, Arizona, and California (Map 1.1c). A sizable immigrant-derived Mexican American population came to completely submerge the old Tejano and Californio populations. However, New Mexico, as well as southern Colorado, which Hispanos meanwhile had colonized, attracted only modest numbers of Mexican immigrants. Once again, in a relative sense, the Hispano subculture remained relatively intact.

Understandably, these twentieth-century immigrants from

---

[4] Richard L. Nostrand, "The Hispano Homeland in 1900," *Annals of the Association of American Geographers* 70 (1980): 384.

[5] Richard L. Nostrand, "Mexican Americans circa 1850," *Annals of the Association of American Geographers* 65 (1975): 383, 390.

Mexico, and in lesser degrees their descendants, had mixed political loyalties. The ideology of the Revolution of 1910, moreover, engendered in them a pride in their *Mexicanidad*—which means in part that they extolled their Indianness and rejected their Spanishness. By contrast, Hispanos in New Mexico, as citizens of the United States since 1848, in the twentieth century have had undivided political loyalties. And as explained below, they identify with their Hispanidad.[6]

Out of the context of the Borderlands, then, come the Hispanos—an indigenous people who evolved from the oldest and largest of the Spanish colonial subcultures and who were relatively unsubmerged by Mexican immigrants and, until the twentieth century, by Anglos. Because of sustained contact with Anglos, Hispanos, like their Mexican American brethren, are a bicultural and bilingual people. Because of their peculiar origins, however, they are different culturally from the larger immigrant-derived Mexican American population. The result is something of a Hispano enclave embedded in the midst of overlapping Latin and Anglo peoples.

A DISTINCTIVE SUBCULTURE

Two reasons, then, explain why Hispanos are culturally distinctive among members of the larger southwestern minority. First, their ancestors came earlier and, with exceptions, more directly from Spain to the Borderlands than did those of Tejanos, Californios, or, of course, of Mexican immigrants, and certain archaic Iberian cultural forms that do not seem to exist elsewhere in the Borderlands remain peculiar to them. This reason can be styled *early diffusion and preservation*. Second, after initial colonization, Hispanos were isolated from outside contact, and their numbers increased—factors that fostered certain indigenous attributes. *Independent invention or modification*, then, is the second reason.

Both reasons explain the distinctiveness of the Hispanos' Spanish language. Juan de Oñate and his colonists took a largely Castilian dialect of Spanish with them to New Mexico in 1598.[7] As the several Spanish dialects evolved in Spain and

[6] Marc Simmons, "Rejoinder" [to Nostrand's "Hispano Cultural Distinctiveness: A Reply"], *Annals of the Association of American Geographers* 74 (1984): 169–70.

[7] Aurelio M. Espinosa, *Studies in New Mexican Spanish*, University of New Mexico Bulletin, Language Series, vol. 1, no. 2, whole no. 53: 53.

her empire, many now-archaic forms were preserved in isolated New Mexico. "I believe there is no modern Spanish dialect, either in Spain or America," wrote Aurelio M. Espinosa, "that can surpass the New Mexican in archaic words and expressions, constructions and sounds."[8] In his glossary of New Mexican Spanish, F. M. Kercheville noted, as archaic words, *truje* (rather than *traje*) for "I brought" and *facer* (rather than *hacer*) for "to do" or "to make." After colonization certain colloquialisms also came to characterize New Mexican Spanish. Kercheville gave as examples *cajete* (as opposed to *baño*) for "tub" and *puela* (as opposed to *sartén*) for "frying pan."[9]

The Hispanos' Spanish surnames are also distinctive, but for reasons that are much less clear. Hispanos have surnames such as García, González(s), López, Martínez, and Sánchez that are among the most common in the Spanish-speaking world, yet they also have surnames like Abeyta, Archuleta, Barela, Maestas, and Tafoya that differentiate them from the larger southwestern minority, Puerto Ricans, and Cubans. The onomatologist Robert W. Buechley identified thirty-nine such "distinctively *New Mexican names*" (Table 1.1). It seems unlikely that these peculiar Hispano surnames are found only among Hispanos because a given source area in Spain was unique to them. Thirty-five of Buechley's thirty-nine names apparently either originated in or are most frequently found in some ten diverse parts of Spain. Rather, it is likely that families with these names converged in Mexico, whence some members joined the New Mexico colonization enterprise but not the subsequent Borderlands entradas.[10] More easily explained

[8] Aurelio M. Espinosa, *The Spanish Language in New Mexico and Southern Colorado*, Historical Society of New Mexico, no. 16: 8–9. Early colonization and subsequent isolation also preserved an archaic French in French Canada.

[9] F. M. Kercheville and George E. McSpadden, *A Preliminary Glossary of New Mexican Spanish, together with Some Semantic and Philological Facts of the Spanish Spoken in Chilili, New Mexico*, University of New Mexico Bulletin, Language Series, vol. 5, no. 3, whole no. 247: 17, 26, 43. *Truje* was also listed under words that have suffered phonetic changes (p. 39). McSpadden noted that *puela* may be an archaism (p. 99). The use of *puela*, Jacob Ornstein noted, is one of many examples separating Spanish spoken north of Socorro from that spoken south of it, linguistic evidence that the Homeland ends at about Socorro; Jacob Ornstein, "The Archaic and the Modern in the Spanish of New Mexico," *Hispania* 34 (1951): 137–38. See also Rubén Cobos, *A Dictionary of New Mexico and Southern Colorado Spanish*, 24, 139, 154.

[10] Robert W. Buechley, "Characteristic Name Sets of Spanish Populations," *Names* 15 (1967): 58, and table 3. These names are low in abundance outside New Mexico,

Table 1.1   Distinctively Hispano Surnames

Abeyta	Archuleta	Bustos
Acuña	Armijo	Chávez
Anaya	Baca	Córdova
Apodaca	Barela	Durán
Aragón	Benavides	Gallegos
Griego	Madrid	Ortiz
Herrera	Maestas	Pacheco
Jaramillo	Mares	Padilla
Lucero	Montaño	Quintana
Luján	Montoya	Romero
Saavedra	Tapia	
Salazar	Trujillo	
Sandoval	Valdez	
Serna	Vigil	
Tafoya		

SOURCE: Robert W. Buechley, "Characteristic Name Sets of Spanish Populations," *Names* 15 (1967), table 3.

are the Hispanos' distinctive given names. Some, such as Esquipula, Secundino, Onofre, and Belarmino, are archaisms. Others, for example Miterio, Ologia, and Abrelio, derive from phonetic changes in New Mexico.[11]

Most of the Hispanos' folklore—for example, their tales, ballads, riddles, proverbs, nursery rhymes, myths, and super-

West Texas, or Arizona, and they have a "specific locality base" in their " 'Spanish-American' rather than 'Mexican' heritage" (p. 58). The thirty-nine-member name set is not exhaustive, as Buechley derived it from 306 Spanish surnames found in California. William W. Winnie, Jr., inferred that differences in Spanish source areas might explain regional variations in southwestern Spanish surnames; "The Spanish Surname Criterion for Identifying Hispanos in the Southwestern United States: A Preliminary Evaluation," *Social Forces* 38 (1959–60): 364. The Spanish source areas for thirty-five of Buechley's thirty-nine surnames were determined in Richard D. Woods and Grace Álvarez-Altman, *Spanish Surnames in the Southwestern United States: A Dictionary*, 1–152. No locational information was available for four of the surnames. As evidence that some remain in Mexico, Buechley found thirty-one of his thirty-nine Hispano surnames in some small number in the México, D.F., telephone directory, and twenty-five in the Guadalajara directory ("Characteristic Name Sets," table 1). The presence of Hispano surnames in the State of Chihuahua, where a Tafoya was once governor, may stem from the time following the Pueblo Revolt of 1680 when some Hispanos, forced to retreat to the Paso del Norte District, continued farther south into Chihuahua. Some of the Hispano surnames are also found in the Southwest; all thirty-nine exist in California.

[11] Arthur Leon Campa, *Spanish Folk-Poetry in New Mexico*, 10. Emiterio, Eulogia, and Aurelio are the root names; Espinosa, *Spanish Language*, 36.

stitions—diffused from Iberia to New Mexico, where it was preserved in an oral tradition. Comparative studies undertaken by Aurelio M. Espinosa suggest that this Spanish peninsular folklore found among Hispanos is like that found elsewhere in Spanish America. In isolated New Mexico, however, certain indigenous folk materials developed. At least two folk plays are New Mexican in origin: *Los Comanches* and *Los Tejanos*, which celebrate Hispano victories over the dreaded Comanches in about 1777 and the hated Texans in 1841. Some of the more than two hundred alabados (religious hymns) collected by Juan B. Rael in New Mexico and Colorado were definitely composed by Hispanos, as were certain folk songs gathered by John David Robb. During the nineteenth century the *décima*, so named for its four ten-verse stanzas that follow a four-verse introduction, was at its height in popularity, and many were composed for all occasions and then sung in monotonous tone by the ubiquitous village *trovadores*. After the arrival of Anglos, some troubadours turned to writing bitter yet good-natured protest folk poetry, some if it in the form of the *décima*.[12]

The most celebrated of the Hispanos' folk arts, the carved and painted religious images known collectively as "*santos*," was neither some archaic craft that was preserved in New Mexico nor an indigenous creation. It stemmed instead from an attempt by local *santeros* in the century before the American takeover to satisfy a need for such icons by imitating seventeenth-century-style *santo* prototypes fashioned in Spain

---

[12] Aurelio M. Espinosa, *The Folklore of Spain in the American Southwest: Traditional Spanish Folk Literature in Northern New Mexico and Southern Colorado*, ed. J. Manuel Espinosa, 30, 63. At least 75 percent of the 518 folktales gathered by Juan B. Rael in northern New Mexico and southern Colorado were of Old World origin; *Cuentos Españoles de Colorado y Nuevo México (Spanish Folk Tales from Colorado and New Mexico): Spanish Language Originals with English Summaries* 1: 2. Aurelio M. Espinosa, *Los Comanches: A Spanish Heroic Play of the Year Seventeen Hundred and Eighty*, University of New Mexico Bulletin, Language Series, vol. 1, no. 1, whole no. 45: 1–46; and Aurelio M. Espinosa and J. Manuel Espinosa, "The Texans: A New Mexican Spanish Folk Play of the Middle Nineteenth Century," *New Mexico Quarterly Review* 13 (1943): 299–308; Juan B. Rael, *The New Mexican Alabado with Transcription of Music by Eleanor Hague*, Stanford University Publications, University Series, Language and Literature, vol. 9, no. 3: 18–19; John Donald Robb, *Hispanic Folk Music of New Mexico and the Southwest: A Self-Portrait of a People*, 7; Arthur L. Campa, *A Bibliography of Spanish Folk-Lore in New Mexico*, University of New Mexico Bulletin, Language Series, vol. 2, no. 3, whole no. 176: 5–8; Arthur L. Campa, "Protest Folk Poetry in the Spanish Southwest," *Colorado Quarterly* 20 (1971–72): 360.

and Mexico.[13] However, because this art form flourished only in the New Mexico portion of the Borderlands, and because a growing literature on the topic associates Hispanos with the craft, *santos* may be regarded as another culturally distinctive Hispano attribute. In New Mexico *santos* were made as flat or modeled panels often used as altar pieces (*retablos*) and as free-standing statutes (*bultos*). Both were carved from pine or cottonwood, were coated with a white gesso made from native gypsum, and were painted in tempera colors.[14] Many *santos* are now in private hands or in museums, yet some are still venerated in homes and churches and are carried in religious processions, including those of the Penitentes.

The Penitente Brotherhood, a lay Hispano society organized for penance and mutual aid, seems not to have been some archaic institution that was preserved in the upper Rio Grande basin, but whether it evolved in New Mexico about 1800 or diffused to New Mexico about that time is in dispute. Following Bishop Jean Baptiste Lamy's arrival in 1851, the prevailing thought among Catholic clergymen and others was that the Brotherhood derived from the Third Order of Saint Francis founded in 1221; Gaspar Pérez de Villagrá's report that Oñate had scourged himself en route to New Mexico in 1598 seemed to confirm the Third Order's long-standing existence in New Mexico, and it was thought that after the Third Order's introduction, its practices had degenerated into the "bloody flagellations and similar tortures" witnessed by Anglos (Fig. 1.1). Marta Weigle cautiously reaffirmed that Penitentes "likely" evolved from lay interpretations of Franciscanism, particularly the Third Order, in the late eighteenth century. However, this "Franciscan theory of origin" is rejected by Fray Angélico Chávez, who documented that the Brotherhood did not exist anywhere in New Mexico in 1776 yet did exist, at least in

---

[13] José E. Espinosa, *Saints in the Valleys: Christian Sacred Images in the History, Life and Folk Art of Spanish New Mexico*, xii, 4, 61; and George Kubler, *Santos: An Exhibition of the Religious Folk Art of New Mexico*, 4, 6, 7. Although *santos* are not peculiar to New Mexico, archaic symbols nevertheless persist there. Mitchell A. Wilder, for example, pointed out that *santeros* represented images of the Holy Trinity as three identical personages, a Byzantine concept banned by Pope Benedict XIV in 1745; Mitchell A. Wilder and Edgar Breitenbach, *Santos: The Religious Folk Art of New Mexico*, text for plates 49 and 63.

[14] E. Boyd, "The Literature of Santos," *Southwest Review* 35 (1950): 128–40; and José Espinosa's bibliography through 1960 in *Saints in the Valleys*, 101–107. The *santero's* technique is discussed in Wilder and Breitenbach, *Santos*, 24–31.

Fig. 1.1 Charles F. Lummis photographed a Penitente crucifixion at San Mateo in New Mexico's Valencia County on Good Friday (March 30) 1888. The man strapped to the cross did not die. Courtesy Southwest Museum, Los Angeles, California, whose glass plate negative 20,141 (SWM 3294/3292) has been cracked since the photograph was published in Lummis, *The Land of Poco Tiempo* (1893; reprint, Albuquerque: University of New Mexico Press, 1966), 101.

the Santa Cruz area, in 1833 and that after it came to exist, Penitente rites in New Mexico were strikingly similar to those practiced, even to this day, in Seville. From this he inferred that about 1800 the Seville-type institution was transported to New Mexico, probably by way of Mexico, where Penitente activities were undergoing a resurgence.[15]

If, on the one hand, Weigle and her like-minded "Third Order" predecessors are correct, then the Brotherhood is a relatively recent and, to some degree, indigenous development and is therefore a culturally distinctive Hispano attribute. If, on the other hand, Chávez's "late transplant" theory is correct, the Brotherhood, like *santos*, may still be considered as a culturally distinctive Hispano phenomenon, for in all the Borderlands, New Mexico was the "hotbed of penitente-ism," as John G. Bourke expressed it in 1896. Indeed, Lamy, as bishop and then archbishop, was unsuccessful in his attempts to suppress the Brotherhood. His successor, Archbishop Jean Baptiste Sal-

[15] Fray Angélico Chávez, "The Penitentes of New Mexico," *New Mexico Historical Review* 29 (1954): 97–99, 105, 108–12, 115, 117–23; Marta Weigle, *Brothers of Light, Brothers of Blood: The Penitentes of the Southwest,* 26, 37–47, 49.

pointe, finally ordered the society to disband in 1889.[16] Yet the Brotherhood flourished well into the twentieth century before membership finally declined, extremist rites were abandoned or practiced covertly, and the Brotherhood was reinstated by the Catholic Church.[17] Priests today willingly accept invitations to celebrate Mass in Penitente *moradas* (quarters) that are located on the outskirts of many villages.

Several additional attributes which appear to have originated on the indigenous side of the ledger differentiate Hispanos culturally (Table 1.2). For example, the patron saint for Hispanos, as for all persons of Spanish-Indian or Mexican descent, is Our Lady of Guadalupe, but for Hispanos, La Conquistadora, a wooden statue so named after being carved in Spain and taken to New Mexico in 1625, also has great importance. Another example is the heavy use of ground dried chili pepper in many Hispano dishes. Evon Z. Vogt, who was raised in Ramah, New Mexico, observed that he had sampled enough food in Mexico and in the Borderlands to know that Mexican cuisine becomes more *picante* the closer one gets to the international boundary in Mexico, and that it has its greatest chili content in New Mexico. The "extravagant" consumption of chili, noted Josiah Gregg in 1844, was already "truly proverbial." And as Munro S. Edmonson pointed out, the use of chili is an important symbol of Hispano identification. Finally, Hispanos, unlike their larger minority brethren, for the most part reject that which is Mexican, as seen in the nonobservance by many of Mexican Independence Day (September 16) as well as Mexico's Cinco de Mayo holiday and by the fact that most take umbrage at being called "Mexican Americans."[18]

[16] John G. Bourke, "Notes on the Language and Folk-Usage of the Rio Grande Valley," *Journal of American Folk-Lore* 9 (1896): 111. The Penitente Brotherhood did apparently exist in California. A letter and an editor's reply which appeared in the *Los Angeles Star* on March 20, 1852, report that people were "flogging" themselves in a church at San Gabriel in "penance preparatory to Passion week." Scotsman Hugo Reid, a resident of San Gabriel and a reliable source, wrote both the letter and the editor's reply; E. Boyd, "Penitentes in California," *El Palacio* 57 (1950): 372–73. The date and the place raise the possibility that Hispanos introduced the institution to California.

[17] Aurelio M. Espinosa, "Penitentes, Los Hermanos," in *The Catholic Encyclopedia* 11: 636. Reinstatement occurred in 1947; Weigle, *Brothers of Light*, xix.

[18] Fray Angélico Chávez, *La Conquistadora: The Autobiography of an Ancient Statue*, 10; Evon Z. Vogt, professor of anthropology at Harvard University, interview with author, University of Massachusetts, Amherst, October 29, 1970. Arthur L. Campa confirms the greater use of chili north of the Rio Grande in "Chile in New

Table 1.2 Hispano Cultural Distinctiveness

Preserved Archaic Forms (Early diffusion and preservation)	Indigenous Attributes (Independent invention or modification)	Items Less Easily Classified (Relative to the larger minority)
Spanish language	Spanish language	Spanish surnames
Spanish given names	Spanish given names	Santos
Folklore examples	Folklore examples	Penitente Brotherhood
		La Conquistadora
		Chili in food
		Nonobservance of Mexican holidays

SOURCES: See text.

SPANISH ETHNICITY

Why Hispanos reject their Mexican heritage and extoll their Spanishness on the surface seems easily explained. During the long Spanish period (1598–1821) these New Mexicans, noted Ramón A. Gutiérrez, considered themselves "Spaniards," a racial designation that included the mestizo majority. In the Mexican period, Antonio Barreiro noted that the Pueblo Indians still called these New Mexicans "Spaniards." In California, however, where frontier society appears to have been more stratified, only the elite were "Spaniards," and to avoid the discrimination of the elite, the "mixed-bloods," according to Manuel Patricio Servín, either late in the Spanish period or early in the Mexican period began to call themselves "Spaniards."[19] Being "Spaniards" in the eyes of other Spaniards may

---

Mexico," *New Mexico Business Review* 3 (April 1934): 61–63. Josiah Gregg, *Commerce of the Prairies*, ed. Max L. Moorhead, 110. Munro S. Edmonson, who spent a year studying three Hispano communities in west central New Mexico during 1949–50, "was asked rather anxiously whether [he] liked chili on every occasion of [his] first meal with a family, without exception!" Munro S. Edmonson, *Los Manitos: A Study of Institutional Values*, 21. Hispanos' noncelebration of Mexican Independence Day and Cinco de Mayo is noted in Leo Grebler, Joan W. Moore, and Ralph C. Guzmán, *The Mexican-American People: The Nation's Second Largest Minority*, 381. The former event commemorates the day Mexico declared herself free from Spain in 1810; Cinco de Mayo observes an important Mexican victory over the French at Puebla in 1862.

[19] Ramón A. Gutiérrez, "Honor Ideology, Marriage Negotiation, and Class-Gender Domination in New Mexico, 1690–1846," *Latin American Perspectives*, issue 44, vol. 12, no. 1 (Winter 1985): 84–85; Antonio Barreiro, *Ojeada . . .* , reprinted in Lansing B.

have played a role in the origin of the New Mexicans' Spanish ethnicity, but if so, it appears to have been minor compared to being "Spanish" in the eyes of Anglos. In New Mexico, then, the concept of being Spanish seems not to be a holdover of "Spaniard" from the Spanish period, but instead stems from contact with Anglos. The evidence for this comes only in fragments, and what follows contains much conjecture and is at best only a tentative explanation.

In the relatively short but critically important Mexican period (1821–46), two processes were going on simultaneously. First, New Mexico's Hispanos were accepting their being Mexican. They called themselves "Mexicans," and they probably thought of themselves as not different from other Mexicans in Mexico or elsewhere in the Borderlands. Indeed, Antonio Barreiro, while on appointment as Mexico's legal advisor in Santa Fe, promoted Mexican nationalism by organizing the Sixteenth of September celebration (in 1832) and by stating the revisionist Mexican view that earlier "Spaniards" were to be condemned for "oppressing" and "exterminating" the "Ancient Mexicans," who in this case were the Pueblo Indians.[20] The second ongoing process was the arrival of Anglo men. A haughty lot, full of attitudes of self-importance and superiority, these Anglos were generally kind in their feelings toward the women, who they sometimes called "Spanish," but almost universally they viewed the men with contempt and referred to them as "Mexicans."[21] To be Spanish was clearly preferable. Thus, in the brief Mexican period New Mexico's Hispanos and their old-stock brethren elsewhere in the Borderlands faced a unique dilemma: whether to be "Mexican" in the eyes of their countrymen or to be "Spanish" in the eyes of an emerging Anglo elite. "Mexican" was the overwhelming choice.

Bloom, trans. and ed., "Barreiro's Ojeada Sobre Nuevo-Mexico," *New Mexico Historical Review* 3 (1928): 88; Manuel Patricio Servín, "California's Hispanic Heritage: A View into the Spanish Myth," in *New Spain's Far Northern Frontier: Essays on Spain in the American West, 1540–1821*, ed. David J. Weber, 127.

[20] Barreiro, *Ojeada*, 73, 75–76, 89.

[21] James M. Lacy, "New Mexican Women in Early American Writings," *New Mexico Historical Review* 34 (1959): 41, 51; and Beverly Trulio, "Anglo-American Attitudes toward New Mexican Women," *Journal of the West* 12 (1973): 229–30, 239. David J. Weber discussed the background of the unflattering Anglo attitudes in "Stereotyping of Mexico's Far Northern Frontier," in *An Awakened Minority: The Mexican-Americans*, 2d ed., ed. Manuel P. Servín, 18–26.

The American takeover (1846) initiated still a third process—that of becoming "American" politically. This new political label was combined rather quickly with Spanish as "Spanish-American." In California, in an editorial in the Los Angeles newspaper *El Clamor Público*, Californio Francisco P. Ramírez used "Spanish-American" to refer to his fellow Californios in 1856. In New Mexico the same term had caught on at least by 1874. "Spanish-American" may also have been used by Tejanos in Texas. At this early point the Spanish-American label was probably less a real identity than simply a self-referent used by the old-stock population usually when speaking in English. The aim for those who used it was to escape from the subordinate status of being Mexican, and as larger numbers of Mexican immigrants arrived, the aim also became one of disassociating oneself from those who were generally of a lower socioeconomic class.[22]

In New Mexico, the use of "Mexican" declined while that of "Spanish-American" gained momentum. By the 1920s "Spanish-American" was widely entrenched. By the twenties, moreover, "Spanish-American" or simply "Spanish" had come to be much more than a euphemism for avoiding "Mexican"; it was now a genuine ethnic identity with overtones that were cultural and racial. Ruth Laughlin Barker pointed out the irony of the situation: while New Mexicans were cultivating their Spanishness, Mexicans in Mexico were cultivating their Mexicanness, so by the 1920s it was no less insulting to call a Mexican "Spanish" than it was to call a Spanish-American "Mexican."[23] "Spanish American" (with or without the hy-

[22] Leonard Pitt, *The Decline of the Californios: A Social History of the Spanish-Speaking Californians, 1846–1890*, 181. Frances Leon Swadesh cited use of "Spanish-American" by a member of the Board of Indian Commissioners, who was referring to Hispanos; *Los Primeros Pobladores: Hispanic Americans of the Ute Frontier*, 89. The reasons for the use of the term are given in Manuel Gámio, *Mexican Immigration to the United States: A Study of Human Migration and Adjustment*, 129, 209; Carey McWilliams, *North from Mexico: The Spanish-Speaking People of the United States*, The People of America Series, 79, 209.

[23] Erna Fergusson, "New Mexico's Mexicans," *Century Magazine* 116 (1928): 437; and Helen Zunser, "A New Mexican Village," *Journal of American Folk-Lore* 48 (1935): 141. Aurelio M. Espinosa (1880–1958), a lifelong student of the language and folklore of his own Hispano people and a Stanford University professor from 1910 to 1947, wrote, "The Spanish inhabitants of New Mexico and Colorado are descendants of the old Spanish families . . . [that] very rarely intermarried with the native Indian population and are, therefore, in every sense of the word, Spanish"; "Speech Mixture

phen) remained the prevailing self-referent until the 1960s, when it began to lose ground, especially to "Chicano" (Fig. 1.2). However, it continues to be the Hispanos' preferred self-referent and the basis for their ethnic identity. And the extreme to which it is carried is found in some circles where Spanish Americans of the middle and upper classes refer to Spanish Americans of the lower class as "Mexican."[24] "Spanish American" is, of course, used by Hispanos when speaking in English. When speaking in Spanish, Hispanos call themselves *mexicanos*, a term that Arthur L. Campa explained does not mean Mexicans, for those people are *mexicanos de México*, but rather is a somewhat vague term for Hispanos themselves.[25]

In California, meanwhile, the use of "Spanish American" or "Spanish" continued into the twentieth century. Joseph E. Spencer recalled that while he attended the Westside School in San Fernando in the 1920s, to call anyone, whether old stock or immigrant, a "Mexican" was to have a fight on your hands. Except among limited numbers of old-stock Californios in places like Santa Barbara, however, "Spanish" in California has all but disappeared, and the self-referents that prevail today among the descendants of Mexican immigrants are "Mexican American" and "Chicano." In Texas "Spanish" seemingly persisted into the present century among a small pocket of old-stock Tejanos in Nacogdoches—possible evidence of a one-time use of "Spanish" in Texas. However, the prevailing self-referent among the immigrant-derived Texans, at least after World War II, was "Latin American," and today, as in California, it is "Mexican American" or "Chicano."[26] These two

---

in New Mexico: The Influence of the English Language on New Mexican Spanish," in *The Pacific Ocean in History* ed. H. Morse Stephens and Herbert E. Bolton, 410, n. 1. Ruth Laughlin Barker, "Where Americans are 'Anglos,' " *North American Review* 228 (1929): 569.

[24] In Albuquerque in 1972, Joseph V. Metzgar found that *Chicano* was gaining at the expense of *Spanish-American* among young male "Nativos"; "The Ethnic Sensitivity of Spanish New Mexicans: A Survey and Analysis," *New Mexico Historical Review* 49 (1974): 55. Nancie L. González, *The Spanish-Americans of New Mexico: A Heritage of Pride*, 209.

[25] "*Mexicano* in Spanish expresses . . . [for the Hispano] a concept of culture that no other term, not even a translation of the same term, can convey"; Campa, *Spanish Folk-Poetry*, 15–16.

[26] Joseph E. Spencer, professor of geography at UCLA, interview with author, August 27, 1969; Richard L. Nostrand, " 'Mexican American' and 'Chicano': Emerging Terms for a People Coming of Age," *Pacific Historical Review* 42 (1973): 396, 397–99, 404–405.

Fig. 1.2 In the 1940s "Spanish-American" was the prevailing self-referent among Hispanos everywhere. These school children photographed by John Collier in Questa (Taos County) in January 1943, when speaking in English, would have called themselves "Spanish-Americans." Courtesy Library of Congress, photograph LC-USW 3–18139-E.

terms are also the preferred self-referents in Arizona. Throughout the Borderlands, then, the prevailing self-referents and the symbols of an ethnic identity among members of the sizable immigrant-derived population are "Mexican American" and "Chicano."

Thus the Spanish ethnicity of the Hispano is the exception in the Borderlands. And significantly its origin seems to be reactive instead of primordial. This Hispano concept of ethnicity is not easily justified because, although Hispanos are *peculiarly* Spanish culturally, given their preserved archaic and indigenous cultural attributes, they are, as Arthur L. Campa pointed out, no *more* Spanish than anyone else, and they are certainly not Spaniards in a racial sense. Not surprisingly, the pretense of superiority that this Spanish ethnic identity implies offends some Mexican Americans, notably the more militant Chicano element, who declare that the Hispanos' Spanishness is a contrived fantasy heritage and a myth and who, with an eye to political unity, think of all Spanish-speaking people in the Borderlands as members of "La Raza"— one people and one culture.[27] But Hispanos, like any other people, have the right to determine their own philosophical outlook and to choose their own ethnic identity, however legitimate it may or may not be. What seems to have happened is that Hispanos not only exercised this right but also, unlike Californios and perhaps Tejanos, had the demographic "clout" to make it stick.

DEMOGRAPHIC CLOUT

The original census returns for 1850 plus estimates for several gaps in the census give 80,302 Mexican Americans in the Southwest. This is the number of Mexicans who, at least nominally, had just become Mexican Americans. Of this total, 54,394 (67.7 percent) were Hispanos who lived in New Mexico Territory north of the Socorro area (Table 1.3). The 54,394 Hispanos accounted for 90.9 percent of the population in their Homeland—a percentage that, given the steady decline in the number of Pueblo Indians to that point and the fact that the major influx of Anglos was yet to occur, was near the four-century high point. The Mexican American total in the 1850 census is definitely an undercount, and a more realistic figure would be at least 100,000.[28] Yet even an altogether accurate 1850 census would show that the old-stock Hispanos were far

---

[27] Sylvia Rodríguez makes the reactive-primordial distinction and has me coming down heavily on the primordial side in her "The Hispano Homeland Debate," SCCR Working Paper No. 17, Stanford Center for Chicano Research, Stanford University (1986), 9; Arthur L. Campa, *The Spanish Folksong in the Southwest*, University of New Mexico Bulletin, Modern Language Series, vol. 4, no. 1, whole no. 232: 32; Campa, *Spanish Folk-Poetry*, 12–13, 16. The view of Hispanos as members of La Raza is expounded by J. M. Blaut and Antonio Ríos-Bustamante, "Commentary on Nostrand's 'Hispanos' and their 'Homeland,' " *Annals of the Association of American Geographers* 74 (1984): 157–64.

[28] Nostrand, "Mexican Americans," 378–90; 393, n. 29.

Table 1.3   Homeland[a] Population Composition, 1850

	Total	Percent
Hispanos[b]	54,394	90.9
Mexican Americans[c]	370	0.6
Pueblo Indians[d]	3,324	5.6
Nomad Indians[e]	164	0.3
Anglos[f]	1,578	2.6
Homeland	59,830[g]	100.0

SOURCE: U.S. Bureau of the Census, Population Schedules of the Seventh Census [1850].
[a] New Mexico Territory north of the Socorro area (1,600 people in Valencia County's Doña Ana, Las Cruces, and Mesilla were excluded in the analysis).
[b] To facilitate their identity and to emphasize their cultural continuity, the modern term *Hispano* is used anachronistically. Hispanos were identified by their nativity (New Mexico Territory), their "color" (white), and their given names and surnames (Spanish).
[c] Mexican Americans were identified by their nativity (Mexico) and their Spanish names, yet a few were born in Spain (10), Texas (4), and California (1). Of the 355 who were born in Mexico, 251 were men, and of that number 110 had formed unions with Hispanas.
[d] Of the twenty Pueblo villages in 1850, only Zuñi, Laguna, Acoma, Santa Ana, San Ildefonso, Pojoaque, Tesuque, Nambe, and apparently Taos were enumerated. Pueblo Indians were identified by their village residences and sometimes by their "color" ("copper"). They were farmers, had Spanish names, and were born in New Mexico Territory. Most Pueblo Indians probably lived in their separate villages in 1850. Because of imprecise locational data, however, their villages were not removed from the Homeland as non-Homeland enclaves as they were in 1900. The inclusion of all enumerated Pueblo Indians in the Homeland in 1850 thus has yielded a Hispano percentage (90.9) that is low relative to 1900.
[e] Only a relatively small number of nomad Indians who were living among Hispanos were enumerated in 1850. Called *genízaros*, most in 1850 were women who were servants in wealthy Hispano households. They were identified by their "color" or by their tribe ("Nabajoe," "Yutaw") under nativity.
[f] Anglos include all non-Indians and persons who were not of Spanish-Indian or Mexican origin. They were identified by their "color," nativity, and names. Over half were military and ancillary military personnel. Most had come recently to New Mexico Territory from the eastern United States, French Canada, and Western Europe. They were largely males, and some of the nonmilitary had formed unions with Hispanas.
[g] This Homeland total is an undercount; Nostrand, "Mexican Americans circa 1850," *Annals of the Association of American Geographers* 65 (1975): 383, 390. Discrepancies between data in this table and those published in 1975 result from the omission of 1,600 people in Valencia County and a careful reexamination in 1986 of the 1850 population schedules.

and away the largest single Spanish-speaking group in the Borderlands, with percentages in their local area that, unlike those in California and Texas, were uniformly high from county to county. Relative to Californios and Tejanos, Hispanos had clout.

The 1900 census, unlike its 1850 predecessor, at least for greater New Mexico appears to be extremely accurate, primarily because Hispanos rather than Anglos were now enumerating other Hispanos (Map 1.2). The original census returns for 1900 give 140,690 Hispanos in a Homeland that by then spread beyond New Mexico Territory to adjacent parts of Colorado,

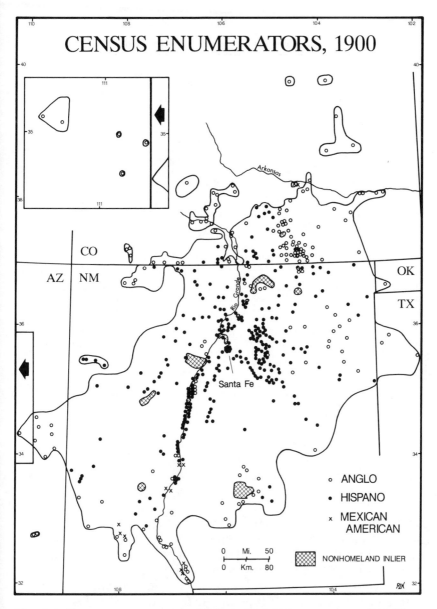

Map 1.2 Census enumerators in 1900. A total 210 enumerators (115 Hispanos, 89 Anglos, and 6 Mexican Americans) took the census in the
Homeland's 485 precincts (which were a minimum 10 percent
Hispano). More than one-third enumerated precincts where they
resided. Symbols are placed at approximate precinct demographic
center points. Source: Population Schedules of the Twelfth Census
[1900].

Table 1.4   Homeland[a] Population Composition, 1900

	Total	Percent
Hispanos[b]	140,690[c]	64.1
Mexican Americans[d]	10,176	4.6
Indians[e]	2,516	1.1
Anglos[f]	66,073	30.1
Homeland	219,455[g]	99.9

SOURCE: U.S. Bureau of the Census, Population Schedules of the Twelfth Census [1900].

[a] A total 485 census precincts wherein Hispanos constituted a minimum 10 percent of the population in New Mexico, Colorado, Arizona, Texas, and Oklahoma.

[b] To facilitate their identity and to emphasize their cultural continuity, the modern term *Hispano* is used anachronistically. Hispanos were identified by their Spanish surnames and given names, their "color or race" (usually "W" for white, but occasionally "M" or "Mex" for Mexican), and by their nativity and parentage (with few exceptions, New Mexico– and Colorado-born or their Arizona-, Texas-, California-, and Oklahoma-born offspring). Anyone who was half or more Hispano was counted as Hispano.

[c] An additional estimated 2,800 Hispanos lived outside the Homeland.

[d] Mexican Americans were identified by their Spanish surnames and given names, their "color or race" (white or Mexican), and by their nativity. With the exception of the New Mexico–born of Mexican parentage in the Homeland's southwestern corner, all Mexican Americans were born outside the Homeland—in Mexico, Texas, Arizona, California, and a few even in Spain; Spaniards were counted as Mexican Americans only if they were living among Mexican Americans or Hispanos.

[e] Indians were easily identified when they were recorded in the "Indian Population" schedules. In the regular schedules they were identified by an "I" or "In" under "color or race." In 1900 most Pueblo and nomad Indians lived alone on reservations, which, because of the absence of Hispanos, were non-Homeland enclaves. This explains the seemingly low Indian population total.

[f] Anglos were non-Hispanos, non–Mexican Americans, and non-Indians.

[g] This Homeland total appears to be highly accurate. Of the 210 Homeland census enumerators, 115 were Hispanos who for the most part were taking the census in their home and neighboring precincts and therefore were knowledgeable about those from whom they were gathering information.

Arizona, Texas, and Oklahoma. Largely because of an influx of Anglos, by 1900 the percentage of Hispanos in the Homeland had dropped to 64.1 percent (Table 1.4). Studies of the sizes of the old-stock Californio and Tejano populations in 1900 have not been made, precluding any comparisons with Hispanos. The sheer number of Hispanos and their relative strength within the New Mexico–centered Homeland, however, would suggest that in 1900 they had the demographic clout to sustain a subculture and to nurture an incipient Spanish ethnicity.

A seventy-two-year confidentiality policy adhered to by the Bureau of the Census will postpone for several decades examination of recent original census returns and the precise data they will contain. Fortunately, however, in 1980 the bureau for the first time asked a 19-percent sample of Americans to self-identify their ancestry or ethnicity, and the results give us some reasonably good up-to-date data (Appendix). By 1980 many Hispanos had left their Homeland and were scattered over much of the American West, but in the Homeland itself, which contained well over half of all Hispanos, 364,545 identified themselves as "Spanish," "Spanish American," and "Hispanic" or "Hispano(a)" (Table 1.5). This figure now represented only 20.0 percent of the total Homeland population. Compared to Mexican Americans, whose numbers in the larger Borderlands had swelled into the millions, the Hispano population in 1980 was indeed small. Compared to the 1,080 who in 1980 in the fifteen western states identified themselves as "Californio," Hispano numbers were impressive. Those who self-identified as "Tejanos" in 1980 were even fewer than Californios, although their exact number cannot be separated from the many entries with which they were coded (Table 1.5). All in all, then, in 1980, although Hispanos demographically were dwarfed by Mexican Americans, they in turn dwarfed the other old-stock populations, and within the Homeland their vitality continued to give them a measure of clout.

Table 1.5 Homeland[a] Population Composition, 1980

	Total	Percent
Hispanos[b]	364,545[c]	20.0
Mexican Americans[d]	200,991	11.0
Anglos and Indians[e]	1,260,300	69.0
Homeland	1,825,836[f]	100.0

SOURCE: U.S. Bureau of the Census, Population Division, Census of Population and Housing, 1980, Summary Tape File (STF) 4 (data for long-form question 14 for fifteen states).
[a] Census County Divisions (CCD) wherein, with one exception (Denver, 7.7 percent Hispano), Hispanos constituted a minimum 10 percent of the population (largely in New Mexico and Colorado).
[b] Persons who reported at least one ancestry to be "Spanish" (code 205), "Spanish American" (code 206), and "Hispanic" or "Hispano(a)" (code 207) in response to question 14 in the long form of the 1980 census.
[c] This number would appear to represent well over half the total Hispano population in the American West.
[d] Persons who reported at least one ancestry to be "Californio" (code 208); "Mexican," "Mexicano(a)," or "Mexico" (code 209); "Mexican American" (code 210); "Nuevo Mexicano," "Tejano(a)," "Aguascalientes" or other states of Mexico (code 211); and "Chicano(a)" (code 212). The preponderance self-identified with labels coded 209 and 210. Very few used labels coded 208 (23 in all of New Mexico; 1,080 in the fifteen western states) and 211 (18 in all of New Mexico; 437 in the fifteen western states).
[e] All others who were not Hispanos or Mexican Americans.
[f] This Homeland total would appear to be based on the most reliable data available. In 1980, for the first time, Americans were asked about their ancestry. Question 14 in the long form, which was asked of 19 percent of the population, requested individuals to self-identify their ancestry or ethnicity regardless of the number of generations that person was removed from his or her country of origin. The Spanish categories were coded 200–43. For this study codes 200–12 were purchased for fifteen states.

GEOGRAPHICAL IMPLICATIONS

Who, then, is the Hispano today? Racially, he is by and large mestizo, different from Mexican Americans only because of a greater nomad Indian admixture. Politically, he is an American, and has been since the mid-nineteenth century, a claim only the descendants of the old-stock populations can make. Six or seven generations of Anglicization have made him bicultural and bilingual, like most other Mexican Americans. Yet culturally he is set apart from Mexican Americans by peculiar preserved and indigenous Spanish attributes—attributes that are different only in subtle ways much like the subtle differences that separate New Englanders or Southerners or Mormons from mainstream Anglo-American society.[29] Finally, in ethnicity the Hispano is different because he identifies with his Spanishness.

These items that set Hispanos apart have implications that are geographical. The Hispanos' identity with their Spanishness, for example, makes their area an "ethnic island." But ethnicity is a fluid sort of thing that is subject to change, and the likelihood that the Hispano area will endure as an ethnic island is low.[30] The Hispanos' sizable population, their distinctive culture, and their deep roots in New Mexico make their area a "cultural region," a concept that has wide acceptance among geographers. As a cultural region the Hispano area will surely endure. In this study I argue that the Hispano area is also their "Homeland." Hispanos adjusted to their natural environment, stamped it with their cultural impress, and created from their natural and cultural surroundings an identity with the land and a sense of place. These things are the ingredients of a "homeland." And the Hispano area as Homeland, like the Hispano area as a cultural region, will surely endure.

The fashioning of a homeland concept, something Hispanos did pretty much by themselves, is the geographical outcome

[29] Marc Simmons made a similar comparison: "The fact is, in spite of a shared language and a common religion, the Hispano is as different from the Mexican-American as an American is from a Canadian"; Buddy Mays and Marc Simmons, *People of the Sun: Some Out-of-Fashion Southwesterners*, 57.
[30] Ellen Churchill Semple identified "ethnic islands" in her *Influences of Geographic Environment*, 210, 224. D. W. Meinig, "Rejoinder" [to Nostrand's "Hispano Cultural Distinctiveness: A Reply"], *Annals of the Association of American Geographers* 74 (1984): 171.

of four centuries of Hispano activity in greater New Mexico. This homeland concept is discussed in chapter 10. The bulk of the study, however, is devoted to the thesis that Hispanos, in interaction with Pueblo and nomad Indians, Anglos, and Mexican immigrants, created a geographical entity, which I call their "Homeland." The eight processes that shaped and reshaped this entity are developed in chapters 2–9. And the major outcomes of these processes are the three morphological zones into which the Hispano region is carved.

CHAPTER 2

✤ ✤ ✤

FORMATIVE COLONIZATION

ABOUT 1550, Juan de Oñate was born into one of the wealthiest families in the Americas. His father, Cristóbal de Oñate, a Basque from the province of Álava, and his mother, Catalina de Salazar, from Granada in Andalucía, had immigrated to New Spain, where they were married, and by the time Juan was born they had a major interest in the silver mines at Zacatecas, where they lived. Appropriate to his station in life, Juan de Oñate was married to Isabel de Tolosa, the daughter of another Zacatecas silver magnate, the granddaughter of Hernán Cortés, and the great-granddaughter of Moctezuma II. When Oñate embarked on his New Mexico enterprise in 1598, his wealth and his position of aristocracy set him apart from those he led, and unlike the majority of the documented early soldier-settlers, he had not been born in Spain. Like the majority of the documented first colonists, however, Oñate was of Spanish parentage.[1]

SOURCE AREAS

Spanish immigration to New Spain began in 1521 when Hernán Cortés conquered the Aztecs. In the sixteenth century all regions of Spain contributed migrants to New Spain, yet 40

---

[1] Facts about the Oñate family are given in Beatrice Quijada Cornish, "The Ancestry and Family of Juan de Oñate," in *The Pacific Ocean in History*, ed. H. Morse Stephens and Herbert E. Bolton, 452–64; Donald Chipman, "The Oñate-Moctezuma-Zaldívar Families of Northern New Spain," *New Mexico Historical Review* 52 (1977): 297–310; and Eric Beerman, "The Death of an Old Conquistador: New Light on Juan de Oñate," *New Mexico Historical Review* 54 (1979): 305–19. Chipman speculated that Catalina de Salazar was a bigamist, for she appears to have abandoned an earlier husband in Granada (pp. 304, 305). Beerman noted that Juan de Oñate died in 1626 at Guadalcanal in Andalucía, Spain (p. 305).

percent were from Andalucía, Spain's southernmost region (Map 2.1). Seville had a monopoly on Spanish trade with the New World, and sheer propinquity to that port city would seem to explain the disproportionate importance of Andalucía as a source area.[2]

In New Spain Spaniards quickly gained control of the *tierra de paz*, the homeland of the peaceful and relatively advanced Aztecs and Tarascans (Map 2.2). Tenochtitlán, the seat of Moctezuma's Aztec state, was transformed into the city of México, after 1535 the seat of the viceroyalty of New Spain. But the discovery of major silver deposits for which New Spain became famous soon lured Spaniards north into the *tierra de guerra*, that dangerous and remote frontier inhabited by hostile nomadic Indians known collectively as the "Chichimecas." Zacatecas (1546) was the first and the largest of the silver strikes, and by the end of the century the Zacatecas region was second only to México as New Spain's leading center of Spanish population.[3]

From Zacatecas, Oñate petitioned to lead, and with his family fortune help finance, a party that would colonize New Mexico. In 1595 he was in México attempting to secure final permission for this proposed venture, and while awaiting the official nod, he recruited colonists, first in México and then in Zacatecas as he progressed to the north from camp to camp. When permission finally came in January 1598, he and his recruits were camped near Santa Bárbara, the important outpost salient on the periphery of New Spain's northern mining frontier.[4]

The party that Oñate led to New Mexico in the spring of 1598 was documented as having 130 soldiers, including Oñate; there is no record of the number of women, children, and servants who accompanied the soldiers. Of the 130, over half

[2] Peter Boyd-Bowman, "Patterns of Spanish Emigration to the Indies until 1600," *Hispanic American Historical Review* 56 (1976): 585, 587, 588. Indeed, the province of Seville (located within Andalucía) led all others in migrants who went to New Spain (pp. 589, 592, 596, 603).

[3] Carl O. Sauer contrasted the "high" cultures of the south and the "ruder" cultures of the north in "The Personality of Mexico," *Geographical Review* 31 (1941): 354–56; Philip Wayne Powell, "Presidios and Towns on the Silver Frontier of New Spain, 1550–1580," *Hispanic American Historical Review* 24 (1944): 199.

[4] George P. Hammond and Agapito Rey, eds., *Don Juan de Oñate, Colonizer of New Mexico, 1595–1628*, Coronado Cuarto Centennial Publications, 1540–1940, ed. George P. Hammond, vol. 5: 7, 14–15.

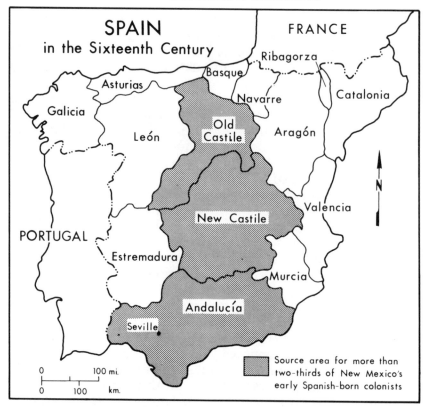

Map 2.1 Spain in the sixteenth century. The majority of New Mexico's early documented colonists were from Spain, more than two-thirds of whom were from Andalucía and Castile. Data derived from George P. Hammond, *Don Juan de Oñate and the Founding of New Mexico*, Historical Society of New Mexico Publications in History, vol. 2: 187–210. Base map from J. H. Elliott, *Imperial Spain 1469–1716*, 4.

were born in Spain (*peninsulares*), and most of the rest, including Oñate himself, were born in New Spain (creoles). One of the *peninsulares* was a mulatto.[5] In 1600, a second party of 80 soldiers, accompanied by some forty-five wives, sisters, children, and servants, joined the original group in New Mex-

[5] This list of 129 soldiers (Oñate was omitted) is in "Inspection Made by Juan de Frías Salazar of the Expedition, September, 1597, to February, 1598," ibid., vol. 5: 199–308. I analyzed Hammond's consolidated list in George P. Hammond, *Don Juan de Oñate and the Founding of New Mexico*, Historical Society of New Mexico Publications in History, vol. 2: 187–200. Of the 129 soldiers, 68 were born in Spain (26 in Andalucía and 22 in Castile), 37 were born in New Spain (14 in the area of México

ico. Documentation exists only for the 80 soldiers, over half of whom were also born in Spain. Of the approximately forty-five people who accompanied them, two were noted to be mulatto and one or two were Indian.[6]

Exactly how many total colonists went with Oñate in 1598, and how many more reinforced his colony in 1600, thus is not known. What is known is that of the 210 for whom documentation exists, more than half were born in Spain, especially in Andalucía and Castile, and most of the rest were born in New Spain, especially in the México and Zacatecas areas. One of the 210 was noted to be a mulatto; most of the rest, surely the majority of the *peninsulares* but also some creoles like Oñate, must have been Caucasian. Further, of those who accompanied the second party, a small number were mulatto and Indian; some of the wives and children must have been mestizo.[7]

New Mexico's early colonists, then, were from two source areas, Spain and New Spain, and of the two, Spain appears to have been the more important. The early colonists, moreover, represented several racial types, of which the Caucasian probably predominated. Significantly, once in New Mexico, attrition from mutinies, battle casualties, and desertions left as a

---

and 13 in the area of Zacatecas), 10 were born elsewhere (eight in Portugal), and the place of birth of 1 was not given. I was unable to locate the places of birth of 13. Oñate was, of course, also born in Zacatecas. Hammond noted that "Indians, mulattos or mestizos were barred from the review unless they made declaration of their status" (p. 87). Oakah L. Jones, Jr., analyzed these same data with different results: of the 129, Jones had 54 born in Spain, 39 born in New Spain, and 37 born elsewhere or at unspecified places; *Los Paisanos: Spanish Settlers on the Northern Frontier of New Spain*, 130.

[6] The second group is given in "Inspection Made by Don Juan de Gordejuela and Juan de Sotelo of the Reinforcements Sent to New Mexico, August 1600," in Hammond and Rey, *Don Juan de Oñate* 5: 514–79, and in consolidated form in Hammond, *Don Juan de Oñate and the Founding*, 201–10. Of the 80, 42 were born in Spain (14 in Andalucía and 16 in Castile), 17 were born in New Spain (9 in Puebla, 5 in the area of México, and 1 in Zacatecas), and 3 were born elsewhere (2 in Portugal). Of the remaining 18, I was unable to locate places of birth for 2, 1 never went to New Mexico, and the places of birth of 15 (2 of whom were listed among the 129 in 1598 and were returning to New Mexico) were not given. (One of the 42 Spanish-born was also noted to be returning to New Mexico, yet he was not among the original 129.) Eleven of the approximately 45 people who accompanied the soldiers were noted to be natives of México or Puebla.

[7] Before 1540 the proportion of women among Spain's emigrants was small; Boyd-Bowman, "Patterns of Spanish Emigration," 598. The shortage of Spanish women in the first several decades after 1521 was one important reason why a mestizo population was created so quickly; C. E. Marshall, "The Birth of the Mestizo in New Spain," *Hispanic American Historical Review* 19 (1939): 164, 167, 171.

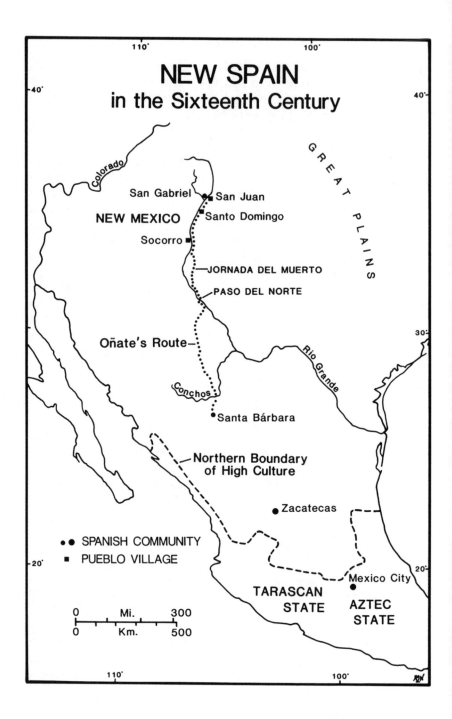

permanent legacy less than forty of the more than two hundred original surnames.[8] That such a sizable percentage had come so early and so directly from Spain to New Mexico, however, left Hispanos with an Iberian legacy that, in a Borderlands sense, made them culturally distinctive.

THE DESTINATION

Late in January of 1598, Oñate's expedition left the Santa Bárbara area, proceeded to the Río Conchos, then struck out on an overland course north to the Rio Grande (then the Río Bravo del Norte—Map 2.2). There, Indians showed Oñate a fording point used by natives for leagues around that was located between modern-day El Paso and Ciudad Juárez. North of the ford, where the Rio Grande was entrenched, Oñate's party left the valley and followed a waterless route later known as the Jornada del Muerto. Several leagues south of Socorro, where the valley of the Rio Grande widened again, Oñate encountered his first Pueblo village. Advancing up the valley, he stopped temporarily at the village of Santo Domingo, and at the junction of the Chama and Rio Grande, at the village of San Juan in the northern portion of the Pueblo Indian realm, he halted his advance party in July.[9]

San Juan, the village that still exists on the east side of the Rio Grande, was Oñate's first headquarters. His permanent headquarters were across the Rio Grande at San Gabriel. San Gabriel (Yungue) and San Juan (Okeh) were two dwelling units of a single Tewa-speaking village. San Gabriel, which today lies in ruin, may have been partially or entirely abandoned when Oñate moved in in the winter of 1600–1601.[10]

---

[8] Fray Angélico Chávez, *Origins of New Mexico Families in the Spanish Colonial Period*, xi.

[9] Hammond and Rey, *Don Juan de Oñate* 5: 15–17.

[10] Florence Hawley Ellis, "The Long Lost 'City' of San Gabriel del Yungue, Second Oldest European Settlement in the United States," in *When Cultures Meet: Remembering San Gabriel del Yunge Oweenge*, ed. Herman Agoyo and Lynnwood Brown, 12, 16, 17, 21.

Map 2.2 (*opposite*) New Spain in the sixteenth century. The northern boundary of high culture is after Carl O. Sauer, "The Personality of Mexico," *Geographical Review* 31 (1941): 355; Oñate's route is after Max L. Moorhead, *New Mexico's Royal Road: Trade and Travel on the Chihuahua Trail*, 10–11.

From San Juan, Oñate quickly visited many Pueblo villages in a broad zone between the Pecos village on the east and the Zuñi and Hopi villages on the west. Some were soon assigned missionaries. From San Gabriel, Oñate later explored an even larger area that stretched from central Kansas west to the Gulf of California. In his travels he found no mineral wealth, and in his absence some colonists deserted the isolated and exposed colony. Further, the Pueblo Indians, who were being exploited for their labor and compelled to provide maize, on occasion became openly defiant. Realizing that he had not been success-ful, Oñate offered his resignation in 1607, which, ironically, coincided with the issuing of an order for his recall. Oñate remained in New Mexico until 1610, during which time the Spanish authorities, persuaded that it would be a mistake to abandon those Indians who had been converted to Roman Catholicism, decided to retain New Mexico as a missionary province.[11]

In 1609, Pedro de Peralta was appointed governor, and the next year he founded Santa Fe, the new provincial capital (Map 2.3). The site chosen for the new *villa* was on a piedmont plain where the Santa Fe River issues from the Sangre de Cristo foothills twenty miles east of the Rio Grande. Following the Laws of the Indies, Santa Fe was laid out with a central *plaza mayor* whose corners pointed weakly in cardinal compass di-rections.[12] Fronting the plaza on the north side was the Palace

---

[11] Hammond and Rey, *Don Juan de Oñate* 5: 17–33. Oñate's resignation was offered apparently without the knowledge that he was about to be recalled; Hammond, *Don Juan de Oñate and the Founding*, 172; George P. Hammond, "The Date of Oñate's Return from New Mexico," *El Palacio* 64 (1957): 142–44.

[12] Lansing B. Bloom, "When Was Santa Fe Founded?" *New Mexico Historical Review* 4 (1929): 188. The reason for Sante Fe's orientation, as stated in "law" 114, was to avoid directly exposing the streets that diverged from the plaza to the four principal winds; Zelia Nuttall, "Royal Ordinances Concerning the Laying Out of New Towns," *Hispanic American Historical Review* 5 (1922): 250. Concerning the *villa* of San Antonio in Texas, Edwin P. Arneson pointed out that a second reason for this peculiar orientation was probably so that streets would be shaded in summer; "The Early Art of Terrestrial Measurement and Its Practice in Texas," *Southwestern Histori-cal Quarterly* 29 (1925–26): 85.

Map 2.3 (*opposite*) New Mexico in 1680. The geography of Spaniards in 1680 directly reflected the location of Pueblo Indians. The Paso del Norte District and the Acoma, Zuñi, and Hopi (not shown) villages are outliers. Sources: see text.

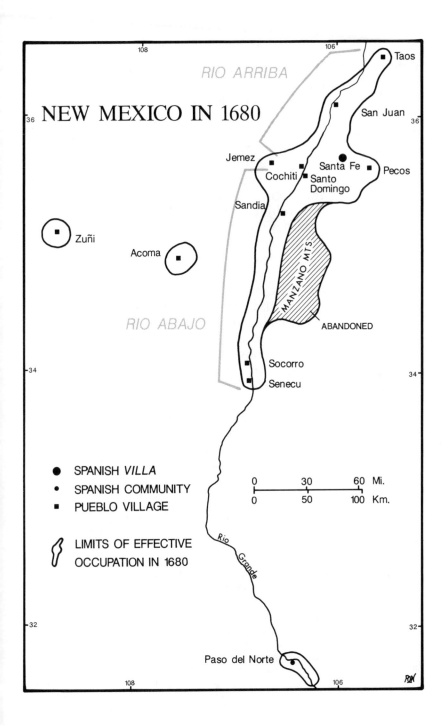

NEW MEXICO IN 1680

RIO ARRIBA

Taos

San Juan

Jemez

Santa Fe

Cochiti

Pecos

Santo
Domingo

Sandia

Zuñi

Acoma

MANZANO MTS.

ABANDONED

RIO ABAJO

Socorro

Senecu

● SPANISH *VILLA*
• SPANISH COMMUNITY
■ PUEBLO VILLAGE

⸨ LIMITS OF EFFECTIVE
OCCUPATION IN 1680

0   30   60 Mi.
0   50   100 Km.

Rio Grande

Paso del Norte

RDN

of the Governors, and located on the east side near the present Cathedral of Saint Francis was the Roman Catholic church (the *plaza mayor* once extended as far east as the present cathedral). Beyond the plaza were the one-story adobe and stone houses of the inhabitants, but these were not arranged in a grid. Once Santa Fe was established, San Gabriel was abandoned, and Santa Fe became the hub of "the Kingdom and Provinces of New Mexico"—the seat of government, the destination of the triennial mission supply trains, and the point from which military and exploratory expeditions departed and to which they returned. Yet there was some dissatisfaction with the *villa's* location, as expressed in a petition (denied in 1620) that proposed moving Santa Fe to a more defensible site.[13]

Both Oñate and Peralta were authorized to award encomiendas or entrustments of Indians, which in New Mexico meant Pueblo villages. The value of such awards was determined by the amounts of annual tribute encomenderos, who were obliged to protect and convert their charges, were allowed to collect. How many encomiendas were awarded, for what amounts of tribute, and exactly what villages were involved is not entirely known, yet it is thought that Oñate gave all of the original colonists encomiendas, and Lansing B. Bloom "conservatively" estimated that before 1680 there were at least one hundred encomiendas held by some fifty to sixty Spaniards. About 1640 the number of encomiendas that would be permitted in New Mexico was limited by the viceroy to thirty-five,

---

[13] Fray Angélico Chávez, "Santa Fe Church and Convent Sites in the Seventeenth and Eighteenth Centuries," *New Mexico Historical Review* 24 (1949): 92 and locational sketch facing 85; Marc Simmons, "Settlement Patterns and Village Plans in Colonial New Mexico," *Journal of the West* 8 (1969): 12. Regarding San Gabriel, see France V. Scholes, "Civil Government and Society in New Mexico in the Seventeenth Century," *New Mexico Historical Review* 10 (1935): 94. The San Gabriel settlers were presumably joined by the nineteen soldiers, nine Franciscan missionaries, and a hundred "Indian attendants" who had accompanied Peralta; Bloom "When Was Santa Fe Founded?" 192. Concerning the dissatisfaction, see Lansing B. Bloom, "A Glimpse of New Mexico in 1620," *New Mexico Historical Review* 3 (1928): 369. The place where Santa Fe might have been relocated is not recorded, yet one could speculate that the Rio Grande valley, with its Pueblo Indians, plentiful river water, and more generous arable floodplain, might have been favored by many. Indeed, in 1692, when Diego de Vargas was about to successfully reoccupy the upper basin, it was suggested by the king "that Cia might be a better site than Santa Fé for the proposed restoration of the Spanish villa"; Hubert Howe Bancroft, *The Works of Hubert Howe Bancroft*, vol. 17, *History of Arizona and New Mexico 1530–1888*, 196.

which must have caused confusion and may have resulted in the dispossession of some awardees. Titles to all encomiendas were abrogated following the Pueblo Revolt of 1680, and after the reconquest only one encomienda seems to have been awarded—to Diego de Vargas in 1698, an award that was never consummated.[14]

In addition to the encomiendas, large grants of land known as estancias were given to soldier-citizens for purposes of stock raising and farming. How many were awarded is not known, but most seem to have been located near the Pueblo villages where Indian labor was available. Many are known to have existed on both sides of the Rio Grande in the vicinity of the Sandia village. The estancia headquarters were probably small, fortified, courtyard-centered dwellings similar to the *"placitas"* or *"restricted plazas"* of the eighteenth and nineteenth centuries.[15]

In 1659 the effectively occupied portion of this basically missionary frontier was extended to include the Paso del Norte District located south of the Jornada. At Paso del Norte (renamed Ciudad Juárez in 1888), near the point where the Rio Grande was forded, friars from New Mexico built a mission, and before 1680 two additional missions were added at points outside the district.[16] Some Spanish colonists were also in the area in 1680 when, in the Pueblo Revolt, Spaniards farther north were suddenly uprooted and were forced to take refuge in the district.

On the eve of the Pueblo Revolt some twenty-five hundred Spaniards inhabited New Mexico. Included in the total were many mestizos, some creoles and *peninsulares,* perhaps a few

---

[14] H. Allen Anderson, "The Encomienda in New Mexico, 1598–1680," *New Mexico Historical Review* 60 (1985): 356, 360. Tribute was paid in mantas (pieces of cotton cloth six palms square) and in maize; one manta was worth one peso; Scholes, "Civil Government and Society," 109; Lansing B. Bloom, "The Vargas Encomienda," *New Mexico Historical Review* 14 (1939): 367, 369, 370. Two Vargas heirs who had legitimate claim to the encomienda may have been awarded annual pensions of four thousand pesos in the eighteenth century (Bloom, "Vargas Encomienda," 371, 382, 402, 414, 416).

[15] Scholes, "Civil Government and Society," 107; Charles Wilson Hackett, *Revolt of the Pueblo Indians of New Mexico and Otermín's Attempted Reconquest, 1680–1682,* Coronado Cuarto Centennial Publications, 1540–1940, ed. George P. Hammond, 8: li, xciv; Bainbridge Bunting, *Taos Adobes: Spanish Colonial and Territorial Architecture of the Taos Valley,* 4; Simmons, "Settlement Patterns," 14.

[16] Anne E. Hughes, *The Beginnings of Spanish Settlement in the El Paso District,* University of California Publications in History, vol. 1, no. 3: 305–10, 388.

blacks and mulattos, some Indians from Mexico, and some local Indians, who were used as domestics. One can only guess what proportions each represented. Santa Fe, the only authorized community in New Mexico, was surely New Mexico's largest Spanish settlement. Outside Santa Fe the remainder of the Spanish population was dispersed in encomiendas, estancias, perhaps small hamlets, and, in the case of friars, missions located at many of the Pueblo villages.[17] The distribution of this population reflected directly the location of the Pueblo Indians who lived, for the most part, in the valley of the Rio Grande and its tributaries.

The area that was effectively occupied, then, extended from Taos south to Socorro and Senecu and from Pecos west to Jemez (Map 2.3). The section of floodplain downriver from Paso del Norte and the Acoma, Zuñi, and Hopi villages were outliers. Before 1680 the area east of the Manzano Mountains had also been temporarily occupied. The total occupied zone, however, represented only a fraction of New Mexico, which reached from the nonexistent Strait of Anián south to the swath of desert that separated the Paso del Norte District from Nueva Vizcaya and stretched from the Great Plains west to the Colorado River. To avoid setting limits on what she claimed, Spain was purposefully vague about New Mexico's boundaries.[18]

SUBREGIONS

In the seventeenth century, then, many of the relatively few Spaniards lived along the cottonwood-lined floodplain of the Rio Grande, where Pueblo Indian labor was available. The dry, grass- and shrub-covered plains and mesas found in gradual ascent away from the bluff-encompassed floodplain were used, with the help of Indians, for livestock grazing. At the apexes

[17] New Mexico's population before 1680 probably never exceeded twenty-five hundred; in the revolt, some four hundred (including twenty-one friars) were killed, a few were held captive, and the remaining approximately two thousand retreated to the Paso del Norte District; Scholes, "Civil Government and Society," 96–97. A second organized community, other than Santa Fe, may possibly have existed (p. 94, n. 39). Santa Fe never had more than a few hundred inhabitants in the seventeenth century (p. 102). Concerning the dispersal of population, see pp. 96; 102, n. 51; 107. See also Bloom, "Vargas Encomienda," 370. Simmons, "Settlement Patterns," 10, stressed the propensity of these colonists to disperse even in the seventeenth century.

[18] Scholes, "Civil Government and Society," 71.

of the alluvial fans and into the juniper- and piñon-covered foothills, small streams and springs sustained additional Pueblo villages—and additional Spaniards, as at Santa Fe. And rising still higher in elevation were the pine-covered mountains that furnished building timber and supported some permanent occupance.[19]

These vertical zones lying between the valley floodplains and mountain summits were, of course, fully appreciated and used by the early Spaniards. The two subregions that they differentiated, however, were the less obvious Rio Arriba (Upriver Country) and Rio Abajo (Downriver Country—Map 2.3). The Rio Arriba was higher in elevation and therefore had a shorter growing season, yet it was wetter and had more plentiful stands of ponderosa and other pines. The Rio Abajo, on the other hand, was lower in elevation, which meant drier and dustier conditions, but it had a longer growing season. Separating the two areas was La Bajada barranca located southwest of Santa Fe. Recognized for their environmental differences, these two subregions were used as administrative districts. From about 1660 onward, for example, the governor commanded military operations in the Rio Arriba, while the lieutenant governor took charge in the Rio Abajo.[20]

REOCCUPATION

In 1680 the Pueblo Indians staged a successful revolt, and some two thousand Spaniards who were not killed or held captive, along with some Pueblo Indians, took refuge in the Paso del Norte District. During several abortive reconquest attempts, more Pueblos were gathered, and all were placed in new villages whose names—Isleta (Ysleta), Socorro, and Senecu, all "del Sur"—denoted the major village sources.[21] The Spanish refugees meanwhile regrouped in several settlements which collectively were elevated to *villa* status and near which a presidio (garrisoned fortification) was established. Soon a

[19] Wilfrid D. Kelley, "Settlement of the Middle Rio Grande Valley," *Journal of Geography* 54 (1955): 388–90.

[20] Scholes, "Civil Government and Society," 91.

[21] Isleta, Socorro, Senecu, and several other Indian settlements were established in an attempt to keep the Indians and Spaniards apart and so avoid problems of Indian exploitation or epidemics; Hughes, *Beginnings of Spanish Settlement*, 321–30. Such attempts were not successful, for as Jones, *Los Paisanos*, 114, pointed out, all were mixed communities of Spaniards and Indians.

string of communities existed on the south bank of the river along some twenty miles of productive floodplain downstream from the ford.[22] This major influx of people to the valley brought to a head the question of whether New Mexico or Nueva Vizcaya had jurisdiction over the Paso del Norte District, an issue that in 1685 was resolved in favor of New Mexico, under whose authority it remained until 1824.[23]

Diego de Vargas led the successful reconquest entradas. In 1692, from the Paso del Norte District, he visited all the inhabited Pueblo villages to the north and obtained nominal agreements of submission to Spanish rule. Late the next year he returned with colonists, soldiers, and friars, but when he tried to reoccupy Santa Fe, the Galisteo Pueblos, who now lived in the *villa*, had to be forced to vacate.[24] That open hostility triggered skirmishes and battles that were widespread and lasted until 1700, when, finally reduced in number and broken in spirit, the Pueblos permanently submitted to Spanish control. Of the seventy families that reoccupied Santa Fe under Vargas, some, with surnames that included Archuleta, Baca, Chávez, Lucero, and Montoya, were pre-1680 colonists who were returning. During the time of exile, a number of original families dispersed south into New Spain, and replacing them were new families, recruited in the city and the valley of Mexico, whose surnames included Aragón, Medina, Ortiz, and Quintana.[25]

At the time Santa Fe was reoccupied, a presidio was established. This presidio was not a formal fortress but instead a company of soldiers whose quarters, guardhouse, and military chapel were somewhat scattered through the *villa*. Before the 1680 revolt a walled adobe fortress had existed immediately north of and contiguous with the Palace of the Governors,

[22] See Jones, *Los Paisanos*, 113. No settlements apparently existed on the north bank until 1827; J. Lawrence McConville, "A History of Population in the El Paso–Ciudad Juarez Area" (master's thesis, University of New Mexico, 1966) 51. El Paso on the north bank was founded in the 1820s in conjunction with the flow of Santa Fe trade goods south into Mexico; Ralph H. Brown, *Historical Geography of the United States*, 78, 393.

[23] Hughes, *Beginnings of Spanish Settlement*, 382–87, 390; Lansing B. Bloom, "Notes and Comments," *New Mexico Historical Review* 17 (1942): 279.

[24] J. Manuel Espinosa, "The Recapture of Santa Fé, New Mexico, by the Spaniards—December 20–30, 1693," *Hispanic American Historical Review* 19 (1939): 443–63.

[25] Chávez, *Origins of New Mexico Families*, x, xii, xiii; Bancroft, *History of Arizona and New Mexico*, 202, 221, 224.

yet that fort was manned by colonists, not by soldiers, and technically was not a presidio.[26] The old fort was partially restored in 1715, yet even after that date the presidio troops seem to have lived at points around the *villa*—until 1791, when a one-hundred man barracks and other modifications were completed in a major two-year renovation. With some one hundred soldiers, the Santa Fe presidio was relatively large, yet so was its charge of protecting colonists, missionaries, and Christianized Indians while subduing the gentiles in the entire Spanish-Pueblo realm north of the Paso del Norte District.[27]

With reoccupation that northern realm saw the creation of additional *villas* and other Spanish settlements. In April 1695, in the Santa Cruz Valley some twenty miles north of Santa Fe, Galisteo Pueblos were dispossessed of a village they had recently occupied, and on the site forty-four families from Santa Fe founded the *villa* of Santa Cruz (Map 2.4). The next month forty-six families (146 people) repopulated Santa Fe. Nearly all were new recruits from the Zacatecas-Sombrerete area, most were mestizos or Spaniards, and among their surnames were Armijo, Vargas, and Vigil. Like Santa Fe, Santa Cruz had a central open plaza and an adjacent Roman Catholic church, and beyond the plaza area its houses were scattered along an irrigation ditch.[28]

Santa Fe and especially Santa Cruz became fountainheads for expansion north. From both, Hispanos advanced into the Española Valley (as that segment of the Rio Grande valley is

[26] Max L. Moorhead, *The Presidio: Bastion of the Spanish Borderlands*, 172–76; Max L. Moorhead, "Rebuilding the Presidio of Santa Fe, 1789–1791," *New Mexico Historical Review* 49 (1974): 123–42. Moorhead, in *The Presidio*, 172, cites Ralph Emerson Twitchell, "The Palace of the Governors," *Historical Society of New Mexico Publications*, 29 (1924): 12–38.

[27] The Santa Fe garrison usually exceeded one hundred men and officers; Max L. Moorhead, "The Presidio Supply Problem of New Mexico in the Eighteenth Century," *New Mexico Historical Review* 36 (1961): 210.

[28] Ralph E. Twitchell, "Spanish Colonization in New Mexico in the Oñate and De Vargas Periods," *Publication of the Historical Society of New Mexico* 22 (1919): 16–28. Jones, *Los Paisanos*, 115, gives the month of settlement of Santa Cruz as April and the number of families as forty-four. The muster roll for the Santa Fe colonists of 1695, which contains information on surnames, source areas, and ethnicity, was found at the Gilcrease Institute in Tulsa, Oklahoma; Clevy Lloyd Strout, "The Resettlement of Santa Fe, 1695: The Newly Found Muster Roll," *New Mexico Historical Review* 53 (1978): 260–70. The surnames Armijo, Vargas, and Vigil belonged to this group; Chávez, *Origins of New Mexico Families*, xiii. Simmons, "Settlement Patterns," 12–13, described the plaza area.

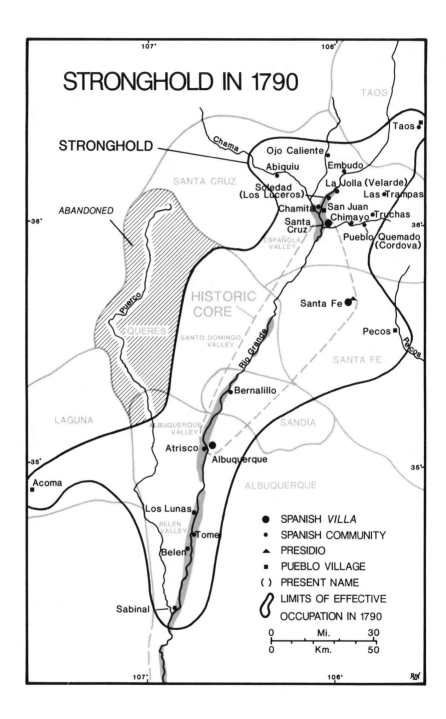

STRONGHOLD IN 1790

TAOS

STRONGHOLD

Chama

Taos

Ojo Caliente

Abiquiu

Embudo

SANTA CRUZ

La Jolla (Velarde)

Soledad
(Los Luceros)

Las Trampas

ABANDONED

Chamita

San Juan

Chimayo

Truchas

Santa
Cruz

ESPAÑOLA
VALLEY

Pueblo Quemado
(Cordova)

HISTORIC
CORE

Puerco

Santa Fe

QUERES

SANTO DOMINGO
VALLEY

Rio Grande

Pecos

Pecos

SANTA FE

LAGUNA

Bernalillo

ALBUQUERQUE
VALLEY

SANDIA

Atrisco

Albuquerque

Acoma

ALBUQUERQUE

Los Lunas

BELEN
VALLEY

Tome

Belen

● SPANISH *VILLA*

• SPANISH COMMUNITY

▲ PRESIDIO

■ PUEBLO VILLAGE

( ) PRESENT NAME

LIMITS OF EFFECTIVE

OCCUPATION IN 1790

Sabinal

| 0 | Mi. | 30 |
| 0 | Km. | 50 |

RIN

known today) to Soledad (Los Luceros) in 1712, to Embudo in 1725, and, probably by 1750, to La Jolla (Velarde). They reoccupied the area around the village of San Juan, whose lands they encroached upon when they founded Chamita in 1724. Apparently by 1735 they had established Ojo Caliente in the Ojo Caliente Valley, and in 1744 they settled at Abiquiu in the Chama Valley. When dislodged from these last two outposts by nomad Indians, the residents took refuge in Santa Cruz, and until the 1790s the settlement history of especially Ojo Caliente was basically a tug-of-war between angry governors, who desired to have a buffer of frontier settlements against the nomad Indians and thus mandated the colonists to reoccupy their "plazas," and recalcitrant one-time residents, who refused to reoccupy because they had lost relatives to the hostile Indians and because they lacked firearms.[29]

From Santa Cruz, Hispanos also spread east up the Santa Cruz Valley (or La Cañada) to Chimayo, which they apparently reoccupied, and beyond Chimayo they followed the Camino Alto to Las Trampas, settled by twelve families from Santa Fe in 1751. Between Chimayo and Las Trampas communities developed at a burned and abandoned Indian village called Pueblo Quemado (Cordova) by 1748 and on the edge of a high mesa at Truchas in 1754. Sometime before 1751, Santa Barbara (location undetermined) in the Peñasco area was reached, perhaps by way of the Rio Grande valley.[30]

The thrust to the north reached all the way to the Taos

---

[29] Lynnell Rubright, "A Sequent Occupance of the Espanola Valley, New Mexico" (master's thesis [geography], University of Colorado, 1967), 76–77, 79, 111; Frank D. Reeve, *History of New Mexico* 1: 322, 324; J. J. Bowden, *Private Land Claims in the Southwest* 4: 1159–60, 1162; E. Boyd, "Troubles at Ojo Caliente, A Frontier Post," *El Palacio* 64 (1957): 347–60; Bowden, *Private Land Claims* 4: 1099.

[30] Bowden, *Private Land Claims* 4: 993, 1010–12. Residents of Pueblo Quemado petitioned to be allowed to abandon their settlement in 1748; Boyd, "Troubles," 347. Tony Hillerman gave 1754 as the date Truchas was founded; "Las Trampas," *New Mexico Quarterly* 37 (1967–68): 26.

Map 2.4 (*opposite*) Stronghold in 1790. The Paso del Norte District and Zuñi village outliers are not shown. The seven *alcaldía* boundaries (Alcaldía de Zuñi not shown) are from the Miera y Pacheco map of 1779 reproduced in Alfred Barnaby Thomas, trans. and ed., *Forgotten Frontiers: A Study of the Spanish Indian Policy of Don Juan Bautista de Anza, Governor of New Mexico, 1777–1787*, back pouch. Sources: see text.

Indian village. The origin of the Hispano community of Taos, however, is somewhat obscure. By 1710, Hispanos had been granted land in the vicinity of the Taos Indian village. By midcentury a Hispano community existed very near and perhaps within the lands belonging to the Taos Indians. Endless nomad Indian raids drove the Hispanos at this outpost into the Taos village itself, where, in 1760 and again in 1776, Hispano families were reported living with the Pueblos. By 1795, however, most if not all of the non-Indian families had moved out of the Taos Indian village, and the next year sixty-three were awarded the Don Fernando de Taos Grant, which contains the present-day community of Taos. That this grant overlaps with the four square leagues belonging to the Taos Indians, and that the Hispano village of Taos is actually located within the southern boundary of the Indian lands, have been the cause of endless Hispano-Pueblo conflict and litigation.[31]

As Hispanos extended their control for a second time in the Rio Arriba, they spread south from Santa Fe to reoccupy the Rio Abajo. In the Albuquerque area Atrisco came to exist by 1703, and on the site of a pre-1680 Spanish settlement, Bernalillo was established by 1706. Bernalillo's existence by 1706 is confirmed by the fact that it contributed some of the thirty-five families (252 people) who came together that year to found "Alburquerque" (the first *r* was dropped from the spelling in the American period). Like Santa Fe and Santa Cruz, Albuquerque was officially designated a *villa*. And as happened in the earlier two *villas*, the houses in Albuquerque were irregularly placed around a central plaza and Roman Catholic church, with many more of them stretching away along an irrigation ditch.[32] Together with Santa Fe, Albuquerque be-

---

[31] Myra Ellen Jenkins, "Taos Pueblo and Its Neighbors, 1540–1847," *New Mexico Historical Review* 41 (1966): 91, 96–100; Bowden, *Private Land Claims* 4: 965; G. Emlen Hall, *Four Leagues of Pecos: A Legal History of the Pecos Grant, 1830–1933*, New Mexico Land Grant Series, 26, 128–38, 248.

[32] Richard E. Greenleaf noted the existence of Atrisco in 1703; "Atrisco and Las Ciruelas, 1722–1769," *New Mexico Historical Review* 42 (1967): 6. Lansing B. Bloom noted that in 1680 a Spanish community had existed at Bernalillo; "The 'Peñalosa' Map," *New Mexico Historical Review* 9 (1934): 229; Lansing B. Bloom, ed., "Alburquerque and Galisteo Certificate of Their Founding, 1706," *New Mexico Historical Review* 10 (1935): 48–50; Richard E. Greenleaf, "The Founding of Albuquerque, 1706: An Historical Legal Problem," *New Mexico Historical Review* 39 (1964): 5, 10; Reeve, *History of New Mexico* 1: 311; Simmons, "Settlement Patterns," 12–13.

came the fountainhead for the spawning of new communities in the Rio Abajo.

From Santa Fe, and undoubtedly from Albuquerque, Hispanos reoccupied the Belen Valley segment of the Rio Grande valley; in lockstep down the valley they founded Los Lunas (1716), Tome (1739), Belen (1742), and Sabinal (1770s). Sabinal appears to have been the southernmost frontier outpost at the end of the century. From Albuquerque, and perhaps from elsewhere, Hispanos crossed west to the middle and upper Puerco Valley, where, for some twenty years in the second half of the eighteenth century, they occupied a dozen villages between Nacimiento (Cuba) and Los Quelites. Meanwhile, the linear string of houses and *placitas* that stretched north from Albuquerque in the eighteenth century came to be known collectively as "Los Ranchos de Albuquerque."[33] Perhaps the "suburbs," as it were, that came to exist at Los Ranchos de Atrisco and Los Ranchos de Tome (now called Adelino) also originated in the eighteenth century.

In much of the eighteenth century dispersed linear settlements called *ranchos* were typical. These "loose agglomerations of small farmsteads," as Marc Simmons characterized them, must have originated as community enterprises, because to construct and maintain the mandatory diversion dams and irrigation ditches was more than one family could manage.[34] The farms in these *ranchos*, which were often established

[33] The dates for Los Lunas, Tome, and Belen are from Allan G. Harper, Andrew R. Córdova, and Kalervo Oberg, *Man and Resources in the Middle Rio Grande Valley,* Inter-American Studies, vol. 2: 18. That Sabinal was populated in the 1770s is in Reeve, *History of New Mexico* 1: 320. Kelley noted the importance of Santa Fe as a source area in "Settlement of the Middle Rio Grande Valley," 393. The dozen Rio Puerco villages, shown in Map 4.4, are described in Jerold Gwayn Widdison, "Historical Geography of the Middle Rio Puerco Valley, New Mexico," *New Mexico Historical Review* 34 (1959): 259–60, 262–63; and Larry López, "The Founding of San Francisco on the Rio Puerco: A Document," *New Mexico Historical Review* 55 (1980): 71, 72. Reeve, *History of New Mexico* 1: 312, told of the growth north from Albuquerque.

[34] There is little doubt that settlements in eighteenth-century New Mexico were "dispersed." Governor Cachupín noted this in his inspection of 1751–52, as did Governor Mendinueta in 1772, and Father Morfí in the 1780s. Scattered houses, noted Morfí, put Spaniards beyond the reach of law and religion and exposed them to Indian raids. See Robert Ryal Miller, trans. and ed., "New Mexico in Mid-Eighteenth Century: A Report Based on Governor Vélez Capuchín's [sic] Inspection," *Southwestern Historical Quarterly* 79 (1975–76): 172; and Bancroft, *History of Arizona and New Mexico* 259, 269. Simmons, "Settlement Patterns," 11; and Marc Simmons, "Spanish Irrigation Practices in New Mexico," *New Mexico Historical Review* 47 (1972), esp. pp. 142–43.

without government sanction, were smaller than the estancias of the seventeenth century, in part because Pueblo Indian labor was less readily available. By the late eighteenth century, however, nomad Indian raids began to force those living in *ranchos* to consolidate in fortified villages known as *plazas*.[35] These villages, which usually were authorized by the government, were composed of houses arranged in contiguous fashion around an open plaza. The outer walls of the houses were windowless, the *plaza* entrances were barred, and a circular *torreón* (tower) outside the compound offered a vantage point for detecting intruders. It is known that in the Rio Arriba subregion, Ojo Caliente, Chimayo, Truchas, Las Trampas, and Taos were *plazas*.

As barriers against hostile incursions, frontier outposts were dangerous places, and understandably Hispanos were reluctant to live in them. Probably for this reason some outposts came to be populated by *genízaros*, nomadic Indians who, usually while children, had been abducted in warfare, ransomed in trade, or purchased by Hispanos and had lost their tribal identities. In the homes of their Hispano masters, whom they served as laborers or domestics, they became Spanish-speaking Christians. Eventually, groups of them were allowed to establish their own settlements, provided these were at frontier locations. Frontier outposts that had reputations for being populated by *genízaros* include Abiquiu, Belen, and Sabinal.[36] After a time each such settlement acquired a Hispano population.

People living in New Mexico in the eighteenth century were isolated within their local districts, yet two annual events that had become institutionalized by the second half of the century brought at least a few together. Each summer Hispanos and nomad Indians came together at Taos to trade Hispano knives, horses, woolen blankets, and beads for nomad Indian deerskins, buffalo robes, and captured slaves. The animal skins and slaves, along with woolen goods, livestock, and wine (made in the Paso del Norte District), were then transported in caravans to Chihuahua, where, at a fair held each January, they would

---

[35] Kelley, "Settlement of the Middle Rio Grande Valley," 393; Simmons, "Settlement Patterns," 13–14, 18.

[36] Sabinal is noted by Jones, *Los Paisanos*, 116.

be exchanged for hardware of all kinds, a variety of textiles, and luxury goods.[37] Representatives of the settlements in New Mexico formed the given caravans that would depart in November and return in April, the trips themselves taking forty days.[38] Products that they traded away, even the slaves and wine, contributed only modestly to the overall economy of New Spain, yet through this trade, and also through the periodic arrival of the mission supply caravans, at least some contact was maintained with the outside world.

The returning trade and mission supply caravans brought relatively few new people to New Mexico.[39] Rather, birth rates that exceeded death rates account for the slow increase in the Hispano population, which, exclusive of the Paso del Norte District, stood at about sixteen thousand in 1790. Hispanos in 1790 apparently represented most racial combinations. The majority were probably mestizo, the *mestizaje* process having advanced with each generation in the México and Zacatecas areas and in New Mexico. Some were also Caucasian, Indian from Mexico, local Indian servants, and mulatto. Sixteen were *peninsulares* and probably Caucasian, and perhaps a handful were black. The three *villas* contained the largest population concentrations, and they were the nuclei of three of eight *alcaldías* (administrative districts) into which New Mexico was divided. Franciscans were, of course, stationed at many of the Pueblo villages, yet some

[37] In his *History of Arizona and New Mexico*, Bancroft discussed both fairs (pp. 276–77), and he noted that sometimes the Indian slaves Spaniards would trade away were acquired through warfare (p. 235). In the seventeenth century, buffalo hides, chamois, candles, coarse woolen cloth, and mantas made by Pueblo Indians were exported from Santa Fe to Parral (near Santa Bárbara); Lansing B. Bloom, trans., "A Trade-Invoice of 1638," *New Mexico Historical Review* 10 (1935): 242–48; Scholes, "Civil Government and Society," 110.

[38] Max L. Moorhead, *New Mexico's Royal Road: Trade and Travel on the Chihuahua Trail*, esp. pp. 42–43. Governor Cachupín noted in the report of his inspection of 1751–52 that representatives of the settlements had to make these annual trips to keep the residents supplied with necessities; Miller, "New Mexico in Mid-Eighteenth Century," 170–71.

[39] Surnames of some who came sporadically with the caravans in the eighteenth century are given in Chávez, *Origins of New Mexico Families*, xiii–xiv; they include two Frenchmen, Alaríe and Labadíe; soldiers at the Santa Fe presidio, including de la O and Villanueva; merchants from Mexico City such as Pino and Gutiérrez; nephews or brothers of missionaries such as Gabaldón and Mariño; and descendants of those who had remained in 1693 at Paso del Norte, including Tapia and Telles.

nonclergy Hispanos also lived there, reportedly to the detriment of the Indians.[40]

Thus the area that was effectively occupied in 1790 was more densely settled than it had been in 1680, for many new communities had been established. Moreover, the outer boundary of the effectively occupied zone now stretched to include frontier settlements such as Ojo Caliente, Abiquiu, Truchas, and Las Trampas in the Rio Arriba, and, for some twenty years it had included much of the Puerco Valley. Since 1680, however, the effectively occupied zone in the Rio Abajo had contracted, for the area south of Sabinal had not been reoccupied. The Zuñi villages and the Paso del Norte District were still outliers, but the western Hopi villages, unwilling to accept missionaries after the reconquest, had been eliminated as an outlier. Most Hispanos in 1790 still lived in the Rio Grande valley and its tributaries, and, indeed, the designations "Rio Arriba" and "Rio Abajo" for the two subregions were common.[41]

A STRONGHOLD

Viewed in the large context of New Spain, New Mexico in 1790 was an isolated, remote, and relatively unimportant frontier outpost. It had produced no mineral wealth to speak of and its missionary activities were a drain on the Spanish treasury, and

[40] Alicia V. Tjarks, "Demographic, Ethnic and Occupational Structure of New Mexico, 1790," *Americas: A Quarterly Review of Inter-American Cultural History* 35 (1978–79): 60–61 (the figure 16,000 is derived from table 2), 79, 81, 82. According to Tjarks, the 1790 census is even more "trustworthy" than is the Domínguez census of 1776 (p. 57). Tjarks pointed out that in 1790 Spaniards were "predominant," yet the term *Spaniards* "probably" included mestizos. Some New Mexicans had Aztec ancestry; Chávez, *Origins of New Mexico Families*, xiv. The sixteen *peninsulares* may have included three priests at Paso del Norte (Tjarks, "Demographic Structure," 81, 81, 86). In 1790, for the first time in any census, the number of inhabitants at Albuquerque and at Santa Cruz surpassed that at Santa Fe; Jones, *Los Paisanos*, 127. The *alcaldías* are shown in the Miera y Pacheco map of 1779, reproduced in Alfred Barnaby Thomas, trans. and ed., *Forgotten Frontiers: A Study of the Spanish Indian Policy of Don Juan Bautista de Anza, Governor of New Mexico, 1777–1787*, end pouch. Writing in the 1780s, Father Morfi noted that Spaniards, who were freely admitted to live in the Pueblo villages, succeeded in making the Indians "practically slaves through debt"; Bancroft, *History of Arizona and New Mexico*, 269.

[41] Bancroft, *History of Arizona and New Mexico*, 222, 246, 266 ff. Oakah L. Jones, Jr., "Spanish Civil Communities and Settlers in Frontier New Mexico, 1790–1810," in *Hispanic-American Essays in Honor of Max Leon Moorhead*, ed. William S. Coker, 49.

although its significance as a colonist province was increasing, because of its modest population growth, still New Mexico's population constituted less than 1 percent of that in New Spain. Perhaps New Mexico's existence did give Spain some tangible basis for claiming the interior of North America, yet its real significance as a portal through which American manufactured goods would enter Mexico was three decades away. In a viceregal sense, then, New Mexico was little more than a "longitudinal . . . terminus" or "the end of the geographic line [in a] system geared upon Mexico City," as D. W. Meinig and George Kubler, respectively, expressed it.[42]

In a more immediate or regional sense, however, Hispanos had created something major. In the area stretching from Taos to Sabinal and from Pecos to Acoma, they had tilled the floodplains, grazed animals on the mesas, and detimbered the mountains as they went about the business of establishing plaza-centered communities, digging irrigation ditches, laying out long-lots for agriculture, and building adobe, stone, and log structures. They had adjusted to and had used effectively an environment that now bore their distinctive impress. By 1790 they were very much entrenched in a "Stronghold" carved out of the upper basin of the Rio Grande—the legacy of two centuries of formative colonization (Map 2.4).[43]

In the middle of that Stronghold was a historic core where the density of Hispano occupance, the intensity of Hispano culture, and the degree of Hispano nodality were seemingly greatest.[44] Santa Fe, politically and economically the focus of this nodality and really the only settlement where colonists were militarily secure, was the cornerstone of this historic core, whose outer boundary encircled Santa Cruz and Albuquerque to enclose a roughly triangular area. In this core, one can safely assume, the three *villas* were centers of innovation and the places where Hispanos forged a major part of their

---

[42] The Revillagigedo census of 1793 gave 30,853 people (excluding nomad Indians) for New Mexico and 4,483,559 for New Spain; Robert Denhardt, "Mexican Demography," *Pacific Historical Review* 7 (1938): 153. D. W. Meinig, *Southwest: Three Peoples in Geographical Change 1600–1970*, 120; George Kubler, *Santos: An Exhibition of the Religious Folk Art of New Mexico*, 1, 4, 6, 8.

[43] "Stronghold" is borrowed from Meinig, *Southwest*, 92.

[44] These three criteria for defining a "core" are from D. W. Meinig, "The Mormon Culture Region: Strategies and Patterns in the Geography of the American West, 1847–1964," *Annals of the Association of American Geographers* 55 (1965): 213, 215.

indigenous cultural institutions. In this core, moreover, the degree of interaction between Hispanos and their sedentary Pueblo Indian allies was probably greatest—a topic that is rooted in the long and complicated process of Hispano-Indian articulation.

CHAPTER 3

✢ ✢ ✢

INDIAN ARTICULATION

IN 1900, in a Homeland by then the size of Utah, only 163 Indians lived among the more than 140,000 Hispanos. Forty of the Indians were married to Hispanos, 42 were boarders (servants, pupils, or relatives) in Hispano homes, and 81 lived in separate but nearby households. Tribal affiliations are known for only 47 of the 163 Indians, and all 47—thirty-nine Navajos, five Apaches, two Cheyennes, and one "Dacota"—were nomad Indians.[1] These data are surprising. They reveal that in 1900 intermixing between Hispanos and the local Pueblo and nomad Indians was almost nonexistent, and, ironically, what little occurred was apparently with members of nomad tribes. They imply, moreover, that in at least the several generations before 1900, examples of unions between Hispanos and the local Pueblo and nomad Indians were few and that such unions had apparently been more frequent with the once nomadic and warlike tribes who lived on the periphery of the Homeland than with the peaceful and contiguous Pueblos.

[1] These were Indians as recorded largely by Hispano census marshals within census precincts that were a minimum 10 percent Hispano—the criterion by which the Homeland was defined. Hispano marshals would have been sensitive to questions of ethnicity, and because they often enumerated their home precincts, they were knowledgeable about those they recorded. On reservations located *outside* the Homeland, only a handful of Hispanos were married to Pueblo or nomad Indians. Population Schedules of the Twelfth Census [1900], Microcopy no. T–623, National Archives. Of the 163 Indians, 123 were identified in the regular schedules; tribal affiliations were given for 7, 5 of whom were married to Hispanos(as). Richard L. Nostrand, "The Hispano Homeland in 1900," *Annals of the Association of American Geographers,* 70 (1980): 388, n. 11. The remaining 40 were identified in the Indian schedules; 36 were Navajos and 4 were Apaches, and all lived in separate households among Hispanos in Mora, Rio Arriba, or San Juan counties in New Mexico or in Las Animas County in Colorado.

PUEBLO INDIAN ARTICULATION

About 1600 perhaps as many as forty-five thousand Pueblo Indians inhabited some eighty compact villages in what was then northern New Mexico. Culturally, these Indians were divided between the Western Pueblos, which included the Zuñis and Hopis, each with their three thousand who spoke one language and lived in half a dozen villages, and the Eastern Pueblos, where probably less than forty thousand lived in sixty or seventy villages in the upper Rio Grande basin. Each of the multistory adobe and stone villages inhabited by the Eastern Pueblos was politically autonomous and economically self-sufficient, and in all, six by-and-large mutually unintelligible languages were spoken (Map 3.1).[2] These sedentary and peaceful Pueblo Indians were, of course, what attracted Oñate and his colonists, and in the seventeenth century they were what kept the New Mexican enterprise alive as a missionary frontier.

Soon after Oñate's arrival, missions began to be built. Located typically at the edges of the Pueblos' villages, from which they were separated by a wall, these missions consisted of a church, the missionary's quarters or convento, corrals, and perhaps a blacksmith shop, weaving shop, and school.[3] By 1616 there were nine such missions at Pueblo villages and a convento and parish church at Santa Fe (Map 3.2). The mission at Santo Domingo was made the ecclesiastical headquarters.[4] By 1629 a cordon of new missions staffed with friars sur-

[2] Edward H. Spicer, *Cycles of Conquest: The Impact of Spain, Mexico, and the United States on the Indians of the Southwest, 1533–1960*, 153–55, 187–90. Spicer noted that at the time of first Spanish contact in 1540 the Zuñis numbered three thousand to thirty-five hundred in six villages, and the Hopis had approximately the same number in seven villages (pp. 187, 189, 190). The forty thousand figure is an estimate for the time of Coronado's arrival (p. 155). Edward P. Dozier reviewed other ways in which anthropologists have subdivided the Pueblo Indians culturally and linguistically; "The Pueblo Indians of the Southwest: A Survey of the Anthropological Literature and a Review of Theory, Method, and Results," *Current Anthropology* 5 (1964): 81–82, 85. The Piro language resembled Tiwa, and Tano and Tewa were mutually intelligible; Spicer, *Cycles of Conquest*, 153.
[3] Spicer, *Cycles of Conquest*, 287, 289, 291, 296, 298.
[4] France V. Scholes and Lansing B. Bloom, "Friar Personnel and Mission Chronology, 1598–1629," *New Mexico Historical Review* 19 (1944): 319–36; 20 (1945): 58–82. Concerning Map 3.2, by 1601, San Gabriel, San Ildefonso, and Jemez had conventos (19: 328). About 1610, the convento at San Gabriel was transferred to Santa Fe (19: 332.). Founded between 1610 and 1613, the San Lazaro convento was apparently

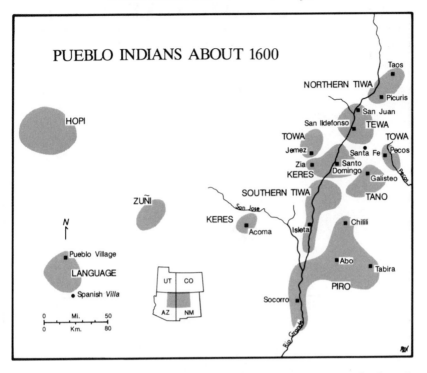

PUEBLO INDIANS ABOUT 1600

Map 3.1 Pueblo Indians about 1600 shown by language groups and selected villages. After Edward H. Spicer, *Cycles of Conquest: The Impact of Spain, Mexico, and the United States on the Indians of the Southwest, 1533–1960,* 154, 190.

rounded the old with outliers at the Zuñi and Hopi villages on the far western frontier. The twenty-five missions with resident friars that existed in 1629 may have been the largest number in the era before the Pueblo Revolt.[5] By 1680 those located east of the Manzano Mountains were abandoned because of Apache raids and drought.

abandoned by friars between 1614 and 1621 (20: 64). The other conventos in 1616 are noted on 19: 335. Concerning Santo Domingo, see France V. Scholes, "Civil Government and Society in New Mexico in the Seventeenth Century," *New Mexico Historical Review* 10 (1935): 108.

[5] Scholes and Bloom, "Friar Personnel," vol. 20. In chronological order, these missions with conventos were Pecos, 1619 (p. 66); Picuris about 1621 (p. 67); Jemez, reestablished in 1621–22 (p. 67); Taos about 1622 (p. 67); Abo by 1622 (p. 68); Socorro by 1626 (p. 78); Querac or Cuarac in the Chilili area 1626–28 (p. 73); Santa Clara about

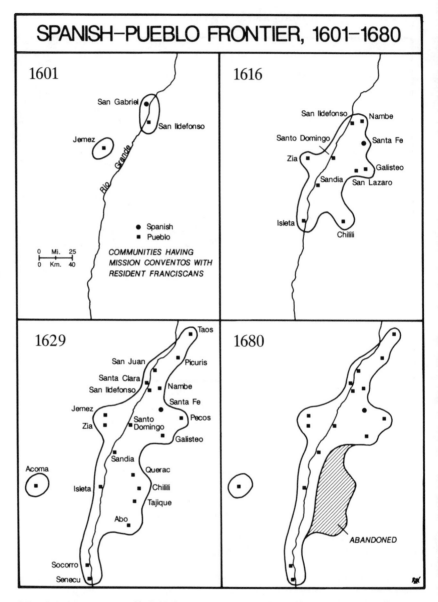

SPANISH–PUEBLO FRONTIER, 1601–1680

1601

San Gabriel

San Ildefonso

Jemez

● Spanish
■ Pueblo

COMMUNITIES HAVING
MISSION CONVENTOS WITH
RESIDENT FRANCISCANS

0   Mi.   25
0   Km.   40

Rio Grande

1616

San Ildefonso   Nambe

Santo Domingo   Santa Fe

Zia   Galisteo

Sandia   San Lazaro

Isleta

Chilili

1629

Taos

San Juan   Picuris

Santa Clara

San Ildefonso   Nambe

Jemez   Santa Fe

Zia   Santo Domingo   Pecos

Galisteo

Sandia

Acoma   Querac

Isleta   Chilili

Tajique

Abo

Socorro

Senecu

1680

ABANDONED

Map 3.2 Missions staffed with Franciscans marked the changing periphery of the incipient Hispano Homeland in the 1600s. Conventos at the Zuñi and Hopi villages are omitted in 1629 and 1680. The Paso del Norte District is not shown in 1680. Data for 1601, 1616, and 1629 are from France V. Scholes and Lansing B. Bloom, "Friar Personnel and Mission Chronology, 1598–1629," *New Mexico Historical Review* 19 (1944): 319–36; 20 (1945): 58–82. The 1680 frame shows the presumed locations of the thirty-three missionaries.

The missionaries who were assigned to the "provinces," as the yet unchristianized Pueblo Indian fields of labor were called, were the one learned class in New Mexico, the Franciscans, the majority of whom during much of the colonial period were born in Spain. Ten Franciscans joined Oñate en route to New Mexico in 1598, another seven were added in 1600, and during the 1600s the number fluctuated with the arrival and departure of the mission supply caravans. The presence of forty-six Franciscans in 1629 may have been the high point in the era before the revolt. These friars converted many Pueblos to Roman Catholicism, and they taught them various trades, music, reading, and writing, but unlike the Jesuits, who were working elsewhere in the Borderlands, they were not interested in learning the Pueblos' languages. Moreover, they exerted strong pressures to repress or eradicate the Pueblos' "pagan" religious beliefs, and they forced their charges to build churches, grow food, and even herd the cattle that some friars exported.[6]

From the beginning, then, Spaniards encroached on the Pueblos' villages. Friars and their soldier-escorts arrived first, and by the 1620s there were also encomenderos and the governor's agents, both groups of whom were bent on extracting tribute. One consequence of this encroachment was that the

1628 (p. 73); Acoma by 1629 (p. 73); Zuñi by 1629 (p. 73); Hopi by 1629 (p. 73); Tajique 1629 (p. 74); Senecu about 1629 (p. 80); and San Juan 1629–33 (p. 73). Located on the far western frontier of New Mexico, the Zuñis and Hopis in 1620 were exempted from payment of tribute; Lansing B. Bloom, "A Glimpse of New Mexico in 1620," *New Mexico Historical Review* 3 (1928): 365. Hubert Howe Bancroft cited a report by Father Alonso Benavides dated 1630 that states that each of the more than ninety Pueblo villages had a church, that all ninety were grouped in twenty-five missions or conventos, and that some fifty friars were ministering to the more than sixty thousand Christian Indians; *The Works of Hubert Howe Bancroft*, vol. 17, *History of Arizona and New Mexico, 1530–1888*, 162. A second peak in the number of conventos with resident friars may have been reached thirty years later. France Scholes noted twenty conventos in a document he translated and dated as 1664; "Documents for the History of the New Mexican Missions in the Seventeenth Century," *New Mexico Historical Review* 4 (1929): 45–51. In a correction, Scholes redated the document as about 1641; "Correction," *New Mexico Historical Review* 19 (1944): 245, 246. More recent evidence would suggest that the correct date is 1656; Stuart J. Baldwin, "A Reconsideration of the Dating of a Seventeenth-Century New Mexican Document," *New Mexico Historical Review* 59 (1984): 412.

[6] Marc Simmons, "New Mexico's Spanish Exiles," *New Mexico Historical Review* 59 (1984): 69; George P. Hammond and Agapito Rey, eds., *Don Juan de Oñate, Colonizer of New Mexico, 1595–1628*, Coronado Cuarto Centennial Publications, 1540–1940, ed. George P. Hammond, 5: 16, 24; Scholes and Bloom, "Friar Personnel," 71–72; Spicer, *Cycles of Conquest*, 158, 160; Dozier, "Pueblo Indians," 81, 90, 91; Scholes, "Civil Government and Society," 78, 106, 108.

Pueblos, who were made to work at different trades, became New Mexico's artisans in the Spanish era. A second was that the Pueblos found it necessary to practice their religion clandestinely. And a third was that the Pueblos quickly began to resent, indeed hate, all Spaniards, including the friars.[7]

On the eve of the Pueblo Revolt, the upper Rio Grande basin may have been the Spaniard's Homeland, but it was hardly their Stronghold, for the twenty-five hundred Spaniards were vastly outnumbered by the Pueblos. Even at Santa Fe, Indians may have been in the majority.[8] Outside Santa Fe, friars and their soldier-escorts, government agents, encomenderos, and other Spaniards were scattered at or near the Pueblos' villages. The geography of Spaniards in 1680, then, directly reflected that of the Pueblo Indians: a discrete point pattern within a Homeland whose periphery was marked by the outermost Indian villages that contained missions staffed with friars (Map 3.2).

When the Spaniards reoccupied New Mexico late in 1693, they found a Pueblo population that was perhaps half what it had been a century earlier. They found that many villages were abandoned, especially those of the Piro and the Southern Tiwa, some of whom had accompanied the Spaniards in 1680. Many Pueblos had regrouped, some at sites atop more defensible mesas. Some had fled to the distant villages of the Hopis, where refugees were always welcome. Yet when the Spaniards and Pueblos finally ceased their fighting about 1700, all but the Hopis, who would never again accept missionaries, had seemingly resigned themselves to the presence of the Spaniards.[9]

By the end of 1694 the Franciscans were once again at their

---

[7] Scholes, "Civil Government and Society," 81, 109; Spicer, *Cycles of Conquest*, 157, 159, 162. In the early 1800s, some Spaniards were carpenters and blacksmiths, but nearly all weaving, tanning, and pottery making was done by the Pueblos; Bancroft, *History of Arizona and New Mexico*, 302–303. See also Marc Simmons, "The Chacón Economic Report of 1803," *New Mexico Historical Review* 60 (1985): 85, 86. Of the thirty-three friars stationed in New Mexico in 1680, twenty-one were killed in the revolt; Spicer, *Cycles of Conquest*, 163.

[8] In 1630, Santa Fe was reported to have had 250 Spaniards and 700 Indians; Bancroft, *History of Arizona and New Mexico*, 164. During the 1600s some of the Indians living in the Indian barrio (district) in Santa Fe were Tlaxcalans brought from central Mexico; Spicer, *Cycles of Conquest*, 300.

[9] Spicer, *Cycles of Conquest*, 162, 164–65, 169. In the upper Rio Grande basin there may have been twenty-five thousand to thirty thousand Pueblos in 1680. Franciscan efforts to return to the Hopi villages ceased in 1782 (p. 196).

missions, whose reconstruction by Pueblos they supervised. But now these friars were more relaxed about executing their policies. Even though their ranks swelled to forty by 1740, perhaps a high point in the second epoch of Spanish occupance, still they took little interest in learning the Pueblos' languages, they built no more schools at the villages, and they were less committed to making conversions.[10] Instead, they placed greater emphasis on ministering to the Hispano population, which was growing relative to that of the Pueblos.

As the friars' relative neglect of the Pueblos mounted, the Pueblo population continued to decline. About 1800 it was again half what it had been about 1700.[11] Meanwhile, the number of villages decreased. By 1752, only twenty-five remained, and by 1811 there were twenty, of which only four (Taos, Picuris, Isleta, and Acoma) were located where they had been when the Spaniards first arrived (Fig. 3.1).[12]

Hispanos capitalized on the Pueblo decline. They infiltrated Pueblo villages, notably those of the Tewas located north of Santa Fe—San Juan, Santa Clara, San Ildefonso, Nambe, Pojoaque, and Tesuque. And they encroached on Pueblo lands to establish their own communities, for which they preempted Pueblo village names—Taos, Pojoaque, Tesuque, San Ildefonso, Galisteo, and, in the early nineteenth century, Pecos.

[10] Ibid., 165, 166, 167; Bancroft, History of Arizona and New Mexico, 212, 241, 269–70; Dozier, "Pueblo Indians," 90; Robert Ryal Miller, "New Mexico in Mid-Eighteenth Century: A Report Based on Governor Vélez Capuchín's [sic] Inspection," Southwestern Historical Quarterly 79 (1975–76): 174. Spicer noted that in 1767 those missions that adjoined Spanish settlements were secularized, which practically ended their mission programs (Cycles of Conquest, 167).

[11] Spicer, Cycles of Conquest, 169. A census taken in 1790 recorded nearly ninety-five hundred Pueblo Indians (as compared to sixteen thousand Spaniards) in New Mexico exclusive of the Paso del Norte District; Alicia V. Tjarks, "Demographic, Ethnic and Occupational Structure of New Mexico, 1790," Americas: A Quarterly Review of Inter-American Cultural History 35 (1978–79): 61. Reasons given for the decline included miscegenation with Europeans, declining birth rates, and increasing mortality rates (p. 59).

[12] Miller, "New Mexico in Mid-Eighteenth Century," 175 (twenty-two of the twenty-five villages in 1752 are listed on p. 177). Pino recorded twenty-two "Indian Pueblos" in 1811; two of them, Abiquiu and Belen, were obviously included because of their genízaro populations; Pedro Bautista Pino, Exposición . . . , in Three New Mexico Chronicles: The Exposición of Don Pedro Bautista Pino 1812; The Ojeada of Lic. Antonio Barreiro 1832; and the Additions by José Augustín de Escudero, 1849, The Quivira Society Publications, vol. 11, trans. and ed. H. Bailey Carroll and J. Villasana Haggard, 27. Spicer noted the four villages that had not been relocated; Cycles of Conquest, 169.

Fig. 3.1 Located on a high mesa, the Acoma village has remained at its pre-Spanish site. The church (center) was built between 1629 and about 1641; John L. Kessell, *The Missions of New Mexico since 1776*, 196. Source: Spence air photograph E–11232, taken June 7, 1941, photograph 4.A.57 courtesy Maxwell Museum of Anthropology, University of New Mexico, Albuquerque.

Such encroachment forced Spanish officials to recognize each Pueblo group as having a minimum four-square-league land base.[13] The ever-growing Hispano population meanwhile filled in, as it were, between the Pueblos, and beginning in the 1790s, in a modest way, Hispanos began to expand beyond the outer-

[13] Myra Ellen Jenkins, "Spanish Land Grants in the Tewa Area," *New Mexico Historical Review* 47 (1972): 114, 117–32; Miller, "New Mexico in Mid-Eighteenth Century," 175. The plaza and many of the houses in Taos (officially, Don Fernando de Taos when the grant was approved in 1796) were within the limits of the Taos Indian grant; Myra Ellen Jenkins, "Taos Pueblo and Its Neighbors, 1540–1847," *New Mexico Historical Review* 41 (1966): 100. Hispanos encroached on the site of Pecos within the Pecos land base beginning in 1815; G. Emlen Hall, *Four Leagues of Pecos: A Legal History of the Pecos Grant, 1800–1933*, New Mexico Land Grant Series, 23ff.; Jenkins, "Spanish Land Grants," 114, asserted that it is a mistaken notion that during Spanish rule each village was awarded a land grant of four square leagues. Rather, Hispanos were to respect as belonging to the Pueblos those areas effectively occupied by them.

most Indian villages. Thus, by the end of the Spanish era, no longer did the geography of Hispanos merely reflect that of the Pueblo Indians, and their numerical superiority ensured that their Homeland was also their Stronghold. The Franciscan ministerial shift to the Hispanos also signaled that New Mexico by 1821 had undergone a transition from a largely missionary to a largely colonist province.

No one knows the exact extent of miscegenation between Hispanos and Pueblos during the Spanish era. This is in part because New Mexican society was "fluid," and through mixed marriages an "Indian" could be transformed to a "Spaniard" in as little as two generations. It does seem, however, that relatively little cultural borrowing took place between Hispanos and Pueblos during Spanish rule. Compared to the one hundred words taken (in Mexico) from Nahuatl to the Spanish spoken in New Mexico and Colorado, only twenty were apparently incorporated from the Pueblo (and nomad) Indian languages, for example.[14] It also seems that most of the miscegenation and cultural borrowing that occurred did so in the seventeenth century.

During the Mexican period the relative neglect of the Pueblos by the church continued. The Franciscans (or religious clergy) sent from Mexico City were gradually being replaced by secular clergy sent by the bishop in Durango. Both were in short supply. For the first time secular clergy who were born in New Mexico began to appear.[15] Given that the ministerial concerns of these New Mexico–born clergy undoubtedly rested with their own people, and given that the Pueblos, who contin-

---

[14] Children of an Indian and a mestizo were classed as mestizo, and those of a mestizo and a Spaniard were accorded Spanish status; such social fluidity also helps to explain the decline in the Indiand population; Robert Archibald, "Acculturation and Assimilation in Colonial New Mexico," *New Mexico Historical Review* 53 (1978): 214. Aurelio M. Espinosa, *The Spanish Language in New Mexico and Southern Colorado,* Historical Society of New Mexico, no. 16, 12–13.

[15] As early as 1797 the Bishop of Durango sent secular clergy (*curas*) to the Hispanic parishes of New Mexico. Chávez labeled the decades 1790–1850 the "Secular Period"; Fray Angélico Chávez, "The Penitentes of New Mexico," *New Mexico Historical Review* 29 (1954): 115. The supply of Franciscans was made even smaller when, in 1828, three or four who were Spanish-born were exiled from New Mexico; Simmons, "New Mexico's Spanish Exiles," 70–72. Bancroft noted that no New Mexico–born priest had been produced in the Spanish period; *History of Arizona and New Mexico,* 304. Father Antonio José Martínez, the best known of the New Mexico–born clergy, was ministering at Taos as early as 1824; Lansing Bartlett Bloom, "New Mexico under Mexican Administration, 1821–1846," *Old Santa Fe* 1 (1913–14): 268.

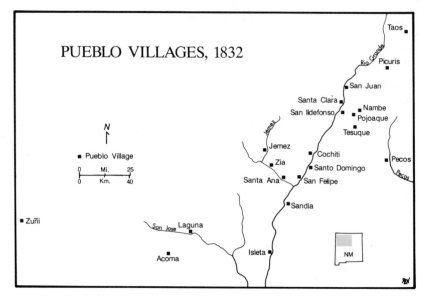

Map 3.3 Pueblo villages in New Mexico in 1832. Antonio Barreiro gave nineteen villages in his *Ojeada* ... (Puebla, 1832), reprinted in "Barreiro's Ojeada Sobre Nuevo-Mexico," trans. and ed. Lansing B. Bloom, *New Mexico Historical Review* 3 (1928): 87. He must have omitted San Juan by mistake. He does not list the Hopis, with whom Hispano contact had ceased.

ued to speak their own languages, were Roman Catholics only in a nominal sense anyway, it is perhaps remarkable that in 1832 five of the twenty Pueblo villages were staffed with clergy (Map 3.3).[16]

In 1850 there were sixteen Roman Catholic clergy in New Mexico. All were born in New Mexico.[17] The following year, French-born Jean Baptiste Lamy took up his duties in Santa Fe, and over the next several decades he greatly increased the number of clergy, nearly all of whom came from Europe. Still,

[16]Antonio Barreiro, *Ojeada* . . . , in "Barreiro's Ojeada Sobre Nuevo-Mexico," trans. and ed. Lansing B. Bloom, *New Mexico Historical Review* 3 (1928): 87, 88. Barreiro noted that five of nineteen Pueblo villages had clergy in 1832. He apparently erred in not including San Juan as a Pueblo village. The five villages with clergy were not named. Barreiro commented that the Pueblos spoke their own languages as well as Spanish.

[17] This was New Mexico exclusive of the El Paso District. Population Schedules of the Seventh Census [1850], Microcopy no. 432 (1963), rolls 467–70, National Archives.

the relative neglect of the Pueblos continued. In 1859, only four of twenty clergy in New Mexico Territory resided in Pueblo villages (Picuris, San Juan, San Ildefonso, and Santo Domingo), and by 1900, only three (all Frenchmen) of forty-seven clergy in New Mexico Territory lived in Pueblo villages (San Juan, Jemez, and Isleta).[18]

The influence of the Roman Catholic church on the Pueblos was sustained, however, through the establishment of schools. In the late 1880s, Archbishop Jean Baptiste Salpointe, Lamy's successor, contracted with the federal government for his archdiocese to run day schools at many of the Pueblo villages and also a boarding school (Saint Catherine School) for Indians at Santa Fe. And in the 1880s acculturation of a different sort was initiated by Pueblo men who began to leave their villages temporarily for wage work among the Anglos. There were also two recognizable geographical changes. The federal government compartmentalized the Pueblos' villages on grants of land, and these villages spread well beyond their original village nuclei as Pueblos chose to live in single-family homes. Of the Eastern Pueblo villages only Taos remained as compact as it once was.[19]

The ever-growing Hispano population meanwhile encroached as blatantly as ever on the tiny, well-chosen lands of the Pueblos. Only Zia and Acoma appear to have been spared as Hispanos squatted on the choice bottomlands, primarily in the second half of the nineteenth century. In the end, 80 percent of the Pueblos' land that Hispanos legally acquired through squatters' rights was in the eight Rio Arriba Pueblo grants (north of Santa Fe), where, by about 1940, approximately 18,200 acres had been awarded in more than two thousand

[18] John Baptist Salpointe, *John Baptist Salpointe: Soldier of the Cross*, ed. Odie B. Faulk, 51; Population Schedules of the Twelfth Census [1900]. In 1900, Jemez and Isleta were technically non-Homeland enclaves, so in chapter 5 their two French-born clergy are not counted among the fifty-six in the Homeland.

[19] Salpointe, *John Baptist Salpointe*, 137–41; Spicer, *Cycles of Conquest*, 176. In 1858, Congress confirmed seventeen Pueblo grants, and ten years later it confirmed the Santa Ana Grant; J. J. Bowden, *Private Land Claims in the Southwest*, 1: 171, 198, 213. Regarding village dispersal, see Dozier, "Pueblo Indians of the Southwest," 92; Spicer, *Cycles of Conquest*, 181; and Marc Simmons, who noted that Pueblo village dispersal coincided with the reduced threat of nomad Indian raids in the second half of the nineteenth century ("Settlement Patterns and Village Plans in Colonial New Mexico," *Journal of the West* 8 [1969]: 19). Regarding Taos, see Spicer, *Cycles of Conquest*, 182.

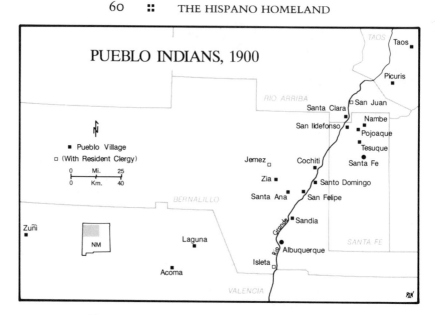

Map 3.4 Pueblo Indians in New Mexico Territory in 1900. Santa Fe and Albuquerque contained three Indian schools (Table 3.1). Source: Indian Schedules, Population Schedules of the Twelfth Census [1900].

largely uncontested private claims that affected an estimated ten thousand Hispanos. Indeed, by 1900, Hispanos living in three of the nineteen Pueblo grants accounted for more than 10 percent of the population: Sandia (12 percent), San Juan (17 percent), and Cochiti (32 percent).[20]

In 1900, 8,488 Pueblos, most of them farmers who lived in "fixed" dwellings, were enumerated in New Mexico Territory (Map 3.4). They lived in nineteen villages and at three schools (Table 3.1). The three schools to which Pueblo students had been attracted were within the Hispano Homeland, as were the Cochiti, San Juan, and Sandia villages, but the other sixteen

[20] Spicer, *Cycles of Conquest*, 172; Alvar W. Carlson, "Spanish-American Acquisition of Cropland within the Northern Pueblo Indian Grants, New Mexico," *Ethnohistory* 22 (1975): 101, 103; Population Schedules of the Twelfth Census [1900]. The Pueblos received compensation for lands that could not be restored; Spicer, *Cycles of Conquest*, 173. For case studies of encroachment on the San Ildefonso and Picuris grants, see Alvar W. Carlson, "El Rancho and Vadito: Spanish Settlements on Indian Land Grants," *El Palacio* 85 (1979): 28–39.

Table 3.1 Pueblo Indians in New Mexico Territory, 1900

Taos	413
Picuris	96
San Juan	379
Santa Clara	215
San Ildefonso	138
Pojoaque	12
Nambe	77
Tesuque	80
Cochiti	198
Santo Domingo	771
San Felipe	514
Santa Ana	228
Zia	114
Jemez	449
Sandia	76
Isleta	1,021
Laguna	1,077
Acoma	492
Zuñi	1,525
Pueblo Indians on Reservations	7,875
Saint Catherine School (Santa Fe)	162
Indian Industrial School (Santa Fe)[a]	245
Albuquerque Indian School[a]	206
Pueblo Indians off Reservations	613
Total	8,488

SOURCE: U.S. Bureau of the Census, Indian Schedules, Population Schedules of the Twelfth Census [1900].
[a] Includes some Pima and Papago from Arizona.

villages fell well below the 10 percent Hispano criterion for belonging in the Homeland and thus were non-Homeland enclaves. Except at the three schools, where Pueblos and Hispanos lived in close proximity, the two peoples appear to have interacted very little and to have lived in quite separate worlds.[21]

In 1980 there were still nineteen Pueblo villages and grants, yet the Pueblo population was 26,283. The number of active clergy in the Archdiocese of Santa Fe, which areally had been

[21] These 8,488 were given in the Indian schedules. Few if any of the 222 Indians identified in New Mexico Territory and Colorado in the regular schedules (123 of whom lived among Hispanos) appear to have been Pueblos; Population Schedules of the Twelfth Census [1900]. See Nostrand, "Hispano Homeland in 1900," 386, 388, 389. Hispanos stayed away from all Pueblo religious ceremonies to which they were not expressly invited; Spicer, Cycles of Conquest, 185.

reduced to about two-thirds of New Mexico, had also grown—
to about 190. In 1900, Archbishop Peter Bourgade of Santa Fe
had invited the Franciscans to return to New Mexico.[22] By
1980 they and religious clergy from a number of additional
orders constituted approximately 40 percent of the 190 total.
Few religious clergy were Hispanos. The secular clergy, on the
other hand, was once again heavily Hispano, including even
Archbishop Robert Sánchez, who was from Socorro. The same
three Pueblo villages (San Juan, Jemez, and Isleta) that had
been staffed with resident clergy in 1900 continued to have
such clergy, yet from nearby parish seats a dozen additional
clergy ministered to many of the remaining Pueblo villages as
well as to Saint Catherine School in Santa Fe. In 1980 the
Pueblos continued to live an isolated existence, speaking their
own languages, practicing their own form of Roman Catholicism, and intermarrying with Hispanos only rarely.[23]

NOMAD INDIAN ARTICULATION

When Spaniards moved in with the Pueblos about 1600, they
and the Pueblos were surrounded by nomad Indians. To the
east and west were several Athapaskan-speaking Apache
groups. One, the Jicarilla Apaches, in about the 1740s was
driven west of the Rio Grande by Comanches, who had come
from the north to dominate the eastern plains. Another, the
ancestors of the Mescalero Apaches, was probably shifting
southward into southern New Mexico at this time. In the
upper reaches of the Chama, northwest of the Spaniards and
Pueblos, were the Navajos, an Athapaskan-speaking offshoot

[22] The figure 26,283 represents the sum of the nineteen Pueblo populations on
reservations in New Mexico; U.S. Bureau of the Census, *Census of Population:
American Indian Areas and Alaska Native Villages, 1980,* Supplementary Report
PC80-S1–13, table 4. The Archdiocese of Santa Fe stretched from the Texas-Oklahoma
border west to the Puerco and from a line drawn south of Socorro-Portales north to
the Colorado border. Data about the clergy in the archdiocese in 1980 are from
[Clergymen in the] "Archdiocese of Santa Fe," typescript, and "Parishes in the Archdiocese of Santa Fe," typescript, in the chancery office, Archdiocese of Santa Fe, Albuquerque. Bourgade's invitation is discussed in John L. Kessell, *The Missions of New
Mexico since 1776,* 22.
[23] In the memories of the oldest inhabitants who were interviewed in the Spanish
villages of the Rio Arriba in 1935, only in "rare instances" had there been intermarriages between Hispanos and Indians; U.S. Department of Agriculture, Soil Conservation Service, *Tewa Basin Study, 1935,* vol. 2, *The Spanish-American Villages,* 33,
reprinted in *Hispanic Villages of Northern New Mexico,* ed. Marta Weigle.

of the Apaches who, during the 1700s, gradually migrated west to relocate in the area north of the Zuñis. And north of the Navajos were the Utes. No one knows how numerous these and other nomad Indians were during the Spanish period.[24]

Basically hunters and gatherers who ranged in small, separate bands, these nomads had long made a practice of raiding the Pueblos for their agricultural stockpiles, and now they looted the Hispanos for their foodstuffs and livestock. The Apaches appear to have been the chief plunderers in the 1600s. Beginning in 1706, the Navajos, newly reconstituted by their absorption of Pueblo refugees after the revolt of 1680, joined in the depredations, sporadically in the 1700s and then quite regularly in the first half of the 1800s. Significant Comanche marauding, meanwhile, seems to have begun in 1716 and ended in 1779. That of the Utes began in the late 1830s after they acquired guns and ammunition from Anglos.[25] One effect of these constant attacks was that Hispanos were severely constrained in their efforts to expand areally. A second was that nomadic Indians carried off large numbers of Hispano children, and the Hispanos, in retaliation, captured (or ransomed) large numbers of nomad children.

The practice of making captives of one another's children for use as domestics or laborers began in the 1600s. In the next two centuries Hispanos came to possess captives, or *genízaros*,

[24] Spicer, *Cycles of Conquest*, 210, 212, 213, 229, 230, 407; Harold Hoffmeister, "The Consolidated Ute Indian Reservation," *Geographical Review* 35 (1945): 601. "La Jicarilla," as Hispanos called the Jicarilla Apache habitat located on the High Plains east of Taos, was vacated sometime after 1727; Jerry N. McDonald, "La Jicarilla," *Journal of Cultural Geography* 2 (1982): 46, 55. Information on the numbers of nomads "is very contradictory"; Tjarks, "Demographic Structure," 50.

[25] Apache raids were the paramount problem in New Mexico in the 1670s (Scholes, "Civil Government and Society," 78); their raids continued well into the 1800s. This information on the Navajos is from Spicer, *Cycles of Conquest*, 211–12, 214; Navajo raids occurred as recently as 1879 (p. 221). In the mid-1800s, the Navajos "openly declare[d] that they would long ago have exterminated the Mexicans [of New Mexico] had it not been deemed more profitable to use them as shepherds"; Bancroft, *History of Arizona and New Mexico*, 459. Josiah Gregg made the same point in his *Commerce of the Prairies*, ed. Max L. Moorhead, 135. The date 1716 for the Comanches is in Bancroft, *History of Arizona and New Mexico*, 235; the date 1779 is in Aurelio M. Espinosa, *Los Comanches: A Spanish Heroic Play of the Year Seventeen Hundred and Eighty*, University of New Mexico Bulletin, Language Series, vol. 1, no. 1, whole no. 45: 13. Ute raiding is in David J. Weber, "American Westward Expansion and the Breakdown of Relations between Pobladores and 'Indios Bárbaros' on Mexico's Far Northern Frontier, 1821–1846," *New Mexico Historical Review*, 56 (1981): 222, 227, 229.

who were Apaches, Comanches, Navajos, Utes, Kiowas, and Pawnees. So large was the exchange of captives between Navajos and Hispanos that by the mid-1800s an entire "Mexican" clan composed of descendants of captive Hispanas lived among the Navajos, while hundreds of Navajos were reported to be harbored by Hispanos. In 1850, as recorded in the census, 164 nomad Indians lived among the Hispanos, and Navajo was the leading tribal affiliation when one was given.[26]

Contact between Hispanos on the one hand and *genízaros* and nomad Indians on the other resulted in much cultural borrowing. From various nomad peoples, for example, Hispanos learned to use wild plants and to make clothing from animal skins. From *genízaros* they incorporated into their folkways certain nomad Indian beliefs and customs. From their contact with Hispanos, meanwhile, the Navajos and especially the Apaches were fundamentally transformed through their acquisition of domesticated animals, notably sheep and horses, and through their adoption of other forms of material culture.[27] This is paradoxical. Contact between Hispanos and the Apaches and Navajos was apparently less intimate and of shorter duration than between Spaniards and any other southwestern Indians save the Yuman-speaking peoples. Franciscans, moreover, were totally unsuccessful in missionizing among them, and never once were Hispanos able to control the Apaches and Navajos politically or to settle among them.[28]

[26] Scholes, "Civil Government and Society," 83–85; Chávez, "Penitentes," 115; Spicer, *Cycles of Conquest*, 213, 217. Scholes notes that Apache (also Pueblo) children were commonly and illegally enslaved in the 1600s. Chávez writes that both the captives and their free descendants were known as *genízaros*. "Hispanos always had more Indian captives than the reverse"; Frances Leon Swadesh, "Structure of Hispanic-Indian Relations in New Mexico," in *The Survival of Spanish American Villages*, Colorado College Studies Number 15, ed. Paul Kutsche, 61. Most of the 164 in 1850 were females (102), and most were servants in relatively wealthy Hispano households (which included a priest in Tome and a priest and the vicar in Santa Fe); Population Schedules of the Seventh Census [1850], rolls 467–70.

[27] Arthur Leon Campa, *Spanish Folk-Poetry in New Mexico*, 5–6; Spicer, *Cycles of Conquest*, 210, 214, 227, 229. Hispanos used all parts of the buffalo, including the meat, lard, suet, wool, horns, and hides; Barreiro, *Ojeada*, 92.

[28] Spicer, *Cycles of Conquest*, 210, 211, 212, 213, 241. Franciscan missions established in 1745 among the Navajos at Cebolleta and Encinal lasted only two years (p. 212). The mission reportedly in existence in 1733 among the Jicarilla Apaches some five leagues from Taos was also apparently short-lived; Oakah L. Jones, Jr., *Los Paisanos: Spanish Settlers on the Northern Frontier of New Spain*, 123.

Such cultural borrowing had probably run its course when the Apaches, Navajos, and other nomad tribes began to be confined to reservations by Anglos.

Nomad peoples were placed on reservations to control their forays and thus to open the frontier to Anglo colonists. By the spring of 1863, four hundred Mescalero Apaches were gathered at the Pecos Valley Bosque Redondo Reservation under the protection of Fort Sumner. The next year these Apaches were joined by eight thousand Navajos. Friction between the two saw the Mescaleros withdraw and, in 1873–74, regroup on a reservation in southern New Mexico. In 1868 the Navajos were permitted to return to their former territory and thus rejoin those who had not relocated. They, too, were given a reservation that, over the next forty years, was enlarged as the Navajos increased numerically. And the Jicarillas and Utes, who were clustered at Indian agencies at Cimarron and Abiquiu (later Tierra Amarilla), also reluctantly moved onto reservations, the Utes in 1878 to one established earlier for other Utes in southwestern Colorado and the Jicarillas in 1880 to one located east of the Navajo reservation (Map 3.5).[29]

In 1900, 4,708 of 5,309 nomad Indians in New Mexico Territory and southwestern Colorado lived on their respective reservations, where they raised sheep, farmed, or, in the case of the Utes and Jicarilla Apaches, were "ration" Indians (Table 3.2). Living with them at the reservation headquarters were some Anglo government agents, traders, and teachers and a few Hispano farmers, teamsters, and laborers. In two places, the Animas Valley of La Plata County and southwestern Archuleta County, both in the Southern Ute Reservation, a few Hispanos, apparently because they were part Ute or were Ute spouses, received allotments of Ute Indian land. In 1900, Hispanos at each of these two places consisted of a dozen families who lived by themselves and owned their own farms. Nomad Indians who lived off their reservations included a number of Navajo sheepmen found in "movable" dwellings in parts of western New Mexico Territory, some Navajo and Apache students in boarding schools at Santa Fe and Albuquerque, and,

---

[29] Spicer, *Cycles of Conquest*, 218–19, 220–23; Bancroft, *History of Arizona and New Mexico*, 662, 730, 732, 737–39, 743, 744.

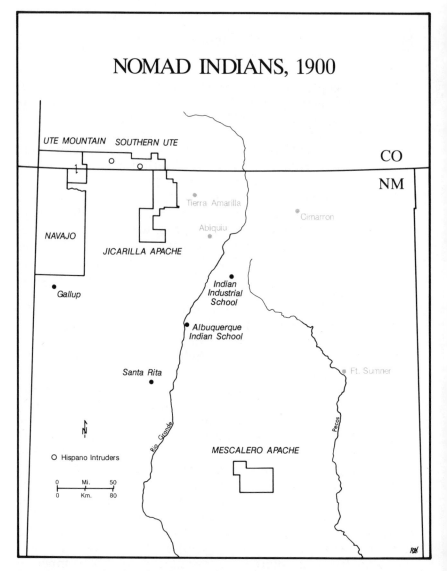

NOMAD INDIANS, 1900

UTE MOUNTAIN SOUTHERN UTE

CO

NM

Tierra Amarilla

Cimarron

Abiquiu

NAVAJO

JICARILLA APACHE

Gallup

Indian
Industrial
School

Albuquerque
Indian School

Santa Rita

Ft. Sumner

N

Rio Grande

Pecos

MESCALERO APACHE

O Hispano Intruders

| 0 | Mi. | 50 |
| 0 | Km. | 80 |

Map 3.5 Nomad Indian locations in New Mexico Territory and southwestern Colorado in 1900 (Table 3.2). Ft. Sumner, Cimarron, Abiquiu, and Tierra Amarilla were former Indian agencies. Source: Indian Schedules, Population Schedules of the Twelfth Census [1900].

Table 3.2   Nomad Indians in New Mexico Territory and Southwestern
Colorado, 1900

Navajos (NMT only)[a]	2,441
Utes (Colorado)[b]	968
Jicarilla Apaches	819
Mescalero Apaches	480
Nomad Indians on Reservations	4,708
Navajos by themselves[c]	470
Boarding school students[d]	93
Living among Hispanos[e]	38
Nomad Indians off Reservations	601
Total	5,309

SOURCE: U.S. Bureau of the Census, Indian Schedules, Population Schedules of the Twelfth Census [1900].
[a] San Juan County (1,731); Bernalillo County (710).
[b] Ignacio Subagency, Southern Ute Reservation, La Plata County (409); Navajo Springs Agency, Ute Mountain Reservation, Montezuma County (559). There were no Indians in the Archuleta County portion of the Southern Ute Reservation.
[c] Gallup area (336); Santa Rita Precinct, Socorro County (134).
[d] Navajos, Apaches, etc., at Indian Industrial School in Santa Fe (60) and Albuquerque Indian School (33).
[e] Navajos (34); Apaches (4).

as noted at the beginning of this chapter, some Navajos and Apaches who lived among or were intermarried with Hispanos.[30]

By 1980 nomad Indians were at least two times more numerous than in 1900. On reservations the Navajos alone numbered

[30] The Hispanos in the Southern Ute reservation had apparently lived on Ute land for more than a full generation. Of the ninety-three Hispanos involved, thirty-seven were born in New Mexico of New Mexico–born parents, forty-two were born in Colorado of New Mexico–born parents, and thirteen were born in Colorado of Colorado-born parents. One was born in Kansas of New Mexico–born parents; Population Schedules of the Twelfth Census [1900], roll 130, Enumeration District (ED) 155, pp. 222A, 223A, 223B. Hispanos in the Animas Valley constituted more than 10 percent of the Ignacio Subagency in La Plata County, thus bringing that area into the Homeland; Nostrand, "Hispano Homeland in 1900," 386, 389. That a few Hispanos or part-Hispanos received allotments is noted by Swadesh in her discussion of La Posta and Cañada Bonita, apparently the communities of these two Hispano groups. Frances Leon Swadesh, *Los Primeros Pobladores: Hispanic Americans of the Ute Frontier*, 118–20. In 1918 the Southern Ute Reservation (La Plata and Archuleta counties) and the Ute Mountain Reservation (Montezuma County) became the Consolidated Ute Indian Reservation, Hoffmeister, "Consolidated Ute Indian Reservations," 601. Only 38 of the 163 Indians discussed in the introduction to this chapter are cited in Table 3.2. Omitted are two Navajos who lived among Hispanos in Colorado outside its southwestern corner and all 123 Indians identified as living among Hispanos in the regular schedules. These data are discussed and mapped in Nostrand, "Hispano Homeland in 1900," 388–89.

31,956 (New Mexico only), the Jicarilla Apaches 1,715, the Mescalero Apaches 1,922, and the Utes (in southwestern Colorado) 1,966.[31] The 1980 census gives no information concerning how many nomad Indians may have been married to Hispanos, but the number was undoubtedly small.

INDIAN ENCLAVES

An evangelical religion and a desire for captive labor compelled the friars and the Spanish soldier-settlers to encroach upon the Pueblo Indians as soon as they reached New Mexico, and by 1680 the geographical arrangement of these intruders directly reflected that of the Pueblos. After the reconquest, however, the friars were less compulsive about making converts, the emerging Hispano population no longer enslaved the Pueblos, and the two peoples increasingly went their separate ways, the greatly reduced Pueblo population maintaining its cultural integrity while the Hispano population settled between and beyond them to create its own regional configuration. Thus, the bulk of the miscegenation and cultural borrowing that took place seems to have occurred in the seventeenth century. Today, Hispanos and Pueblos share the same region, yet geographically they live apart, and socially they are kept apart by strong feelings of animosity engendered most recently by competition for land.

Articulation between Hispanos and nomad Indians, on the other hand, went a different direction. Until the 1790s Hispanos were areally contained on all sides by hostile nomadic tribes. From raids by Hispanos to capture Indians, however, detribalized nomadic children became servants in Hispano households, giving rise to a *genízaro* population that intermarried with Hispanos. Ironically, then, after the seventeenth century the degree of miscegenation, and perhaps also of cultural borrowing, between Hispanos and nomad Indians may have been greater than between Hispanos and Pueblos. Today, the

---

[31] The breakdown was as follows: Navajos: Alamo Reservation, Socorro County, 1,062; Cañoncito Reservation, Bernalillo and Valencia counties, 969; Navajo Reservation, San Juan and McKinley counties, 28,762; Ramah Community, Valencia and McKinley counties, 1,163; Jicarilla Apache Reservation, Rio Arriba and Sandoval counties, 1,715; Mescalero Apache Reservation, Otero County, 1,922; Utes: Southern Ute Reservation, La Plata and Archuleta counties, 855; Ute Mountain Reservation, Montezuma County, 1,111. U.S. Bureau of the Census, *American Indian Areas . . . 1980*, table 4.

Hispano–nomad Indian *mestizaje* is what differentiates Hispanos, racially, from their larger-minority brethren.

Today both Pueblo and nomad Indians are compartmentalized on reservations. Both have had their reservations encroached upon by Hispanos. Yet even in those reservations where encroachment has been greatest, Hispanos and Indians live apart geographically and socially. Thus, these Indian reservations are enclaves that are either embedded in the Hispanos' Homeland, as is the case with the Pueblos, or are located on the periphery of that Homeland, as is the case with the nomad Indians. After four centuries of articulation, the Hispano-Indian geographical legacy is one of relic Indian islands in a heavily Hispano sea.

CHAPTER 4

⊹ ⊹ ⊹

CONTIGUOUS EXPANSION

SOUTH OF MORA a century ago three villages named Cebolla stretched along the Cebolla Valley floor: Abuelo Cebolla (Grandfather Wild Flower—of the onion family), San Jose Cebolla (Saint Joseph Wild Flower), and El Oro Cebolla (Golden Wild Flower).[1] That each of these villages was named Cebolla suggests that one of them, perhaps San Jose Cebolla, later renamed Ledoux, was the parent village, the others its offspring. That all had such delightfully unpretentious names further suggests that their colonizers were a good-natured folk people who were close to the earth and to their religion. Significantly, this string of small "wild flowers" is a microcosm of a powerful yet little-appreciated Homeland-shaping process: the village-by-village contiguous expansion of a folk society that, in a period of about a century, spontaneously yet dynamically came to blanket much of New Mexico and parts of four adjacent present-day states.

A STOCKMENS' FRONTIER

The year 1790 marked the beginning of relatively peaceful times in New Mexico. Governor Juan Bautista de Anza had led successful military campaigns against the Comanches and Apaches during the dozen years before 1790, ending a period of exceptionally bloody warfare. Heavily armored caravans, meanwhile, had been inching their ways to and from Chihuahua each year to enable Hispanos to exchange their sheep,

---

[1] *Cebolla*, which means "onion," in New Mexico place names has a shaded meaning of "wild flower of the onion family"; Fray Angélico Chávez, "Neo-Mexicanisms in New Mexico Place Names," *El Palacio* 57 (1950): 70. *Abuelo* (grandfather) is also a New Mexican expression for "bogeyman" (p. 67).

animal skins, and woolen goods for hardware, textiles, and luxury goods. Encouraged by the Chihuahua market, and sustained by a growing population of some sixteen thousand, Hispanos took advantage of the comparative calm to expand cautiously their settlement frontiers.[2]

The process went something like this: stockmen in quest of suitable pasture for their flocks would venture across a divide to the next valley, where they would build adobe shelters, irrigate patches of land, and eventually attract others. In this fashion, stockmen from Taos settled Arroyo Hondo in 1815. Or, to be closer to their grazing lands, several stock-raising families would migrate up or down a valley to a point where floodplain cropland and a village site were available. So it was that families primarily from San Miguel founded El Cerrito down the Pecos Valley probably in the 1830s. Or, rather than return home from their summer grazing lands, a stock-raising family would build a jacal (house with walls made of upright poles chinked and covered with mud) and remain permanently, as happened in 1859 (perhaps 1861) at La Plaza de los Leones (modern-day Walsenburg), Colorado.[3] Through a process sometimes called "splinter diffusion," largely stockmen from parent villages created offspring villages; Taos gave rise to more than a dozen such offspring, and San Miguel parented at least a dozen. The source area for La Plaza de los Leones is not known.

Title to much of the land over which Hispanos spread was secured in land grants. Arroyo Hondo and El Cerrito were located within community grants awarded to groups of set-

[2] The military campaigns are in Max L. Moorhead, *The Apache Frontier: Jacobo Ugarte and Spanish-Indian Relations in Northern New Spain, 1769–1791*, The Civilization of the American Indian Series, vol. 90: 277, 283–84; Oakah L. Jones, Jr., "Pueblo Indian Auxiliaries in New Mexico, 1763–1821," *New Mexico Historical Review* 37 (1962): 93, 95, 98, 107. Anza was governor from 1778 to 1788. Oakah L. Jones, Jr., documented population growth between 1790 and 1810 in "Spanish Civil Communities and Settlers in Frontier New Mexico, 1790–1810," in *Hispanic-American Essays in Honor of Max Leon Moorhead*, ed. William S. Coker, 40, 41, 54. The figure sixteen thousand is derived from table 2 in Alicia V. Tjarks, "Demographic, Ethnic and Occupational Structure of New Mexico, 1790," *Americas: A Quarterly Review of Inter-American Cultural History* 35 (1978–79): 60–61.

[3] Francis T. Cheetham, "The Early Settlements of Southern Colorado," *Colorado Magazine* 5 (1928): 1; Olen Leonard and C. P. Loomis, *Culture of a Contemporary Rural Community: El Cerrito, New Mexico*, Rural Life Studies, no. 1: 10; Louis B. Sporleder, "La Plaza de los Leones," *Colorado Magazine* 10 (1933): 28, 34, 35. El Cerrito's existence in 1844 is documented in Hubert Howe Bancroft, *The Works of Hubert Howe Bancroft*, vol. 17, *History of Arizona and New Mexico, 1530–1888*, 312.

tlers, whereas La Plaza de los Leones was located within a private grant made to individuals. In the former case the original grantees and their descendants owned their village house lots (solares) and their floodplain planting lots (suertes), while grazing lands were held in common. In the latter case the individual grantees were to develop their property, yet the colonists at La Plaza de los Leones apparently settled there without the knowledge of the grantees and later acquired title to their land through preemption.[4] Not all of the land Hispanos encroached upon was granted by official decree, however. After 1848, for example, the Hispano stockmen who ventured east across the High Plains and west across the Colorado Plateau settled on ungranted land.

In the first several decades of expansion after 1790, the villages themselves were of the fortified *plaza* variety common in the late eighteenth century. Taos and San Miguel were *plaza* communities. Consisting of central open spaces (or plazas) surrounded on four sides by houses whose outer walls were windowless, *plazas* were reached through one or more heavy gates. Outside the compound a high, round *torreón* (tower) sometimes gave added protection. Given the Hispanos' penchant for living on their own irrigated tracts, however, *rancho* settlements, which predated the *plaza* types, were reinstituted as quickly as pacification of nomad Indians allowed. These *ranchos* consisted of farmsteads that were strung out at irregular intervals along a linear irrigation ditch, with a church, eventually a school, and perhaps a store and a blacksmith shop grouped at some point near an open plaza, which was the village focus. Among Hispanos the term "plaza" was used rather loosely to refer to both compact *plazas* and semidispersed *ranchos*.[5]

[4] These land grants are described in Marc Simmons, "Settlement Patterns and Village Plans in Colonial New Mexico," *Journal of the West* 8 (1969): 8. J. J. Bowden, *Private Land Claims in the Southwest*, discussed the San Miguel del Vado Grant (which included El Cerrito) in vol. 3: 734–44, and the Arroyo Hondo Grant in vol. 4: 927–35. The land grant which included La Plaza de los Leones is called both the Las Animas Grant, as discussed by Bowden, *Private Land Claims* 6: 1794–1805, and the Vigil and St. Vrain Grant, as discussed by LeRoy R. Hafen, "Mexican Land Grants in Colorado," *Colorado Magazine* 4 (1927): 87–88.

[5] Simmons noted that Taos was a *plaza*; "Settlement Patterns," 14. E. Boyd affirmed the same for San Miguel; "The Plaza of San Miguel del Vado," *El Palacio* 77, no. 4 (1971): 17. Simmons described both *ranchos* and *plazas* in "Settlement Patterns," 11–15. That *rancho* settlements were called plazas is nicely illustrated by La Loma (near Del Norte, Colorado), which acquired the nickname "Seven-Mile Plaza"; Frances

Villages in at least the Rio Abajo were unequally divided between a small, relatively wealthy *patrón* class and a large, relatively poor *peón* class. The two stock-owner heads of households at El Cerrito were the *patrones*, and the stock-herder heads of households were the *peones*. *Patrones* employed and otherwise took responsibility for *peones* and their families; indeed, the reputation of a given village often depended on the personality and behavior of a given *patrón*. The dependent *peones*, on the other hand, were an obedient and loyal source of labor, for which they were usually compensated in goods. A contract institution known as the *partido* also existed whereby a *patrón* would lease his sheep to a *peón* for a guaranteed rental in kind.[6] In this way an enterprising *peón*, who perhaps was not favored by having a generous *patrón* as a relative, could acquire a flock of his own.

Each average-sized village was basically self-sufficient. Among its heads of households were a merchant, a blacksmith, and a carpenter, and by the second half of the nineteenth century there were often a schoolteacher (usually a married man), a cobbler, a mason, perhaps also a fiddle-playing musician, and a saloon keeper. Single women were usually laundresses or seamstresses.[7] As the century progressed, larger villages were designated as parish seats, and resident priests would visit their half-dozen outlying *visitas* or chapels once a month and on special occasions. By the late 1800s a village hierarchy and geographical network also developed around the presence or absence of schools and post offices.

The majority of the heads of households in any given village,

---

Leon Swadesh, *Los Primeros Pobladores: Hispanic Americans of the Ute Frontier*, 138.

[6] Paul Kutsche, "Introduction: Atomism, Factionalism, and Flexibility," in *The Survival of Spanish American Villages*, Colorado College Studies, no. 15, ed. Paul Kutsche, 15; Leonard and Loomis, *Culture of Contemporary Rural Community*, 10, 30–31, 57–59; Clark S. Knowlton, "Patron-Peon Pattern among the Spanish Americans of New Mexico," *Social Forces* 41 (1962–63): 13, 14. The *partido* institution was established in New Mexico at least as early as 1760. In the twentieth century the guaranteed rental in kind was commonly twenty lambs for each one hundred ewes; Ralph Charles, "Development of the Partido System in the New Mexico Sheep Industry" (master's thesis [economics], University of New Mexico, 1940), 9, 18, 63.

[7] These occupations are found in the 1790, 1850, and 1900 censuses; Jones, "Spanish Civil Communities," 51–52; Population Schedules of the Seventh Census [1850], Microcopy no. 432, 1963–64, rolls 467–70, National Archives; Richard L. Nostrand, "The Hispano Homeland in 1900," *Annals of the Association of American Geographers* 70 (1980): 392–93.

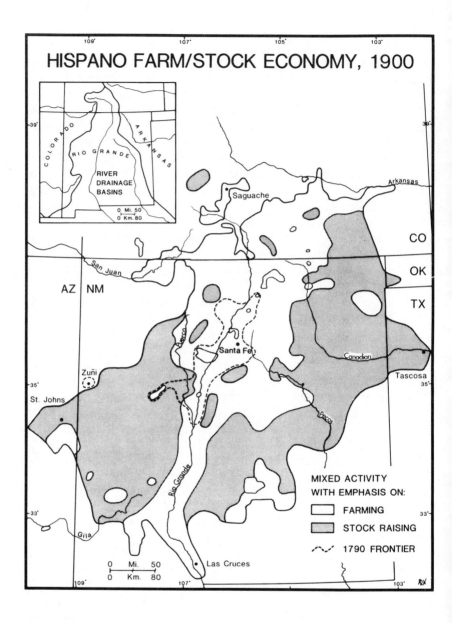

HISPANO FARM/STOCK ECONOMY, 1900

RIVER
DRAINAGE
BASINS

0 Mi. 50
0 Km. 80

COLORADO

ARKANSAS

RIO GRANDE

Saguache

Arkansas

CO

OK

AZ | NM

San Juan

TX

Santa Fe

Canadian

Zuñi

Tascosa

St. Johns

Pecos

Rio Grande

MIXED ACTIVITY
WITH EMPHASIS ON:

☐ FARMING

▨ STOCK RAISING

⌇ 1790 FRONTIER

Gila

0 Mi. 50
0 Km. 80

Las Cruces

however, were farmers, stockmen, or those noted somewhat elusively in census returns as "day laborers." In 1790 the majority of the heads of households in New Mexico were farmers or day laborers; stockmen, as Oakah L. Jones, Jr., pointed out, were surprisingly few. During the century of expansion after 1790, however, the number of stockmen dramatically increased, as did the number of sheep.[8] By 1900, over a decade after the process of contiguous expansion had run its course, Hispano farmers were still more numerous than stockmen, but only in the interior of their Homeland. In the region's outer margins, where the contiguous expansion had occurred, stockmen heavily outnumbered farmers (Map 4.1).[9]

[8] Jones, "Spanish Civil Communities," 51. Firsthand accounts of large numbers of sheep are given in 1827 by José Augustín de Escudero, *Additions*, in *Three New Mexico Chronicles: The* Exposición *of Don Pedro Bautista Pino, 1812; the* Ojeada *of Lic. Antonio Barreiro, 1832; and the* Additions *by Don José Augustín de Escudero, 1849*, The Quivira Society Publications, vol. 11, trans. and ed. H. Bailey Carroll and J. Vissasana Haggard, xxi, 40, 90; and in 1832 by Antonio Barreiro, *Ojeada . . .* , "Barreiro's Ojeada Sobre Nuevo-Mexico," trans. and ed. Lansing B. Bloom, *New Mexico Historical Review* 3 (1928): 93. William M. Denevan discussed the increasing number of sheep in "Livestock Numbers in Nineteenth-Century New Mexico, and the Problem of Gullying in the Southwest," *Annals of the Association of American Geographers* 57 (1967): 695–96, 699. The increases in stockmen are documented in decennial census returns beginning in 1850.

[9] Nostrand, "Hispano Homeland in 1900," 392, 394. At the time of the 1880 census, the century of Hispano expansion had not yet run its course, especially to the west. Because the original population schedules of the 1890 census were largely destroyed by fire (in the Commerce Department Building in 1921), the 1900 schedules contain data closest to the termination of the expansion.

Map 4.1 (*opposite*) In 1900 Hispano male heads of households were overwhelmingly farmers/farm laborers or stock raisers/herders. Both activities were carried on simultaneously, yet stock raising (largely sheep) predominated in the more recently settled periphery of the Homeland. The Hispanos' outward contiguous expansion was incomplete in 1880, and because the original census data for 1890 do not exist, the Homeland's outer boundary is shown for 1900, by which time Anglos had attracted Hispanos to parts of the region's periphery (chapter 6). Shown are five of thirteen Homeland outliers and all thirteen non-Homeland inliers. The limit of Hispano settlement in 1790 is drawn to exclude the upper Puerco Valley but to include the Zuñi outlier. Sources: Population Schedules of the Twelfth Census [1900], and Richard L. Nostrand, "The Hispano Homeland in 1900," *Annals of the Association of American Geographers* 70 (1980): 383. Inset map is after U.S. Geological Survey, *Twelfth Annual Report to the Secretary of the Interior* (1891), part 2, plate 58.

The evidence that stock raising, instead of farming, pro-pelled most of the Hispanos who expanded their frontiers thus is both direct and indirect. Examples of the direct evidence include the three local situations in which stockmen initiated territorial expansion: testimony taken in land grant litigation, as cited by Francis T. Cheetham in his discussion of Arroyo Hondo; oral histories gathered and used by Olen E. Leonard and Charles P. Loomis in their discussion of El Cerrito; and recollections of the Anglo pioneer Louis B. Sporleder, a lifetime resident of Walsenburg who lived among and knew the His-panos and their Spanish language. Indirect evidence is to be found in the reports of nineteenth-century chroniclers, who lamented that Hispanos farmed only out of necessity and only at subsistence levels, while at the same time they were trailing sheep by the thousands to Mexico in the Mexican era, to California in the 1850s, and to various Rocky Mountain and Great Plains states in the 1870s and 1880s.[10] More powerful indirect evidence lies in the occupational shift that saw farm-ers decrease and stockmen increase during the period and the corroborating point that stockmen greatly outnumbered farm-ers in the periphery of the Hispano region at the end of the period.

It seems then that once pacification of the nomad Indians made limited expansion possible, an emergent class of stock-men, whose desire it was to add to their grazing lands, led the way. Ironically, in cases in which grazing lands were held in common (or were not owned at all), livestock rather than the lands themselves were the measure of one's wealth. By the time Anglos blunted this expanding frontier between the 1860s and the 1880s, Hispano stockmen had made impressive ad-vances in every direction.

[10] "Agriculture is utterly negelected," wrote Barreiro in 1832 (Ojeada ..., 95). Writing in 1857, Davis reported that "no branch of industry in New Mexico has been more negelected than that of agriculture ... [which is] pursued merely as a means of living"; W. W. H. Davis, El Gringo: New Mexico and Her People, 195. In 1883, Hispanos were still being criticized for being little more than subsistence farmers; see Alvin R. Sunseri, "Agricultural Techniques in New Mexico at the time of the Anglo-American Conquest," Agricultural History 47 (1973): 337. Concerning the trailing of sheep, see John O. Baxter, Las Carneradas: Sheep Trade in New Mexico 1700–1860, esp. pp. 103, 121; Alvar Ward Carlson, "New Mexico's Sheep Industry, 1850–1900: Its Role in the History of the Territory," New Mexico Historical Review 44 (1969): 26–28, 32–34.

EXPANSION EAST

In Santa Fe in 1794, fifty-two individuals, some of whom owned land in the capital, successfully petitioned for a grant of land that straddled the Pecos in the vicinity of an important *vado* (ford). Just when they established their village of San Miguel del Vado is apparently unrecorded, yet by 1803 they were put into possession of agricultural plots along the Pecos, and by 1807 their church in the middle of the plaza seems to have been completed. San Miguel prospered in part because many of its inhabitants were *genízaros* who had better relations with the nomad Indians than did the Hispanos. As the Pecos Pueblo declined—to the point of extinction in 1837— San Miguel emerged as the major outpost on the eastern frontier in late Spanish and Mexican times (Map 4.2).[11]

San Miguel became the springboard for village founding in the upper Pecos watershed. On the San Miguel del Vado Grant itself, it was the parent to most if not all villages established before American acquisition: El Gusano, Las Mulas, Entrañosa (location undetermined), and San Jose north of San Miguel; El Pueblo, Puertecito (Sena), La Cuesta (Villanueva), and El Cerrito on the Pecos below San Miguel; and Bernal on Bernal Creek. It was the source area for colonists who in 1822 were awarded land down the Pecos at Anton Chico. It was the parent village to Tecolote on Tecolote Creek about 1838.[12] And it also contributed colonists to Las Vegas.

Las Vegas replaced San Miguel as the major springboard leading east. In 1823 a family from Peña Blanca apparently received land that included a large vega (meadow) on the high plains just east of the front range, but nomad Indians drove the family back to San Miguel. In 1835 the coveted area was

[11] "Bowden, *Private Land Claims* 3: 733–34; Boyd, "Plaza of San Miguel," 17, 18; Robert Archibald, "Acculturation and Assimilation in Colonial New Mexico," *New Mexico Historical Review* 53 (1978): 211, 212; G. Emlen Hall, *Four Leagues of Pecos: A Legal History of the Pecos Grant, 1800–1933*, New Mexico Land Grant Series, 60. Boyd suggested that the community was settled in 1794, recorded that baptismal records appear after 1799, and noted the apparent completion of the church before 1807.

[12] Bowden, *Private Land Claims* 3: 690, 738. Bowden lists all the grant villages save El Cerrito. Lynn I. Perrigo, in a letter to the author, November 12, 1984, stated that San Miguel was the parent village to Tecolote. Malcolm Ebright noted that Tecolote came to exist after a community grant was issued in 1838; "The Tecolote Land Grant," unpublished paper read at the Historical Society of New Mexico Annual Conference, Montezuma, June 7, 1986.

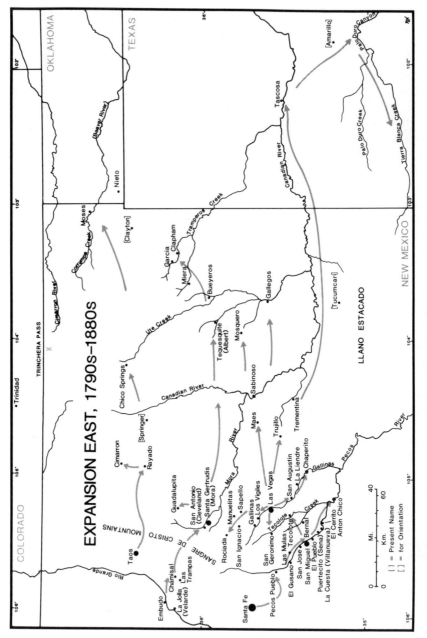

Map 4.2 Hispano expansion to the east resulted in the greatest territorial gains. Sources: see text.

regranted as a community tract to twenty-nine petitioners who founded Las Vegas.[13] A small village in the Mexican period, Las Vegas grew rapidly after 1846 to outstrip San Miguel much as San Miguel had eclipsed the Pecos village. Aggressive Anglo and Hispano merchants preempted trade with the Santa Fe–bound caravans that pulled through the Las Vegas plaza; Las Vegas was elevated to a parish seat; it was named the county seat; and when the Atchison, Topeka, and Santa Fe Railroad (AT&SF) skirted both Las Vegas and San Miguel in 1879, the depot community that emerged at East Las Vegas flourished, whereas the one at San Miguel Station (Ribera) experienced only modest growth.[14]

From Las Vegas groups of families splintered off to form villages over much of San Miguel County.[15] Along the Gallinas River upstream from Las Vegas they founded Los Vigiles and Gallinas, and downstream they established San Augustin, La Liendre, and Chaperito. West of Las Vegas on upper Tecolote Creek, San Geronimo became a Las Vegas satellite, as did Rociada to the north and perhaps also Sapello, Manuelitas, and San Ignacio lying in that direction. These communities and many more contributed to a village network in western San Miguel County that was one of the densest in the entire Hispano Homeland. East of Las Vegas, where villages were sometimes large but much more widely spaced, Trujillo and Maes were Las Vegas offspring.

Meanwhile, in the Arkansas River basin across a low drain-

---

[13] Milton W. Callon, *Las Vegas, New Mexico: The Town That Wouldn't Gamble*, 4–7. Regranting the area was but one reason for endless litigation over rightful ownership of the grant; Clark S. Knowlton, "The Town of Las Vegas Community Land Grant: An Anglo-American Coup d'Etat," *Journal of the West* 19, no. 3 (July 1980): 12–21.

[14] Between 1847 and 1853, five Anglo families moved to Las Vegas, opened mercantile stores, and proceeded to monopolize the Santa Fe trade; the parish seat was apparently created in 1852; F. Stanley [Crocchiola], *The Las Vegas (New Mexico) Story*, 55, 280. The county seat was moved from San Miguel to Las Vegas briefly in 1860–61, then permanently in 1864; F. Stanley [Crocchiola], *The San Miguel del Bado New Mexico Story*, 18.

[15] Information on this expansion is from Lynn I. Perrigo, in a letter to the author, November 12, 1984. Dr. Perrigo, professor emeritus of history at New Mexico Highlands University in Las Vegas, directed many student papers and theses on local history. One student, Andrés S. Hernández, noted that La Liendre was settled in 1870 by people from Las Vegas; "This They Said (A Report of Interviews with Old-Time Residents of Las Vegas and San Miguel County, New Mexico)" (seminar paper, New Mexico Highlands University, June 1, 1955), 4.

age divide just north of Las Vegas, another important springboard leading east developed at Mora (Map 4.1 inset). As early
as 1816 or 1817, families from the La Jolla (Velarde) and Embudo area in the Rio Grande Valley, and from Las Trampas,
Chamisal, and Santa Barbara (present Peñasco area; location
undetermined) in southern Taos County, crossed the Sangre
de Cristo Mountains to the Mora Valley, and by 1835 the
villages of San Antonio (Cleveland) and Santa Gertrudis (Mora)
had been founded. Additional families crossed the mountains
from Las Trampas to the Guadalupita Grant in 1837 and from
Taos to Rayado in 1848. Although eclipsed by Cimarron by
the late 1850s, Rayado was the first permanent settlement on
the Beaubien-Miranda Grant, and it appears to have been the
first Hispano community to have been established on the initiative of Anglos who had become part of the Hispano society.[16]
Of these Canadian drainage subbasin settlements, Mora
emerged as the major central place, and from it family groups
hived off to create local villages, or they regrouped at points
that stretched across the broken High Plains to the east.

From Las Vegas and Mora, also from Taos and from other
settlements as well, Hispanos as early as the 1860s trailed
sheep east across the entire northeastern corner of New Mexico. Their plazas, which sometimes were mere *placitas* containing no more than an extended family, were nestled in the
valleys of perennial streams or at springs, and they grazed their
sheep and cattle on the grass-covered, ungranted open range.
Before the Denver and Fort Worth Railroad reached Clayton
in 1888, these Hispanos hauled their wool clips, sheep skins,
and hides by wagon to Las Vegas and Springer or across Trinchera Pass to Trinidad. Among the larger plazas were Trementina
and Sabinoso on the Canadian River and its tributaries; Chico
Springs, Tequesquite (Albert), Bueyeros, Mosquero, and Galle-

---

[16] Fray Angélico Chávez, "Early Settlements in the Mora Valley," *El Palacio* 62
(1955): 319–22; Bowden, *Private Land Claims* 4: 824–25; Lawrence R. Murphy, "Rayado: Pioneer Settlement in Northeastern New Mexico, 1848–1857," *New Mexico
Historical Review* 46 (1971): 38. Rayado was founded by Lucien B. Maxwell, the son
of an Irish immigrant and his wife, the daughter of Pierre Menard, a wealthy French
Canadian merchant of Kaskaskia, Illinois; Maxwell had married Luz Beaubien, the
daughter of French Canadian Charles Beaubien and his Hispana wife, Paulita Lobato;
Jim Berry Pearson, *The Maxwell Land Grant*, 4, 9–10. At Rayado, where Maxwell
lived from 1848 to 1857, were Hispano family members and sheepherder employees,
Anglos such as Kit Carson and Carson's Hispana wife (residents between 1849 and
1853), and Indians; Murphy, "Rayado," 40, 42–43, 49, 52.

gos on Ute Creek and its tributaries; Miera, Garcia, and Clapham on Tramperos Creek (known in Texas as Punta de Agua
Creek) and its tributaries; and Moses on Corrumpa Creek
(known in Oklahoma as the Beaver River).[17] Few plazas were
apparently established on the high and flat Llano Estacado
located south of the Canadian River and east of the Pecos.

This thrust to the east carried New Mexican pastores
(herdsmen) well into the panhandles of Texas and modern-
day Oklahoma. In the 1860s sheepmen from Taos, Mora, and
probably Las Vegas descended the Canadian Valley to the vicinity of Tascosa.[18] In lush riverbottom vegas on the south
bank of the Canadian opposite Tascosa, a dozen or more family
placitas with their adobe homes, irrigation ditches, and ceme-
teries were reported in the early 1870s. The Tascosa plaza itself
was settled in 1877 when a half-dozen Hispano families and
two Anglo merchants converged on the north bank. Beyond
Tascosa, Hispanos advanced to the head of Palo Duro Canyon;
their seasonal grazing circuits carried them southeast into the
drainage systems of the Red and the Brazos. The 1880 census
shows them spread thinly across the entire panhandle of Texas.
By 1872 or earlier sheepmen meanwhile had moved down the
Beaver River to establish plazas including Nieto in the far
western panhandle of Oklahoma.[19] The Hispanos in Oklahoma
seem to have prevailed longer than those in Texas; in the
Tascosa area, skirmishes with Anglos, who began to arrive in
late 1875 or early 1876, prompted some Hispanos to return to
New Mexico as early as 1877. The clash was between newcomer Anglo cattlemen, who were buying and fencing range
land, and shallow-rooted Hispano sheepmen, who had done

[17] Goldianne (Mrs. Harry) Thompson and William H. Halley, *History of Clayton
and Union County, New Mexico*, 5, 6, 8, 12, 19. Barry Newton Alvis noted that
southern Union County was settled earlier than northern Union County; "History of
Union County, New Mexico," *New Mexico Historical Review* 22 (1947): 247–48.

[18] The route from New Mexico lay entirely on the south side of the Canadian; José
Ynocencio Romero (as told to Ernest R. Archambeau), "Spanish Sheepmen on the
Canadian at Old Tascosa," *Panhandle-Plains Historical Review* 19 (1946): 47. The
information on Tascosa is from John L. McCarty, *Maverick Town: The Story of Old
Tascosa*, 8, 15–16, 21, 29, 32, 34, 37–40, 46, 53.

[19] Paul H. Carlson, *Texas Woollybacks: The Range Sheep and Goat Industry*,
93; Ernest R. Archambeau, "The First Federal Census in the Panhandle—1880,"
Panhandle-Plains Historical Review 23 (1950): 26. In Beaver County (the entire panhandle of Oklahoma) in the 1900 census, 1872 was the earliest date that a child was
born in Oklahoma to New Mexico–born Hispano parents; Population Schedules of
the Twelfth Census [1900], Microcopy no. T–623, n.d., roll 1335: 37A, 37B, 38A, 38B.

neither. Stifled by the Anglos, the Hispano population in the Texas Panhandle peaked well before 1900.[20]

EXPANSION NORTH

Expansion to the north stemmed from Taos, the Hispano community located within the lands of the Taos Indians. From Taos, the late–1790s frontier salient of the north, stockmen settled Arroyo Seco and Arroyo Hondo in 1815 (Map 4.3). That same year a settlement was established on the Red River, but nomad Indians forced its abandonment several years later. Next among the permanent settlements came San Antonio (Valdez) and San Cristobal, and in 1842 the Red River was regained when, near the ruins of its ephemeral predecessor, colonists from Taos founded San Antonio (Questa). Just south of New Mexico's present-day northern boundary—established in 1861 along the thirty-seventh parallel—Costilla, a community that eventually grew north of the line into Colorado, was established in 1849. By that point Anglo men who had married Hispanas were directly involved in the founding of some of these basically Hispano communities. Charles Beaubien, for example, a naturalized Mexican of French Canadian descent who lived in Taos and who owned the Sangre de Cristo Grant on which Costilla was located, founded Costilla.[21]

Beaubien also directed the founding of plazas north of the thirty-seventh parallel, which his land grant straddled. In 1851 families from Taos (and Mora) established San Luis, Colorado's oldest settlement, on Culebra Creek. Along the Culebra and its tributaries additional families from Taos and elsewhere in northern New Mexico established plazas at San Pedro, San Pablo, and San Acacio in 1852–53 and at Chama and San

[20] Romero, "Spanish Sheepmen," 62, 68. In the twenty-six Texas Panhandle counties in 1880, there were 358 Hispanos, most of them in Oldham (Tascosa) and Hartley counties located adjacent to New Mexico; Archambeau, "First Federal Census," 27. By 1900, in the same area, the number had dwindled to 158, with the majority continuing to live in Oldham and Hartley counties; Population Schedules of the Twelfth Census [1900], rolls 1627 (Deaf Smith County), 1628 (Donley County), 1643 (Hartley, Hemphill, and Moore counties), 1663 (Oldham County), and 1665 (Potter, County). By comparison, in 1900, 156 Hispanos were recorded in the extreme western panhandle of Oklahoma; Population Schedules of the Twelfth Census [1900], roll 1335 (Beaver County).

[21] This paragraph draws heavily on Cheetham, "Early Settlements of Southern Colorado," 1, 2, 5. Edmond C. van Diest noted that Costilla was largely "Mexican"; "Early History of Costilla County," Colorado Magazine 5 (1928): 141.

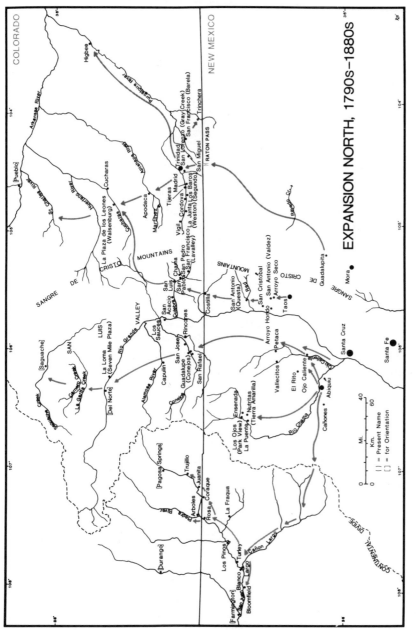

Map 4.3 Demographically, the Hispanos' northern frontier was the most dynamic. Sources: see text.

Francisco (Lavalley) in 1854–55. So great was the threat of nomad Indian attack that colonists united for protection while cultivating crops, husbanding sheep and goats, and making bows and arrows.[22]

West of San Luis on the opposite side of the San Luis Valley, as the Colorado portion of the upper Rio Grande basin is called, another complex of plazas meanwhile emerged in the vicinity of Conejos. The lower Chama Valley, notably Abiquiu, was the major source area, although Ojo Caliente and plazas that led in the direction of Conejos, including Vallecitos (1824) and Petaca (1836), contributed. Small El Llanito (location undetermined) in the Ojo Caliente Valley, for example, seems to have supplied the first settlers, who in August of 1854 were recruited and led to the Conejos River by José María Jáquez.[23] On the north bank of the Conejos a fortified *plaza* called Guadalupe (Conejos) was built late in 1854. The dates of water appropriations are clues to the chronology of the plazas that followed: San Jose and San Rafael, 1856; Rincones, 1857; San Juan, 1861 (location undetermined); and Los Sauces, 1867. This activity west of the Rio Grande resulted in the permanent occupance of the Conejos Grant, a tract that had seen several unsuccessful colonizing efforts since its award in 1833.[24]

[22] Cheetham, "Early Settlements of Southern Colorado," 5; van Diest, "Early History of Costilla County," 141, 142; Louis E. Bernal, "Los Vallejos and San Pablo," *Colorado Magazine* 22 (1945): 178. Emilia Gallegos Smith gave Taos and Mora as the source areas; "Reminiscences of Early San Luis," *Colorado Magazine* 24 (1947): 24. That San Luis is Colorado's oldest settlement is noted by LeRoy R. Hafen, "Colorado Cities—Their Founding and the Origin of Their Names," *Colorado Magazine* 9 (1932): 182. From interviews with local Hispanos, John Philip Andrews noted Chamita, San Juan, Ojo Caliente, Tierra Amarilla, El Rito, and Plaza Rota as additional source areas in New Mexico; "History of Rural Spanish Settlement and Land Use in the Upper Culebra Basin of the San Luis Valley, Costilla County, Colorado" (master's thesis [geography], University of Colorado, 1972), 34.

[23] Swadesh, *Los Primeros Pobladores*, 79–80. Vallecitos was settled by families from Santa Cruz; Bowden, *Private Land Claims* 4: 1046. Much information in this paragraph is from Melitón Velásquez, "Guadalupe Colony Was Founded 1854," *Colorado Magazine* 34 (1957): 264–67. Velásquez noted that the initial leadership of this enterprise was entirely Hispano; Lafayette Head, an Anglo who became locally prominent, did not join the colony until October (p. 265). Swadesh, *Los Primeros Pobladores*, 77, cited conflicting evidence about the founding of Guadalupe (Conejos). She had Atanacio Trujillo of El Rito leading colonists to the Conejos, where they founded Rincones, San Rafael, Mesitas, and Mogote. No date is given.

[24] Cheetham, "Early Settlements of Southern Colorado," 7; Purnee A. McCourt, "The Conejos Land Grant of Southern Colorado," *Colorado Magazine* 52 (1975): 37–39. "Mexican settlements" shown in township and range survey plats (1858) and in "early maps" included Servietta, Brazoso (?), San Francisco, Cañon, and Mazeta on

The northern reaches of the never-patented Conejos Grant around Del Norte and on north to Saguache were theaters of continued colonization. In the 1860s, Hispanos, largely newcomers from New Mexico, founded two villages (one was La Loma, nicknamed Seven Mile Plaza) east of Del Norte on the upper Rio Grande. By the late 1860s colonists had established themselves along La Garita Creek, Carnero Creek, and Saguache Creek. Meanwhile, they also settled in the Capulin District along the Alamosa River. Paralleling this occupation of the west side of the San Luis Valley in the 1860s was a more modest advance north from the Culebra Creek area along the east side of the valley.[25] The close of the 1860s marked the end of formative Hispano colonization in this uppermost portion of the Rio Grande basin.

As Hispanos pushed north in the San Luis Valley, they made territorial gains east of the Sangre de Cristo Mountains in the Arkansas basin. In the fall of 1860, Felipe Baca of Guadalupita in Mora County staked out a farm in the upper valley of El Rio de las Animas Perdidas en Purgatorio (the Purgatoire River) in southern Colorado. When he returned permanently the next spring, he found Anglos living in the area. What evolved was the bicultural community of Trinidad. In 1862 a dozen additional families from Guadalupita and the Rayado Creek area crossed through Raton Pass into the Arkansas watershed, establishing plazas at Madrid, San Miguel, and Apodaca. In the decade that followed, the upper reaches of the Purgatoire, the Apishapa River, and various tributary valleys came to be lined with plazas, including Martinez, Vigil, La Junta (Weston), Cordova, Los Baros (Segundo), Tijeras, San Lorenzo (Gray Creek),

---

the Rio Conejos and San Antonio on the Rio San Antonio (shown in Map 4.3); Forbes Parkhill, "Colorado's First Survey," *Colorado Magazine* 33 (1956): 177.

[25] Swadesh, *Los Primeros Pobladores*, 79, noted La Loma, Piedra Pintada, and Las Garritas as having been founded in the Del Norte area by Hispanos from the San Luis and Conejos areas. David William Lantis emphasized the New Mexico derivation of these colonists and gave as a second name for Seven Mile Plaza, "Plaza la Valdeza"; "The San Luis Valley, Colorado: Sequent Rural Occupance in an Intermontane Basin" (Ph.D. diss. [geography], Ohio State University, 1950), part 1: 146, 148, 149–50. A map entitled "Settlements and Roads in the San Luis Valley 1870," drawn in 1934 by Charles E. Gibson, Jr., showed Carnero and Saguache to exist in 1870; Civil Works Administration Pionier Interviews, pamphlet 349, Alamosa, Conejos, and Costilla counties, interview no. 18: 73, in the Documentary Resources Department, Colorado Historical Society, Denver. Anglos founded the community of Saguache in 1867; Hafen, "Colorado Cities," 181. Settlement of the Capulin District and Culebra Creek is in Lantis, "San Luis Valley," 150–51, 171, 182, 189.

San Francisco (Barela), and Trinchera. In the mid-1860s a mixed Hispano-Anglo population moved down the Purgatoire to "Nine Mile Bottom" near Higbee.[26] Felipe Baca of Trinidad, meanwhile, became a highly successful sheep rancher. Even before the founding of Trinidad, sheepmen used the Cucharas Valley to the north for summer pasture. Along its banks in 1859 (perhaps 1861), members of the Atencio family located permanently at a site known after 1866 as La Plaza de los Leones (renamed Walsenburg in 1873). Soon, additional plazas came to dot the valleys of the upper Cucharas and Huerfano. One, Cucharas, was settled by the Vallejos brothers, who originally hailed from Taos County but had spent some fifteen years at San Pablo in the San Luis Valley.[27]

This thrust to the north along the eastern piedmont of the Sangre de Cristo Mountains reached almost to the Arkansas Valley. Along the Saint Charles River and its tributaries south and west of present-day Pueblo, Hispanos seem to have been entrenched by 1880.[28] Those along the Saint Charles were located within the Gervacio Nolán Grant (1843), and those in the higher valleys to the south were within the Cornelio Vigil–Cerán St. Vrain (Las Animas) Grant (1843). Hispanos had pre-empted land on both grants. Altogether, they had founded thirty-seven plazas on this lee side of the Sangre de Cristo Mountains. About 1870, when the two grants were adjudi-

[26] Luis Baca, "The Guadalupita Colony of Trinidad," Colorado Magazine 21 (1944): 22–26 (published posthumously, this paper is by the son of Felipe Baca); Morris F. Taylor, Pioneers of the Picketwire, 3–56.

[27] Sporleder, "La Plaza de Los Leones," 28, 35; Hafen, "Colorado Cities," 183; Louis B. Sporleder, "A Day and a Night on Spoon River," Colorado Magazine 9 (1932): 104; Bernal, "Los Vallejos and San Pablo," 179. Sporleder ("La Plaza de Los Leones," 35) noted that the Cucharas Valley was used for summer pasture before 1859 and that Oso, Hermanes Plaza, and Tequesquite were all founded in 1863.

[28] Anglos were living along the Saint Charles in 1870; Joseph O. Van Hook, "Mexican Land Grants in the Arkansas Valley," Southwestern Historical Quarterly 40 (1936–37): 71. The Hispano male heads of households who also lived in rural Pueblo County (apparently including along the Saint Charles) in 1870 were farm laborers, which implies that they had been attracted to the area to work for Anglos. By 1880, however, many Hispano heads of households in rural Pueblo County (apparently including those along the Saint Charles) were farmers, which suggests that they arrived as part of the spontaneous folk emigration. Few Hispanos lived in Pueblo itself in either 1870 or 1880; Population Schedules of the Ninth Census of the United States [1870], Microcopy no. M–593, 1965, roll 95: 458A–489B; Population Schedules of the Tenth Census of the United States [1880], Microcopy no. T–9, n.d., roll 92: 228A–308B.

cated, the Hispano settlers filed preemption and homestead claims for their plazas and adjacent lands.[29]

Expansion to the north veered off in still a third direction—to the northwest. Abiquiu, which by the 1790s was a composite of nine separate plazas, was the secondary springboard beyond Santa Cruz leading northwest. From Abiquiu sheepmen in the early 1800s trailed flocks to the upper Chama Valley around Tierra Amarilla for summmer grazing. By 1814 they were petitioning for land. In 1832 the substantial Tierra Amarilla Grant was awarded, but nomad Indians prevented settlers from establishing anything but summer sheep camps until the 1850s. Land allotments on the grant were conveyed between 1861 and the early 1870s. Even before 1861, however, stable communities probably existed at Nutritas (Tierra Amarilla), La Puente, Los Ojos (Park View), Ensenada, Cañones, and Barranco (location undetermined). The lower Chama Valley contributed the bulk of these colonists, much as it had been the major contributor to the Conejos Valley portion of the San Luis Valley.[30]

From the Chama Valley Hispanos crossed the Continental Divide to the upper reaches of the San Juan—which may have marked their debut in the basin of the Colorado River. The major source area for the San Juan Valley once again was the Lower Chama, although some Hispanos went indirectly to the San Juan after stopovers in the San Luis Valley. Facilitating the thrust was the opening of a wagon road from Abiquiu over the divide and down the Cañon Largo in 1876. The authority on Hispanos in the San Juan Valley, Frances Swadesh (Quintana), noted that the details of the settlement history of the area may never be fully known.[31] The Turley area on the San Juan may have been settled first in the 1860s. By 1872, Hispanos from the Abiquiu–El Rito area, who had resided in Huerfano County in Colorado, settled on the San Juan across from Bloomfield. In the 1870s loosely agglomerated settlements (called plazas)

---

[29] Hugh Burnett and Evelyn Burnett, "Madrid Plaza," *Colorado Magazine* 42 (1965): 224, gave the number thirty-seven; they also traced the chronology of the filing of the homestead claim (p. 227) and other events at Madrid. Van Hook, "Mexican Land Grants," 64–65, 70–71.

[30] Swadesh, *Los Primeros Pobladores*, 50–51, 62, 79–82, 145.

[31] Ibid., 82, 91–94, 97–105.

then came to line the San Juan at Bloomfield, Blanco, Largo, Los Pinos, Rosa, and Coraque. Juanita, Trujillo, and La Fraqua were added after 1880. In 1883 Hispanos on the Piedra River above Arboles were forced to relocate because they were within the Southern Ute Reservation, created in 1877. Thus, about 1880, the length of the San Juan from Bloomfield to Trujillo (but not to Pagosa Springs) was heavily Hispano.

EXPANSION WEST

Albuquerque (and the Albuquerque Valley) was the fountain-head for peopling lands to the west. For a brief time in the 1740s, Franciscans maintained missions to the Navajos at Cebolleta and Encinal (Map 4.4). Permanent occupation happened by 1804 when some thirty families from the Albuquerque-Atrisco area, on a land grant issued in 1800, founded Cebolleta. On a second land grant, sixty-one families, also from greater Albuquerque, settled Cubero in 1833. From Cebolleta and Cubero, Hispanos encroached on lands belonging to the Laguna Pueblos. And as conditions became more peaceful under American control, families from Cebolleta established San Mateo in 1862.[32]

By 1860 Hispanos from the Albuquerque area were beginning to reoccupy the Puerco Valley. For twenty years in the second half of the eighteenth century, a dozen villages had lined the Puerco between Nacimiento (Cuba) and Los Quelites. Navajos drove the Hispano occupants back to the Rio Grande valley, however, and in the first half of the nineteenth century they continued to thwart Hispano attempts to resettle their grants. Safer times after 1860 allowed Hispanos to return to their old villages (although San Fernando and Poblazon were not resettled), to which they added Los Cerros. Unfortunately, their large flocks of sheep exceeded the carrying capacity of the local Puerco basin, for overgrazing seems to have triggered

---

[32] Founded in 1745, the Navajo missions lasted about two years; Edward H. Spicer, *Cycles of Conquest: The Impact of Spain, Mexico, and the United States on the Indians of the Southwest, 1533–1960*, 212. The Cebolleta and Cubero settlements are noted in Myra Ellen Jenkins, "The Baltasar Baca 'Grant,' History of an Encroachment," *El Palacio* 68 (1961): 57–58, 63. Cebolleta was founded from the Albuquerque-Atrisco area "as early as 1804"; Marc Simmons, *Albuquerque: A Narative History*, 131. Jenkins, "The Baltasar Baca 'Grant,' " 55, 60, 88, 92, discusses the movement into Laguna lands, and San Mateo settlement is in C. C. Marino, "The Seboyetanos and the Navahos," *New Mexico Historical Review* 29 (1954): 9, 27.

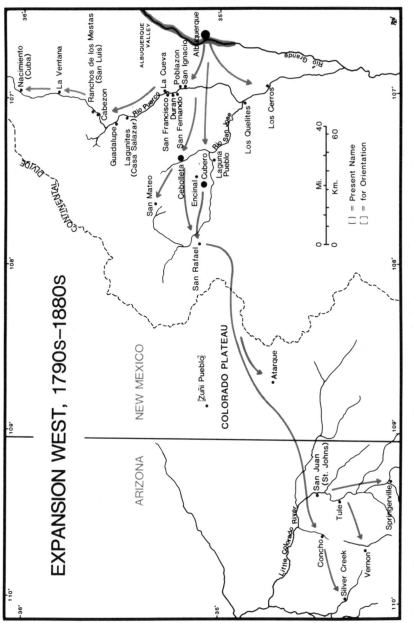

EXPANSION WEST, 1790s–1880s

36°

Nacimiento
(Cuba)

La Ventana

Ranchos de los Mestas
(San Luis)

ALBUQUERQUE
VALLEY

Cabezon

Guadalupe

Lagunites
(Casa Salazar)

Rio Puerco

San Francisco · La Cueva
Duran
San Fernando

Poblazon
San Ignacio

Albuquerque

35°

Rio Grande

San Jose

Los Cerros

San Mateo

Cebolleta

Encinal

Cubero

Laguna
Pueblo

Los Quelites

Rio

40

Mi.

60

Km.

( ) = Present Name
[ ] = for Orientation

0

0

San Rafael

COLORADO PLATEAU

Atarque

NEW MEXICO

[Zuñi Pueblo]

ARIZONA

San Juan
(St. Johns)

Little Colorado River

Concho

Silver Creek

Vernon

Tule

Springerville

CONTINENTAL DIVIDE

108°

109°

110°

36°

35°

107°

107°

108°

109°

110°

RDM

Map 4.4 Expansion to the west saw Hispanos spread thinly across the Colorado Plateau: Sources: see text.

Fig. 4.1 Sheep and a sheepman in the Puerco Valley at the base of Cabezon Peak at Cabezon. The photographer, Henry A. Schmidt (1861–1944), took pictures between about 1890 and 1924. This photograph was taken early in that period, because the deep channel of the Puerco at Cabezon, which does not appear in the photograph, began to be cut between 1885 and 1892, and by 1910 it was about thirty-five feet deep (Kirk Bryan, "Historic Evidence on Changes in the Channel of Rio Puerco, a Tributary of the Rio Grande in New Mexico," *Journal of Geology* 36 (1928): 274, 279). Photograph 50-P courtesy Center for Southwest Research, General Library, University of New Mexico, negative 000–179–0717.

the rapid runoff that caused the Puerco to cut deeply into its alluvium-filled valley (Fig. 4.1). As the Puerco incised itself in a headward direction, villagers could no longer divert irrigation water to their fields by simple gravity flow, and beginning in the late 1880s, one by one from south to north, the villages were abandoned or severely depopulated.[33] By the 1950s the only viable community left was Cuba.

[33] Larry López, "The Founding of San Francisco on the Rio Puerco: A Document," *New Mexico Historical Review* 55 (1980): 72. Concerning attempts to reoccupy Cabe-

The thrust to the west took Hispanos across the Continental Divide and far onto the Colorado Plateau in eastern Arizona Territory, a migration that stemmed from Cebolleta and Cubero. In 1866, Juan Candelaria of Cubero trailed seven hundred sheep to a point several miles south of Concho. Gradually, Hispanos established themselves in the upper reaches of the Little Colorado at Concho, San Juan (Saint Johns), Tule, Springerville, Vernon, and Silver Creek. And from Cubero in 1882 an extended family of Garcias (initially from Cebolleta) and Landavazos settled the area of Jaraloso Canyon and nearby Atarque, which lay in the direction of the Arizona villages.[34] On the Colorado Plateau Hispanos located villages either at springs or at points in arroyo bottoms where intermittent streams could be dammed.

As Hispanos moved onto the Colorado Plateau, they came into contact with Anglos, largely Mormon farmers. Saint Johns is a classic example of the convergence of these two frontiers. In 1872, Hispanos preempted land along the Little Colorado in the vicinity of Saint Johns. About a year later in a card game, a German Jew named Solomon Barth won from these Hispanos several thousand head of sheep and squatter's rights to twelve hundred acres of bottomland.[35] Together with his brothers and some Hispano laborers, Barth built a dam and dug acequias,

---

zon, see Jack D. Rittenhouse, *Cabezon: A New Mexico Ghost Town*, 19. The reoccupation of the villages after 1860 is detailed in a thoroughly enjoyable study (based on a master's thesis in geography at the University of Colorado) by Jerold Gwayn Widdison, "Historical Geography of the Middle Rio Puerco Valley, New Mexico," *New Mexico Historical Review* 34 (1959): 248–84. The Puerco Valley information in Map 4.4 is drawn from Widdison. Abandonment of the villages is in Kirk Bryan, "Historic Evidence on Changes in the Channel of Rio Puerco, a Tributary of the Rio Grande in New Mexico," *Journal of Geology* 36 (1928), esp. pp. 279–81.

[34] Bert Haskett, "History of the Sheep Industry in Arizona," *Arizona Historical Review* 7 (July 1936): 19; Florence Rockwood Kluckhohn, "Los Atarqueños: A Study of Patterns and Configurations in a New Mexico Village" (Ph.D. diss. [sociology], Radcliffe College, 1941) 1: 81–85. The original population schedules of the 1900 census show a Hispano living in Vernon, Apache County, Arizona, who in 1865 was born in Arizona to New Mexico–born parents; Population Schedules of the Twelfth Census [1900], roll 45, ED 3: 34B.

[35] John Baptist Salpointe gave June 24, 1872, for the founding of Saint Johns; *John Baptist Salpointe: Soldier of the Cross*, ed. Odie B. Faulk, 126. What follows is drawn from N. H. Greenwood, "Sol Barth: A Jewish Settler on the Arizona Frontier," *Journal of Arizona History* 14 (1973): 366–69. Barth was born in Posen (Poznań), Poland (then a part of the German empire); Floyd S. Fierman, "Jewish Pioneering in the Southwest: A Record of the Freudenthal-Lesinsky-Solomon Families," *Arizona and the West* 2 (1960): 57.

and amongst Hispano homes on the site of San Juan (his choice of names was soon Anglicized to Saint Johns) he built an adobe mansion (in 1874) and a mercantile outlet. He also married a Hispana from the Landavazo family. To the chagrin of the Hispanos, in 1879 Barth sold his bottomland to Mormon farmers, who in 1880 platted their own addition to Saint Johns. Meanwhile, Texas cattlemen, some of them Mormon converts, entered the area, and to arbitrate the range disputes that quickly pitted cattlemen against sheepmen, a man who was half Hispano and half Anglo was elected Apache County sheriff. Almost from the beginning, then, Saint Johns was bicultural, and not always congenially so. To this day it is part Hispano and part Mormon.[36]

EXPANSION SOUTH

The southernmost Hispano outpost in 1790 was apparently Sabinal in the Belen Valley (Map 4.5). About 1800, Hispanos pushed south of Sabinal into the southern Belen and Socorro valleys, where they reoccupied sites that had been abandoned for more than a century—Alamillo (1800), Socorro (1800?), and La Joya (by 1811). South of Socorro, Valverde was occupied about 1819, although nomad Indians drove the colonists off in 1824, leaving Socorro as the southernmost outpost until perhaps as late as 1840, by which time Luis Lopez and San Antonio had been founded. Farther downstream Paraje was added in 1857, San Marcial in about 1864, and Rio Palomas (Las Palomas) in 1866; Valverde had been reoccupied by 1860, and Contradero existed by 1870. Las Palomas completed the spontaneous Hispano thrust down the Valley of the Rio Grande. Meanwhile, on a grant issued in Chihuahua, Old Mexico colonists from the El Paso District founded Doña Ana in 1842, and within a decade they had spread to Las Cruces (1848

---

[36]The sheriff was John Lorenzo Hubbell, who was born in Pajarito, New Mexico, to a Vermont-born Santa Fe Trail freighter and a Hispana and who had married Lena Rubi of Cebolleta; Dorothy E. Albrecht, "John Lorenzo Hubbell, Navajo Indian Trader," *Journal of Arizona History* 4 (1963): 33–40. At the turn of the nineteenth century, 1,239 Hispanos lived in a wedgelike part of the Homeland that extended from New Mexico into Apache and a tiny part of Navajo counties (Map 4.1). Of these, 388 lived in Concho (76 percent Hispano) and 414 lived in Saint Johns (46 percent Hispano); Population Schedules of the Twelfth Census (1900), rolls 45 (Apache County) and 46 (Navajo County).

or 1849), Mesilla (1849 or 1850), and a string of small villages below Mesilla in the Mesilla Valley. Attracted to the Mesilla Valley in the late nineteenth century, Hispanos seem never to have been dominant in this zone of converging subcultures.[37]

Probably from the Belen Valley, Hispanos moved east to the lee side of the Manzano Mountains, where they settled Manzano by 1816. Forty years later the Belen Valley and Manzano served as springboards for a seemingly undocumented thrust in which Hispanos headed southeast across rugged basin and range country to the lee side of the Sacramento and Capitan mountains. There, La Placita (renamed Lincoln in 1869) was established on the Rio Bonito in the late 1850s within the protective range of Fort Stanton (1855). East of La Placita on the Rio Hondo, at a point where the floodplain widened sufficiently for agriculture, families from Manzano arrived in the 1860s to found San Jose. A relatively large but short-lived plaza, San Jose was called

---

[37] See Frank D. Reeve, *History of New Mexico* 1:320 for Sabinal and 1:431 for Luis Lopez and San Antonio; some sixty-two families reoccupied Alamillo by March, 1800 (1:427). George Kubler recorded the Socorro church as being reoccupied in 1800; *The Religious Architecture of New Mexico in the Colonial Period and Since the American Occupation*, 125. Writing about 1811, Pino noted the presence of seven soldiers at Sevilleta, which Carroll and Haggard identify as present-day La Joya; Pedro Bautista Pino, *Exposición . . .*, in Carroll and Haggard, *Three New Mexico Chronicles*, 69, 209. A list of settlements in New Mexico in 1840 is given by Escudero, *Additions*, in Carroll and Haggard, *Three New Mexico Chronicles*, 91–93 (Luis Lopez and San Antonio are noted on p. 93). See also Lansing Bartlett Bloom, "New Mexico under Mexican Administration 1821–1846," *Old Santa Fe* 1 (1913–14): 12, 13. In 1850 a conscientious census marshal named John R. Tulles, who enumerated south to Las Cruces and Mesilla, did not list any of these settlements along the Rio Grande; *Population Schedules of the Seventh Census* [1850], roll 470: 411–765. Valverde and a place called La Parida are recorded in 1860; *Population of the United States in 1860; Compiled from the Original Returns of the Eighth Census . . .*, 571, table 3. In 1870, Paraje (which is equated with La Parida of the 1860 census), Contadero (*sic*) and San Marcial are given, as is Rio Polomas (*sic*; the original name for Las Palomas) in Doña Ana County. *Population of the United States . . . Compiled from the Original Returns of the Ninth Census . . .*, 1870, 1: 204, 206, table 3. John P. Wilson gave the specific dates for Paraje, San Marcial, and Las Palomas (which he notes was originally called Rio Palomas) in "How the Settlers Farmed: Hispano Villages and Irrigation Systems in Early Sierra County, 1850–1900," *New Mexico Historical Review* 63 (1988): 335, 337, 344. In 1900, Las Palomas (Sierra County) was the southernmost of the Hispano plazas in the Rio Grande Valley. Derry (Sierra County), the next village downstream, was half Hispano and half non-Hispano. For Las Palomas, see *Population Schedules of the Twelfth Census* [1900], roll 1002, ED 132, Precinct 4:195B–197B. For the Mesilla Valley villages, see Maude Elizabeth McFie Bloom, "A History of Mesilla Valley," (bachelor's thesis, New Mexico College of Agriculture and Mechanic Arts, Mesilla Park, 1903), 23–24, 30, 55; Nostrand, "Hispano Homeland in 1900," 395.

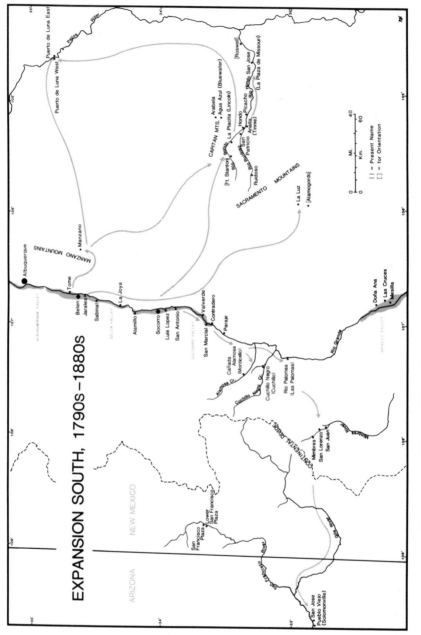

Map 4.5 Least well documented is the diffuse Hispano expansion to the south. Sources: see text.

"La Plaza de Missouri" because some men had been freighters to and from Kansas City and Saint Joseph.[38] The push down the Hondo reached the Pecos Valley: two plazas and their acequias existed in the 1860s within several miles of later-day Roswell. The high country west of the Pecos, meanwhile, came to be sprinkled with plazas including Ruidoso, San Patricio, Hondo, Analla (Tinnie), Picacho, Arabela, and Agua Azul (Bluewater). Added to them was La Luz (located north of modern-day Alamogordo), founded in 1863 on the windward side of the Sacramento Mountains by families who had crossed from Jarales in the Belen Valley. Also in 1863, families from the Rio Bonito valley moved far to the north to establish Puerto de Luna West on the Pecos; they were soon joined across the Pecos at Puerto de Luna East by families from the Rio Grande valley (likely the Belen segment).[39]

Hispano expansion southwest from the Rio Grande valley appears to be even less well documented than that to the southeast. In the 1860s Hispanos seem to have crossed the Continental Divide to the Gila valley, where, thirty miles into Arizona, they established San Jose and Pueblo Viejo (renamed Solomonville in 1878). Between these two most distant Hispano outposts and the Rio Grande valley itself a number of villages were established. From east to west these included Cañada Alamosa (Monticello; 1864) on Alamosa Creek; Cuchillo Negro (Cuchillo; 1871) on Cuchillo Negro Creek; Mimbres, San Lorenzo, and San Juan on the Mimbres River; San Francisco Plaza and Lower San Francisco Plaza on the San Francisco River; and several scattered settlements on the upper Gila.[40]

---

[38] Reeve, *History of New Mexico* 1: 432; Tom Sheridan, *The Bitter River: A Brief Historical Survey of the Middle Pecos River Basin*, 35, 76; James D. Shinkle, *"Missouri Plaza," First Settled Community in Chaves County*, 11, 14, 23. Shinkle shows that the diversion of water by Anglos and Hispanos upstream from San Jose literally dried up the Hondo and forced the plaza's abandonment in the 1870s (p. 24).

[39] Linda Reese, "Anglo Intrusion to Hispanic Roswell: Frontier Articulation in Nineteenth-Century New Mexico" (unpublished paper read at the Eleventh Comparative Frontier Symposium, University of Oklahoma, Norman, April 5, 1985), 3–4; Emily Kalled Lovell, *A Personalized History of Otero County, New Mexico*, 10; Fabiola Cabeza de Baca, "Puerto de Luna," *New Mexico Magazine* 36 (October 1958): 20.

[40] Isador E. Solomon was the local merchant (by 1876) and postmaster (after 1880) at Pueblo Viejo; Fierman, "Jewish Pioneering," 64, 65. He had entered the Gila Valley with his sheep in 1868; Haskett, "Sheep Industry in Arizona," 2. The dates for Monticello and Cuchillo are from Wilson, "How the Settlers Farmed," 336, 340.

THE STRONGHOLD ENLARGED

As the century of Hispano expansion evolved, a hierarchy of village source areas emerged whose pattern can be likened to a fireworks display of shooting stars: each star that shot into space gave rise to several new stars, which in turn parented stars of their own, all headed in the same direction. Santa Fe, Santa Cruz, and Albuquerque were the oldest and largest of the stars, the veritable fountainheads of colonist production. Beyond them was a constellation of lesser magnitude, the major village springboards that included San Miguel, Las Vegas, Mora, Taos, Trinidad, Abiquiu, Cebolleta, Cubero, and probably Belen and Socorro. Beyond these villages were still smaller starlike springboards such as Manzano, which gave rise to La Plaza de Missouri. As has been documented for the westward movement of Anglos, families involved in this process were sometimes repeat migrants. The Vallejos family, for example, moved first from Taos County to San Pablo and then to Cucharas. Thus, some villages were steppingstones as well as springboards.

The decade of greatest areal gains was the 1860s; gradual containment of nomad Indians by Anglo soldiers facilitated expansion in that decade. Each enlarging frontier, however, had its own characteristics. The northern frontier was the most dynamic demographically; of 140,690 Hispanos in 1900, 23,315 (16.5 percent) lived in southern Colorado.[41] Nevertheless, this higher and relatively well watered country also attracted Anglos, who by the early 1860s were blunting Hispano expansion. Hispanos spread rather thinly across the plains to the east, and their numbers were even smaller on the Colorado Plateau to the west. Yet in the west they stood their ground when Anglo colonists confronted them, whereas in the east, Anglo cattlemen were rolling back the Hispano frontier as early as the 1870s. To the south, large numbers of Hispanos moved into the Socorro Valley, but in the Mesilla Valley, where the potential for substantial gains was greatest, Hispanos were not the first colonists, and those who were attracted were in the minority.

[41] Tabulated from Population Schedules of the Twelfth Census [1900], rolls 117–30. Hispanos in Colorado were largely Colorado- and New Mexico-born; see Nostrand, "Hispano Homeland in 1900," 384, 385.

Hispano expansion did not end in the 1880s, but after that time it took a new form. Anglos who had moved to the outer margins of the Homeland now attracted Hispanos through employment opportunities, including work on railroads, ranches, and farms and in sawmills, mines, and industry. Indeed, this peripheral attraction began in a small way in the 1830s, when Anglo traders hired Hispano masons to build their posts. What did end in the 1880s, however, was the spontaneous and contiguous village-by-village expansion of a folk people. The legacy of place names is sometimes deceptive: a Walsenburg rather than a La Plaza de los Leones, a Saint Johns rather than a San Juan, a Lincoln rather than a La Placita, a Solomonville (today Solomon) rather than a Pueblo Viejo. Yet in their expanding Stronghold, Hispanos were the initial colonists, the dominant people in a broadening region. In one century they founded hundreds of new villages in parts of five states. Not all the areal gains made by 1900 were the result of village-by-village expansion; in perhaps 15 percent of the Homeland's outer margins, Anglos had attracted Hispanos. Between 1790 and 1900, however, as shown by Map 4.1, this remarkably dynamic people had increased their entire Homeland region from approximately 5,350 square miles (an area the size of Connecticut) in 1790 to 85,000 square miles (an area the size of Utah) in 1900.

CHAPTER 5

✠ ✠ ✠

ANGLO INTRUSION

AT A LARGE spring that overlooked the Estancia valley, His-panos, probably from Tome, laid out the fortified *plaza* of Man-zano. Their grant petition of 1829 suggests that this happened before 1824. When the 1850 census was taken (in January 1851), Manzano claimed 403 residents, of whom all were Hispanos save three, who had been born in Mexico. By 1853, however, an American hunter named Fry had moved in. Other "Anglos" soon followed: a Polish-born priest named Alexander Grzela-chowski in the mid-1850s; a merchant named Charles Beach before the Civil War; a New York–born postmaster and newspa-per publisher named Charles L. Kusz, Jr., in the early 1880s; lumbermen attracted by the pine-covered Manzano Mountains also in the 1880s; and a Syrian-born merchant named Tenos Tabet, who, with his Syrian-born wife, opened a general store in 1902. By 1940, some Hispanos in Manzano were part Irish and French, and of the now 802 villagers, sixteen adults, presumably also some children, were Anglos. And by 1980, with village numbers now substantially reduced because of emigration, 14 of the 118 Manzaneños were Anglos. Although some typical intruders, such as the Chinese laundrymen who were once ubiq-uitous in larger communities, seem to have bypassed Manzano, the village nevertheless illustrates how an isolated and to this day highly Hispano community was gradually encroached upon by Anglos, a phenomenon that by 1980 had Anglicized Hispanos and had transformed virtually the entire Hispano Stronghold into an Inland.[1]

---

[1] This paragraph draws heavily on Wesley Robert Hurt, Jr., "Manzano: A Study of Community Disorganization" (master's thesis [sociology], University of New Mexico, 1941), 26, 28–29, 34, 101–102, 201. In his *History of New Mexico* 1: 432, Frank D.

EARLY INTRUDERS

In New Mexico an "Anglo" is anyone who is not Indian or of Spanish-Indian or Mexican descent. Even blacks are "Anglos"; in her *New Mexico* (1951), Erna Fergusson, a lifetime resident of Albuquerque, quoted a black bootblack as saying "us Anglos." No one seems to know when the term *Anglo* first came into use; presumably, it was after the American takeover in 1846.[2] Because New Mexicans use it in such a liberal way demographically, for the present purpose perhaps it can also be stretched chronologically, to include those earliest alien intruders who began to trickle into the Homeland after the reconquest.

In this sense, the first Anglo intruders appear to have been two Frenchmen, Jean L'Archeveque (Archibeque) and Jacques Grolé (Gurulé), who were members of Robert Cavelier, Sieur de La Salle's ill-fated expedition. Surrendering themselves to Spaniards in Texas, they were taken to Mexico City and Spain before they ended up in the 1690s in New Mexico, where they were married and left offspring. Bent on establishing trade between Louisiana and New Mexico, a party of eight or nine Frenchmen from Canada led by Pierre and Paul Mallet reached Santa Fe in 1739. They remained for nine months, and at least one, Juan Bautista Alarí (Alarid), was married, had children, and remained permanently.[3]

Reeve asserted that Manzano was founded by 1816. Concerning 1850, Population Schedules of the Seventh Census [1850], Microcopy no. 432, 1963, roll 470: 746–55. Concerning Fry, see James Henry Carleton, "Diary of an Excursion to the Ruins of Abó, Quarra, and Gran Quivira, in New Mexico, under the Command of Major James Henry Carleton, U.S.A.," *Ninth Annual Report of the Board of Regents of the Smithsonian Institution* . . . , 304. Concerning Grzelachowski, see Francis C. Kajencki, "Alexander Grzelachowski: Pioneer Merchant of Puerto de Luna, New Mexico," *Arizona and the West* 26 (1984): 246–47. Concerning Beach, see F. Stanley [Crocchiola], *The Manzano, New Mexico, Story,* 12. Concerning Kusz, see Peter Hertzog, *The Gringo and Greaser,* Western Americana Series, no. 6: 3. Concerning the lumbermen and Tabet, see Hurt, "Manzano," 83, 92–93. The 1980 data are from Mrs. Juanita Candelaria, director of the Senior Citizens' Center, Manzano, New Mexico, interview with the author, August 14, 1980.

[2] Erna Fergusson, *New Mexico: A Pageant of Three Peoples,* 217. No clue about the first use of "Anglo" is found in such likely sources as Ruth Laughlin Barker, "Where Americans Are 'Anglos,'" *North American Review* 228 (1929): 568–73; and Burl Noggle, "Anglo Observers of the Southwest Borderlands, 1825–1890: The Rise of a Concept," *Arizona and the West* 1 (1959): 105–31.

[3] Fray Angélico Chávez, *Origins of New Mexico Families in the Spanish Colonial Period,* 122, 129, 193; Henri Folmer, "The Mallet Expedition of 1739 through Nebraska, Kansas and Colorado to Santa Fe," *Colorado Magazine* 16 (1939): 161, 167–69.

The French traders who followed were apparently less fortunate; Spain's mercantile policy forbade would-be traders from breaching her frontier, and in the 1740s and '50s those who ventured into Santa Fe seem to have had their goods confiscated and were imprisoned. In 1766, however, another Frenchman named Domingo Labadía (Labadíe) was married in Santa Fe and left heirs with his family name. And, as Zebulon Pike was being escorted through New Mexico in 1807, he recorded the presence of additional intruders, including one Baptiste LaLande, a trader from Kaskaskia who had been detained in New Mexico since about 1804, and one James Purcell (called "Pursley" by Pike), a trader as well as a carpenter from Kentucky who had been interned since 1805.[4] Craftsmen like Purcell, always in short supply in New Mexico, were spared imprisonment in Chihuahua, the apparent fate of many of the interlopers.

Newly independent Mexico abruptly reversed Spanish policy and in 1821 opened her northern frontier to foreigners. Late that year, on the south side of Raton Pass, a detachment of soldiers from New Mexico encountered a party from Missouri led by William Becknell. The soldiers invited the party to Santa Fe, where Becknell traded goods intended for barter with the Comanches. Word of Becknell's reception (and profits) spread quickly after his return to Missouri early in 1822. Thus was initiated the famous trade that soon plied a two-way wagon trail between the Missouri River towns (ultimately Saint Louis) and Santa Fe—although in time Santa Fe was less a terminus than a way station, for many wagons continued down the Camino Real to Chihuahua (Map 5.1).[5]

In Santa Fe in July and August, in shops on or near the

[4] For the French traders, see Herbert E. Bolton, "French Intrusions into New Mexico, 1749–1752," in *The Pacific Ocean in History*, ed. H. Morse Stephens and Herbert E. Bolton, esp. pp. 393–400; and Henri Folmer, "Contraband Trade between Louisiana and New Mexico in the Eighteenth Century," *New Mexico Historical Review* 16 (1941): 263–64, 272. Chávez casts some doubt on the extent to which French intruders may have been imprisoned when he recorded the marriages of Frenchmen Louis Febre (Luis Febro) and Jean Mignon (Juan Miñon) in New Mexico in 1750 and 1752, respectively; *Origins of New Mexico Families*, 174, 231; he mentions Labadía on p. 202. Zebulon Montgomery Pike, *The Journals of Zebulon Montgomery Pike, with Letters and Related Documents*, ed. Donald Jackson, 1: 388–90; 2: 59–62; and David J. Weber, *The Taos Trappers: The Fur Trade in the Far Southwest, 1540–1846*, 35–38.

[5] Max L. Moorhead, *New Mexico's Royal Road: Trade and Travel on the Chihuahua Trail*, 76 ff.

plaza, traders exchanged their textiles, hardware, and liquor for woolen and leather goods, livestock, and silver bars or coin. According to Josiah Gregg, author of the epic firsthand account of the Santa Fe trade, between 50 and 350 traders and teamsters were engaged in this commerce each year between 1822 and 1843. A small number remained in New Mexico, primarily in Santa Fe (for example, Spanish-born Manuel Álvarez) but also along the trail itself, as in Las Vegas (L. J. Keithly) and San Miguel (Thomas Rowland).[6]

Trappers, meanwhile, were entering New Mexico. Indeed, trappers and traders were sometimes the same people. Members of the first three parties to enter Santa Fe in late 1821 and early 1822 (Becknell, McKnight-James, and Glenn) engaged in both enterprises. Unlike the traders, whose focus was Santa Fe, most trappers congregated in Taos, a logical choice given its history as a rendezvous point and its strategic location as the gateway to the southern Rockies. And unlike the Santa Fe trade, which continued down to the arrival of the AT&SF in 1879, trapping was already in decline by the early 1830s, in part because the most sought animal, the beaver, was becoming less plentiful. As the major entrepôt for the trappers, Taos came to contain a large number of Anglos, including Quebec-born Charles Beaubien, Missouri-born Cerán St. Vrain, Virginia-born Charles Bent, and Kentucky-born Christopher (Kit) Carson. Besides being prominent, what these four Taoseños had in common was that each was a one-time trapper who was married to (or cohab-

---

[6] Josiah Gregg, *Commerce of the Prairies*, ed. Max L. Moorhead, 332. Manuel Álvarez was born in Spain in 1794, went to New York in 1823, entered the Santa Fe trade in 1824, petitioned to be a Mexican citizen in 1825 and again in 1826, then applied for U.S. citizenship in Saint Louis in 1834, was the American consul in Santa Fe between 1839 and 1846, and for some thirty years was a major mercantile proprietor in Santa Fe, where he died in 1856. Harold H. Dunham, "Manuel Alvarez," in *The Mountain Men and the Fur Trade of the Far West: Biographical Sketches of the Participants by Scholars of the Subject and with Introductions by the Editor*, ed. LeRoy R. Hafen, 1: 181, 182, 190, 193, 194, 197. Moorhead asserted that Álvarez acquired U.S. citizenship in 1842; *New Mexico's Royal Road*, 128–29. L. J. Keithly, a Santa Fe trader, in 1840 was the first American to open a store in Las Vegas; F. Stanley [Crocchiola], *The Las Vegas (New Mexico) Story*, 67. Thomas Rowland, an American who was married to a Hispana, by 1839 was a merchant in San Miguel (where he was murdered in 1858); F. Stanley [Crocchiola], *The San Miguel del Bado, New Mexico, Story*, 10, 11, 16. That Thomas Rowland was a Santa Fe trader is noted in David J. Weber's account of a brother, John Rowland, who lived in Taos and was married to a Hispana; "John Rowland," in Hafen, *Mountain Men* 4: 276, 279.

NEW MEXICO TRADE LINKAGES,
1821–1846

SANTA FE TRAIL

Independence

Missouri

St. Louis

Raton Pass

UNITED STATES

Taos

Santa Fe

Las Vegas

San Miguel

Arkansas

← ADAMS–ONIS BOUNDARY (1819)

MEXICO

CAMINO REAL

Mississippi

Chihuahua

Rio Grande

| 0 | Mi. | 200 |
| 0 | Km. | 300 |

Map 5.1 New Mexico's trade linkages in the Mexican era. Wagon trails connected Santa Fe with both Missouri and the "States" and with Chihuahua and Mexico. The Mountain Division of the Santa Fe Trail, which followed the U.S. side of the Arkansas River into Colorado before crossing through Raton Pass, was used earlier than the shorter but more dangerous Cimarron Division. Las Vegas came to exist about 1835; Texas won her independence in 1836 and was annexed to the United States in 1845; and Westport Landing supplanted Independence in 1844. The Santa Fe Trail is modified from Josiah Gregg, *Commerce of the Prairies,* ed. Max L. Moorhead map between pp. 58 and 59; the Camino Real is after Max L. Moorhead, *New Mexico's Royal Road: Trade and Travel on the Chihuahua Trail,* 104–105.

itated with) a Hispana, and two of them (Beaubien and St. Vrain) were also naturalized Mexicans.[7]

Until 1846, the intruders who remained in New Mexico were primarily Americans (many of French extraction), French Canadians, or Frenchmen. Most lived in the larger communities located in the Rio Arriba, notably Taos and Santa Fe. That very few lived in the Rio Abajo, and that they had entered New Mexico from the northeast, nicely illustrates the principle of "distance-decay": the greater the distance from the "States," the fewer the Anglos. Almost to a person these intruders were men, many of whom formed unions with Hispanas; to an important degree they had assimilated with the dominant society; and their offspring were Hispanicized. Because many were educated, possessed skills, had access to American markets, or had connections with the elite of New Mexico's society, these early intruders wielded power and influence that were disproportionate to their small numbers.[8] And in a small way they started the process whereby Hispanos became Anglicized.

[7] Weber, Taos Trappers, 53–55, 210; in Hafen, Mountain Men, see Harold H. Dunham, "Charles Bent," 2: 27, 44; Harold H. Dunham, "Ceran St. Vrain," 5: 297, 300, 306, 316; Lawrence R. Murphy, "Charles H. Beaubien," 6: 23, 25, 26, 27; and Harvey L. Carter, "Kit Carson," 6: 105, 107, 117.

[8] From an analysis of new surnames in New Mexico in the church records of the Archdiocese of Santa Fe for the period 1820–50, Chávez found that Taos was the major destination, with Santa Fe "a far second," for those having "French-Canadian, U.S. American, and some North European" surnames. Numerically, these surnames exceeded the "new Spanish or Mexican surnames," yet they represented only those who had come in contact with the church through baptism or marriage. Chávez noted specifically the absence of many new non-Spanish or Mexican surnames in the Rio Abajo; Fray Angélico Chávez, "New Names in New Mexico, 1820–1850," El Palacio 64 (1967): 291–92.

Craver examined 122 unions between Anglo men and Hispanas in New Mexico's Rio Arriba between 1821 and 1846. She concluded that Anglos had, to an important but uncertain degree, assimilated with the Hispano society, and that their offspring were Hispanicized. For example, of at least 273 children born to 88 of the 122 unions, with rare exceptions all married Hispanos(as). Craver also gave the states from which Americans among these 122 Anglos had originated. In order of frequency, they were Missouri, Kentucky, Tennessee, Pennsylvania, Virginia, New York, Vermont, Ohio, Illinois, and Maryland; Rebecca McDowell Craver, The Impact of Intimacy: Mexican-Anglo Intermarriage in New Mexico, 1821–1846, Southwestern Studies Monograph no. 66: 6, 37–38, 46–47. For more on the influence of the Anglos, see Moorhead, New Mexico's Royal Road, 193; and David J. Weber, The Mexican Frontier, 1821–1846: The American Southwest under Mexico, Histories of the American Frontier, 128, 180, 183. Reporting on New Mexico in 1831–32, Barreiro listed among the trades of the Anglos tailors, carpenters, gunsmiths, blacksmiths, hatters, tinsmiths, and shoemakers; Antonio Barreiro, Ojeada . . . , in "Barreiro's Ojeada Sobre Nuevo-Mexico," trans. and ed. Lansing B. Bloom, New Mexico Historical Review 3 (1928): 96.

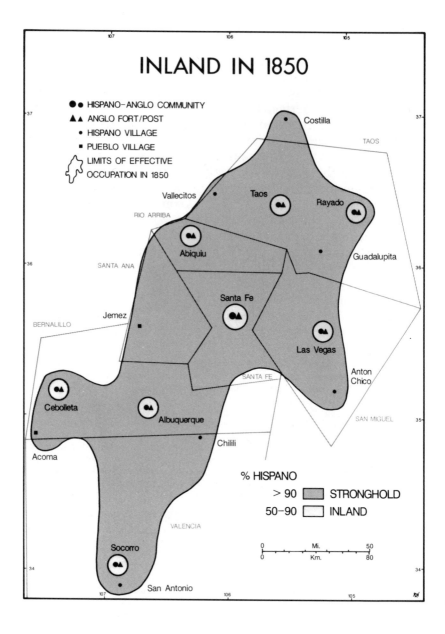

INLAND IN 1850

● ● HISPANO–ANGLO COMMUNITY
▲ ▲ ANGLO FORT/POST
● HISPANO VILLAGE
■ PUEBLO VILLAGE
LIMITS OF EFFECTIVE
OCCUPATION IN 1850

Costilla

TAOS

Vallecitos Taos Rayado

RIO ARRIBA

Abiquiu

Guadalupita

SANTA ANA

Santa Fe

Jemez

BERNALILLO

Las Vegas

Anton
Chico

SANTA FE

Cebolleta Albuquerque

SAN MIGUEL

Acoma

Chilili

% HISPANO

> 90 STRONGHOLD
50–90 INLAND

VALENCIA

Socorro

0 Mi. 50
0 Km. 80

San Antonio

The year 1846 saw invading American soldiers rapidly take control politically as well as militarily. Over the next four years troop numbers fluctuated and their locations changed, but by late 1850 or early 1851, when the census was taken, in the area north of Socorro soldiers were found at Fort Marcy (located on the old presidio grounds behind the Palace of the Governors) and at seven posts in Taos, Abiquiu, Cebolleta, Albuquerque, Socorro, Las Vegas, and Rayado (Map 5.2). With the possible exception of Rayado, all eight garrisons were located within the Hispano communities. Although definitely an undercount, the 1850 census records a military population of 895, including 617 officers and soldiers (entirely men) and 278 ancillary personnel (largely men, including teamsters, clerks, carpenters, blacksmiths, laundrywomen, and interpreters; Table 5.1). The several officers were born in the United States, but, significantly, nearly two-thirds of the soldiers were born in Europe, primarily in Ireland (195) and Germany (113). Interaction between the soldiers and the Hispano population was common, and at least an occasional soldier married a Hispana.[9]

[9] George Archibald McCall, *New Mexico in 1850: A Military View*, ed. Robert W. Frazer, 34–37. Frazer seemed to suggest that the post at Rayado was not located in the basically Hispano community of Rayado. Lawrence R. Murphy noted, however, that mounted dragoons were stationed at newly founded Rayado from the winter of 1849–50 until August 1851, "Rayado: Pioneer Settlement in Northeastern New Mexico, 1848–1857," *New Mexico Historical Review* 46 (1971): 42–43, 49. Taken by six Anglo assistant marshals, the 1850 census was probably more accurate for its Anglo component than for its Hispano and Pueblo Indian components. McCall (*New Mexico in 1850*, 34) noted that there were 1,019 officers and men in New Mexico Territory in 1850. This compares with 617 given by the census takers. Troops garrisoned at three posts south of Socorro (Doña Ana, El Paso, and San Elizario) explain part of the

Map 5.2 (*opposite*) The Inland (intruder zone) in 1850. Anglo intruders had recently created discontinuous islands of "Inland" (50–90 percent Hispano) within the Stronghold (greater than 90 percent Hispano). Imprecise census data preclude showing any of the twenty Pueblo villages as non-Homeland inliers. Sources: Population Schedules of the Seventh Census [1850]; troop locations are from George Archibald McCall, *New Mexico in 1850: A Military View*, 34–37; county boundaries (presumably drawn by James S. Calhoun) are from the J. W. Abert and W. G. Peck map of New Mexico Territory in 1846–47, reproduced as map no. 2 (in pocket) in Annie Heloise Abel, ed., *The Official Correspondence of James S. Calhoun while an Indian Agent at Santa Fe and Superintendent of Indian Affairs in New Mexico*.

Table 5.1   Anglos in the Homeland,[a] 1850

County	Non-Military[b]	Military[c] Officers/Soldiers[d]	Ancillary[e]
Bernalillo[f]	38	290	39
Rio Arriba	21		
San Miguel	118		
Santa Ana	7		
Santa Fe[g]	336	225	207
Taos	99		
Valencia[f]	64	72	32
Homeland	683	617	278

SOURCE: U.S. Bureau of the Census, Population Schedules of the Seventh Census [1850].
[a] New Mexico Territory north of the Socorro area.
[b] Overwhelmingly men whose places of birth were United States (451), foreign (208—many in Ireland and Germany), or unknown (24); 96 were either married to or lived with Hispanas.
[c] Enumerated were the United States garrisons in Albuquerque and Cebolleta (Bernalillo County), Santa Fe, and Socorro (Valencia County).
[d] Entirely men whose places of birth were United States (195), foreign (380), unknown (42).
[e] Largely men whose places of birth were United States (76), foreign (42), unknown (160).
[f] One hundred sixty-two persons enumerated in western Bernalillo County by the Valencia County assistant marshal were removed from the total for Valencia County and were added to the total for Bernalillo County.
[g] All military and 310 of 336 nonmilitary Anglos were located in the City of Santa Fe, which had a total population of 4,846.

The attitudes of the soldiers towards the Hispanos, as recorded about 1846–49 in letters, diaries, and accounts, were fairly uniform, and they were the same attitudes expressed earlier by many traders and trappers. What these intruders believed was that they represented a superior civilization, and with contempt they described New Mexico's "Mexicans" as indolent, degenerate, undependable, dishonest, improvished, and addicted to gambling and other vices. However, these traders, trappers, and soldiers often complimented the women, who, out of respect for their beauty, grace, and caring, they sometimes referred to as "Spanish." Not surprisingly, the atti-

---

difference. Still, no military personnel were reported in the census schedules for Taos, Rio Arriba, and San Miguel counties, which would suggest that Rayado, which was already founded, was by-passed and that the posts at Taos, Abiquiu, and Las Vegas either were not yet established or, more likely, were by-passed by the assistant marshals. The census in all seven counties was taken between October 1850 and January 1851; Population Schedules of the Seventh Census [1850], rolls 467–70. For intermarriage, see John P. Bloom, "New Mexico Viewed by Anglo-Americans, 1846–1849," *New Mexico Historical Review* 34 (1959): 191.

tude of Hispanos towards Anglos was equally unfavorable: "*Americanos,*" as all were called, were thought to be arrogant, rude, insolent, economic materialists, religious heretics, and cultural barbarians.[10]

What had happened, of course, was that when the strikingly contrasting Latin and Anglo cultures came into contact, conflict and discrimination were two results. A third was an early realization that between the two cultures was a genuine contrast in values. Fences, which were prominent features in most landscapes in the States, are a case in point. Anglos Josiah Gregg, Lewis H. Garrard, and James William Abert were all struck by the absence of fences around the agricultural plots of Hispanos. Explained Gregg, "Instead of the cultivator's having to guard his crop from the cattle as with us, the owners of these are bound to guard them from crops."[11] Among Hispanos, in other words, it was the livestock owner's responsibility, not the farmer's, to keep his animals away from a farmer's crops, which explained the absence of fences (and the ubiquitous shepherd) in New Mexico.

By 1850, then, in a Homeland that was overwhelmingly Hispano, Anglos had established footholds. The largest was at Santa Fe, where 772 military and nonmilitary Anglos (half of all 1,578 Anglos in the Homeland) represented 15.9 percent of the town's population (Table 5.1). After Santa Fe, data in the 1850 census would suggest the following combined military-nonmilitary Anglo hierarchy: Albuquerque, 183; Cebolleta, 162; Socorro, 150; Las Vegas, 85 (nonmilitary

---

[10] Concerning traders, see Moorhead, *New Mexico's Royal Road*, 192. Concerning trappers and "mountain men," see Lewis H. Garrard, *Wah-to-Yah and the Taos Trail*, 189, 222. Concerning soldiers, see Bloom, "New Mexico Viewed by Anglo-Americans, 1846–1849," 173, 182; and Noggle, "Anglo Observers," 114. Concerning the women; see James M. Lacy, "New Mexican Women in Early American Writings," *New Mexico Historical Review* 34 (1959): 41, 51; and Bloom, "New Mexico Viewed by Anglo-Americans, 1846–1849," 188, 191, 194. Beverly Trulio found that the Anglo males' favorable impression of the Hispana, as characterized by James Lacy, has been overstated; "Anglo-American Attitudes toward New Mexican Women," *Journal of the West* 12 (1973): 229–30, 239. For examples of Hispanos' opinions of Anglos, see Thomas Maitland Marshall, "St. Vrian's Expedition to the Gila in 1826," *Southwestern Historical Quarterly* 19 (1915–16): 257, 258; and Moorhead, *New Mexico's Royal Road*, 193. Gregg noted that all foreigners were called Americanos; *Commerce of the Prairies*, 262, n. 11.

[11] Gregg, *Commerce of the Prairies*, 107; Garrard, *Wah-to-Yah*, 166, 168; J. W. Abert, *Abert's New Mexico Report, 1846–'47*, 37, 38, 41.

only); and Taos, 50 (nonmilitary only). Anglos probably exceeded 10 percent of the population in all these communities save perhaps in Taos.[12]

Indeed, although a few nonmilitary Anglos were thinly scattered over much of the Homeland, most nonmilitary and all military Anglos were clustered residentially, and these clusters were always in close proximity to the Hispano elite (those who owned considerable real estate and used nomad Indian domestics). Wherever Anglos exceeded 10 percent of a community's population, there existed an intruder zone or "Inland," defined here as the zone where Hispano percentages had dropped to between 50–90 percent (Map 5.2). Geographically a series of discontinuous islands, this Inland in 1850 had just been created out of the Stronghold (over 90 percent Hispano). Thus, ignoring the Pueblo Indians, whose twenty villages are not shown as non-Homeland inliers because of an absence in the census of precise Hispano-Indian locational data, Hispanos in 1850 were everywhere in the majority, yet in their largest towns their dominance was eroding.[13] And this erosion was only beginning.

[12] Charles Blumner, a German-born merchant who lived with his Hispana wife (Feliciana) and daughter (Carlota) in Santa Fe, was the census taker in Santa Fe County; Population Schedules of the Seventh Census [1850], roll 468: 748. Blumner was both knowledgeable about Spanish and accurate. He noted precisely where Santa Fe (total population 4,846) began and ended, and in the left schedule margins he even noted whether certain establishments were groceries, bakeries, boarding houses, and so on. In a biographical profile of Blumner, Thomas Jaehn said that Blumner (1805–76) was more successful as a public servant (territorial treasurer, U.S. marshal, and tax collector) than as a merchant; "Charles Blumner: Pioneer, Civil Servant, and Merchant," *New Mexico Historical Review* 61 (1986): 319–27. Like Blumner, John R. Tulles, the census taker for Valencia County, conscientiously noted places being enumerated, as did James D. Robinson in a cruder way for San Miguel County. But, with minor exceptions, the other assistant marshals omitted locational data, making it impossible to determine Anglo percentages, whether Hispanos lived on Pueblo lands, and so on. Estimates of total populations for all but Cebolleta are given in John P. Bloom, "Note on the Population of New Mexico, 1846–1849," *New Mexico Historical Review* 34 (1959): 200–202. (That Bloom is the author is noted in the same issue on p. 174, n. 22.)

[13] In March 1850, James S. Calhoun, the Indian agent in New Mexico Territory, noted the existence of twenty-two pueblos exclusive of the Hopis. Two, Socorro (del Sur) and Isleta (del Sur), were in the El Paso District. The others were Taos, Picuris, San Juan, Santa Clara, San Ildefonso, Pojoaque, Nambe, Tesuque, Cochiti, Santo Domingo, San Felipe, Sandia, Santa Ana, Cia, Jemez, Isleta, Leutis (in same district with Isleta), Laguna, Acoma, and Zuñi; Annie Heloise Abel, ed., *The Official Correspondence of James S. Calhoun while Indian Agent at Santa Fé and Superintendent of Indian Affairs in New Mexico*, 175–77.

INTRUDERS, 1850–1900

After 1850, Anglo intruders increased in both number and variety, and perhaps the incoming Roman Catholic clergymen most dramatically illustrate how this hastened the Anglicization process. In 1850, fifteen priests and one vicar (in Santa Fe) were ministering in the Homeland, and all sixteen were Hispanos. By 1900, of fifty-six Catholic clergy in the Homeland, only three were Hispanos. Practically all of the Anglo clergy were born in Europe, most of them in France (Map 5.3). What had happened was that in 1849 New Mexico was placed under the jurisdiction of the Roman Catholic church in the United States. The next year French-born Jean Baptiste Lamy, who had just spent eleven years as a missioner priest in Ohio and Kentucky, was appointed the vicar apostolic and bishop of New Mexico, and in 1851 when Lamy arrived in Santa Fe he was appalled by what in his opinion were debased values of the local clergy and by the seemingly barbaric practices of the Penitentes. Lamy, whose tenure as bishop and eventually archbishop lasted until 1885, replaced the local clergy with those from Europe, many from his home diocese of Clermont-Ferrand. To his credit, Lamy insisted that his clergy learn Spanish (and English), yet the local resentment against him ran high, and the outcome was that in every major Hispano community, the best educated and most influential person— whose persuasive powers included the ability to swing votes at election time—was no longer a Hispano, and unlike the situation in the Spanish period was not even a person who spoke Spanish as a native language.[14]

[14] All sixteen of the clergymen in 1850 were born in New Mexico, had Spanish names, and (under "color") were white. At least one of the sixteen was located at a Pueblo village (San Ildefonso); Population Schedules of the Seventh Census [1850], rolls 467–70. The nativity of the fifty-six clergymen in 1900 was as follows: thirty-two, France; eight, Italy; four, Germany; two, Belgium; one, Holland; one, Ireland; one, French Canada; one, Costa Rica; one, "South America"; two, Illinois; and three, New Mexico. Of the three born in New Mexico, one, a thirty-six-year-old priest in Trinidad, may not have been a Hispano. Both his parents were given as New Mexico–born, which is why he is counted as a Hispano, yet his name was Albert Gilbert. One of the fifty-six clergymen was located at a Pueblo village (San Juan); Population Schedules of the Twelfth Census [1900], Microcopy no. T–623, n.d., rolls 45–46, 117, 120–21, 124–29, 999–1003, 1335, 1643, 1663. Lamy's biographer is Paul Horgan, *Lamy of Santa Fe: His Life and Times*, 69, 73, 114, 128, 149, 183, 184, 188. In 1939 an elderly priest in the El Cerrito area told Olen E. Leonard that "he could swing the votes of his followers toward any political candidate he chose," and Leonard speculated that the influence of the church was even stronger fifty years earlier; Olen E. Leonard, *The*

With the American takeover there also came a new group of Anglo merchants who were notable because so many were German-born Jews. In the vanguard was Solomon Jacob Spiegelberg, who arrived in Santa Fe in 1844, set up a business in 1846, and about then was appointed sutler to Fort Marcy. By 1850 sixteen definite or possible Jews, two of them Spiegelberg's brothers, Levi and Elias, were in New Mexico, and all sixteen were young, German-born men who were either merchants or clerks. The 1850s and '60s found the Seligmans, Staabs, Ilfelds, and others opening mercantile houses on the plazas of Santa Fe and Las Vegas. What set the Jews apart from the other Anglo merchants, and what probably explains why so many were successful, was that their businesses were family enterprises. Brothers were the partners; relatives in Baltimore, Philadelphia, or New York were the supply agents; and when branch stores or new outlets were opened on the plazas of the smaller villages, relatives or Jewish friends got the financing.[15]

During the second half of the nineteenth century, according to William J. Parish, no fewer than eighty-seven New Mexican communities had at least one German Jewish merchant, and

---

Role of the Land Grant in the Social Organization and Social Processes of a Spanish-American Village in New Mexico, 55, 71–72.

[15] Henry J. Tobias, *A History of the Jews in New Mexico*, 25, 29, 30, 34, 36–37, 40, 41ff. All sixteen of these men are recorded in the Population Schedules of the Seventh Census [1850], rolls 467–70. In Santa Fe in 1867, according to Nathan Bibo, the mercantile firms of the Spiegelberg brothers, Staab brothers, Ilfeld brothers, Simon Seligman, Elsberg and Amberg, and Johnson and Koch all were located around the plaza; Floyd S. Fierman, ed., "Nathan Bibo's Reminiscenses of Early New Mexico," *El Palacio* 68, part 1 (1961): 242. For more on the business relationships of these men, see William J. Parish, "The German Jew and the Commerical Revolution in Territorial New Mexico, 1850–1900," *New Mexico Historical Review* 35 (1960): 18–19, 19–20, 22.

Map 5.3 (*opposite*) Roman Catholic clergymen in the Homeland, 1850 and 1900. Between 1850 and 1900, the number of clergy grew from sixteen to fifty-six, but the proportion that was Hispano declined precipitously. In 1850 the location of five of the sixteen clergy is known only for the county. In 1900, omitted are eight of thirteen Homeland outliers (which contained one Illinois-born priest at Winslow, Arizona) and all thirteen non-Homeland inliers (which contained two French-born priests at Jemez and Isleta villages). Places having more than one clergy are named. By 1900 the Homeland stretched well beyond New Mexico Territory, and it also exceeded the limits of the Archdiocese of Santa Fe. Sources: Population Schedules of the Seventh [1850] and Twelfth [1900] censuses.

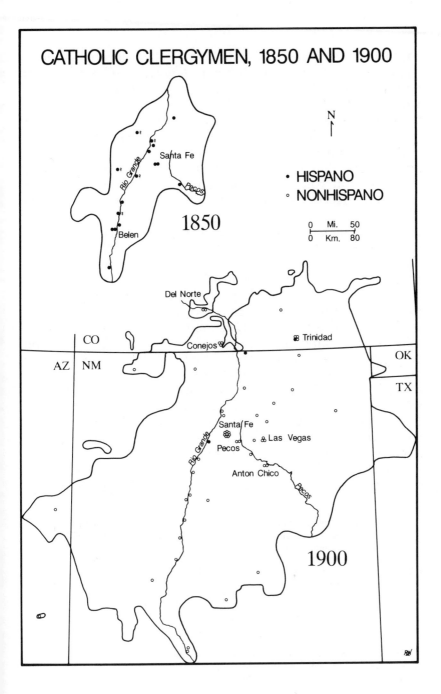

CATHOLIC CLERGYMEN, 1850 AND 1900

N

• HISPANO
○ NONHISPANO

Santa Fe

Rio Grande

Pecos

Belen

1850

0   Mi.   50
0   Km.   80

Del Norte

CO

Conejos

Trinidad

AZ   NM

OK

TX

Santa Fe

Rio Grande

Pecos

Las Vegas

Anton Chico

Pecos

1900

Santa Fe, Las Vegas, and Albuquerque had dozens of them. There emerged a network wherein Jewish merchant-bankers on the smaller plazas sold (bartered) their merchandise for the wool and sheep of the local Hispanos and, in turn, exchanged these Hispano products for new merchandise at the major Jewish wholesale houses on the large plazas. Occasionally these German merchants were the only non-Hispanos in a given village. Some were married to Hispanas.[16] And symbolic of their vital role as middlemen were their stores, which invariably faced right onto the all-important village plaza (Fig. 5.1).

Other Anglos penetrated the Hispanos' villages just as directly as did the Catholic clergymen and the Jewish merchants, but they were both less cohesive and less influential. Further, these other Anglos were usually born in the States instead of Europe, and unlike the clergy and merchants, they reached even the smallest villages. By 1900, almost every village had its handful of them.[17] Farmers, and to a lesser extent stock raisers, were found in the largest numbers, yet carpenters, who curiously were often born in Kentucky, and blacksmiths, who just as curiously were often born in Pennsylvania, were also often present. Occasionally there were teachers, millers, or miners, and very occasionally there was a doctor, a lawyer, or a Protestant minister. Except for the teachers, who were usually single women from one of the eastern states, most of these Anglos were men, and many of them were married to Hispanas.

Additional Anglos were meanwhile arriving in the periphery of the Homeland. Among the first were cattlemen. Lured by

[16] These eighty-seven communities are listed in Parish, "The German Jew," 133–35, table 3 (that these merchants were German Jews is stated on p. 17). In 1850, Moses Sachs, a single German-born merchant of twenty-eight, and a man born in Mexico were the only non-Hispanos in Los Lunas, a village of 226 people in Valencia County; Population Schedules of the Seventh Census [1850], roll 470: 732. Sachs is mentioned in Tobias, *A History of the Jews*, 45. In 1900, one S. (?) Christopher, a single, German-born, thirty-nine-year-old merchant, was the only non-Hispano in the Valencia County precinct of Jarales, with 848 people; Population Schedules of the Twelfth Census [1900], roll 1003, ED 168, precinct 3: 77A. Christopher may not have been Jewish. On intermarriage, see Parish, "The German Jew," 23, 129, 150; and Tobias, *A History of the Jews*, 39, 88.

[17] Population Schedules of the Twelfth Census [1900], rolls 45–46, 117, 120–21, 124–29, 999–1003, 1335, 1643, 1663. See also Richard L. Nostrand, "Hispano Homeland in 1900," *Annals of the Association of American Geographers*, 70 (1980): 393.

Fig. 5.1 Jewish merchants on the north side of the Las Vegas plaza about 1880. Photograph by James N. Furlong, courtesy Denver Public Library, Western History Department (F 24018). According to William J. Parish, Samuel Kohn, Marcus Brunswick, and Charles Ilfeld were Jews, the last two being closest friends. Ilfeld eventually became the largest general merchandise wholesaler in New Mexico. Parish, "The German Jew and the Commercial Revolution in Territorial New Mexico, 1850–1900," *New Mexico Historical Review* 35 (1960): 12, 19, 27 (n. 91).

government contracts to supply beef to soldiers at various army forts and also the Indians at Bosque Redondo in the Pecos valley, Charles Goodnight, Oliver Loving, and John S. Chisum all trailed cattle from Texas to the Fort Sumner area in the middle Pecos valley in 1866 (Map 5.4). Chisum was to remain permanently along the middle Pecos, and during the 1870s he was the undisputed "cattle king" in what had become the heart of New Mexico's open-range industry. The 1870s saw cattlemen from Texas reach eastern Colfax, Mora, and San Miguel counties, an area that boomed in the 1880s under large cattle company control and expanded national markets. Likewise, western Socorro, Sierra, and Grant counties saw the range cattle industry flourish in the late 1880s and early '90s. Contact between Anglo cattlemen and Hispano sheepmen was often some confrontation over the control of a spring or water hole.[18]

To the Homeland's periphery there also went farmers. The earliest ones, for example those at Trinidad in 1861, simply preempted the land, as did their Hispano neighbors.[19] The completion of the township and range surveys enabled them and later arrivals to file for quarter sections, and what was created in the periphery of the Homeland was the discontinuous pattern of dispersed farmsteads found in much of the American West. Because they lived in villages rather than in dispersed farmsteads, Mormons, on the other hand, were atypical Anglo farmers in the Homeland.

It was rare for a Mormon village to be embedded within the Homeland, and Fairview (1895), located near Española, was short-lived (Map 5.4). Instead, Mormons were found in the periphery of the Homeland. In the San Luis Valley were Manassa (1879), Sanford (1885), and East Dale (1893). Lacking any Hispanos in 1900, these villages were outside the Homeland, yet Mormons and Hispanos were sufficiently mixed at La Jara (Conejos County) and Zapato (Costilla County) to meet the minimum 10 percent Hispano criterion for inclusion in the Homeland. Mormon farm villages with the requisite Hispano percentage were also found in the Homeland's western periphery, where farming could be combined with missionary work among the Navajos and Zuñis. In New Mexico these villages included Bloomfield in the San Juan Valley, Wingate and Coolidge east of Gallup, Ramah east of Zuñi, Bluewater in Valencia County (the one area village located east of the Continental Divide), and Luna in western Socorro County. Ramah (1881) appears to have been established earliest. In Arizona, the Mormon-Hispano village echelon included Saint Johns, Concho, Springerville, and Greer in Apache County; Silver Creek and Heber in Navajo County; and Solomonville and San Jose in Graham County. To be sure, conflicts erupted between Mor-

[18] The three foregoing areas of expansion of open-range cattle ranching are discussed by Gerald Robert Baydo, "Cattle Ranching in Territorial New Mexico" (Ph.D. diss. [history], University of New Mexico, 1970), 39, 44, 46, 49, 54, 70–71, 74, 76, 90, 93, 96, 97. Concerning confrontations, see, for example, Dorothy Virginia Morton, "A History of Quay County, New Mexico" (master's thesis [history], University of Colorado, 1938), 39–40.

[19] Luis Baca, "The Guadalupita Colony of Trinidad," Colorado Magazine 21 (1944): 23, 27.

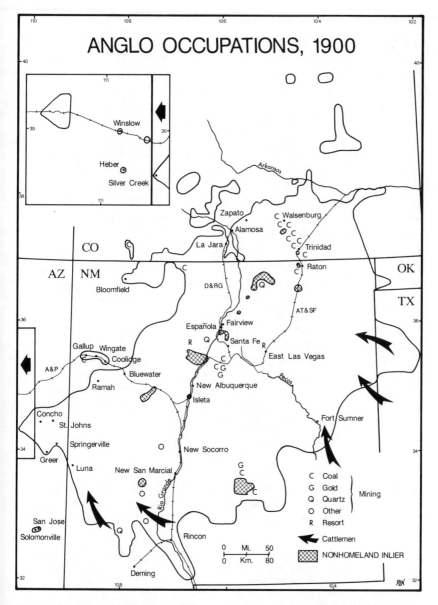

ANGLO OCCUPATIONS, 1900

Winslow

Heber

Silver Creek

Zapato

C Walsenburg
C C
C C C
Alamosa C C
C C
C Trinidad
C

La Jara

CO

AZ | NM

Bloomfield

D&RG

Q

Raton

OK

TX

AT&SF

Española | Fairview

R Q

Santa Fe R

East Las Vegas

Gallup Wingate

Coolidge

A&P

Bluewater

Ramah

C
C G
G

New Albuquerque

Isleta

Concho
St. Johns

Fort Sumner

Springerville

O

New Socorro

Greer

Luna

New San Marcial

New San Marcial

G
C

C

C Coal
G Gold
Q Quartz
O Other
R Resort

Mining

San Jose

Solomonville

Q

Rincon

Cattlemen

NONHOMELAND INLIER

| 0 | Mi. | 50 |
| 0 | Km. | 80 |

Deming

RJ

Map 5.4 Selected occupations that prompted Anglo intrusion by 1900. Occupations in places that are named are given in the text. Omitted are the ubiquitous farmers (except for Mormons) and stock raisers. Also omitted are the lesser railroad, sawmill, and steel mill communities and the great variety of occupations held by Anglos in urban areas. The Homeland and its thirteen outliers are a minimum 10 percent Hispano per census precinct. Source: Population Schedules of the Twelfth Census [1900].

mons and Hispanos, intermarriages were rare, and there were examples of segregation, as at Bluewater, where Hispano children attended their own school, yet there were also examples of cooperation, as in the Conejos basin, where Hispanos gave dairy cows to initial Mormon colonists, loaned them tools and oxen, and sold them land and irrigation water rights.[20]

Railroad promoters and builders were among the next to enter the Homeland. Through Raton Pass came the AT&SF to reach Las Vegas in 1879 and Albuquerque in 1880. (Bypassed because of difficult grades, Santa Fe was later connected by an eighteen mile spur; Map 5.4.) In 1880 the Atlantic and Pacific (A&P) began building west from Albuquerque (actually Isleta) and the Denver and Rio Grande (D&RG) reached Española from Alamosa, and the next year the AT&SF was extended down the Rio Grande to El Paso, with a main-line branch from Rincon to join the Southern Pacific at Deming. These major carriers and the lesser ones that followed brought truly profound changes. Along the AT&SF, for example, new depot-centered Anglo communities were grafted to the old plaza-centered Hispano communities at East Las Vegas, New Albuquerque, New Socorro, and New San Marcial. Although in 1900 New Socorro had little more than a railroad station and a stockyard, the other three, also Anglo-created Alamosa, Raton, Gallup, and Winslow, contained major railroad yards. Scores of Anglos worked as superintendents, yardmasters, roadmasters, station agents, car inspectors, telegraph operators, office clerks, dispatchers, callmen, switchmen, engineers, conductors, firemen, brakemen, porters, pumpers, machinists, boiler makers, carpenters, painters, and section foremen. Some Hispanos also worked for the railroads, but with rare exceptions they were only laborers or section hands. Nor had Hispanos

[20] Population Schedules of the Twelfth Census [1900], roll 1001, ED 82, precinct 7 (Española): 25B, 26A; and Lynnell Rubright, "A Sequent Occupance of the Espanola Valley, New Mexico" (masters thesis [geography], University of Colorado, 1967), 113. Mormons at Ephriam (1880) and Richfield (1881) regrouped in 1885 to form Sanford; David William Lantis, "The San Luis Valley, Colorado: Sequent Rural Occupance in an Intermountain Basin" (Ph.D. diss. [geography], Ohio State University, 1950), 203, 204, 205, 208, 212, 219, 220, 222–23, 224. Near Ramah were two ephemeral predecessors, Savoya and Navajo, which were founded about 1874; H. Mannie Foster, "History of Mormon Settlements in Mexico and New Mexico" (master's thesis [history], University of New Mexico, 1937), 68, 86.

been hired to grade the rights-of-way and lay the main-line tracks. For that, the AT&SF and the A&P used only Irish.[21]

By the time the AT&SF entered the Homeland, Anglos were mining coal at major deposits in the Walsenburg-Trinidad area (Map 5.4). Indeed, to tap the Raton portion of the same lucrative coal field, the AT&SF had built south through rugged Raton Pass rather than follow the easy grade of the Cimarron Division on the Santa Fe Trail. By constructing branches to the mines themselves, railroads facilitated both the coal mining operations and the arrival of workers, who by 1900 were heavily foreign-born, especially in Italy but also in Austria, Wales, England, Scotland, Poland, Germany, and Ireland. Three major mining sites also had blacks brought in from the South.[22] Anglo-Hispano communities, some of them quite picturesque, evolved (Fig. 5.2). A few Hispanos were miners, yet most had menial jobs as watchmen, laborers, and burro packers. In 1900 perhaps the one nontraditional activity in which Hispanos instead of Anglos were the bosses was the fabricating of railroad ties, an occupation that was especially well represented in the villages of high, pine-covered western San Miguel County.

As the procession of Anglos entered the Homeland between 1850 and 1900, fundamental changes occurred, and the pivotal decade was the 1860s. Before the 1860s, Hispanos attracted Anglos, many of whom arrived to carry on trade and to implement military control. These Anglos went directly to the Hispano communities. Most were single men, and a high percentage formed unions with Hispanas. After the 1860s, although some Anglos continued to be drawn by Hispanos to the interior of the region, resources located largely in the Homeland's pe-

[21] William S. Greever, "Railway Development in the Southwest," *New Mexico Historical Review* 32 (1957): 161–64, 200. The Anglos' job descriptions at the major yards were listed in the Population Schedules of the Twelfth Census [1900]. In 1900, Roswell, Deming, and Lordsburg, located just outside the Homeland, also had major railroad yards.

[22] Coal was mined in Las Animas County beginning in 1873, Wilbur Fisk Stone, ed., *History of Colorado* 1: 449. The AT&SF reached Pueblo in February 1876, then built south through Raton Pass; Greever, "Railway Development," 159. The three sites were Walsen Mines and Pryor in Huerfano County (fifty blacks each) and Gardiner in Colfax County (over three hundred blacks). Some black laborers were also found in the larger communities, notably Trinidad, New Albuquerque, and East Las Vegas. By contrast, in all of the Stronghold in 1900, there were only thirteen blacks; Population Schedules of the Twelfth Census [1900].

Fig. 5.2 Chloride, a quartz mining community in Sierra County, was photographed in the 1890s by a resident, Henry A. Schmidt. With adobe and framed structures laid out in the orderly fashion characteristic of Anglo communities, Chloride by 1910 was about one-third Hispano (Population Schedules of the Thirteenth Census [1910], roll 918, ED 239, Precinct 11; 29–31). Photograph 13780 courtesy Museum of New Mexico, Santa Fe.

riphery became the bigger magnet. The availability of land lured farmers and ranchers; coal, gold, silver, copper, and quartz attracted miners; timber attracted lumbermen; while potential profits from transporting commodities attracted railroad promoters and builders who crisscrossed the Homeland with their tracks. These later arrivals included families as well as single men. Intermarriages with Hispanas were not common. After the 1860s, moreover, the source areas for intruders broadened to include, among others, Italians from Italy and blacks from the South. This shift to the periphery was readily apparent in the Homeland patterns of 1900.

By 1900, in a Homeland that was still heavily Hispano, 66,073 Anglos now represented 30.1 percent of the population (Table 1.4). Those who had gone directly to the Hispanos' villages had enlarged and further diluted the islands of Inland within the Stronghold. Those larger numbers who had gone to the periphery, notably the coal mining areas, had transformed large areas from Stronghold to Inland (Maps 5.5 and 5.6). Albuquerque (New and Old, 5,316) now led the Anglo settlement hierarchy, followed by Trinidad (4,789), Las Vegas (East and Old; 3,454), and Raton (3,110), all on the AT&SF main line. Santa Fe, with only 1,355 Anglos, was a distant seventh (Map 5.5). Pueblo and Denver, with many times more Anglos than Albuquerque, had attracted few Hispanos and were outside the Homeland. As seen in Map 5.6, the geographical interdigitation between Hispanos and Anglos was most complex in the northern third of the Homeland, a still somewhat unstable zone where two dynamic frontiers had recently met head-on. In 1900, the Inland, which altogether represented 21.4 percent of the Homeland areally and was 72.3 percent Hispano and 24.3 percent Anglo, was clearly the ethnically vibrant part of the Homeland, the zone where Hispanos and Anglos shared in political control, social prestige, and the rewards of economic activity.[23] By 1900, although the Stronghold was still intact, the process of Anglicization was well on its way.

AFTER 1900

After 1900 the process of intrusion accelerated, both in tempo and volume, to the point where sorting out intruder types, their source areas, destinations, and degrees of intermarriage is next to impossible. Several census takers in 1900, for example, illustrate the extent to which Anglo-Hispano intermarriage had already progressed by the turn of the century. Of the 155 census marshals in the New Mexico portion of the Homeland, at least seven, John Florence (49, farmer, La Cueva), O. P. Hovey (39, salesman, Las Placitas), J. Felipe Hubbell (39, farmer, Pajarito), Henry P. McKenzie (25, teacher, Española), George W. Metzgar (34, day laborer, New Albuquerque), Eugenio Rudulph (47, stock raiser, Las Vegas), and Alexander Read (49, attorney, Los Ojos or Park View) were the offspring of an Anglo father and a Hispana mother and thus were second-

---

[23] Nostrand, "Hispano Homeland in 1900," 392, 393, 395. The Hispano and Anglo numerical and proportional breakdowns by Homeland zone are given on p. 393. Of the 66,073 Anglos in the Homeland in 1900, 53,651 (64.8 percent) were in the Outland, discussed in chapter 6. The Inland had 10,120 (24.3 percent), while the Stronghold had only 2,302 (2.4 percent).

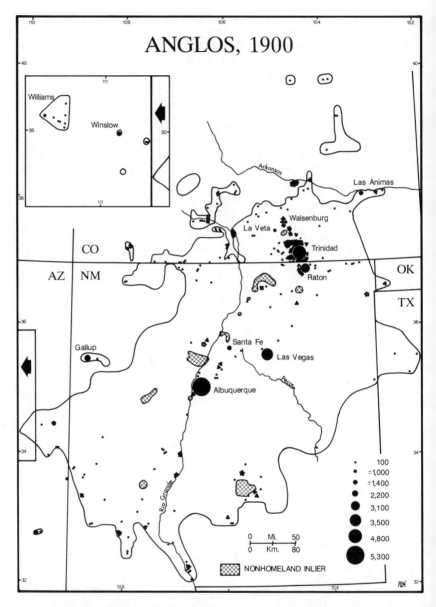

Map 5.5 Anglo numbers in 1900. Anglos were all people who were not Hispanos, Mexican Americans, or Indians. Places with more than approximately one thousand Anglos are named. Old and New Albuquerque and Old and East Las Vegas are represented by single dots. The Homeland and its thirteen outliers were a minimum 10 percent Hispano per census precinct. Source: Population Schedules of the Twelfth Census [1900].

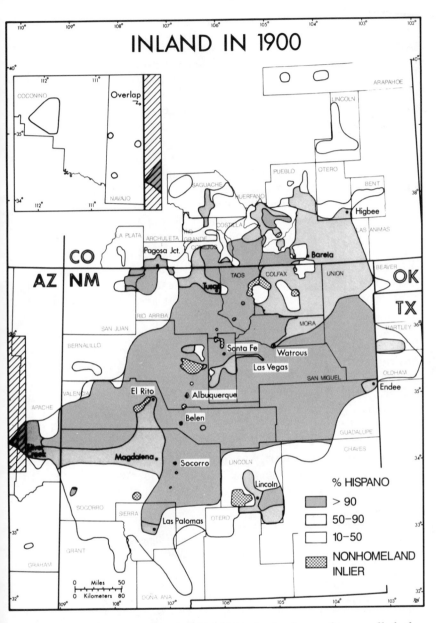

INLAND IN 1900

% HISPANO
- > 90
- 50–90
- 10–50
- NONHOMELAND INLIER

Map 5.6 The Inland (intruder zone) in 1900. As Anglo numbers swelled, the Inland (50–90 percent Hispano) grew areally at the expense of the Stronghold (greater than 90 percent Hispano). Interdigitation between the Inland and the Stronghold was most complex in the northern third of the Homeland, and major Hispano communities had become islands of Inland within the Stronghold. The Homeland and its thirteen outliers are a minimmum 10 percent Hispano per census precinct. Source: Population Schedules of the Twelfth Census [1900].

generation New Mexicans on the father's side. And at least three more, Juan R. Charette (22, saloonkeeper, Cimarron), Joseph P. Conklin (at home, José was reported to be his given name, 27, apothecary, Santa Fe), and Lorenzo R. Labadíe (29, farmer, Puerto de Luna West), because their surnames were Anglo and because both parents were born in New Mexico, on the father's side were at least third-generation New Mexicans.[24] Seven of these ten enumerators were married to Hispanas (Hubbell was married to an Anglo, while Conklin and Labadíe were single), nine lived in heavily Hispano communities (not Metzgar, who lived in New Albuquerque), and all probably identified with their Hispano heritage. Moreover, all were literate in both Spanish and English (a requirement of the job), and all were part of the establishment (a necessity to be offered the job). Examples of a new Hispano-Anglo population, these ten individuals represented several generations of cultural borrowing. Learning English and acquiring Anglo surnames were but two examples of borrowing.

For Hispanos, learning English happened earliest in the larger or the less isolated communities. The lag in the spread of English to the smaller, more remote villages is nicely illustrated by what happened in El Cerrito. In 1900, census taker Néstor Sena, a resident of San Jose located up the Pecos from El Cerrito, reported that not one of the 136 villagers in El Cerrito could speak English. By 1940, when sociologists Olen E. Leonard and Charles P. Loomis lived in El Cerrito, some men who had temporarily taken jobs outside the village knew a little English, and because English was now the medium of instruction in the village grade school, the children were

[24] Population Schedules of the Twelfth Census [1900], Florence, French Canada–born father, roll 1001, ED 72, precinct 5: 103B; Hovey, English-born father, roll 999, ED 13, precinct 16: 149B; Hubbell, Vermont-born father, roll 999, ED 5, precinct 11: 51B; McKenzie, Illinois-born father, roll 1001, ED 82, precinct 7: 24A; Metzgar, Pennsylvania-born father, roll 999, ED 18, precinct 26: 211A; Rudulph, Maryland-born father, roll 1002, ED 101, precinct 26: 81B; Read, Maryland-born father, roll 1001, ED 89, precinct 18: 105A; Charette, roll 1000, ED 33, precinct 3: 73B; Conklin, roll 1002, ED 127, precinct 17: 143B; and Labadíe, roll 1000, ED 62, precinct 10: 217B. Labadíe on his father's side would have been about a sixth-generation New Mexican. Reconstructing these family genealogies would be rewarding. In Santa Fe in 1850, for example, one Oliver P. Hovey, twenty-five, Vermont-born, a printer, had a Hispana wife and a son, Juan, three, while one Wilnor Rudulph, twenty-three, Maryland-born, was a clerk in the Quartermaster Department; Population Schedules of the Seventh Census [1850], roll 468: 685, 713.

learning English. Indeed, in the opinion of the older villagers, the main benefit of children going to school was for them to learn English, because English would facilitate obtaining an outside job.[25] By 1980, when I lived in El Cerrito, the older villagers (in their seventies) spoke Spanish almost exclusively and knew very little English. The middle-aged villagers (thirties and forties), meanwhile, were bilingual, the degree of comfort in one language or the other depending on what they had spoken as children (in El Cerrito or in Pueblo, Colorado). And the children (under ten), although exposed to Spanish, generally had the greater facility in English. Given this trend, a transition from only Spanish to only English among Hispanos in El Cerrito was well underway.

Besides English, Anglos of course introduced their material culture. American-style shirts and coats replaced sarapes, iron stoves supplanted corner adobe fireplaces, and pitched roofs replaced flat roofs. Pre-1846 descriptions of Santa Fe, San Miguel, and Socorro note only flat roofs. Hispanos knew that a pitched roof meant one did not have to shovel off snow or hang a *mantilla* (cloth) at the ceiling to catch dust, yet an absence of roofing materials seems to have precluded their construction. Responding to the need for roofing, enterprising Santa Fe traders began to wagon in terneplate made of lead and tin, and after 1880 railroads introduced corrugated iron. Pitched roofs began to appear in Santa Fe as early as 1850.[26] The obvious benefits of pitched roofs and the availability of roofing material ensured their diffusion. A lack of capital rather than remoteness ex-

[25] Population Schedules of the Twelfth Census [1900], roll 1002, ED 97, precinct 23: 4B (Néstor Sena); ED 108, precinct 37: 147A, 147B, 148A (El Cerrito); Olen Leonard and C. P. Loomis, *Culture of a Contemporary Rural Community: El Cerrito, New Mexico*, Rural Life Studies, no. 1: 13, 30, 32, 52.

[26] Sarapes were "gradually disappearing" in Santa Fe by the mid-1850s; W. W. H. Davis, *El Gringo: New Mexico and Her People*, 189–90. In 1807, Pike likened the flat-roofed rectangular houses that stretched three streets wide for a mile in Santa Fe to a fleet of flatboats descending the Ohio River; Pike, *Journals*, 1: 391. In 1837–38, Francisco Perea reported that Santa Fe had only flat roofs; W. H. H. Allison, "Santa Fe as It Appeared during the Winter of the Years 1837 and 1838 . . . as Narrated by the Late Colonel Francisco Perea," *Old Santa Fe* 2 (1914–15): 177, 178. In 1844, Marmaduke reported only flat roofs in San Miguel; E. Boyd, "The Plaza of San Miguel del Vado," *El Palacio* 77, no. 4 (1971): 19. And in 1846, George Frederick Ruxton described Socorro as having "houses all of adobe . . . one story high and with the usual . . . flat roof," *Wild Life in the Rocky Mountains*, 51. Pitched roofs are described in Beverly Spears, *American Adobes: Rural Houses of Northern New Mexico*, 45; terneplate and corrugated iron are noted on pp. 51, 52.

plains the gradual switch to pitched roofs in El Cerrito. When Irving Rusinow photographed El Cerrito in 1941, a few houses still had flat roofs (Fig. 5.3). By 1980, however, all houses had pitched roofs.

If intruding Anglos brought certain benefits, they also brought much grief. Land grants are a case in point. Under the Treaty of Guadalupe Hidalgo (1848), the United States was obligated to investigate and confirm valid land grants in the area ceded to it by Mexico. When the legal machinery for this was set in motion, Hispanos were made to prove ownership of their grants, a task not easily accomplished. According to J. J. Bowden, between 1858 and 1879, under the adjudication of the surveyors general of the several territories, sixty-five grants (9.65 million acres) were patented largely in New Mexico Territory, and between 1891 and 1904, under the Court of Private Land Claims, an additional eighty-two grants (1.93 million acres) were patented (although subsequent appeals reversed some of these latter decisions) just in New Mexico Territory. And according to Victor Westphall, the later eighty-two grants amounted to 1.93 million acres confirmed of 34.65 million acres claimed (5.58 percent).[27] Not only were entire grants rejected, but many of the grants that were awarded were substantially reduced in size. The descendants of the grantees who lived in ten villages on the San Miguel del Vado Grant, for example, were awarded only their small village sites and adjacent floodplains, not their extensive grazing lands. To be sure, lands that were not confirmed became part of the public domain and could be filed for by Hispanos or Anglos. But relatively few Hispanos seem to have done this, and by the early twentieth century, outmanuevered by Anglos, Hispanos had lost most of their land base.

By 1980, the 1,260,300 Anglos and Indians who lived in the Homeland accounted for 69.0 percent of the population (Table 1.5). They were located primarily in the region's periphery in a zone which had seen Anglos attract Hispanos (Map 5.7). In 1980, Denver (407,001) led the Homeland's Anglo-Indian settlement hierarchy, followed by Albuquerque (226,796), Pueblo (67,521), Roswell (27,235), Farmington (27,044), Las

[27] J. J. Bowden, *Private Land Claims in the Southwest*, 1: 216–19, 243–48, maps on pp. 217 and 244; Victor Westphall, *Mercedes Reales: Hispanic Land Grants of the Upper Rio Grande Region*, New Mexico Land Grant Series, 258, 265.

Fig. 5.3 Village of El Cerrito in April 1941 (above) and March 1980 (below), looking northeast. Houses with flat roofs had to be shoveled of snow, and a *mantilla* hung at the ceiling caught any dust. By 1980 all occupied buildings had pitched roofs covered with sheet iron or aluminum. Upper photograph by Irving Rusinow, National Archives Neg. 83-G–37795; lower photograph RLN, March 31, 1980.

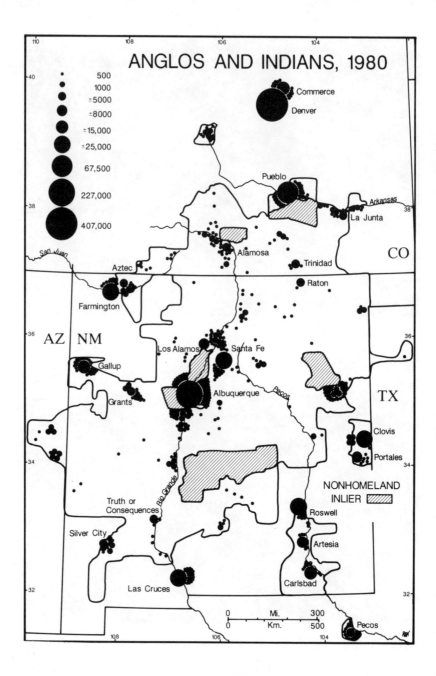

ANGLOS AND INDIANS, 1980

Cruces (25,605), Clovis (24,318), and Santa Fe (23,407).[28] The remainder of the Anglos in 1980 were found in the centrally positioned Inland, an area of eleven counties that was split along the Rio Grande and had two outliers at Belen and Bayard (Map 5.8). This still importantly Hispano Inland was the new heart of the Homeland. Overrun by Anglos after 1900, the Stronghold by 1980 was a mere relic of its former size; only the one census county division (CCD) of Chimayo, located in southeastern Rio Arriba County, was more than 90 percent Hispano.

THE INLAND

The term *Inland* suggests a direction of movement: Anglos coming into the Homeland. The term also stands for the geographical outcome of that movement—the subregion created by the interplay of an intruding minority Anglo population and an indigenous majority Hispano population. In 1850 this subregion amounted to only a handful of Anglo footholds in the major Hispano communities. By 1900 additional intruders had enlarged these initial footholds and had elsewhere created a patchwork of intruder zones that was most complex in the northern third of the Homeland. And by 1980 so massive had Anglo intrusion been that Hispanos now constituted a majority population only in rural portions of eleven partially contiguous counties. The result was an Inland that in 1980 was the crux of the Homeland. Except for the one small remnant of

---

[28] These Anglo-Indian figures are population totals less totals for Hispanos and Mexican Americans, as explained in Table 1.5; U.S. Bureau of the Census, Population Division, Census of Population and Housing, 1980, Summary Tape File (STF) 4 (data for long-form question 14 for fifteen states). In Map 5.7 places with more than approximately five thousand Anglos and Indians are named.

Map 5.7 (*opposite*) Anglo and Indian numbers in 1980. Anglo and Indian data for CCDs and places within CCDs were derived by subtracting Hispanos (codes 205–207) and Mexican Americans (codes 208–12) from the population totals. Indians could not be removed from the Anglo population. With the exception of Denver (7.7 percent Hispano), the Homeland is a minimum 10 percent Hispano per CCD. Five Homeland outliers in Colorado, Utah, Wyoming, Kansas, and Texas are omitted. Source: U.S. Department of the Census, Population Division, Census of Population and Housing, 1980, Summary Tape File (STF) 4 (data for long-form question 14 for fifteen states).

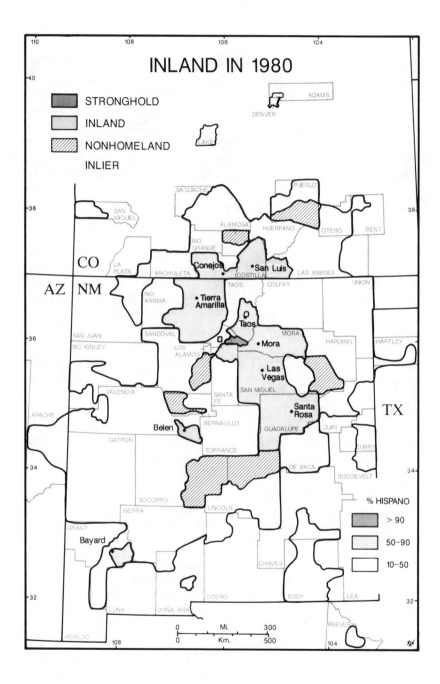

INLAND IN 1980

Stronghold, this Inland represented the best preserved portion of an old cultural region. It was the zone where neither Hispanos nor Anglos were wealthy, yet where both had risen in social prominence. It was also the zone where Hispanos, now several generations wiser and desperately in need of employment, held the reins of political control. And, because of its Hispano-Anglo proportions, the Inland was the domain of the least Anglicized of the Homeland's Hispanos and the most Hispanicized of the Homeland's Anglos.

In the Homeland as a whole, the assimilation that resulted from the coming together of Anglos and Hispanos cut in two directions. Until the 1860s and probably longer, the thrust was for Anglos to be Hispanicized. The relatively small number of early Anglo intruders were usually single men. They learned Spanish and many were married to Hispanas. Perhaps to facilitate being married, some became Roman Catholics. The offspring of these unions, with surnames like Hubbell and Rudulph, were given Spanish Christian names and were brought up in Spanish-speaking households. Thus, the early intruders in degrees were themselves Hispanicized, and their offspring constituted an entirely new subpopulation that, like the offspring of Spanish-Indian unions of an earlier time, were also Hispanicized.

But the dominant process, the one that gained in momentum after the 1860s, was for Hispanos to be Anglicized. So thorough was this process that by 1980 most Hispanos could be characterized as bicultural. So pervasive was its reach that Hispano villagers even in remote Manzano had been significantly Anglicized. In a study based on 1970 census data, A. J. Jaffe, Ruth M. Cullen, and Thomas D. Boswell analyzed indices of assimilation for Mexican Americans, Puerto Ricans, Cubans,

---

Map 5.8 (*opposite*) The Inland (intruder zone) in 1980. After 1900, the Inland grew areally at the expense of the Stronghold, which by 1980 was reduced to the Chimayo CCD in southeastern Rio Arriba County. Hispanos are those who self-identified as Spanish (205), Spanish American (206), or Hispanic/Hispano(a) (207). With the exception of Denver (7.7 percent Hispano), the Homeland is a minimum 10 percent Hispano per CCD. Four distant Homeland outliers in Utah, Wyoming, Kansas, and Texas are omitted. Source: U.S. Department of the Census, Population Division, Census of Population and Housing, 1980, STF4.

Central and South Americans, and New Mexico–centered Hispanos. What they found was that Hispanos were "converging" with the larger society more rapidly than were the other subcultures. This convergence was seen in their increased educational attainment, their increased occupational similarity, and their decreased fertility. More to the point, of these several Hispanic subcultures, Hispanos had the highest rate of outmarriage, compared to Mexican Americans they had a higher incidence of non-Spanish surnames, and among just Hispanos their use of English in the home was increasing rapidly.[29] Modern-day statistics were affirming what one would have anticipated after more than a century and a half of relentless Anglo intrusion.

[29] A. J. Jaffe, Ruth M. Cullen, and Thomas D. Boswell, *The Changing Demography of Spanish Americans*, Studies in Population Series, 4, 21, 28, 64, 73, 75, 85, 89, 98, 109, 114, 116–17, 311, 336. The nature of the data analyzed made it impossible for the three coauthors to compare all five Hispanic subcultures in each of the indices of assimilation.

CHAPTER 6

✛ ✛ ✛

PERIPHERAL ATTRACTION

ON THE GRASS-COVERED High Plains east of Denver were three sparsely populated Homeland outliers in 1900. Living in them were 144 Hispanos, all of whom were men, nearly all of whom were born in New Mexico, and most of whom were married but without their wives or families. As the boarder-employees of twenty-six Anglo sheep raisers, these Hispano males were in Colorado to earn money.[1] That nearly all were born in New Mexico suggests that they had traveled north several hundred miles from their New Mexican villages; that most were married but without their families suggests that they were in Colorado only temporarily. This example of peripheral attraction is somewhat extreme: families often accompanied the male heads of households; jobs were often found in cities; distances traveled were often less great. Nevertheless, the example does capture the essence of still another Homeland-shaping process—namely, Hispanos being lured mainly to peripheral locations by Anglo economic opportunity. Whether they remained temporarily or permanently, Hispanos in many areas became sufficiently numerous to constitute a minimum

[1] The largest outlier areally was in Lincoln County (Colorado) and contained 79 Hispanos in three contiguous precincts (Limon, 19 percent Hispano; Rush Creek, 43 percent Hispano; Sanborn, 12 percent Hispano). Due east of Denver in Arapahoe County were the two smaller outliers which contained 65 Hispanos in two separate precincts (Bennett, 27 percent Hispano; Deer Trail, 14 percent Hispano). Of the 144 Hispanos, all but one (a railroad section hand in Limon) were ranch employees—sheepherders, ranch hands, sheepshearers, plus one "sheep foreman" (Bennett) and one "ranch under manager" (Rush Creek). They worked for twenty-six Anglos, nine of whom were born in Scotland. Of all the Hispanos, 116 (80.6 percent) were born in New Mexico and the rest in Colorado. Population Schedules of the Twelfth Census [1900], Microcopy no. T–623, n.d., roll 117, ED 132 (Arapahoe County) and roll 126, ED 181 (Lincoln County), National Archives.

10 percent of the population, the criterion for being included in the Homeland.

EARLY CONNECTIONS

In what was one of the first examples of peripheral attraction, Californios instead of Anglos actually did the attracting, yet Anglos were behind it. Anglo traders in Santa Fe in the 1820s were eager to exchange their goods for horses and mules, and their demands for these animals exceeded the local supply. Thus, in the winter of 1829–30, some sixty enterprising Hispanos under the leadership of Antonio Armijo pioneered a pack trail that led to a California source.[2] Known as the "Spanish Trail" because its first long leg followed an already established fur- and slave-hunting route northwest into Utah, this pack trail angled southwest from Utah across rugged desert before finally entering Southern California through Cajon Pass (Map 6.1).[3] It took about a month and a half for the pack animal caravans to traverse the one thousand miles in each direction, which they traveled in the winter months when temperatures were cooler and forage was more plentiful. Caravans are reported to have used the trail annually down to the winter of 1847–48.

In California the Hispanos exchanged their woolen sarapes, *fresadas* (blankets), and colchas (embroidered hangings or coverlets) for the Californios' horses and mules. Some even traded for silk and other Chinese goods brought to California in Manila galleons. Los Angeles was the focus of the trade, yet Hispanos bartered all along the coast from San Diego to Sonoma. Within a few years the Hispanos acquired a reputation for thievery, and by 1833 Californios were insisting that they

[2] LeRoy R. Hafen and Ann W. Hafen, *Old Spanish Trail: Santa Fé to Los Angeles,* The Far West and the Rockies Historical Series, 1820–75 vol. 1: 155–94. J. J. Warner, a resident of Los Angeles after 1831, reported that in Southern California by about 1825 wild horses were so numerous that they had to be slaughtered because they so depleted the forage; "Los Angeles County from September 8th, 1771, to January, 1847," chapter 1 in J. J. Warner, Benjamin Hayes, and J. P. Widney, *An Historical Sketch of Los Angeles County California,* 16–17, 34–35.
[3] The Armijo expedition of 1829–30, unlike subsequent parties going to California, did not head northwest into Utah, but followed a more southerly course west of the San Juan River; Joseph J. Hill, "The Old Spanish Trail," *Hispanic American Historical Review* 4 (1921): 465, 467–68. LeRoy R. Hafen follows Armijo's route in Antonio Armijo; "Armijo's Journal of 1829–30: The Beginnings of Trade between New Mexico and California," trans. Arthur Campa, *Colorado Magazine* 27 (1950): 124–31.

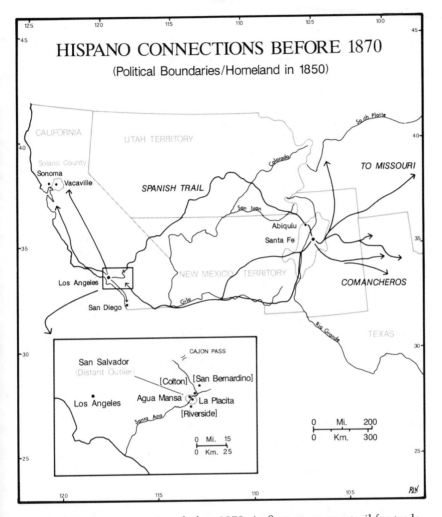

Map 6.1 Hispano connections before 1870. At first a two-way trail for trade, the Spanish Trail also became a one-way trail for Hispano migrants, who were most numerous at the two villages known collectively as San Salvador. Other connections found Comancheros going to Texas, traders and students to Missouri, workers to the Arkansas and South Platte, and sheepmen to California along the Gila. The Spanish Trail is after LeRoy R. and Ann W. Hafen, *Old Spanish Trail: Santa Fé to Los Angeles*, 371; Comanchero routes are after J. Evetts Haley, "The Comanchero Trade," *Southwestern Historical Quarterly* 38 (1934–35): 161–62; and the Gila route is after Ralph P. Bieber, ed. *Southern Trails to California in 1849*, 389.

check the brands of animals against the evidence of purchase before the Hispanos be allowed to depart for New Mexico. The customary inspection point was in the area of "La Puerta del Cajon."[4] Significant because it represents the first sustained contact between any two Borderlands subcultures, this trade is also a classic example of peripheral attraction: Hispanos, mainly men, were attracted by an Anglo-inspired activity to some peripheral location where they remained temporarily—but in time left a residue.

At least a few of the Hispanos who went to California with the trade caravans remained permanently. Antonio Armijo seems to have located north of Suisun Bay in Solano County, where, in 1850, at the age of fifty-nine, he was a farmer. LeRoy R. Hafen wrote that there is little in the New Mexico records about Armijo, and if this Antonio Armijo is the same person who led the California expedition in 1829–30, which seems likely, then his residency in northern California would explain why. A second Hispano to arrive with the trading caravans and remain permanently was Julián Chaves, in 1850, at the age of forty-three, a farmer in the city of Los Angeles who lived with California-born Dorotea (age thirty-six) and their five California-born children. J. J. Warner noted that Chaves served many terms as Los Angeles county supervisor or common councilman. Another example is Hipólito Espinosa, who by 1840 was a farmer in the upper Santa Ana Valley south of modern-day Colton. The ages of children born in California to various Hispano parents suggest that Hispanos began to remain permanently as early as the mid-1830s.[5]

---

[4] The coastal points and the trading for silk are noted by Warner, "Los Angeles County," 34. On the checking of brands, see Eleanor Lawrence, "Mexican Trade between Santa Fe and Los Angeles 1830–1848," *California Historical Society Quarterly* 10 (1931): 29, 32, 36.

[5] On Armijo, see Population Schedules of the Seventh Census [1850], Microcopy no. 432, 1964, roll 36: 14, National Archives; Armijo, "Armijo's Journal of 1829–30," 122, n. 6. Bancroft's biographical sketch of Antonio Armijo (in his Pioneer Register and Index, 703) does not definitely resolve the matter of identity; Hubert Howe Bancroft, *The Works of Hubert Howe Bancroft*, vol. 29, *History of California*, vol. 2, 1801–1824. On Chaves, see Population Schedules of the Seventh Census [1850], roll 35: 32–33. In the census, Chaves is spelled "Chavis." Whether couples were married was not asked in the 1850 census. Warner noted that Chaves arrived with one of the trading caravans; "Los Angeles County," 34. On Espinosa, see Joyce Carter Vickery, *Defending Eden: New Mexican Pioneers in Southern California 1830–1890*, 15. In 1850, "Hippolito" Espinosa, age fifty, lived with thirty-six-year-old María, who had been born in New Mexico; Population Schedules of the Seventh Census [1850], roll 35: 71. At least two cases

Besides leaving a residue in California, traders back in New Mexico spread the word of California's amenities and successfully induced many Hispanos to migrate. In 1843, two Hispanos who had been to California in the trading season of 1841–42 led a party of *genízaro* colonists from Abiquiu to the banks of the Santa Ana near Hipólito Espinosa's farm. Augmented by additional arrivals, the *genízaro* nucleus within several years had spread downstream to establish Agua Mansa (northwest bank) and La Placita de los Trujillos (southeast bank), villages known collectively as San Salvador (Map 6.1 inset).with the Rowland-Workman party of 1841, meanwhile, came one Manuel Baca, the Hispano for whom Vacaville in Solano County is named. When the 1850 census was taken, 213 Hispanos were recorded in California, 172 of them in Los Angeles County, which contained San Salvador (Table 6.1). And by 1900, in San Bernardino, Riverside, Los Angeles, and Orange counties there were hundreds of people noted to be California-born of New Mexico–born parents.[6]

The Hispano colonists at San Salvador were an anomaly. They had acquired land, presumably also water rights, from members of the Lugo family and from Juan Bandini, Californio ranchers who wished to make the area more secure against marauding Indians. Once in place, they did much what they

in the 1850 census and two more in the 1900 census substantiate that Hispanos remained in California as early as the mid-1830s. In 1850 the oldest of five California-born children in the Julián Chaves household was fourteen (Population Schedules of the Seventh Census [1850], roll 35: 32–33), and in what was apparently the extended household of Antonio Armijo were New Mexico–born Juan, age twenty, and California-born Jesús, either age nineteen or fourteen, roll 36: 14. And in the 1900 census, a man who was born in California in 1835 to two New Mexico–born parents lived in El Moro, Las Animas County, Colorado (Population Schedules of the Twelfth Census [1900], roll 126, ED 68, precinct 16:332A), while in Gallina, Rio Arriba County, New Mexico, there lived a woman who had been born in California to a New Mexico–born father and a California-born mother in 1836 (roll 1001, ED 91, precinct 24:123B).

[6] One of the leaders of the 1843 colonists, José Antonio Martínez de la Rosa, had accompanied the regular trade caravan led by Francisco Esteván Vigil, and the other, Lorenzo Trujillo, had accompanied the Rowland-Workman party. Concerning this and San Salvador, see Vickery, *Defending Eden* 3, 4, 20–25, 50. Concerning Baca, see Hubert Howe Bancroft, *The Works of Hubert Howe Bancroft*, vol. 22, *History of California*, vol. 5, 1846–1848, 753–54. Listed in the 1850 census in Solano County was Manuel Vaca, fifty-seven, farmer, owning real estate valued at $30,000 and living with Juana, thirty-one, born in California; Population Schedules of the Seventh Census [1850], roll 36: 13. There were only twenty-one New Mexico–born Hispanos in the four California counties in 1900, which suggests that the migration to California had pretty much run its course; Population Schedules of the Twelfth Census [1900], rolls 88–92: 95–97.

Table 6.1 Hispanos[a] in California, 1850

Coastal counties[b]	
Los Angeles	172[c]
Marin	1
Mendocino	4
Monterey	7
Napa	3
Solano	17
Gold rush counties[d]	
Butte	1
Calaveras	1
Mariposa	1
Tuolumne	4
Yuba	2
Total	213

SOURCE: U.S. Bureau of the Census, Population Schedules of the Seventh Census [1850].
[a]New Mexico–born with Spanish given names and/or surnames.
[b]Largely men (a few having formed unions with Californias), some women (a few having formed unions with Anglos); families and single people; heads of households largely farmers and laborers.
[c]Of 172, 23 in City of Los Angeles, and most of the rest in San Salvador.
[d]All men, seven of them miners.

would have done had they colonized somewhere in New Mexico: in linear fashion along hand-dug irrigation ditches they built adobe houses, a church, a school, and a saloon, and meanwhile they engaged in subsistence agriculture while husbanding sheep and cattle on a nearby mesa.[7] These were not male Hispano traders or employees of Anglos who had gone to California, but colonist families who were farmers and stock raisers. Unlike the handful of Hispano men in the gold rush counties who in 1850 were clearly on a distant frontier mining with Anglos, these San Salvadorans, although on a distant frontier, lived in a self-contained community and exhibited all the attributes of their traditional folk culture. Born in the context of peripheral attraction, yet having all the characteristics of villages spawned from contiguous expansion, San Salvador constituted a distant Homeland outlier. The traders and gold seekers were spread too thinly and did not.

[7] Vickery, *Defending Eden*, 24, 28, 57, 58, 68, 73, and map on p. 115. Like so many villages in New Mexico, San Salvador also had an Anglo priest and an Anglo merchant. Further, the agricultural plots of land that the villagers were put in possession of were, according to the description given by Harold A. Whelan, much like the narrow linear "long-lots" of New Mexico, "Eden in Jurupa Valley: The Story of Agua Mansa," *Southern California Quarterly* 55 (1973): 420.

The connection between New Mexico and California had a fallout back in the Homeland. In 1900, forty-four Hispanos who had been born in California to New Mexico–born parents now lived in the New Mexico–centered Homeland (Map 6.2). Their presence confirms a "reverse" migration from California. That in at least two instances these California-born children of Hispanos were living with their New Mexico–born parents back in the Homeland also confirms something of a "return" migration from California. Unfortunately, the census schedules shed little light on the magnitude of this return migration.[8] It seems likely, however, that at least some of the reverse migrants were living in the villages of their parents. If so, then perhaps some of the communities shown in Map 6.2, especially those in the part of the Homeland where the Spanish Trail began (Santa Fe, Santa Cruz, Coyote, Gallina, La Jara), contributed some of the California-bound traders and colonists.

Even before Hispanos were being attracted to California, other peripheral connections had developed. Perhaps as early as 1786, Hispanos who were known as "Comancheros" began to venture east onto the High Plains to trade with Comanches, an activity that was in its heyday between 1850 and about 1870. Sometime after 1821, Hispanos began to engage in the Santa Fe trade, which led them across the steppe- and prairie-covered plains to Missouri. As early as 1831 the sons of wealthy Hispano families were being sent to Missouri to be educated. By 1834, Hispano masons from Taos were building adobe trading posts on the Arkansas, and by 1842 they were working for Anglo traders on the South Platte. And, in the 1850s, Hispanos trailed their sheep west along the Gila River to California, where there was a booming market along the Sierra Nevada foothills.[9] To be sure, Comanches, not Anglos, attracted the

[8] Without genealogical research, we find that Hispanos who were born in the Homeland and who may at one time have lived in California can be identified in the census schedules of the Homeland counties only if their California-born children lived with them. One case in which this happened was that of two California-born children who were with their New Mexico–born father and California-born mother in Badito, Huerfano County, Colorado (Population Schedules of the Twelfth Census [1900], roll 124, ED 144, precinct 2:252A); a second was that of a California-born child who lived with his New Mexico–born father and California-born mother in Jicarilla, Lincoln County, New Mexico (roll 1001, ED 67, precinct 7:42B).

[9] On the Comancheros, see Marc Simmons, "On the Trail of the Comancheros," *New Mexico Magazine* 39 (May 1961): 30, 39. The story of Hispano freighters and

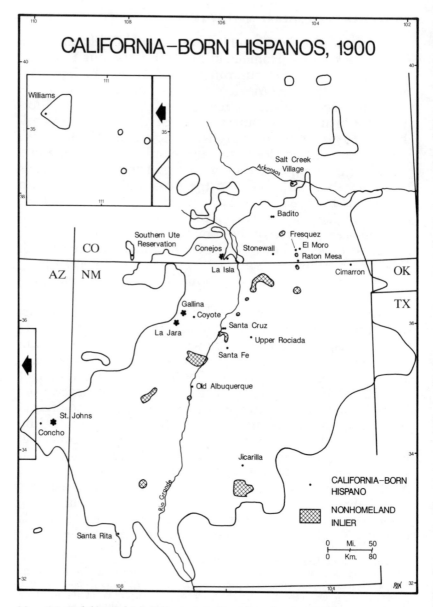

Map 6.2 California-born Hispanos in the Homeland in 1900. All forty-four
were the children of at least one New Mexico–born Hispano parent.
Some communities shown may have supplied the California-bound
parents. Source: Population Schedules of the Twelfth Census [1900].

Comancheros, and possibilities for an education, not direct economic gain, pulled away the sons of the wealthy. Yet in all these examples primarily male Hispanos were being lured to distant locations. In each, however, save for San Salvador in California, the Hispanos involved seem to have remained only temporarily and to have left merely a residue.

CONNECTIONS BEFORE 1900

The several examples of early connections affirm that Hispanos were willing to travel long distances to trade or to take Anglo jobs. Beginning in the 1870s such linkages with peripheral locations became more numerous, and the seasonal pulsations out of the villages became more regular. One reason for this was a push factor: men villagers began to seek outside employment as the economic base on which their livestock raising depended was eroding away by rejected land grant petitions and other legal maneuverings.[10] For some, a willingness to take Anglo jobs became a necessity. But a second and more powerful reason for the intensification of the peripheral attraction process after 1870 was a pull factor: the arrival of more Anglos, especially north of the Homeland, meant more potential jobs, and to work for an Anglo seasonally, despite all

outfitters between Santa Fe and the United States has yet to be told; David A. Sandoval, "Who is Riding the Burro Now? A Bibliographic Critique of Scholarship on the New Mexican Trader," *The Santa Fe Trail: New Perspectives*, Essays in Colorado History, no. 6: 75–86. David A. Sandoval, a historian at the University of Southern Colorado in Pueblo, generously shared a list of twenty-four New Mexican males (thirteen total surnames) who attended Saint Louis College/University between 1831 and 1853. The list was compiled by Catherine Weidle, Pius XII Library, Saint Louis University, and was transmitted to Sandoval on October 5, 1987, by William Barnaby Faherty, S.J., of the Jesuit Community at Saint Louis University. The student in 1831 was Nepomuceno Alário of Santa Fe. Narciso Beaubien, oldest son of Charles Beaubien and Paulita Lobato, was a recent graduate of Cape Girardeau College in Missouri, where he had been a student for five years, when he was killed in the Taos rebellion of January 1847; Lawrence R. Murphy, "The Beaubien and Miranda Land Grant, 1841–1846," *New Mexico Historical Review* 42 (1967): 39–40. In 1834, John Gantt hired Hispano adobe masons from Taos to build his Fort Cass, located on the Arkansas six miles below the mouth of Fountain Creek; Janet Lecompte, *Pueblo, Hardscrabble, Greenhorn: The Upper Arkansas, 1832–1856*, 10–12. And in the summer of 1842, Rufus B. Sage found a "large number of Mexicans" from New Mexico "doing the drudgery" at different trading posts on the South Platte; Alvin T. Steinel, *History of Agriculture in Colorado . . . 1858 to 1926*, 24. On the sheep trailing, see Alvar Ward Carlson, "New Mexico's Sheep Industry, 1850–1900: Its Role in the History of the Territory," *New Mexico Historical Review* 44 (1969): 28.

[10] This point is made by Rodman W. Paul, "The Spanish-Americans in the Southwest, 1848–1900," chapter 2 in *The Frontier Challenge: Responses to the Trans-Mississippi West*, ed. John G. Clark, 37, 52.

the hardships of leaving the family, was simply more remunerative than to work in the village all year. The men villagers of El Cerrito, for example, took jobs as day laborers with the AT&SF when that line first built into New Mexico in 1879– 80.[11] This was years before the 1904 decision that stripped them of their mesa land.

The examples are numerous of Hispanos who, like the men of El Cerrito, left their villages for basically rural jobs. Hispano herders were used by Horace C. Abbot to trail his sheep from Trinidad to Union County in 1878; Hispano laborers were hired by the D&RG to construct its narrow-gauge line between Chama and Durango in 1881; Hispano freighters were employed by Frederick Gerhardt to haul his wool from the Fort Sumner area to Las Vegas after 1882.[12] By 1900, Hispano farm laborers, ranch laborers, sawmill laborers, railroad laborers, and those engaged in mining were sufficiently numerous and clustered in given rural locations to be mapped (Map 6.3 and Fig. 6.1). Hispano freighters, by contrast, were spread too thinly to be shown. Most of these Hispanos were men who were away from their villages temporarily or seasonally, and all worked for Anglos. Their numbers were largest in southern Colorado, suggesting that the network of linkages between southern Colorado and villages of the Rio Arriba was especially dense.

The most extreme examples of the peripheral attraction phenomenon by 1900 were the six areas where all or nearly all of the Hispanos were men (Map 6.3). Three of these areas were noted at the outset of this chapter. In these six areas most Hispanos lived in groups, most were born in New Mexico, many were married, and all were employed by Anglo ranchers,

[11] Olen E. Leonard, *The Role of the Land Grant in the Social Organization and Social Processes of a Spanish-American Village in New Mexico*, 149–50, 162–63. Leonard pointed out that working for the railroad paid considerably more than herding sheep (p. 150). See also Olen Leonard and C. P. Loomis, *Culture of a Contemporary Rural Community: El Cerrito, New Mexico*, Rural Life Studies, no. 1: 4, 12. As early as 1882, in the area between Raton and Albuquerque, the AT&SF hired Hispanos for its track crews, and Hispanos dominated these crews to the end of the century, James H. Ducker, *Men of the Steel Rails: Workers on the Atchison, Topeka & Santa Fe Railroad, 1869–1900*, 27.

[12] Concerning Abbot, see Barry Newton Alvis, "History of Union County, New Mexico," *New Mexico Historical Review* 22 (1947): 250. Concerning the D&RG, see Frances Leon Swadesh, *Los Primeros Pobladores: Hispanic Americans of the Ute Frontier*, 98. And concerning Gerhardt, see Lillie Gerhardt Anderson, "A New Mexico Pioneer of the 1880's," *New Mexico Historical Review* 29 (1954): 251.

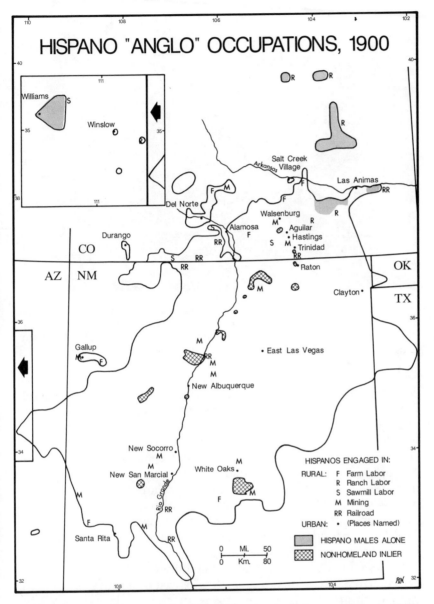

Map 6.3 Hispano males employed by Anglos in "Anglo" occupations in 1900. Besides those occupations listed as rural, urban occupations included day laborers, sheepshearers, and steel mill laborers. Source: Population Schedules of the Twelfth Census [1900].

Fig. 6.1 Hispanos were employed in sawmills such as this one owned by W. W. McAlpine near Catskill in northern Colfax County, New Mexico, about 1893. Photographer unknown. Courtesy of Museum of New Mexico, Santa Fe, photograph 14258.

sawmill owners, or railroad construction or section gang bosses. For two reasons the outlier in Arizona was different (Map 6.3 inset). It contained an urban center, Williams, and besides its more than 250 Hispanos, it contained more than two hundred Mexican, Japanese, Chinese, and Indian (probably Navajo) males who were also living in groups without their families. The Chinese were cooks or laundrymen, and the others were railroad construction laborers, section hands, or ranch laborers.[13] So many men without families suggests that few if any intended to remain permanently, a rootlessness that in the long run left only a residue.

Roots were deeper for Hispanos who were attracted to urban areas. Already by 1870 a few New Mexico–born families and men without families were living in places like Cañon City and Pueblo, where they were farm laborers, brickyard laborers,

[13] Population Schedules of the Twelfth Census [1900], roll 45, ED 12 (Williams) and ED 13 (east of Williams).

and adobe makers.[14] And by 1900 literally hundreds of Hispanos lived in urban centers all around the periphery. There were railroad laborers in Alamosa, Gallup, and Winslow; coal miners in Aguilar, Hastings, and White Oaks; day laborers in Walsenburg, Trinidad, and Raton; quartz miners in Santa Rita; farm laborers in Del Norte; ranch laborers in Las Animas; sawmill laborers in Williams; sheepshearers in Clayton; and both steel mill workers and day laborers in Durango and on the south side of Pueblo in Salt Creek Village (Map 6.3). In all these communities families, who usually lived in rented houses, were far more numerous than were men without families. And except in Aguilar, Santa Rita, and perhaps Clayton, where Hispanos were only mildly clustered residentially, in all these communities Hispanos had strongly clustered patterns and were therefore segregated residentially.

Not all Hispanos who were lured from their villages were pulled to the periphery. The four "new towns" that the AT&SF had laid out alongside some "old towns" were themselves magnets for Hispanos. With major railroad shops, East Las Vegas, New Albuquerque, and New San Marcial had the greatest power to attract, yet by 1900 even New Socorro, which had only a railroad station and a stockyard, had its Hispano population. Indeed, in 1900 more Hispanos lived in New Albuquerque than in Old Albuquerque (Table 6.2). In each of the four new towns Hispano families far outnumbered single men. And in each new town Hispanos were residentially segregated. Hispano heads of households in the new communities were commonly day laborers, although some worked for the railroad and in East Las Vegas there was an especially large contingent of wool washers, sorters, and haulers.

The recency of the phenomenon of peripheral attraction by 1900 is highlighted by Hispano nativity patterns. In 1900, Hispanos who lived in New Mexico had been born in New Mexico (Table 6.3). Some New Mexico–born Hispanos had, of course, moved within their territory, yet New Mexico's

[14] Population Schedules of the Ninth Census [1870], Microcopy no. M–593, 1965, roll 95, Cañon City, Fremont County, 235A–238B; Pueblo, Pueblo County, 481A–489B, Colorado.

Table 6.2   Old Town-New Town Populations, New Mexico, 1900

Community	Hispano	Percentage	Anglo	Mexican American	Indian	Total
Old Albuquerque	927	77.8	224	36	4	1,191
New Albuquerque	1,097	17.6	5,071	69	1	6,238
Total						7,429
[Old] Las Vegas	2,699	82.9	502	46	7	3,254
East Las Vegas	620	17.4	2,952	2		3,574
Total						6,828
[Old] Socorro	920	70.7	358	23		1,301
New Socorro	100	47.4	110	1		211
Total						1,512
Old San Marcial	379	90.5	16	24		419
New San Marcial	101	16.9	498			599
Total						1,018

SOURCE: U.S. Bureau of the Census, Population Schedules of the Twelfth Census [1900], Old/New Albuquerque, roll 999, ED 9, precinct 12; ED 10, precinct 13; ED 18, precinct 26; [Old]/East Las Vegas, roll 1002, ED 101, precincts 5, 26, 64; ED 104, precinct 9; ED 113, precinct 29; [Old]/New Socorro, roll 1003, ED 135, precincts 1, 24; Old/New San Marcial, roll 1003, ED 145, precincts 13, 14.

population was basically old and stable. The one important exception were the 1,098 Colorado-born "reverse" migrants—Hispanos whose parents had been born in New Mexico and who were themselves now living in New Mexico, usually just across the Colorado border in New Mexico.[15] In Colorado, on the other hand, although two-thirds of the Hispanos were born in Colorado, fully one-third had been born in New Mexico. More of the Colorado-born were of the second generation (of New Mexico–born parents) than of the third generation (of Colorado-born parents), yet all the New Mexico–born in Colorado were, of course, only of the first generation. More recent yet were Hispanos living in Arizona, Texas, and Oklahoma, where one-half or more were New Mexico–born, the rest being their Arizona-, Texas-, and Oklahoma-born children. It is revealing that as the distance

[15] If these Colorado-born were with their New Mexico–born parents, then their parents were "return" migrants, which was sometimes the case. The communities along the northern tier (for example, Lumberton, Los Pinos, and Raton), where the Colorado-born were most numerous, were likely source areas for those who went to Colorado; Richard L. Nostrand, "The Hispano Homeland in 1900," Annals of the Association of American Geographers, 70 (1980): 385, 386.

Table 6.3   Hispano Nativity in the Homeland, 1900

Place of Birth	State/Territory of Residence				
	New Mexico	Colorado	Arizona	Texas	Oklahoma
New Mexico	113,906	8,049	1,095	51	100
Colorado	1,098	15,239	5	2	5
Arizona[a]	45	1	876		
Texas[a]	51	5	4	50	4
Oklahoma[a]	4				35
California[a]	21	14	9		
Other[a,b]	14	7			
Homeland	115,139	23,315	1,989	103	144

SOURCE: U.S. Bureau of the Census, Population Schedules of the Twelfth Census [1900].
[a] The offspring of New Mexico- and (occasionally) Colorado-born parents.
[b] Arkansas (1), Kansas (3), Missouri (1), Montana (1), Nebraska (2), Nevada (3), North Dakota (2), Wyoming (4), Washington (2), District of Columbia (1), Italy (1).

beyond New Mexico increased, so did the percentage of Hispanos who were New Mexico–born.

By 1900, then, a newly settled peripheral zone which can fittingly be called the "Outland" had been added to the Homeland (Map 6.4). Like the Stronghold and Inland, this Outland is defined by rigid proportional criteria: a lower limit of ten, the minimum for Hispano significance, and an upper limit of fifty, for the Hispano intruders were a minority. Theoretically, the whole of the Outland was created when Hispanos were pulled to Anglos by economic opportunity. In actuality, perhaps half of the Outland (definitely the panhandles of Oklahoma and Texas; Lincoln, Chaves, and Otero counties in New Mexico; the Saint Johns and Solomonville areas in Arizona; and the Walsenburg area in Colorado) was initially lightly settled by Hispanos in their contiguous expansion—and was then overrun by Anglos to the point that the Hispanos became a minority. That much of what is shown, however, was the outcome of peripheral attraction is substantiated by the strong correlation between the Outland and large numbers of Hispanos holding "Anglo" jobs (Maps 6.3 and 6.4). Representing 28.9 percent of the Homeland areally, the Outland in 1900 contained 13.1 percent of all Hispanos.[16] In rural areas these

[16] In the Outland, 18,363 Hispanos constituted 22.2 percent of the population, while 53,651 Anglos constituted 64.8 percent of the population; Nostrand, "Hispano Homeland in 1900," 392, 393, 395.

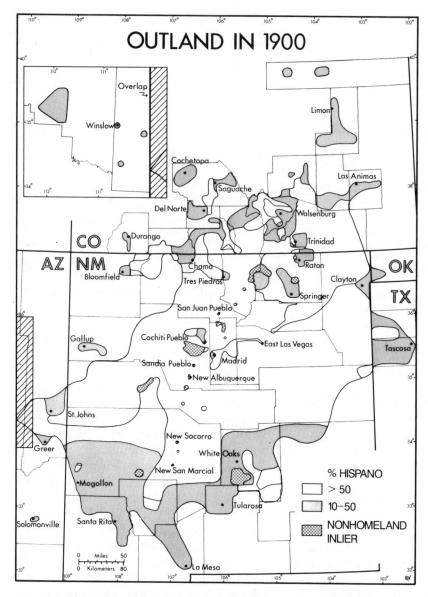

Map 6.4 The Outland in 1900. Located mainly in the Homeland's outer margins, the Outland (10–50 percent Hispano) was the zone to which Anglos pulled Hispanos. Communities locate the Outland. The Homeland and its thirteen outliers were a minimum 10 percent Hispano per census precinct. Source: Population Schedules of the Twelfth Census [1900].

Hispanos were primarily men who were boarders and who were away from their villages temporarily, and in urban centers these Hispanos were primarily family units who lived in rented houses and who had apparently relocated permanently.

CONNECTIONS AFTER 1900

After 1900, identifying Hispano connections and delimiting an Outland become increasingly difficult. What is especially needed are census data to reconstruct the Outland in 1920, when peripheral attraction was at a high point, and in 1940, when the phenomenon was practically dead; the Bureau of the Census will not be releasing the original census returns for 1920 and 1940 until about 1992 and 2012. And when the returns are released, it may turn out that Hispano-Anglo intermarriage had become so prevalent that to identify many who were Hispanos is next to impossible. What is also needed is a way to come to grips with just what is Outland without relying on Hispano population proportions. Even though special ancestry data make it possible to map Hispano percentages in 1980, by that date the influx of Anglos had so reduced Hispano percentages in the Homeland that to define an Outland as the area where Hispanos were a significant minority population would be meaningless.

Despite the problems, several trends after 1900 are clear. One is that substantial numbers of Hispanos became seasonal wage-worker migrants in Colorado. In 1900, Hispanos entered the sugar beet districts of the Arkansas Valley downstream from Pueblo. There, and in the valley of the South Platte north of Denver, where they had gone as early as 1903, they contracted by the acre to bunch, thin, hoe, weed, pull, and top sugar beets during the growing season (Map 6.5). In the early 1900s Hispanos, including families, also began to migrate seasonally within the San Luis Valley, where they performed stoop labor for potato and vegetable growers. They were joined in the 1920s by men and whole families from northern New Mexico who had come to plant and harvest these crops and to work in the packing sheds.[17]

[17] Sarah Deutsch noted that in 1900, Hispano laborers who had been recruited by a sugar beet company in Rocky Ford were then driven from the town by Anglo residents; *No Separate Refuge: Culture, Class and Gender on an Anglo-Hispanic Frontier in the American Southwest, 1880–1940*, 33; Paul S. Taylor, "Mexican Labor in the United States: Valley of the South Platte, Colorado," University of California

By 1915, sugar beet and smelting companies in Colorado were actively recruiting seasonal Hispano laborers in New Mexico, and in the 1920s livestock companies and the D&RG paid transportation costs for those going from New Mexico to Colorado. From sample surveys it is estimated that during the 1920s, from New Mexico's upper Rio Grande basin alone, some 12,500 Hispano workers obtained outside seasonal work each year, and that between 7,000 and 10,000 of these workers migrated to points outside New Mexico. These points were mainly in Colorado. After about World War I, Hispanos began to form communities and to stay permanently in Colorado's sugar beet districts or in nearby towns. In the San Luis Valley by the end of the 1920s some were remaining permanently in Monte Vista, Center, and Del Norte.[18]

A second trend after 1900 is that Hispanos were now attracted to entirely new states. In the early 1900s they were pulled from Rio Arriba County (Abiquiu, Coyote, Gallina, Tierra Amarilla) to the southeastern corner of Utah, where they worked for Mormon sheep ranchers. Monticello became their focus (Map 6.5). By 1918 some sixty apparently Hispano families lived next to their source of employment, a sugar beet factory at Garland in northern Utah, and by 1920 Hispanos were going to Salt Lake City. In the 1920s the D&RG, of the several railroad companies the significant employer of Hispanos, each year pulled hundreds of Hispanos out of New Mexico's upper Rio Grande basin to be its track laborers in Utah. Meanwhile, Hispanos were being lured to Wyoming,

---

Publications in Economics, vol. 6, no. 2: 104–105. On labor in the San Luis valley, see Alvar W. Carlson, "Seasonal Farm Labor in the San Luis Valley," *Annals of the Association of American Geographers*, 63 (1973): 100.

[18] U.S. Department of Agriculture, Soil Conservation Service, *Village Dependence on Migratory Labor in the Upper Rio Grande Area*, Regional Bulletin no. 47, Conservation Economics Series, no. 20: 2, 6, 16, 22, 24–25, 30; the portion of the Rio Grande basin being studied was the watershed between Elephant Butte Reservoir and the Colorado boundary (p. 29); Carlson, "Seasonal Farm Labor," 101.

Map 6.5 (*opposite*)Hispano connections, 1900–30. The Rio Grande basin, including its San Luis Valley portion in southern Colorado, was a major source area for seasonal wage workers. After 1900 new ties were made with Utah and Wyoming. Sources: see text; Rio Grande basin, which excludes the Pecos watershed, is from U.S. Department of Agriculture, Soil Conservation Service, *Population of the Upper Rio Grande Watershed*, map before p. 1.

HISPANO CONNECTIONS, 1900–1930

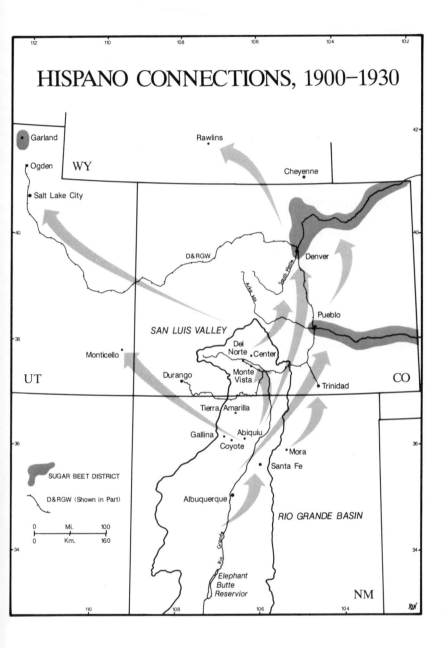

especially to railroad jobs in Rawlins and Cheyenne. The major source areas appear to have been the San Luis Valley for Rawlins and Mora County for Cheyenne.[19] By 1930, Hispano sheepherders, sugar beet workers, and miners were also found in Montana, Idaho, Nevada, and probably in other states.

In the early 1930s, however, peripheral attraction came almost to a standstill. A severe national economic depression coupled with a prolonged regional drought caused an immediate drop in the demand for wage laborers. Villages became swollen with men and families who were forced to return. To alleviate conditions, various New Deal relief programs were instituted, and the phenomenon of peripheral attraction was thereby perpetuated, but only in a limited way. If the villagers of El Cerrito are representative, then knowledge was widespread of the requirements and benefits of each government program, which included the Work Projects Administration (WPA), the National Youth Administration (NYA), the Civilian Conservation Corps (CCC), the Farm Security Administration/Rehabilitation (FSA/FSR), and the Agricultural Conservation Program (ACP).[20] Although these agencies paid less well than did the relatively few conventional outside jobs, only a fortunate few were hired, which left the majority of the villagers economically destitute.

Not surprisingly, then, when wartime activities in the early 1940s rejuvenated the economy, the Hispano villages quickly emptied out. Renewed seasonal farm labor migrations took some of the villagers.[21] Railroads hired additional villagers (Fig. 6.2). But most left permanently for war-related industries in urban centers, for reopened mines, and for new facilities like

[19] Vincent V. Mayer, Jr., ed., *Utah: A Hispanic History*, 37, 39; William H. González and Genaro M. Padilla, "Monticello, the Hispanic Cultural Gateway to Utah," *Utah Historical Quarterly* 52 (1984): 9–12; Paul Morgan and Vince Mayer, "The Spanish-Speaking Population of Utah: From 1900 to 1935," in *Working Papers toward a History of the Spanish-Speaking People of Utah*, 37, 46–48; U.S. Department of Agriculture, *Village Dependence*, 6, 24. By 1946, Hispanos from the Trinidad-Walsenburg area were also mining coal at Rock Springs, yet they appear to have arrived in the 1940s. T. Joe Sandoval, "A Study of Some Aspects of the Spanish-Speaking Population in Selected Communities in Wyoming" (master's thesis [education], University of Wyoming, 1946), 18, 19, 31, 33.

[20] Leonard and Loomis, *El Cerrito*, 6, 32, 33, 35.

[21] In the San Luis Valley, Hispanos were again the largest seasonal migrant group from after World War II until the 1960s; Carlson, "Seasonal Farm Labor," 102–104, 106.

Fig. 6.2 Jacob Chaves of Torreon (left) and Luis Baca of Willard were section
gang workers for the AT&SF when photographed by Jack Delano in
New Mexico (between Clovis and Vaughn) in May 1943. Courtesy
Library of Congress, photograph LC-USW 3–20684-E.

Los Alamos. By the 1950s the steady exodus left many villages
severely depopulated and a few completely abandoned (chapter
8). At some point between about 1900 and 1930 the push
factors began to outweigh the pull of the Anglo: small irrigated
plots made even smaller by a growing population that practiced
equal inheritance had precluded anything but subsistence agriculture. And except for those few who had forsaken precious

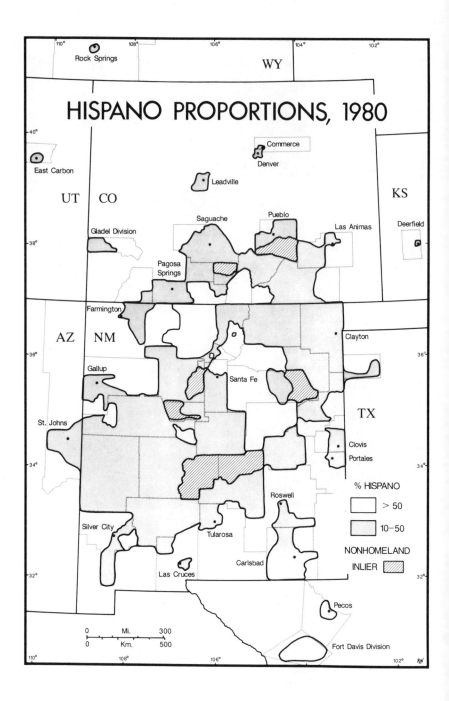

HISPANO PROPORTIONS, 1980

110° 108° 106° 104° 102°

Rock Springs

WY

40°

Commerce

Denver

East Carbon

Leadville

KS

UT CO

Saguache

Pueblo

Las Animas

Deerfield

Gladel Division

38°

Pagosa
Springs

Farmington

AZ NM

Clayton

36° 36°

Gallup

Santa Fe

St. Johns

TX

34° 34°

Clovis

Portales

% HISPANO

> 50

Silver City

Roswell

10–50

Tularosa

NONHOMELAND

Carlsbad

INLIER

32° Las Cruces 32°

Pecos

0   Mi.   300

0   Km.   500

Fort Davis Division

110° 108° 106° 102°

village ties to homestead rangeland or who were favored with the means to buy or lease rangeland, the loss of common grazing lands as a result of land grant denials or sales had removed the stock raising option.[22] Thus, before 1930 wage incomes from outside sources had artificially postponed the villagers' exodus, during the 1930s villagers could not leave, and after 1940, when economic rejuvenation made it possible to leave, the exodus was massive and permanent.

The pattern shown for 1980 gives an impression of where Hispanos went largely after 1940 (Map 6.6). In the contiguous Homeland, this was, for example, to Pueblo, Pagosa Springs, Farmington, and Silver City. In the nearer Homeland outliers this was to Denver and Commerce, Leadville and all of Lake County, the Gladel division in western San Miguel County (Colorado), the Clovis-Portales area, and the Roswell-Carlsbad area. And in the more distant Homeland outliers this was to East Carbon in Utah, Rock Springs in Wyoming, Deerfield in Kansas, and Pecos and the Fort Davis division in Texas. In all of these peripheral areas Hispanos constituted a significant minority, yet to characterize these places as Outland would be inaccurate. In 1980, Hispanos in these areas were there because of push as well as pull reasons, they were not recent arrivals, they did not work only for Anglos, and they did not necessarily live outside the Anglo society and polity.

Back in 1900 the outer boundary of the Homeland was like a cliff, inasmuch as very few Hispanos lived beyond it. By 1980, however, the outer boundary was more like a severely eroded bank, in that Hispanos were now strewn throughout the American West and were piled especially high in California. California was the big magnet after 1940, yet it is an enigma for lack of study. By September of 1942 two-thirds of the thirty-five

---

[22] Kalervo Oberg, "Cultural Factors and Land-Use Planning in Cuba Valley, New Mexico," *Rural Sociology* 5 (1940): 441.

Map 6.6 (*opposite*) Hispano proportions in 1980. By 1980 heavy Anglo intrusion had so reduced Hispano percentages that in major parts of the Homeland Hispanos were a minority population. Hispanos are those who identified themselves as Spanish (205), Spanish American (206), or Hispanic/Hispano(a) (207). With the exception of Denver (7.7 percent Hispano), the Homeland is a minimum 10 percent Hispano per CCD. Source: U.S. Department of the Census, Population Division, Census of Population and Housing, 1980, STF4.

hundred Hispano men who had taken special wartime vocational training at nine schools in New Mexico had taken jobs in California. William W. Winnie, Jr., found that between 1940 and 1950 California was the most important receiving state for the estimated thirty thousand Hispanos who left New Mexico.[23] And by 1980, Hispanos in California (those identifying their ancestry as "Spanish," "Spanish American," and "Hispanic/Hispano(a)," although everywhere less than 1 percent of the population, were nevertheless very numerous, especially in the Los Angeles lowland, the Bay Area, the San Joaquin Valley, and the Tulare Basin. Moreover, by 1980 many Hispanos who had lived in California were now back in the Homeland, much as had happened in the nineteenth century. Perhaps with them came low riders and Chicano graffiti. The little-known California connection is probably the most significant outcome of peripheral attraction in the twentieth century.

THE OUTLAND

The term *Outland*, like the term *Inland*, suggests a direction of movement—in this case, Hispanos bound for areas initially beyond their Homeland. The term *Outland* also stands for the geographic outcome of that movement—the Homeland subregion created as Hispanos were pulled to Anglos. Before 1870, Hispanos who were pulled beyond their Homeland, except at San Salvador, left merely a residue. After 1870, however, they began to constitute significant minority populations, and gradually a peripheral zone was added to the Homeland. The extent of this peripheral zone is difficult to document after 1900, and after 1930 its existence is curtailed by a regional drought and a national economic depression. Nevertheless, during its time of peak importance, which was from 1870 to 1930, the wage incomes generated in the Outland were what fueled the village economies of the Stronghold and Inland. And while fulfilling this critical role of keeping the villages economically viable, linkages were forged which to this day tie Outlanders to their home villages and bind the periphery

---

[23] Charles P. Loomis and Nellie H. Loomis, "Skilled Spanish-American War-Industry Workers from New Mexico," *Applied Anthropology* 2, no. 1 (October, November, December 1942): 34; William W. Winnie, Jr., "The Hispanic People of New Mexico" (master's thesis, University of Florida, 1955), 98, 102–103.

with the central Homeland. To speak of "connections" rather than destinations in the peripheral attraction process is appropriate.

It would be inappropriate to ascribe to the economic pull of Anglos the entire explanation for the formation of an Outland between 1870 and 1930. It does seem that the availability of wage incomes earned on the outside offset the loss of grazing lands that resulted from the denial of land grants. It also seems that such wage incomes compensated somewhat for the small plots of irrigated land that were being made smaller by equal inheritance. But the likely importance of other potential push factors is simply not known. Hispano villages are often divided between two antagonistic clans. In El Cerrito, the division was between the Quintanas and the Manzanareses, and by 1900 all but one Manzanares family had given up the struggle and had moved away from the village.[24] Did this contribute to the peripheral attraction process? Did Hispanos who were movers share some common psychological makeup that would explain their behavior? Were there other push factors?

More could also be known about the Outland itself. It seems clear that in the Outland Hispanos were at the mercy of Anglos economically, they lived outside the Anglo establishment socially, they were leaderless politically, and most were landless materially. It also seems clear that Hispanos left their villages with great reluctance, and while they were away, their loyalties weakened only gradually.[25] But did the Outlander Hispanos perceive themselves to be different? By living among Anglos on the margins of their Homeland did they feel less Hispano? Did a general incompatibility with Anglos—and with "Mexicans," as discussed in chapter 7—artificially prolong their strong village identities and their continuing village connections? Research on these aspects of the process would add to our understanding of the subregion.

[24] Leonard and Loomis, *El Cerrito*, 57, 63; Population Schedules of the Twelfth Census [1900], roll 1002, ED 108, precinct 37:147A.
[25] The first three points are made by D. W. Meinig, *Southwest: Three Peoples in Geographical Change, 1600–1970*, 55–56. In her synthesis of materials gathered about Hispanos in the Harvard "Values Study," Margaret Mead noted the Hispanos' reluctance to leave their villages. Margaret Mead, ed., *Cultural Patterns and Technical Change*, 168–69.

CHAPTER 7

✠ ✠ ✠

MEXICAN IMMIGRATION

NICOLÁS DE JESÚS PINO and María Juana Rascón were married in Santa Fe in 1842. The social elite in the capital city probably took note, because the groom, a Santa Fean of twenty-two, was the son of wealthy and esteemed Pedro Bautista Pino. The bride, who was only about twelve, was not a Santa Fean, however. She had been born in Old Mexico. The couple may well have met in Santa Fe. Justo Pastor Pino, an older nephew who lived in Santa Fe, had married Juana's older sister, Gertrudis Rascón, and the parents of Gertrudis and Juana, José María Rascón and Josefa Sáenz, seem to have gone back and forth between Old Mexico, where they were born, and Santa Fe, where a third daughter had been baptized in 1832 and where they were living in 1850. Whatever the circumstances that brought the couple together, Nicolás was an example of the small number of New Mexican men of means whose wives were immigrants from Old Mexico, a phenomenon that explains a small but important part of yet another Homeland-shaping process.[1]

---

[1] Nicolás Pino and María Juana Rascón marriage, February 16, 1842, Santa Fe Marriages, Archives of the Archdiocese of Santa Fe (AASF), reel 31, frames 861–62. Nicolás de Jesús Pino baptism, December 6, 1819 (two days old), Santa Fe Baptisms, AASF, reel 16, frame 402. Juana Pino, age twenty in 1850, was born in the Republic of Mexico, Population Schedules of the Seventh Census [1850], Microcopy no. 432, roll 468: 703. Census of Santa Fe, 1841, Mexican Archives of New Mexico (MANM), reel 30, frame 363, shows Justo Pastor Pino married to Gertrudis Rascón. Baptism of two-day-old María del Refugio Estefana Micaela Rascón August 5, 1832, Santa Fe Baptisms, AASF, reel 16, frame 954. José María Rascón, occupation "soapfacterer," and Josefa, both born in the Republic of Mexico, residents of Santa Fe in 1850, Population Schedules of the Seventh Census [1850], roll 468: 689.

SPANISH AND MEXICAN PERIODS

In this chapter, "Mexican" is used as an umbrella label for all Spanish-speaking migrants who went to the Homeland, no matter what their source area. And the process of going to the Homeland is referred to as "immigration," although migrants who entered the Homeland before the American takeover were, of course, colonists headed for a northern frontier, not immigrants going to a foreign country. The leading Spanish-speaking migrant source area was always New Spain or Mexico, which explains the emphasis here on Mexicans. After 1845, 1848, and 1853, Mexican Americans from Texas, Arizona, and California augmented the flow going north from Mexico. A few Spaniards from Spain were also always present, while the number from all other Spanish-speaking countries was always negligible.[2]

In Spanish and Mexican times Mexican immigration contributed only modestly to Hispano population growth. Except for the two relatively large surges that carried Spaniards north to New Mexico with the conquest (1598/1600) and the reconquest (1693/1695), the migrant flow to the Homeland was but a trickle each year. In the 1790 census, for example, of some 16,000 Spanish-origin people enumerated in New Mexico exclusive of the Paso del Norte District, apparently only 25 were born in Mexico south of the Paso del Norte District, and apparently only 16, several of whom probably lived in the Paso del Norte District itself, were born in Spain. When the first American census was taken in 1850, the relative size of the immigrant population was not much larger: 370 "Mexicans" accounted for only 0.6 percent of a total Homeland population of 59,830 (Table 1.3).[3]

---

[2] "Psychologically and culturally," wrote Carey McWilliams, "Mexicans have never emigrated to the Southwest: they have returned"; North from Mexico: The Spanish-Speaking People of the United States, The People of America Series, 58; Richard R. Greer, "Origins of the Foreign-born Population of New Mexico during the Territorial Period," New Mexico Historical Review 17 (1942): 281–87.

[3] Fray Angélico Chávez, Origins of New Mexico Families in the Spanish Colonial Period, xi–xiii; Oakah L. Jones, Jr., "Spanish Civil Communities and Settlers in Frontier New Mexico, 1790–1810," in Hispanic-American Essays in Honor of Max Leon Moorhead, ed. William S. Coker, 48; Alicia V. Tjarks, "Demographic, Ethnic and Occupational Structure of New Mexico, 1790," Americas: A Quarterly Review of Inter-American Cultural History 35 (1978–79): 59, n. 33; 60–61; 81; Population Schedules of the Seventh Census [1850], rolls 467–70.

Data in the 1850 census schedules give an interesting profile of the Homeland's Mexican immigrant population at the end of the Mexican era. The 370 Mexicans recorded in New Mexico Territory north of the Socorro area included 355 born in Mexico, 10 born in Spain, 4 born in Texas, and 1 born in California. Of the 355 born in Mexico, 251 (70.7 percent) were men, of whom 110 (43.8 percent) were married to New Mexican–born Hispanas.[4] Most of the Mexican-born men were laborers and farmers; some were servants; a number were shoemakers, tailors, blacksmiths, and carpenters; and a few were masons, weavers, musicians, silversmiths, and merchants. Those possessing skills were especially numerous in Santa Fe, where two of the merchants lived. Even little Tome, however, had a Mexican-born merchant and a Mexican-born schoolmaster.

All 104 Mexican-born women in the Homeland in 1850 apparently worked in the home, because none was recorded as having an occupation. Most (73, or 70.2 percent) appear to have been single, widowed, or divorced. Of the 31 who were married, 15 had Mexican-born husbands (with whom they had probably come north as couples), 4 had Anglo husbands, and 12 had Hispano husbands. Nine other Mexican-born women, because they were the heads in households that contained New Mexican–born children, may have been widowed from Hispano husbands. Significantly, most of the male spouses of the 31 married women were men of means, as determined by dollar amounts given under "value of real estate owned." Nicolás Pino was the wealthiest of the dozen Hispano spouses. Thus, the 1850 census contains twelve examples of well-to-do Hispano men who had taken Mexican-born women for their wives and nine additional possible examples of such combinations.[5]

Ten Mexican states were listed as places of birth for the 355 Mexican-born in New Mexico in 1850.[6] Chihuahua, including the El Paso District, was far and away the leader, followed

---

[4] The 1850 census did not ask whether people were single, married, divorced, or widowed. These 110 Mexican-born men were heads of households, and immediately below them were listed New Mexican–born women. That they were married is assumed.

[5] That New Mexico's men secured wives from Old Mexico is noted by Arthur Leon Campa, *Spanish Folk-Poetry in New Mexico*, 7, and by Chávez, *Origins of New Mexico Families*, xiv.

[6] In the census specific Mexican states were given for 114 (32.1 percent) of the 355 Mexican-born; Population Schedules of the Seventh Census [1850].

by Durango and Sonora, with small numbers coming from Zacatecas, Jalisco, San Luis Potosí, Querétaro, Vera Cruz, Nuevo León, and Coahuila. Mexico's north central states were clearly the major immigrant source area. The destination for the majority was the Homeland's many villages, where the Mexican-born were spread rather thinly. Of the 355, however, 154 (43.4 percent) lived in Santa Fe. Significantly, in Santa Fe the Mexican-born were residentially clustered, and their clusters correlated areally with the residential clusters of the Hispano and Anglo elite populations. This geographical correlation suggests that the relatively few Mexican-born in Santa Fe were part of the city's establishment, and that like the small number of Anglo men who were living in Santa Fe, these Mexican-born had also been pulled to this midpoint in the trading corridor that linked the "States" with Mexico.

AMERICAN PERIOD

The creation of a new international boundary in 1848 seems to have had little effect on the influx of Mexicans to the Homeland. The migrant flow, at least until the 1890s, continued to be a trickle each year, as verified by data on year of immigration routinely obtained from all foreign-born persons, including the Mexican-born, in the 1900 census schedules.[7] One exception was a curiously large number of Mexican-born people who were living in the Mesilla Valley (Las Cruces, Doña Ana, Mesilla) in 1900. These people noted that they had immigrated between 1848 and 1853, a paradox that begs investigation because that was the very time and place from which at least some Mexicans who wished to remain citizens of Mexico were presumably repatriating. Mesilla itself was reportedly settled by repatriates from Doña Ana in 1850.[8] Otherwise, the annual flow to destinations throughout the Homeland, as reported in the 1900 schedules, was small and continuous.

The birthplaces for a small sample of Mexican immigrants

[7] Population Schedules of the Twelfth Census [1900], Microcopy no. T–623, n.d.
[8] Mesilla and the west side of the Mesilla Valley were part of Mexico before the Gadsden Purchase of 1853. A flood in 1865 put Mesilla on the east side of the river; P. M. Baldwin, "A Short History of the Mesilla Valley," *New Mexico Historical Review* 13 (1938): 317–20. Sigurd Johansen stated that Mesilla was settled from Doña Ana in 1850; *Rural Social Organization in a Spanish-American Culture Area*, University of New Mexico Publications in Social Sciences and Philosophy, no.1: 51.

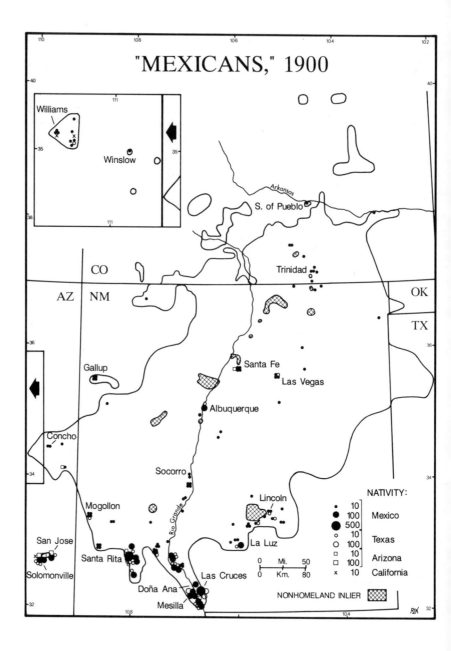

"MEXICANS," 1900

Williams

Winslow

S. of Pueblo

Arkansas

CO

Trinidad

AZ NM

OK

TX

Gallup

Santa Fe

Las Vegas

Albuquerque

Concho

Socorro

Lincoln

Mogollon

Rio Grande

La Luz

San Jose

Santa Rita

Las Cruces

Solomonville

Doña Ana

Mesilla

NATIVITY:

• 10	
● 100	Mexico
● 500	
○ 10	
○ 100	Texas
□ 10	
□ 100	Arizona
× 10	California

0 Mi. 50
0 Km. 80

NONHOMELAND INLIER

RN

in the 1900 schedules suggest further that after 1850 the immigrant source area in Mexico did not change. Census takers in 1900 were instructed to record only the *country* of birth of foreign-born people. For the Mexican-born, most enumerators noted "Mexico" or "Old Mexico." However, nine census takers, seven of them Hispanos and two who were themselves born in Mexico, recorded the Mexican *state* of birth for forty people who lived in fifteen precincts in six of New Mexico's counties.[9] Of the forty, thirty-three were born in Chihuahua, five in Durango, and one each in Sonora and Tamaulipas. These same census takers also noted that at least several parents of those they were enumerating had been born in Zacatecas. Although the sample is small, Mexico's northern plateau states, notably Chihuahua, Durango, and Zacatecas, were apparently the heavy migrant suppliers in the second half of the nineteenth century.

In the 1890s the migrant volume out of Mexico increased somewhat because of the pull of Anglo-related job opportunities. The destination for this added influx was the southern tier of Homeland counties (Map 7.1). The newcomers were largely couples whose male breadwinners were for the most part employed by Anglo farmers, miners, and railroaders. Farther north, by contrast, the Mexican-born continued to be relatively few in number. Largely men who were farmers, stockmen, and laborers, these Mexicans were married to Hispanas and were spread thinly through the Hispano villages. A forty-year-old "bullfighter" in Belen could lay claim to this

---

[9] These precincts and counties were Raton in Colfax County; Georgetown, Mimbres Mill, and San Lorenzo in Grant County; El Oro Cebolla in Mora County; Los Torres, Chaperito, El Aguilar, Tecololito, and South Las Vegas in San Miguel County; Cañoncito and Galisteo in Santa Fe County; and Limitar, Paraje, and Canta Recio in Socorro County. No Mexican states were noted as places of birth in Homeland counties in Colorado, Arizona, Texas, or Oklahoma; Population Schedules of the Twelfth Census [1900].

Map 7.1 (*opposite*) "Mexican" numbers in 1900. The New Mexico–born children of Mexican parentage are omitted; they were as numerous as their parents and their plotting would have doubled the Mexican-born intensity. Las Cruces (723) and Santa Rita (621) led in numbers of Mexicans, who were identified by their nativity, Spanish names, and "color or race." The Homeland and its thirteen outliers were a minimum 10 percent Hispano per census precinct. Source: Population Schedules of the Twelfth Census [1900].

lightly settled area's most unusual occupation.[10] By 1900, the Mexican-born population of Santa Fe had dwindled to a mere thirty-six, all of whom were residentially integrated with the Hispano majority. No Mexican was part of the elite group in Santa Fe in 1900.

By 1900, 10,176 "Mexicans" accounted for 4.6 percent of the Homeland's 219,455 people (Table 1.4). The breakdown by nativity was as follows: 4,432 Mexican-born (43.6 percent), 4,540 New Mexico–born children of the Mexican-born (44.6 percent), 727 Texas-born (7.1 percent), 398 Arizona-born (3.9 percent), fifty-four California-born (0.5 percent), twenty-two Spanish-born (0.2 percent), and three born elsewhere. Children born in New Mexico to Mexican-born parents were counted as Mexicans only in selected precincts in seven counties located close to Mexico.[11] The area south of Socorro—in its own right a veritable borderland between Hispanos and Mexicans—by 1900 contained so many first-generation Mexicans that to assume that their children had been absorbed into the Hispano population, as happened farther north, seemed unreasonable. Categorizing their New Mexico–born children as "Mexicans" nearly doubled that subpopulation; without the New Mexico–born children in this southern edge of the Homeland, "Mexicans" in 1900 would have accounted for only 2.6 percent of the total Homeland population.

After 1900, Anglo-created economic opportunities continued to pull Mexicans into the Homeland, and distant Colorado soon became a major destination. Sugar beets, a labor-intensive crop, had come to dominate agriculture in the valleys of the South Platte northeast of Denver and the Arkansas east of Pueblo. Before World War I, German-Russians, Japanese, and "Northern" Mexicans, as Anglos called Hispanos from New

[10] Compared to the Outland, where 9,079 Mexican Americans lived in 1900, few lived in the Stronghold (349) and Inland (748); Richard L. Nostrand, "The Hispano Homeland in 1900," *Annals of the Association of American Geographers*, 70 (1980): 393. The bullfighter was Antonio Fuentes (immigration date 1896) of Belen, Valencia County; Population Schedules of the Twelfth Census [1900], roll 1003, ED 168, precinct 2:85B.

[11] Those born in Texas, Arizona, California, and elsewhere were the offspring of Mexico-, Texas-, Arizona-, or California-born parents. The seven counties were Coconino and Graham, Arizona, and Doña Ana, Grant, Otero, Sierra, and Socorro, New Mexico; Nostrand, "The Hispano Homeland in 1900," 384, 386.

Mexico and Colorado, provided most of the needed hand labor, but after the war the German-Russian and Japanese labor pools declined, and thousands of "Southern" Mexicans from Mexico were brought in to augment the Northern Mexicans. In El Paso, San Antonio, and Dallas–Fort Worth, agents of the Great Western Sugar Company, which controlled much of the industry, recruited trainloads of Southern Mexican "solos" (singles) before 1920, then families (because they were more stable) after 1920. Some stayed only for the sugar beet season, May to November, others worked winters in the coal mines, and many eventually found their ways to urban centers, including Pueblo and Denver.[12] Elsewhere around the Homeland periphery Mexicans were drawn by urban jobs to Gallup, Clovis, Roswell, and Carlsbad, while Las Cruces and Silver City were prime destinations in the southern tier. Because of its sheer size, Albuquerque drew Mexicans to the center of the region, but Colorado and the periphery as a whole drew the largest numbers.

The periphery of the Homeland was, of course, the Hispanos' Outland, and in that Outland Hispanos had preceded Mexicans everywhere except in the southern reaches. Like Mexicans, Hispanos worked for Anglos, were usually residentially segregated, and were on the bottom rung of the socioeconomic ladder. Not surprisingly, when the two groups came into contact, competition for jobs and for status brought them into conflict. In Colorado, for example, "old Mexico Mexicans" referred to Hispanos as *pochos*, which meant Mexicans who were "Americanized" (more literally, Mexicans who were bleached or faded because of their proximity to whites). To "protect" their heritage, Old Mexico Mexicans in places like Pueblo founded Honorific Commissions to promote the speaking of Spanish, the celebration of Mexican holidays like the Sixteenth of September, and the fostering of patriotic feeling for the *"madre patria."* Hispanos, on the other hand, called the Mexicans *surumatos*, which meant people from the south—and was understood to carry a degree of opprobrium. Hispanos claimed superiority over Mexicans on the grounds

[12] Paul S. Taylor, "Mexican Labor in the United States: Valley of the South Platte, Colorado," University of California Publications in Economics, vol. 6, no. 2: 99, 104–105, 113, 115, 116, 121, 123, 130–31, 134.

of better language, education, cleanliness, culture, and citizenship.[13] Cultural differences between Hispanos and Mexicans, if only nuances in the meaning of a word like *calzones* (Hispano Spanish for men's trousers, Mexican Spanish for women's panties), exacerbated the intergroup friction in Pueblo, as alluded to in chapter 9.

Animosity between Mexicans and Hispanos in the Homeland's periphery was directly related to accelerated immigration after 1900. Because of many unrecorded legal entries and large numbers of illegal entries, the number of migrants who went to the Homeland after 1900 is largely guesswork.[14] In a relative sense, however, the importance of New Mexico and Colorado as destinations is clear. Between 1900 and the 1920s Texas was definitely the major immigrant destination, followed by Arizona and California. A migrant stream that led to several Midwestern states, notably Illinois (and Chicago), developed after World War I. In the 1920s the major flow to Texas diminished while the California stream grew. By the 1950s California had become the leading immigrant destination by a considerable margin, a position it holds today. New Mexico and Colorado, meanwhile, were only minor destinations.[15] It was as though migrant floodgates along the United States–Mexico border had been opened wide for Texas and

[13] The use of *pocho* and the goals of the Comisión Honorífica in Pueblo were discussed by the commission's president, Guadalupe Salas Villarreal, an immigrant from Parral, Chihuahua, and a resident of Pueblo after 1919, in an interview with Arthur F. Corwin in 1974; Corwin, ed., *Immigrants—and Immigrants: Perspectives on Mexican Labor Migration to the United States*, 305–11. Taylor, "Mexican Labor . . . Valley of the South Platte," 184, also noted the existence of honorific commissions in the 1920s in Longmont and Brighton. Concerning Hispano attitudes toward Mexicans, see Taylor, "Mexican Labor . . . Valley of the South Platte," 213–14. According to Manuel Gamio, *surumato* was derived from Zurumate, the name of a hacienda in Michoacán from which many Mexicans emigrated; *Mexican Immigration to the United States: A Study of Human Migration and Adjustment*, 233. In a letter to the author, September 29, 1969, George I. Sánchez, a Spanish American from New Mexico and Professor of Latin American Education in the University of Texas at Austin, noted that *surumato* was the term by which "Spanish Americans . . . referred to all Mexican immigrants"; it was "comparable to 'poor white trash' of the south."

[14] Corwin, *Immigrants*, 108–35. Parker Frisbie reported that for illegal immigrants, whose numbers going to the United States were an estimated eight times greater than the legal entries between 1946 and 1965, push factors in Mexico were greater than pull factors in the United States; "Illegal Migration from Mexico to the United States: A Longitudinal Analysis," *International Migration Review* 9 (1975): 4, 5, 13.

[15] Leo Grebler, *Mexican Immigration to the United States: The Record and Its Implications*, Advance Report no. 2: 51, 52.

California, much less wide for Arizona and the Midwest, and almost not at all for New Mexico and Colorado. Southern New Mexico to a degree held its own, but northern New Mexico and Colorado are voids in any map that shows where the Mexican-born went.[16]

For purposes of mapping "Mexicans" in the Homeland in 1980, ancestry data were used—data that lump together all generations of people of Mexican descent, including the first-generation immigrant. In 1980, 200,991 such Mexicans resided in the Homeland, defined as those CCDs where, with the exception of the Denver CCD, Hispanos constituted a minimum 10.0 percent of the population (Map 7.2). This number represented 11.0 percent of the total Homeland population of 1,825,836 (Table 1.5). Mexican-origin Americans in 1980 were those who self-identified at least one ancestry to be Mexican. The five categories used by the Bureau of the Census, and the numbers responding to each, were as follows: "Californio," 39; "Mexican," "Mexicano(a)," or "Mexico," 138,305; "Mexican American," 56,667; "Nuevo Mexicano," "Tejano(a)," "Aguascalientes," etc. (states of Mexico), 9; and "Chicano(a)," 5,971.[17]

Mexicans in the Homeland in 1980 were heavily concentrated in urban areas, which, with the major exception of greater Albuquerque and the much lesser exception of Santa Fe, were located around the region's periphery. Of the eleven urban centers labeled in Map 7.2, Mexicans outnumbered Hispanos in seven: Denver, Pueblo, Silver City, Las Cruces, Roswell, Carlsbad, and Pecos (Texas). Amazingly, more Mexicans lived in the Homeland's periphery than did Hispanos in 1980. The southern tier of counties—which included Las Cruces, Roswell, Carlsbad, and Pecos, all outliers—continued to have large numbers. By 1980, however, the pull to the north had been so great that Denver and Pueblo contained the first- and

[16] One map example which draws on 1970 data is in Thomas D. Boswell and Timothy C. Jones, "A Regionalization of Mexican Americans in the United States," *Geographical Review* 70 (1980): 94, 96.

[17] U.S. Bureau of the Census, Population Division, Census of Population and Housing, 1980, STF 4 (data for long-form question 14 for fifteen states). In the 1960s *Chicano(a)* emerged as a self-referent among younger minority members, who used it when speaking in English or Spanish; Richard L. Nostrand, "'Mexican American' and 'Chicano': Emerging Terms for a People Coming of Age," *Pacific Historical Review* 42 (1973): 398–99.

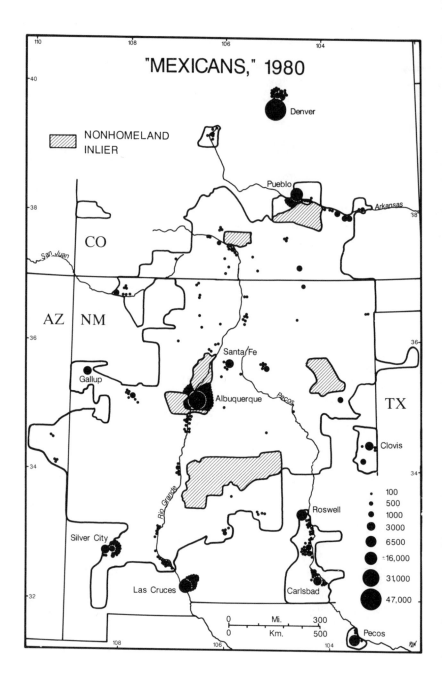

"MEXICANS," 1980

NONHOMELAND
INLIER

Denver

Pueblo

Arkansas

CO

San Juan

AZ   NM

Santa Fe

Gallup

Albuquerque

Pecos

TX

Clovis

Rio Grande

Roswell

Silver City

Las Cruces

Carlsbad

Pecos

100
500
1000
3000
6500
±16,000
31,000
47,000

0   Mi.   300
0   Km.   500

third-ranking Mexican populations, and the Colorado part of the Homeland contained nearly as many Mexicans (80,367) as it did Hispanos (86,139).[18] Clearly, Mexican immigrants in the twentieth century had reinforced Mexican numbers in the southern tier of counties and had leaped beyond to urban areas and their Anglo-generated jobs all around the region's periphery.

ACCOMMODATION

As a Homeland-shaping process, then, Mexican immigration worked in two fundamentally different ways. On the one hand, small numbers of basically single Mexican men with ordinary occupations who had been attracted by the Hispano population intermarried with Hispanas, had offspring, and generation by generation, over a long time span, were absorbed into the Hispano population. This, of course, is what happened in the region's interior. Two anomalies were Santa Fe during the Mexican period, where a small Anglo-Hispano elite seems to have attracted a small but important group of skilled Mexicans who were themselves part of the elite, and greater Albuquerque during the twentieth century, which like a huge urban-industrial magnet pulled in large numbers of Mexican immigrants.

In the periphery of the Homeland, on the other hand, Anglos did the attracting, immigrants were usually couples, numbers were recent and large, and penetration of the periphery, at first quite shallow, eventually reached the entire outer rim. Competition for the Anglos' jobs and for status led to friction, and friction resulted in a standoff pattern of Mexican-Hispano

---

[18] The percentage breakdown by state of Mexicans within the Homeland was as follows: New Mexico, 55.6 percent; Colorado, 40.0 percent; Texas, 3.7 percent; and Arizona, Utah, Kansas, and Wyoming, 0.5 percent; Bureau of the Census, Census of Population and Housing, 1980, STF 4.

Map 7.2 (opposite) "Mexican" numbers in 1980. Places with more than approximately 3,000 Mexicans are named. The leaders were Denver (47,357), Albuquerque (31,263), Pueblo (17,758), Las Cruces (13,583), and Roswell (6,817). Mexicans are those who identified themselves as Californio (208), Mexican/Mexicano(a)/Mexico (209), Mexican American (210), parts of Mexico (211), or Chicano(a) (212). Four distant Homeland outliers in Utah, Wyoming, Kansas, and Texas are omitted. Source: U.S. Department of the Census, Population Division, Census of Population and Housing, 1980, STF 4.

coexistence with very little intermarriage. The number of immigrants going to the periphery, although quite small by California and Texas standards, was impressive by Homeland standards and explains why in 1980 all generations of Mexicans constituted 11.0 percent of the Homeland's total population, while Hispanos constituted only 20.0 percent.

The outcome of the process, then, might be characterized as accommodation, which in the interior of the region meant absorption and in the periphery meant coexistence. Whether the outcome was one or the other was largely a function of the size of the immigrant population. All in all, the significance of Mexican immigration as a process is that it contributed in a modest way to Hispano population growth. Ironically, the influx of Mexicans in the early decades of the twentieth century probably strengthened the Hispanos' rapidly intensifying identification with their Spanish ethnicity. And the sheer weight, as it were, of large numbers of Mexicans all around the periphery of the Homeland only widened the seam that already separated the Outland, with its recent Hispano arrivals, from the Stronghold and Inland, with their deeply rooted Hispanos.

CHAPTER 8

✛ ✛ ✛

VILLAGE DEPOPULATION

FLORENCIO QUINTANA was born in the village of El Cerrito in 1902. When he was twenty, he was married to Agneda Gonzá-lez of Variadero (now La Garita), another San Miguel County village, and over the next twenty-eight years they had seven-teen children. From time to time Forencio found it necessary to leave El Cerrito for employment. With his family he traveled as far as California and New York state, and once he stayed in Denver for six years, but he always returned to El Cerrito. As his children became young adults, however, they left the vil-lage permanently. In 1980, besides Florencio and Agneda, only one son remained in El Cerrito; of the other ten surviving children, six lived in Albuquerque, two in Denver, one in Pueblo, and one had left the Homeland entirely.[1] Thus, through the example of his immediate family, Florencio Quintana had witnessed in his lifetime a Homeland-shaping process of profound significance: the depopulation of villages by primarily young people who were bound for the city.

EL CERRITO

What happened in El Cerrito is well documented. In 1900, 136 people (thirty families) lived in El Cerrito, a number that probably accounted for all villagers. All were Hispanos who, for the most part, were related; all owned their homes free of mortgage; and all probably owned several acres of irrigable floodplain on which they grew household foodstuffs and live-stock forage. Each person apparently lived in the compact little

---

[1] The one who had left the Homeland lived in Alaska. This information was obtained during numerous interviews with Florencio and Agneda Quintana in El Cerrito in 1980.

village that lay nestled on a terrace within a meander of the Pecos River (Map 8.1).[2]

Eighteen of the thirty heads of households were stockmen—ten stock raisers and eight stock herders. The stock raisers grazed their large flocks of sheep and smaller herds of cattle on the surrounding higher mesa, and they probably employed all eight of the stock herders. Four heads of households were "day laborers," two were farmers, one was a blacksmith, one was a carpenter, and four—all sixty-five or older—had no occupation. About 1900, a man, reportedly a cruel person, was the schoolteacher, but no one with that occupation was listed in the census schedules of 1900.[3]

[2] Excellent village data exist for 1900 and 1940, and I gathered my own in 1980. Census enumerators in 1900 were apparently instructed to ignore the one or several villages that may have existed within their precincts, and data can be tabulated for villages only when an especially conscientious enumerator recorded their presence. Fortunately, in the headings for all three census schedules labeled precinct 37, Néstor Sena, the "day laborer" from San Jose who took the census in El Cerrito, wrote "El Cerrito" in the blank spaces that designated an "incorporated city, town, or village," signaling that El Cerrito and precinct 37 were one and the same. Population Schedules of the Twelfth Census [1900], Microcopy No. T–623, n.d., roll 1002, ED 108, precinct 37: 147A, 147B, 148A. Between October 1939 and November 1940 two Department of Agriculture social scientists, Olen E. Leonard and Charles P. Loomis, lived in El Cerrito for seven and six months, respectively, at which time they wrote their comprehensive and insightful *Culture of a Contemporary Rural Community: El Cerrito, New Mexico*, Rural Life Studies, no. 1. (In the foreword to this book, Carl C. Taylor erred when noting that Leonard and Loomis lived in El Cerrito in 1939 for five and three months, respectively; in a letter to this author dated August 25, 1980, Leonard said that he "spent slightly over 7 months in El Cerrito arriving there in October of 1939 and leaving in early May of 1940," and in a letter to this author dated December 27, 1980, Loomis reported that his diary entries for El Cerrito are most complete for the months of February, March, April, June, October, and November, 1940.) A companion volume of photographs was taken April 10–16, 1941, by Irving Rusinow; *A Camera Report on El Cerrito, a Typical Spanish-American Community in New Mexico*, Miscellaneous Publication no. 479. A dissertation by Leonard and two articles by Loomis stemming from a restudy of El Cerrito in the summer of 1956 are noted below. The census reveals that no family in 1900 was without its male head of household. Whether entire families were temporarily away from the village is not known, but if they were, the number would have been small; Population Schedules of the Twelfth Census [1900], 147A, 147B, 148A. The removal of a few El Cerrito families from the village to the mesa seems to have occurred about 1916 when mesa land was opened to homesteading. Families that homesteaded mesa land lived on their claims at least long enough to obtain patents; Leonard and Loomis, *El Cerrito*, 15. Because of site constraints, El Cerrito is more compact than the typical Hispano community.

[3] The stock raisers may well have employed more than eight stock herders. This analysis is based only on heads of households and ignores thirteen sons or sons-in-law whose occupations were stock herder (seven), day laborer (four), farmer (one), and

The villagers thought of themselves as stockmen, not as farmers, and wool was El Cerrito's single important product (Fig. 8.1). Both these conditions were soon altered when the villagers lost all of their common mesa land. In 1904 only 5,148 of 315,300 acres claimed were confirmed by the Court of Private Land Claims to residents of the San Miguel del Vado Grant. Most of the awarded acreage was Pecos valley floodplain, along which most of the grant's inhabitants lived. El Cerrito, one of ten land-grant villages, received a roughly circular 117.65-acre tract that contained only the village and its *solares* and the small irrigated plots located on the adjacent constricted floodplain. After 1904 some villagers were able to purchase or lease mesa land, and after 1916 many families homesteaded mesa tracts of from 40 to 640 acres, but the homesteaded tracts were scattered in a "crazy-quilt" pattern, many had no water, and in the end only two stock raisers were able to piece together the large contiguous holdings needed for successful ranching in a semiarid environment.[4]

The full impact of the loss of the common mesa land was not immediately felt. Until 1916, the stock raisers apparently continued to graze their livestock on what was now public domain. The early decades of the twentieth century were prosperous times when many male villagers readily found temporary employment cutting railroad ties or working for railroads

stock raiser (one). One widowed daughter was also a laundrywoman; Population Schedules of the Twelfth Census [1900], 147A, 147B, 148A. The report of the schoolteacher is in Leonard and Loomis, *El Cerrito*, 13. In 1900 schooling was in Spanish. The census schedules reveal that in 1900 not one of the 136 villagers could speak English; Population Schedules of the Twelfth Census [1900], 147A, 147B, 148A.

[4] Leonard and Loomis, *El Cerrito*, 6, 14, 21, 23, 70. The General Land Office Record of Patents, Private Land Claims Docket No. 119, New Mexico, dated January 6, 1910, and available at the Bureau of Land Management, Santa Fe, gives the figure 5,147.73 acres. Olen E. Leonard noted the figure 315,300 acres in his *The Role of the Land Grant in the Social Organization and Social Processes of a Spanish-American Village in New Mexico*, a doctoral dissertation filed in 1943 at Louisiana State University and reprinted with minor modifications by Calvin Horn, 104. Plat of the San Miguel del Vado Grant, tracts 1, 3, 4, 5, 6, 7, 8, 9, and 10, as surveyed by Wendell V. Hall, December 9, 1902–February 8, 1903, approved by the Court of Private Land Claims on June 14, 1904, available at the Bureau of Land Management, Santa Fe. Tract No. 1 was El Cerrito's grant. Tract No. 2 is shown in the Villanueva fifteen-minute quadrangle map, U.S. Geological Survey, 1960. Water rights to 113.34 acres were adjudicated in the Hope Decree of 1933 and are shown in the Pecos Hydrographic Survey Map Sheet No. A–15, May 1922; both these documents are available at the State Engineer's Office in Santa Fe.

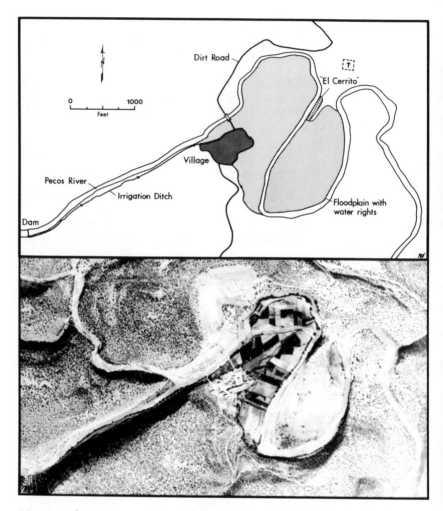

Map 8.1 El Cerrito setting. Between the dam and the village the Pecos valley is deep and narrow. Downstream from the village, where the river meanders, the valley widens and villagers have water rights to some 113 floodplain acres. In 1980 water was conducted through the gravity-flow ditch only to the floodplain adjacent to the village. The air photo shows this also to have been the case in 1939. The cemetery lies atop the mesa near an isolated valley *cerrito* (small hill), after which the village is named. The map is based on field work in 1980; the vertical air photograph, No. 1689, CHX 3 146, was taken September 21, 1939 by the Agricultural Adjustment Administration, courtesy Jack Lanstra.

Fig. 8.1 Wagons loaded with wool at Charles Ilfeld's wool warehouse on Valencia Street (just north of Ilfeld's main building on the plaza) in Las Vegas, 1904. Photographer unknown. Courtesy Museum of New Mexico, Santa Fe, photograph 11987.

in New Mexico, picking cotton in Texas, or working in sugar beet fields and steel mills in Colorado. However, access to the mesa land was curtailed by homesteading after 1916, the temporary jobs disappeared with the Great Depression in the late 1920s, and economic conditions became desperate. Only after 1933, when government relief programs began, was a temporary outside source of income again available to heads of households. By enrolling at government camps, boys and girls supplemented family incomes as well.[5]

In 1940 the number of villagers was unchanged: 135 people (twenty-one families) resided permanently in El Cerrito (Fig. 8.2). An additional five men, each of whom constituted a family, had moved away, yet they continued to own, and occasionally to revisit, their village homes. As in 1900, all villagers were Hispanos, practically everyone was related, and all owned their own homes and their several-acre floodplain tracts, or they were in line to inherit them. And nearly all families lived in the compact village.[6]

[5] Leonard and Loomis, El Cerrito, 4, 6, 12, 32, 33, 35, 60, 69.
[6] In 1940 there were twenty-six permanent and nonresident families in El Cerrito; Charles P. Loomis, letter to author, August 12, 1980. Leonard and Loomis, El Cerrito,

Fig. 8.2 Villagers during Easter week in April 1941. Following services it was customary for the men, who sat in the rear of the church and exited first, to converse
in front of the church until each had had his say. Photograph by Irving
Rusinow, National Archives Neg. 83-G–37865.

Only two families in 1940 owned sheep and cattle, and the
one "big sheepman" employed three laborers, the village's only
full-time employees.[7] Some heads of households had temporary employment; one male schoolteacher/principal from the
village presumably received an outside income; for a fee, one
family boarded the second schoolteacher, a woman from Vil-

7, noted that two families had moved from the village permanently in the fifteen years
before 1940, explaining some of the decrease from the thirty families reported in the
1900 census. Leonard wrote that six families had moved from the village permanently,
but no time frame was given; Role of the Land Grant, 117. On the homes, see Leonard
and Loomis, El Cerrito, 8, 14, 21, 41; the smallest one-family irrigated tract and house
lot was one-fourth acre. Three families lived on their mesa land; Leonard, Role of the
Land Grant, 115. Leonard and Loomis emphasized that family and community ties
were so strong in El Cerrito that removing to the mesa meant great family hardships;
El Cerrito, 46.
  [7] Leonard and Loomis, El Cerrito, 28, 31. Leonard characterized these employees
as part-time laborers in Role of the Land Grant, 142.

lanueva; and a local woman was paid a small sum by the church to conduct services in the absence of the priest. But the majority barely survived by irrigating their one- to four-acre floodplain tracts and by dry farming portions of their home-steaded mesa tracts. A little cash income was derived from the sale of peaches and beans and from piñon nuts that were gathered on the mesa. Some of the younger people who had recently spent time in government camps or had been away to school were now expressing a preference to live outside the village, but very few families were considering leaving it. Al-though aware of their plight, most villagers clung tenaciously to their irrigated land as they searched for outside employ-ment. Everyone knew that some major change was inevitable.[8]

That change happened almost immediately, and it took the form of a major exodus of families (Fig. 8.3). The war effort in the early 1940s provided defense-related construction jobs at airfields and in airplane factories in New Mexico, caused mines to reopen in Arizona, and brought about farm labor jobs in Colorado. By September 1942 a number of El Cerrito men, some with their families, were apparently engaged in all three enterprises. Gradually, however, villagers gravitated to the cities as men obtained work, established "beachheads," and later brought families and relatives from El Cerrito.[9] The long-term results of the exodus were clear by the summer of 1956: of the twenty-six permanent and nonresident families present in 1940, fifteen had moved away, about four-fifths of them going to Pueblo and the rest to Denver, Albuquerque, and Las Vegas; three had died out; and only eight remained, four of which were older couples. These eight families represented one-fourth of El Cerrito's 1940 population. More villagers now lived in Pueblo than in El Cerrito. Indeed, in 1956 half of the

[8] Leonard and Loomis, El Cerrito, 7, 8, 9, 15, 20, 21, 24, 28, 31, 33, 34, 45, 52, 54, 60, 72. In 1940, a state law required that only English be spoken in schools, a regulation that was not always adhered to. The school's primary function was considered to be teaching English, and by 1940 many villagers knew English, yet seldom did a local child attain any degree of proficiency in it. The priest came once a month from Villanueva.

[9] Data for El Cerrito and the nearby village of El Pueblo are aggregated in table 2 by Loomis in his survey of wartime village emigration conducted in 1942, and one cannot say how many El Cerrito villagers had taken what jobs where. Some villagers had also joined the armed forces; Charles P. Loomis, "Wartime Migration from the Rural Spanish Villages of New Mexico," Rural Sociology 7 (1942): 386, 390, 391, 393; Charles P. Loomis, "Systemic Linkage of El Cerrito," Rural Sociology 24 (1959): 54.

Fig. 8.3 No photograph was found that showed a family as it was moving from El Cerrito. Here, the Maclovio Martínez family is leaving Cordova (Rio Arriba County) for a new location on September 21, 1939. Courtesy Museum of New Mexico, Santa Fe, photograph 9053.

eight families remaining in El Cerrito wanted to leave. The exodus obviously continued, because about 1968–69 only five people in two families remained—the nadir of twentieth-century population.[10]

About the time El Cerrito's population reached its lowest

[10] Charles P. Loomis, "El Cerrito, New Mexico: A Changing Village," *New Mexico Historical Review* 33 (1958): 55, 66, 68, 71–72, 74; Loomis, "Systemic Linkage of El Cerrito," 54; Margie Quintana, interview with author, El Cerrito, March 29, 1980. El Cerrito was also apparently restudied in 1949 by Frank E. Wilson in an unpublished study entitled "El Cerrito: A Changing Culture." Several authors, including John Burma, Juan Hernández, Leo Grebler, et al., cite this elusive manuscript as a master's thesis filed in 1949 at New Mexico Highlands University (NMHU) in Las Vegas. In May 1949, Wilson was awarded a master's degree with a major in Latin American civilization at NMHU, but that institution's registrar reported in 1980 that no thesis was noted in Wilson's record, and its library has no record of the thesis. Lynn I. Perrigo, professor emeritus of history at NMHU, recalled that the study was a paper in one of his seminars, but he has no record of it; Perrigo letter to the author, April 4, 1980.

ebb, Anglos began to buy parts of the village. In about 1965 and 1968, two Anglo parties purchased *solares*, irrigated land, and mesa land from villagers, but neither moved into the village.[11] A hippie pair known as Mad John and Dirty Barry, who rented a village house for some six months in 1970, were the first (nonacademic) Anglos to live in El Cerrito. During the next few years five additional Anglo parties, a dozen people in all, rented houses in the village for as long as several years, and one, a couple who arrived in late 1971, remained permanently. With three couples and a bachelor (in all, six Anglos and three Hispanos), the permanent couple purchased five *solares* and some irrigated land in 1972. By 1980, then, six Anglo parties had lived in the village, one remaining permanently, and three Anglo parties (the last being the mixture of Anglos and Hispanos) owned seven of the village's approximately twenty-six *solares*, 28.5 of some 113 acres having water rights, and mesa land.[12]

When the census was being taken in 1980, eleven people (five families) resided in El Cerrito (Fig. 8.4). Nine were Hispanos, most of whom were related, and two were Anglos. Although the two Anglos were neither Roman Catholic nor fluent in Spanish, they were very much accepted by the villagers and an integral part of the community. Soon after moving to El Cerrito, the husband worked for many days to help repair the dam, residents respected him for his technical skills and grantsmanship abilities, and by 1980 he had been elected president of the community acequia commission. His wife, moreover, was in charge of the community well.[13] In 1980 all villag-

[11] The information about Anglos in El Cerrito was obtained in numerous interviews during 1980 with Jack and Heidi Lanstra, El Cerrito's permanent Anglo couple. Originally from the states of Washington and Hawaii, they had met while students at NMHU. I was unable to verify the 1965 and 1968 dates in the county assessor's, clerk's, or treasurer's offices in the San Miguel County courthouse in Las Vegas.

[12] Records that show the number and location of the *solares* were not found at the San Miguel County courthouse in Las Vegas or through interviews with Locario Huertado of San Miguel (April 26, 1980) and Tobias Flores of Villanueva (May 17, 1980), president and treasurer, respectively, of the San Miguel del Vado Grant Commission.

[13] Of the nine Hispano villagers, the three oldest understood but spoke very little English. Of the remaining six, five were bilingual, but one was more comfortable in Spanish, and another, who had grown up in Pueblo, was more comfortable in English; the one child spoke English almost exclusively. The community well had been dug in 1949; Loomis, "El Cerrito, New Mexico," 60–61. A strong feeling of interdependence and cooperation existed among the villagers, and there was an absence of friction between Hispanos and Anglos. On May 17, 1980, for example, Luis Roberto Aragón,

Fig. 8.4 Eight of the thirteen who attended El Cerrito's Patron Saint's Day *función* (December 8), which in 1980 was celebrated a day early, were permanent villagers. The procession of twelve was about to reenter the church as Florencio Quintana rang the bell. Photograph RLN, December 7, 1980.

ers (or members of their extended families) owned their homes and their irrigation plots, and all lived in the compact village.

Of the five heads of households, two were primarily irrigation farmers and cattle ranchers. One, the son of a villager who had grown up in Pueblo, had recently installed a pipeline across the Pecos in an ambitious attempt to transfer water from the village irrigation ditch to the fifty-acre neck of bottomland lying just downstream from the village. Two others were primarily farmers. One, also the son of a villager who had moved from Pueblo to live with his elderly aunt, was a student at New Mexico Highlands University in Las Vegas. The second farmer was the Anglo. And the last head of household, Florencio Quintana, was now retired.

Besides the five permanent families, El Cerrito had fourteen

a village rancher-farmer, and Linda Quintana, both of Pueblo, were married in the first wedding to be held in El Cerrito since 1958, and Jack and Heidi Lanstra, the Anglos, were best man and matron of honor.

nonresident families (approximately sixty-five people) in 1980. Nine lived in Pueblo, Las Vegas, and Albuquerque, and the remainder lived in other New Mexico and Colorado communities. All fourteen families owned houses in El Cerrito, some were registered users of irrigation water, and some owned mesa land on which they ran cattle. On weekends and during vacations, most of these families returned to El Cerrito to maintain their properties, and half planned to retire in El Cerrito.[14]

By 1980, then, El Cerrito had undergone severe depopulation, yet many departed families continued to be active nonresidents. The presence of nonresidents explains why, four decades after depopulation began, the village had changed so little in appearance. For although a few new structures, such as the well house, had been added and a few old ones, including the one two-story house, had almost melted away, and all buildings standing in 1980 now had pitched roofs, the village of 1940 was still immediately recognizable in 1980 (Fig. 5.3). On the other hand, depopulation did leave its mark in occupance patterns. The consolidation of several homes between 1940 and 1980 complicates generalizing, yet the number of permanently occupied houses decreased from twenty-one to five, the number used by nonresidents increased from five to fourteen, and a number were now in substantial ruin (Map 8.2).[15]

In 1940 the villagers perceived that their economic woes were directly attributable to the loss in 1904 of their common grazing land. The failure of all but two stock raisers to acquire viable grazing land units out of the public domain after 1916,

[14] In 1980, fifteen parties were registered users of irrigation water in the village; Jack and Heidi Lanstra, interview with author, August 12, 1980. As in 1956, nonresidents who did not use their arable lands sometimes leased them to residents; Loomis, "Systemic Linkage of El Cerrito," 57. Altogether, villagers owned some thirty-five hundred to thirty-eight hundred acres of mesa land in 1980, but none owned sheep. As an example of the returnees, on Easter Sunday (April 6) in 1980, twelve people, only five of whom were permanent villagers, attended church. Of the seven from outside the village, four were from Los Alamos, two were from Las Vegas, and one was from Pueblo. This pattern of villagers returning to El Cerrito when possible also occurred in 1956; Loomis, "El Cerrito, New Mexico," 66.

[15] El Cerrito's school has eroded away. It was closed in the early 1950s, after which children were bused to Villanueva; Loomis, "El Cerrito, New Mexico," 59–60. According to Leonard, the row of contiguous houses developed as married sons built homes adjacent to those of their parents; *Role of the Land Grant*, 27, 45.

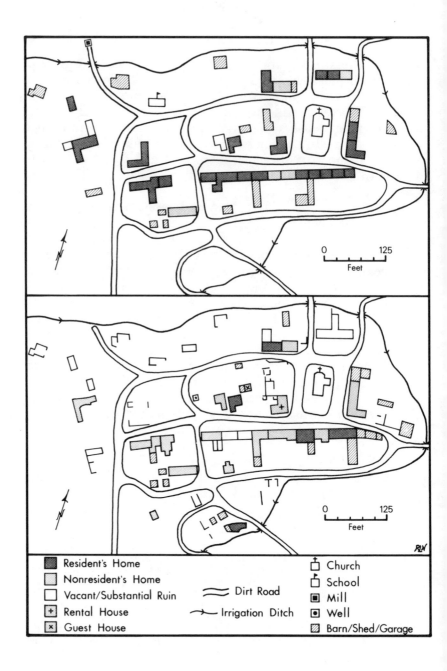

▉ Resident's Home		✟ Church
▨ Nonresident's Home		School
☐ Vacant/Substantial Ruin	≈ Dirt Road	▣ Mill
⊞ Rental House	⤙ Irrigation Ditch	⊡ Well
⊠ Guest House		▨ Barn/Shed/Garage

and a general unwillingness among most heads of households to use their arable floodplain more efficiently, however, must not be ignored. Indeed, the economic vitality of this stock-raising community before 1904 is brought into question when one discovers that, as early as the 1870s, El Cerrito men had taken temporary railroad construction jobs and had supplied ties to the AT&SF Railroad.[16] Thus, a combination of economic and cultural village "push" factors and city "pull" forces seem to explain El Cerrito's dramatic population loss after 1940.

OTHER VILLAGES

Taken together, Hispano villages range along a continuum from those that have undergone complete abandonment, as in the case of La Ventana in the Puerco Valley, to those that have experienced substantial population growth, as, for example, at Santa Rosa in the Pecos Valley. El Cerrito, having suffered severe depopulation, lies near the abandonment end of the continuum, somewhere between San Luis, which has been almost completely abandoned, and Manzano, which has suffered substantial population losses. Examples of villages that represent other points along the continuum are Chamisal, which represents a little better than a population status quo, and Peñasco, which has experienced modest population growth (Map 8.3).

San Luis

San Luis is located in the Puerco Valley some fifty miles north-west of Albuquerque. It came to exist when the site of an

[16] Leonard, Role of the Land Grant, 48, 149–50. See comments of villagers in Leonard and Loomis, El Cerrito 34. The twenty-one permanent families in 1940 had some 113 irrigable acres at their disposal, an average of more than 5 acres per family. The Amish of Pennsylvania, also the subject of one of the rural life studies of the Department of Agriculture Bureau of Agricultural Economics in the early 1940s, claimed that one Amish family could easily make a living on five good irrigated acres. See comments by Loomis in Charles Loomis and Glen Grisham, "The New Mexican Experiment in Village Rehabilitation," Applied Anthropology 2, no. 3 (April–June, 1943): 16.

Map 8.2 (opposite) Village of El Cerrito in 1940 (above) and 1980 (below). The 1940 map is after Olen Leonard and C. P. Loomis, Culture of a Contemporary Rural Community: El Cerrito, New Mexico, 38, and is somewhat speculative. For example, the condition of the mill is not known, and the existence of a plank bridge over the irrigation ditch above it is only assumed. The 1980 map is based on field work; not shown are corrals (unless they were in substantial ruin), greenhouses, outhouses, minor ruins, and driveways.

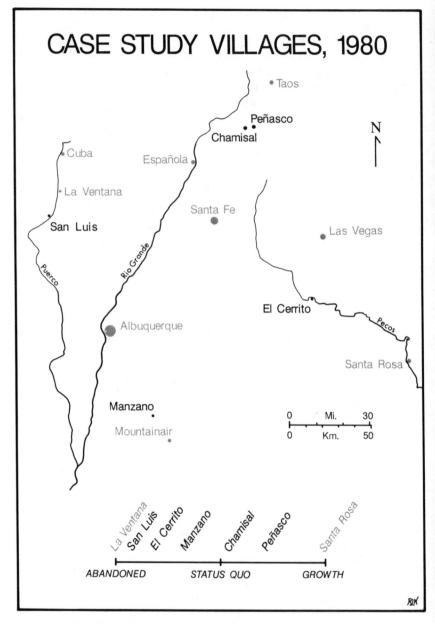

Map 8.3 Case study villages in 1980. Shown are the locations of the five case
study villages (bold lettering) and their relative positions along the
abandonment-growth continuum.

ephemeral eighteenth-century Hispano settlement, Ranchos de los Mestas, was reoccupied in the early 1870s. By 1900, San Luis had more than one hundred residents (over twenty-five families), all Hispanos who lived in houses that stretched for more than three miles along the village acequia west of the Rio Puerco.[17] Approximately half of the village's heads of households were sheep raisers or sheep herders, and half were farmers or farm laborers.

The sheep and cattle population of the Puerco Valley apparently peaked about 1900. These livestock exceeded the carrying capacity of the range, the range vegetation was seriously overgrazed, and this depletion in part precipitated the severe gully erosion which had begun to accelerate between 1885 and 1890. By 1957, the Rio Puerco had entrenched itself into the valley alluvium to depths of fifty feet. Erosion carried away much of the valley's floodplain cropland, flash floods destroyed dams, and entrenchment made dam reconstruction increasingly difficult. The San Luis villagers fared better than their downstream village brethren, however, for in the mid-1930s they alone were able to secure Soil Conservation Service help to build a new dam. In 1936, San Luis had 190 people.[18]

[17] Jerold Gwayn Widdison, "Historical Geography of the Middle Rio Puerco Valley, New Mexico," *New Mexico Historical Review* 34 (1959): 259, 260, 275. Only approximate information is available for San Luis in 1900. Epifanio Gallegos, a resident of Cabezon, the larger and more compact downstream village, took the census in San Luis in 1900. Like most census enumerators that year, Gallegos did not specify where given villages began and ended. However, he did note in the schedule headings, "Tijera Town," a post office name by which San Luis was known, and one has some clue about what data pertain to San Luis from the names of people known to have resided in Cabezon and from gaps of several days on either side of Gallegos's apparent visit to San Luis; Population Schedules of the Twelfth Census [1900], roll 999, ED 17, precinct 21: 181B, 182A, 182B.

[18] Widdison, "Middle Rio Puerco Valley," 253, 265, 272, 273, 277; Kirk Bryan, "Historic Evidence on Changes in the Channel of Rio Puerco, a Tributary of the Rio Grande in New Mexico," *Journal of Geology* 36 (1928): 279–80. Bryan noted that overgrazing precipitated gullying, but that the ultimate cause lay in cyclic fluctuations of climate, for the Puerco Valley had already gone through a cycle of arroyo cutting and sediment filling (p. 281). Much has been written on the subject; from his review of the livestock population history of New Mexico, Denevan concluded that modern gullying was probably caused by a combination of overgrazing, drought, and high-intensity rains; William M. Denevan, "Livestock Numbers in Nineteenth-Century New Mexico, and the Problem of Gullying in the Southwest," *Annals of the Association of American Geographers*, 57 (1967): 702, 703. The population figure is from a Soil Conservation Service Human Dependency Survey conducted in the middle and upper Puerco Valley in 1936; U.S. Department of Agriculture, Soil Conservation Service, *A Report on the Cuba Valley*, Regional Bulletin no. 36, Conservation Economics Series, no. 9: 26. Widdison reported that there were forty-four families in San Luis in 1939; "Middle Rio Puerco Valley," 281.

In the 1940s some San Luis villagers began to move to larger centers, but the exodus seems not to have become massive until after a July 1951 flood destroyed the Soil Conservation Service dam. The dam was not rebuilt, and by 1957 only two families remained, both of them stock raisers who ran cattle on the upland and on the former cropland. After 1969, San Luis had only one villager, and in 1980 its appearance suggested that it was on the verge of becoming a ghost town.[19] Like El Cerrito, however, San Luis had many active nonresidents, and on weekends as many as a dozen families, all Hispanos, returned from Albuquerque, Bernalillo, or Cuba to maintain their homes, care for their cattle, and congregate at the village bar. During Easter week each year, moreover, former Penitente villagers observe rites at the local morada, and on June 24 of each year more than two hundred former villagers reunite from as far away as California to celebrate the village's patron saint's day.[20] In 1980, San Luis was nearly abandoned but was not about to die.

Manzano

In late January of 1851, John R. Tulles took the census in Manzano, a village located on the remote eastern flank of the high Manzano Mountains some thirty-five miles southeast of Albuquerque. "Mansana," as Tulles spelled it, was the penultimate of forty communities which he, the Valencia County census marshal for 1850, had been enumerating since the previous October. Unlike all other census marshals in New Mexico Territory that year, Tulles conscientiously identified every place he visited, and the following is what he recorded at

---

[19] There were still "lots" of villagers left in 1949 when Rafelita Lovato Taylor, who had been born in San Luis in 1930, was married and left San Luis; Rafelita Lovato Taylor, Cuba, New Mexico, interview with author, August 17, 1980. The 1951 flood that destroyed the San Luis dam and its aftermath are noted by Widdison, "Middle Rio Puerco Valley," 277, 279, 281. The one villager in 1969 was Mel Lovato, who was born in San Luis in 1917, left for California and other places on the West Coast in 1937, but returned to be a cattle rancher in 1969; Mel Lovato, San Luis, New Mexico, interview with author, August 17, 1980. In 1980, Mel's family home was one of some thirty (one-third of them in ruins) that were located along both sides of four miles of linear village road.

[20] The Reverend Howard Meyer, Immaculate Conception Church, Cuba, New Mexico, interview with author, October 27, 1979. On both occasions every year Father Meyer conducts services at San Luis.

Manzano: 403 residents (ninety-one families), 400 of whom were Hispanos and 3 of whom were Mexican-born men.[21] Of the ninety-one heads of households, forty-nine were farmers and the rest were the usual assortment of carpenters, shoemakers, tailors, schoolmasters, musicians, and laborers; curiously, none were recorded as being stockmen, yet sheep and cattle raising appear to have been Manzano's leading economic activity. All 403 villagers probably lived in the community itself; Navajo depredations were frequent, and in 1850 Manzano was constructed as a fortified *plaza* with a fort and *torreón* in one corner.[22]

By 1900 the Manzaneños had apparently dispersed beyond their village. Juan C. Jaramillo, a merchant from neighboring Torreon who took the census that year, recorded a population of 399 (ninety-six families) in the village and an additional 250 people (fifty-four families) in Manzano Precinct. In the village the only non-Hispanos were a Tejano who was married to a Hispana and a French-born Roman Catholic priest, whose presence gives some measure of the local importance of Manzano.[23] Elsewhere in the precinct everyone was a Hispano except for five Mexican-born men, all of whom were (or had been) married to Hispanas. As in 1850, the majority of the heads of households (in the precinct as a whole) were farmers, yet ten were identified as sheep raisers and two as cattle raisers. Man-

[21] Eight of the forty communities were actually in Bernalillo County. Tulles was probably not from New Mexico, for he lacked a spelling knowledge of Spanish, and he apparently had some assistance, as the schedules contain several different handwritings; he was in Manzano on January 26, 27, and 29; Population Schedules of the Seventh Census [1850], Microcopy no. 432, 1963, roll 470: 746–55. Two of the Mexican-born were laborers who boarded in Hispano homes, and the third was a farmer who was married to a Hispana. One of the boarders had been born in Sonora; Population Schedules of the Seventh Census [1850], 750, 752.

[22] Wesley Robert Hurt, Jr., "Manzano: A Study of Community Disorganization" (master's thesis [sociology], University of New Mexico, 1941), 52. Navajo raids continued at Manzano until about 1870 (p. 41). Hurt presents a map of Manzano about 1850 in an end appendix (map 4).

[23] In the schedule headings and by a "here ends" note in the schedules, Jaramillo clearly differentiated the "Town of Manzano" from the remainder of the Manzano Precinct; Population Schedules of the Twelfth Census [1900], roll 1003, ED 173, precinct 15: 152B to 156A (town) and 156B to 158B (precinct). The priest, Father José Gauthier, age twenty-eight, had migrated to the United States in 1895 (p. 153B). Records for the Manzano Roman Catholic parish begin in 1867; the present Manzano church was built in 1885; the Reverend John R. Conway, Saint Alice Church, Mountainair, New Mexico, interview with author, October 22, 1979.

zaneños could also boast about their five merchants, a justice of the peace, two lawyers, and an architect, not to mention the usual cadre of freighters (who were probably engaged in hauling railroad ties then being cut in the Manzano Mountains), black-smiths, carpenters, saloon keepers, and musicians. Only one individual was noted to be a "pensioner."

By 1940, Manzano had grown to 802 people, some 565 of whom lived in the village. As in 1900, Manzaneños were largely Hispanos, for of 366 registered adult voters in the precinct in 1939, only 16 were Anglos, including five Syrians, the offspring or relatives of Tenos Tabet, a Manzano merchant between 1902 and 1912. Unlike 1900, however, the Manzaneños were now heavily dependent on government financial support, for of the 125 village families, 119 received incomes from the following sources: welfare, 53; relief work, 29; and other employment, largely farmers and stockmen, 37.[24]

Manzano's excessive dependence on government help forebode a gloomy future. After 1940, a substantial exodus of Manzaneños took place. By 1980 only ninety-four people (thirty-one families) remained in the village, and only twenty-four people (ten families) still resided within several miles of the village. Two of the villagers were Anglos, as were half of those who lived outside the village; one Californio also lived in the village. Most Manzaneños in 1980 were older people who lived on welfare, retirement pensions, or social security. Half a dozen of the villagers and two who lived near the village had full-time employment, and three villagers had part-time employment, but to hold these jobs required commuting to Estancia, Mountainair, or Albuquerque. Manzano's only local employer was the Senior Citizens' Center (opened in the mid-1970s), where an additional half-dozen villagers had part-time work. Manzano's school had been closed in 1955, and its children were now bused to Mountainair; the parish priest had

[24] Hurt, who gathered his data between June 1938 and August 1940, gave the figure 802, "Manzano," 34. He did not differentiate between village and nonvillage precinct population totals, yet he noted that there were 125 households (families) in the village (p. 134) and that the average size of each household was 4.52 (p. 104); 565 is the product of 125 and 4.52. On p. 106, Hurt noted that there were ninety-seven houses in the village and that some contained multiple families; his map 3 in an end appendix shows these houses in 1939. The number of voters is from p. 102; Tabet is discussed on pp. 92–95; and incomes on pp. 134–35.

been relocated to Mountainair in 1972; and in 1980 the now decimated community was economically depressed.[25] The limited number of job-providing communities within reasonable commuting distances was certainly one explanation for Manzano's dilemma.

Chamisal

Chamisal is located several miles west of Peñasco in southern Taos County. In 1900, according to José J. Lucero, a conscientious Hispano census marshal from Taos, 704 people lived in the four villages and "town" that comprised Chamisal Precinct.[26] The "town" (Chamisal) had 232 residents in fifty families, and like all others in the precinct, all were Hispanos. Of the fifty heads of households, twenty-nine were farmers or farm laborers, eighteen were day laborers, one was a grocer, and one (an elderly widow) was a wool spinner. A second elderly widow apparently had no occupation.

In 1935 a team of researchers in the Soil Conservation Service, U.S. Department of Agriculture, undertook to survey a number of Hispano villages in New Mexico's northern Rio Grande basin. They found at least 350 people (approximately seventy families) living in Chamisal. They published no information on the ethnic composition of Chamisal, nor did they give a breakdown of occupations by heads of households, but they did note that in the "Rio Pueblo District," which included Chamisal, agriculture was the predominant activity, several wealthy local contractors employed some tie cutters, and some men had other jobs, but 70 percent of the population in the district was on relief.[27] Since the turn of the century Chamisal

[25] Most of the information in this paragraph is from Mrs. Juanita Candelaria, interview with author, Manzano, New Mexico, August 14, 1980. Mrs. Candelaria and her husband, Eleno, were instrumental in the establishment of Manzano's Senior Citizens' Center. Ethel L. Floyd and R. T. Floyd, eds., *Torrance County History*, 31, noted the school's closing; Father Conway documented the parish seat relocation, interview with author, October 22, 1979.

[26] In the census schedule headings and by "here ends" notes in the schedules José J. Lucero clearly identifies every community; Population Schedules of the Twelfth Census [1900], roll 1003, ED 158, precinct 9: 242B–44B (Chamisal town).

[27] The results of this survey were published by the U.S. Department of Agriculture, Soil Conservation Service, *Tewa Basin Study, 1935*, vol. 2, *The Spanish-American Villages*, 29–212, reprinted in full in *Hispanic Villages of Northern New Mexico*, ed. Marta Weigle, hereafter cited as Weigle, *Hispanic Villages*. Chamisal and its neighboring village of Ojito had a combined population of 565 (114 families) in 1935;

had grown demographically but apparently had stagnated economically.

After 1935, Chamisal's total population increased a little. In 1980, 386 people (ninety-eight families) lived there. Of this number 17 people (five families) were Anglos who had moved to Chamisal within the last several years and who worked locally or in Taos.[28] The rest were Hispanos, nearly all of whom had been born locally and resided there permanently. Many of the Hispanos were older people who lived on social security or retirement pensions, and some twenty Hispano families were on welfare. However, nearly fifty of the Hispano heads of households (also some wives) were employed, thirty locally as by the Forest Service and the Peñasco Independent Schools while another twenty commuted to Taos, Dixon, Española, Los Alamos, and Santa Fe. The availability of jobs at places within reasonable commuting distances would seem to explain why Chamisal, unlike Manzano, had maintained an approximate population status quo since about 1940.

Peñasco

Chamisal's neighboring "town" of Peñasco represented a higher order in the central place hierarchy even in 1900. Although José J. Lucero found only slightly more people in Peñasco than in Chamisal—238 (fifty-five families) as compared to 232 (fifty families)—in Peñasco four heads of households were merchants (two general merchants and two grocers), two were blacksmiths, one was a saloon keeper, one was a "preacher," and one was a clerk, apparently in a store belonging to one of the merchants. Peñasco, moreover, was more "worldly," for although both it and Chamisal were purely Hispano, 36 people spoke English in Peñasco as compared to

---

Weigle, *Hispanic Villages*, p. 207. In 1900, Ojito had a population of 142; Population Schedules of the Twelfth Census [1900], 249A–250B. The figure 350 for Chamisal in 1935 assumes that Ojito and Chamisal grew at the same rate after 1900.

[28] The 1980 data are from Mrs. Olivama J. Atencio, a lifetime resident of the Chamisal area and for the last twenty-one years Chamisal's postmistress; interview with author, Chamisal, New Mexico, August 15, 1980. In 1980, according to Mrs. Atencio, Ojito (Upper and Lower) had a population of only seventy-eight (twenty-two families). One Anglo family of seven from Oklahoma was headed by a Pentecostal minister. George Lucero, owner of Lucero's Grocery in Chamisal, said that the first Anglo to live in Chamisal had moved there in 1943 and had married a local Hispana; interview with author, Chamisal, New Mexico, October 16, 1979.

only 11 in Chamisal. Indeed, Peñasco was more affluent, as four of its families had "servants," an occupation not found in Chamisal.[29] Peñasco's function as a trade center for the surrounding villages foreshadowed its modest sustained growth.

By 1935, Peñasco had 373 people in seventy-four families. The team of Soil Conservation Service researchers left no published record of Peñasco's ethnic composition or of its occupational breakdown by family, but two facts suggest that in the midst of the Great Depression Peñasco enjoyed relative economic prosperity: a parochial Catholic school with 350 students, the area's one large school, was located in Peñasco, and Peñasco's post office transacted six times more business than did the one in Chamisal.[30]

By 1980, Peñasco had grown to at least 481 people (135 families). Twenty-seven of the residents were Anglos, among whom were thirteen members of three Lebanese-derived merchant families and two nuns who taught in the parochial school. As at Chamisal, many of the Hispanos were older people who lived on social security or retirement pensions. But compared to Chamisal, fewer families were on welfare; fewer were commuting to jobs in Taos, Questa, or Los Alamos; and many more were locally employed. In 1980, students from all of southern Taos County—some eight hundred of them— were bused each day to a consolidated public school complex in Peñasco.[31] Peñasco was also the location of Saint Anthony's,

[29] Peñasco also had the usual large number of farmers or farm laborers (twenty-nine) and day laborers (seventeen). In Peñasco Precinct, José J. Lucero again clearly identified the precinct's two communities, Peñasco "town" and Copper Hill Mining Camp. In Peñasco, a thirty-eight-year-old merchant named Smith was the son of a Missouri-born father and thus was only half Hispano, and a sixty-nine-year-old farm laborer named Abreu was the son of a Mexican-born father. The "servants" in Peñasco were usually girls or young women; Ramón Sánchez, one of Peñasco's merchants, had four servants, while the other three families had one each; Population Schedules of the Twelfth Census [1900], roll 1003, ED 158, precinct 10, 239B–41B (Peñasco town).

[30] Weigle, Hispanic Villages, 207, 210, 211.

[31] These 1980 population figures are probably undercounts. They are derived from an initial list of Peñasco residents supplied by the Reverend Roger Martínez of Saint Anthony's Roman Catholic Church in Peñasco, as reviewed and added to by Mrs. Theresa Miera, Peñasco's elementary school principal, and by Mrs. Annabelle Torres, the owner of one of Peñasco's grocery stores. The last two informants were interviewed in Peñasco on August 16, 1980. A 1979 Taos County telephone directory was also helpful in compiling the list of Peñasco residents. The territory of the Peñasco Independent Schools even encompassed the village of Ojo Sarco, which is located in Rio Arriba County near the Taos County boundary. This school system (K–12) employed some

a parochial school with an attendance of one-hundred (K–6); it was the parish seat for the Roman Catholic church, which served nine communities; and it was the location of a Carson National Forest ranger station. All these functions, plus Peñasco's continued role as the local trade center, explain why it had experienced modest population increases since 1935.

DISPLACEMENT

The foregoing case studies suggest that village depopulation was characterized by large numbers of especially young people, who, whether alone or in families, left their villages and moved permanently to urban centers beginning about 1940. When the process had pretty much run its course two or three decades later, two interesting things happened. First, some one-time villagers who had kept their village properties and had maintained active ties as nonresidents in the 1970s began to return to their natal homes to retire. Some of their city-bred children also chose to live in their parents' former villages in the 1970s. Second, as early as the 1960s some Anglos, a share of them representatives of countercultures, were opting to live in these now depopulated villages, or at least were purchasing land in them. By 1980, then, some villages were showing modest signs of rejuvenation, and their ethnic compositions were changing.[32]

Both push factors at the village level and the pull of the city prompted the depopulation phenomenon. In some villages, such as El Cerrito, the ownership of common grazing land was withdrawn by court action, while in others, such as San Luis, land that could be irrigated was lost to erosion.[33] Additional powerful push forces were village overpopulation and the further subdivision of precious arable floodplain into plots that,

---

forty teachers and a number of administrators, secretaries, bus drivers, cooks, janitors, and maintenance men, many of whom lived in Peñasco; Mrs. Theresa Miera, interview with author, Peñasco, New Mexico, August 16, 1980.

[32] Paul Kutsche attributed the vitality of these villages to the flexibility of the Hispanos' social structure. The "strengths of social organization" constitute the "proposition" that authors of the essays Kutsche edits were invited to "test"; see his "Introduction: Atomism, Factionalism, and Flexibility," in Paul Kutsche, ed., *The Survival of Spanish American Villages*, Colorado College Studies, no. 15: 7–19 and subsequent essays.

[33] See Clark S. Knowlton, "Causes of Land Loss among the Spanish Americans in Northern New Mexico," *Rocky Mountain Social Science Journal* 1, no. 2 (April 1964): 201–11.

by about 1940, were almost too small for many families to subsist on. Cities, on the other hand, offered possibilities of steady employment, and in them villagers could maintain familial ties. The degree to which given villages emptied out seems to have been related to urban propinquity: the farther away or the less accessible a village was to a larger center, the greater its population loss.

The outcome of village depopulation, then, was for large numbers of Hispanos to be geographically displaced within their Homeland. The process was rapid and decisive. Village houses were boarded up, the countryside was left behind, and villagers regrouped in cities. An agrarian and traditional Hispano society was rather quickly transformed to an industrial and more Anglo-oriented society. Somewhat belatedly, Hispanos had joined the rural-to-urban tide that was sweeping America. For Hispanos, however, urbanization—the counterpart process to village depopulation—brought revolutionary changes.

CHAPTER 9

✚ ✚ ✚

URBANIZATION

LUIS ARAGÓN and Estefanita Quintana were an industrious and thrifty couple. As newlyweds about 1916 they were homesteading 160 acres on the mesa just north of Estefanita's home village of El Cerrito. By 1935 they were acquiring pieces of El Cerrito's irrigable floodplain. When their sons Cirilio, Candido, and Teodoro (born in 1921, 1923, and 1925) were old enough to work outside the village, their earnings were pooled with family resources to buy more land. By the 1950s the extended Aragón family was second only to the Quintanas in village family wealth.[1] And by the 1980s they and the Quintanas were strong village rivals. Meanwhile, 260 miles north of El Cerrito in Pueblo, where most of the one-time villagers had moved during the 1940s and '50s, and where Cirilio and Candido had put in thirty-year careers, all this business about land and rivalries in El Cerrito seemed of little consequence. Most villagers in Pueblo in the 1980s had long since turned their backs on that tiny place in New Mexico. They had fond memories of El Cerrito, but their homes were now in Pueblo. What happened to the El Cerrito villagers in Pueblo gives insight to urbanization, the most recent of the Homeland-shaping processes.

---

[1] Born in Aguilar, Luis Aragón (1891–1978) was raised by godparents in Chupinas; both small villages are located east of Anton Chico. Estefanita Quintana (1889–1982), daughter of Anastacio and Felipa Quintana, was born in El Cerrito. Between 1919 and 1934 the couple had five daughters and three sons. The couple's dates are from the El Cerrito cemetery, and the other facts are from Aragón family members. The family's wealth is discussed in Charles P. Loomis, "El Cerrito, New Mexico: A Changing Village," *New Mexico Historical Review* 33 (1958): 70; see also pp. 62, 65, 71, 73.

PUEBLO, COLORADO

At the junction of the Arkansas River and Fountain Creek, long an important crossroads for traders, ten or twelve Anglo men moved into a new fort by September 1842. Several owned the *plaza*-like compound, the rest probably rented space in it, and all planned to trade that winter with local Indians and Hispanos in Taos. Most of the dozen Anglos were married to (or had formed unions with) Hispanas from Taos. All apparently employed Hispano laborers, some of whom were probably the adobe masons hired in Taos to build the fort. Thus, Pueblo, as the tiny community was immediately known, from its inception was bicultural, its Hispano element undoubtedly outnumbering its Anglo. However, as often happened in peripheral areas to which Anglos had attracted Hispanos, Pueblo's Hispano element was to dwindle.[2]

A year after its founding, in July 1843, Pueblo's population composition had not changed when John C. Frémont noted that Pueblo's residents were "Americans . . . who had married Spanish women from the valley of Taos." By 1847, however, Pueblo's Hispano element was in relative decline. Indian Agent Thomas Fitzpatrick reported that of some sixty men in Pueblo (also in its neighbor community, Hardscrabble), at least ten had Indian wives and two had American wives. The relative decline continued. By 1870, only 60 of Pueblo's 660 residents were Hispanos, which meant that the Hispano proportion had dropped to nine. And a rootless minority those 60 Hispanos were: all the adults had come from New Mexico, all the men worked as laborers for Anglos, no Hispano owned real estate, and no Hispana was married to an Anglo. In the late 1870s Pueblo's economy began to boom, at first a result of the smelting of metals (gold, silver, copper, lead) mined near the headwaters of the Arkansas, and sustained by an integrated

---

[2] In her *Pueblo, Hardscrabble, Greenhorn: The Upper Arkansas, 1832–1856*, 35, 37, 42, 44, 54, 73, 263–64, Janet Lecompte documented unions between Hispanas from Taos and four Anglos: George Simpson, Robert Fisher, Mathew Kinkead, and John Brown. This paragraph relies heavily on her pp. 35, 47, 52, 54, 56, and 66. Like Pueblo, Rayado (1848) began as a largely Hispano community founded by Anglo initiative. Unlike Pueblo, however, Rayado was established in the context of contiguous expansion, and its Hispano population remained large (chapter 4). In their separate contexts, both Pueblo and Rayado apparently deserve the honors of being "first."

Fig. 9.1 This panoramic view of Pueblo's Goat Hill in 1900 is attributed to the renowned photographer William Henry Jackson. The ubiquitous *horno* (outdoor beehive-shaped oven) is strong evidence that the people shown were Hispanos. Courtesy Denver Public Library, Western History Department, photographs F16864 and F16865.

iron and steel industry that exploited nearby coal, iron ore, and limestone. By 1900 metropolitan Pueblo's population had soared to nearly thirty thousand, yet its Hispano component, now 515 strong, amounted to less than 2 percent of the total.[3]

In 1900 metropolitan Pueblo's 515 Hispanos were highly

[3] Lecompte, *Pueblo,* 102 (quoting Frémont), 203–204. Fitzpatrick's report, dated September 18, 1847, lists ten tribes from which the Indian wives had come; the two American wives were Mormons. The combined population of Pueblo and Hardscrabble was about 150. Of the 60 Hispano residents in 1870, 32 were men, women, and children in nine family units, 26 were single men (or men without their families), and two were teenaged girls. All the men (heads of households or single) were laborers, usually on farms or in a brickyard. The two teenaged girls were domestics in Anglo homes. Save for four Colorado-born children, all 60 were born in New Mexico. Besides these 60, the one other non-Anglo in Pueblo was a Mexican-born teamster; Population Schedules of the Ninth Census [1870], Microcopy no. M–593, 1965, roll 95: 481A– 489B. David Thomas Bailey noted that in the 1870 census real and personal property were to be recorded if either one was valued at more than one hundred dollars; "Stratification and Ethnic Differentiation in Santa Fe, 1860 and 1870" (Ph.D. diss. [sociology], University of Texas at Austin, 1975), 44. Pueblo's economic boom of the late 1870s is described in Roger Thomas Trindell, "Sequent Occupance of Pueblo,

segregated. Of the 147 enumerated in the City of Pueblo (28,172 total population and located just outside the Homeland), 52 lived in Ward 1 in the East 15th Street "Mexican Settlement," almost exclusively a Hispano barrio where heads of households were laborers in the steel works or hauled wood, while 61 lived largely outside of Ward 3 on Goat Hill, a heavily Italian neighborhood where many Hispano and Italian heads of households were laborers at a smelter (Fig. 9.1). Meanwhile, south of the Arkansas near Colorado Fuel and Iron (CF&I), through mergers now the giant of the iron and steel industry in Pueblo, 368 Hispanos lived in three county precincts (44, 50, and 51 and located within the Homeland). Of this number about 330 were clustered in Salt Creek Village. Primarily family units whose heads of households were often laborers in the iron and steel works, metropolitan Pueblo's Hispanos were born largely in Colorado (327 of 515), which would suggest some length of residency in Colorado, if not in Pueblo, and a dozen Hispanas were married to Anglos, which would indicate

Colorado" (master's thesis [geography], University of Colorado, 1960), 66–72. For the 1900 population, see Population Schedules of the Twelfth Census [1900], Microcopy no. T–623, n.d., roll 128, EDs 93–108, wards 1–8 (Pueblo); and roll 128, ED 109, precincts 44, 50, 51 (south of Pueblo).

a beginning of assimilation. Significantly, all twenty-four Mexican Americans (twenty-two of them born in Mexico) in metropolitan Pueblo in 1900 resided with the Hispanos, into which group several had married.[4] By the turn of the century, then, Pueblo had three heavily Hispano barrios, and significant Mexican immigration was yet to happen.

A rather comprehensive survey undertaken in metropolitan Pueblo in 1930 shows that Mexican Americans then outnumbered Hispanos. Of an estimated five thousand Spanish-speaking people in greater Pueblo, 63 percent were Mexican-born. Most of the rest, perhaps two thousand, were born in New Mexico and Colorado and were, therefore, largely Hispanos—which in 1930 would have represented 3 percent of metropolitan Pueblo's 66,038 total. That Hispanos were referred to by the Mexican-born as *comprado*, meaning "bought," suggests some degree of animosity between the two groups. The 1930 study says little about residential patterns. Heavy Spanish-speaking enrollments in grade schools serving Bessemer, a south-side community annexed to Pueblo in 1894, and Salt Creek Village, also on the south side but outside the city limits, would suggest that a majority of the five thousand Mexican Americans and Hispanos lived south of the Arkansas.[5] Two-thirds of the Spanish-speaking work force was employed in the iron and steel industry, while most of the rest worked either for sugar beet growers or for the railroads. Into this context, then, came the villagers from El Cerrito.

Members of the Armijo family, who for many years had sought seasonal agricultural employment in the Arkansas Valley, seem to have been the first El Cerrito villagers to move permanently to Pueblo. They probably did so about 1942 or 1943. Within a decade Quintana, Vigil, Tapia, Torres, and

---

[4] One, Mexican-born Peter Deus, a forty-year-old teacher who lived on Beech Street on the edge of the Italian-Hispano Goat Hill barrio, took the census in the county precincts south of Pueblo (44, 50, 51, 52), which included Salt Creek Village (50); Population Schedules of the Twelfth Census [1900], roll 128, ED 97: 82B. The Colorado-born Hispanos were, for the most part, the children of New Mexico-born Hispanos.

[5] This paragraph draws heavily on Donald S. Howard, "A Study of the Mexican, Mexican-American and Spanish-American Population in Pueblo, Colorado, 1929–1930" (master's thesis [sociology], University of Denver, 1930), 6, 7, 8, 25, 29, 52, 78. Howard gathered his data in house-to-house surveys conducted in January 1930, and from school and industry records. Concerning Bessemer, and for the 1930 figure for metropolitan Pueblo, see Trindell, "Pueblo, Colorado," 65, 92. The idea behind *comprado*, according to Howard, was that Hispanos had not repatriated in 1848.

Aragón family members had also moved to Pueblo. During this period a number of Quintanas reached Pueblo after removing first to ranches near La Garita in eastern San Miguel County, and some El Cerrito women who had married men from Villanueva and elsewhere also went indirectly to Pueblo. In Pueblo, the villagers located wherever they could afford housing, which was nearly always in the relatively poor districts on the east side. When nine El Cerrito families in Pueblo were interviewed in 1959, their residences were scattered within Pueblo, and two families lived outside the city limits. Eight of the nine families owned or were buying their modest but well-kept homes.[6]

Notwithstanding their scattered residential pattern, the villagers in Pueblo in 1959 were extremely cohesive socially. Social interactions in Pueblo were almost exclusively between extended family members and compadres (godparents) from El Cerrito. If a man or a family arrived from El Cerrito, he or they would be put up by relatives until a job and a house were found. The major problem in 1959 was underemployment. Only two of the heads of households interviewed had full-time jobs, both at the large army ordnance depot located fifteen miles east of Pueblo. Most of the other seven worked only irregularly, yet the older children, who were employed at the ordnance depot, in the steel works, in construction, or in farming, were also contributing to the family incomes. Despite their struggle to make a living, only one family (the one that had not bought a house) planned to return to El Cerrito. Indeed, when revisiting "La Placita," as villagers in Pueblo affectionately called El

---

[6] Several informants, who were interviewed in July 1988 and whose names are given below, provided the information on the Armijos. Charles P. Loomis, who restudied El Cerrito in the summer of 1956, confirmed that the migration to Pueblo began in the early 1940s; "Systemic Linkage of El Cerrito," *Rural Sociology* 24 (1959): 54. Exemplary of that migration, the entire Eliodoro Quintana family of eight moved in 1942 from El Cerrito to La Garita, from which a number eventually went to Pueblo; Mary Quintana Sena, Pueblo, Colorado, interview with author, July 8, 1988. Audry Torres, who married Frank Gallejos of Villanueva, moved to Pueblo in 1946; Macario Torres, Pueblo, Colorado, interview with author, July 6, 1988. The fortunate study of the El Cerrito families in Pueblo was undertaken in the summer of 1959 by Julian Samora and Richard F. Larson, "Rural Families in an Urban Setting: A Study in Persistence and Change," *Journal of Human Relations* 9 (1960–61): 494–503. Under Samora's direction, one Mose [sic] Trujillo of Denver conducted most of the interviews. Samora and Larson noted that there were "probably less than twenty" El Cerrito families in Pueblo in 1959. The average educational attainment of the nine heads of households interviewed was five years.

Cerrito, most felt mild contempt for those who were still living in El Cerrito and who had not opted for the better life in Pueblo.[7]

The better life in Pueblo since the early 1940s had attracted large numbers of Hispanos from northern New Mexico and southern Colorado. By 1950, 9,196 Hispanos represented 10.2 percent of metropolitan Pueblo's 90,188 total. Their numbers continued to grow. In 1980, of 116,095 people in metropolitan Pueblo, those who self-identified their ancestry to be Hispano numbered 17,947, which amounted to 15.5 percent of the total. And in 1980 those who self-identified their ancestry to be Mexican in origin now numbered 19,656 (16.9 percent).[8] Both of these minority populations in 1980 were very much integrated residentially with the Anglo majority. Still, there were districts that were heavily Hispano and Mexican American (Map 9.1): Clockwise from Fountain Creek, they were Eastside, Lower Eastside, Dogpatch (renamed Eastwood Heights), Penjamo Village (cut off from Dogpatch by U.S. 50 Bypass), The Lanes or The Mesa (Saint Charles Mesa), Lombard Village, Blende, Salt Creek Village or "Salado," Bessemer, Westside, Sanders Division, Goat Hill, and The Grove. The general perception was that Salt Creek Village and Bessemer were more heavily Mexican American.

In 1988, I interviewed nine El Cerrito families who lived in Pueblo or who had lived there.[9] Most of the first-generation

[7] This paragraph is drawn largely from Samora and Larson, "Rural Families," 494–503.

[8] The 9,196 figure is the total of native-born white persons of Spanish surname, which would have been largely Hispano; U.S. Bureau of the Census, Census of Population: 1950, vol. 4, Special Reports, part 3, chapter C, "Persons of Spanish Surname," p. 44, table 7. The 90,188 total for metropolitan Pueblo in 1950 is from Trindell, "Pueblo Colorado," 103. The figure for Hispanos (17,947) is the sum of codes 205, 206, and 207, as explained in Table 1.5. The totals for metropolitan Pueblo, as opposed to the data for the City of Pueblo given below, were arrived at by adding figures for two CCDs: Pueblo (16,651 Hispanos; 106,998 total) and Saint Charles Mesa (1,296 Hispanos; 9,097 total). The figure for Mexican-origin people (19,656) is the sum of codes 208, 209, 210, 211, and 212, as explained in Table 1.5. In the Pueblo CCD, 18,084 Mexican-origin people were enumerated, and in the Saint Charles Mesa CCD, the figure was 1,572; U.S. Bureau of the Census, Population Division, Census of Population and Housing, 1980, Summary Tape File (STF) 4 (data from long-form question 14 for fifteen states).

[9] Interviewed in July, seven of these families were first-generation migrants, and two were their children. The families were Candido and Mary Barela Aragón (Pueblo), Luis and Linda Quintana Aragón (El Cerrito), Elvira Corrales Quintana (widow of Perfecto; Rocky Ford), Eduardo E. and Jesucita Gutiérrez Quintana (Pueblo), Florencio

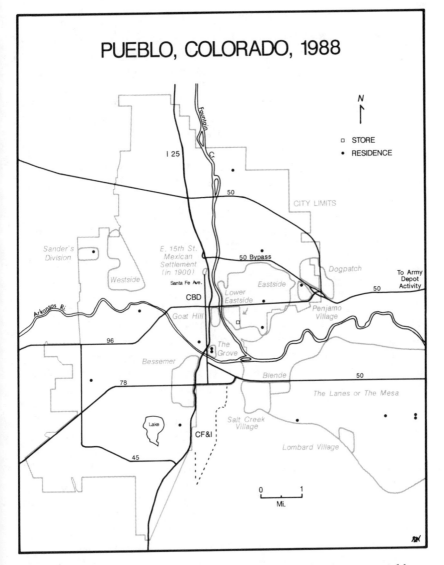

PUEBLO, COLORADO, 1988

N

□ STORE
• RESIDENCE

I 25

50

CITY LIMITS

Sander's
Division

Westside

E. 15th St.
Mexican
Settlement
(in 1900)

50 Bypass

Dogpatch

To Army
Depot
Activity

Santa Fe Ave.

Eastside

50

CBD

Lower
Eastside

Arkansas Ri.

Goat Hill

Penjamo
Village

96

The
Grove

Bessemer

Blende

50

78

The Lanes or The Mesa

Lake

Salt Creek
Village

CF&I

Lombard Village

45

0   1
Mi.

Map 9.1 Pueblo, Colorado, in 1988. Shown are heavily Hispano neighborhoods and the 1988 known residences (plus one store) of sixteen
first-generation El Cerrito villagers who went to Pueblo largely between 1947 and 1953. Clustering occurs among siblings. Source: see
text.

villagers who were still alive had retired from jobs at the army ordnance depot, now called the Pueblo Army Depot Activity; CF&I, now a mere vestige of a once great enterprise; and a meat packing plant on Santa Fe Avenue that had gone by several names and was now closed. These first-generation villagers in 1988 lived mainly in lower-middle-class neighborhoods on the east side of Pueblo (Map 9.1). Their large numbers of children and grandchildren appeared to live throughout Pueblo, some had gone to college, and many had moved away to cities like Denver, Los Angeles, and New York. Because all whose roots could be traced to El Cerrito were in some way related, when there was an important occasion like a graduation, a wedding, a funeral, even an occasional family reunion, members of all three generations would come together. Few occasions for social interaction seemed otherwise to present themselves. By 1988 villagers from El Cerrito in Pueblo no longer constituted a cohesive subsystem.

The first-generation migrants in 1988 held differing degrees of loyalty for El Cerrito, which they were now calling "The Ranch." All remembered when El Cerrito was a very special place. All realized that practically everyone had left and that the orchards were gone. All also seemed to think that New Mexico was nicer than Colorado as a place to live. Those who had revisited El Cerrito often and who planned to retire in the village expressed strong feelings of pride that they were from El Cerrito.[10] Those who had revisited El Cerrito only infrequently and had sold their land also expressed pride in being from El Cerrito, and some had regrets that their land had been sold. But at least some who had not returned to El Cerrito and who probably never would were embarrassed to have once been so poor and to have come from such a small place. To the disbelief of other first-generation villagers, when asked by some new acquaintance where they were from, these villagers would answer "Las Vegas." Feelings of embarrassment were foremost behind this response, but there was also the matter of naming

and Helen Baca Quintana (Pueblo), Rick and Repita Chacón Quintana (El Cerrito), Joe and Mary Quintana Sena (Pueblo), Abel and Josie Martínez Tapia (Pueblo), and Macario and Rose Sandoval Torres (Pueblo).

[10] In July 1988 two Pueblo couples, both first-generation villagers, were planning to retire in El Cerrito: Macario and Rose Torres (in 1989) and Florencio and Helen Quintana (in 1994).

a place that was large and about which few would inquire further.

Feelings between the "Spanish" villagers and "white" people in Pueblo had improved since the villagers first arrived. One informant recalled that when she lived in Pueblo during World War II, Spanish people had to sit in the balconies of movie theaters, and they would not be waited on in downtown department stores. This was no longer true when she returned to Pueblo in 1953. But still there were the recent examples of Spanish children in school being punished more severely than Anglo children or of Spanish children being refused permission to go to the bathroom. And there were the white in-laws who had never spoken to the Spanish in-laws. Whatever the feelings, contact between the two groups by 1988 had resulted in a clear linguistic transition of Spanish to English. The first-generation villagers in Pueblo all knew English well but were usually more comfortable speaking in Spanish, which many still spoke at home. The second generation were usually bilingual but spoke English in their own homes. And the third generation, having heard much less Spanish than their second-generation parents, could understand Spanish but usually could not speak it. The transition from Spanish to English, then, had gone forward much more rapidly in Pueblo than it had back in El Cerrito.

There was general agreement among the first-generation villagers in Pueblo in 1988 that "Spanish" and "Mexican" people did not get along. Members of the two groups had intermarried. In one case a Mexican-descent woman from Colorado who had married a first-generation villager from El Cerrito knew that her mother-in-law back in El Cerrito never would accept her simply because she was of Mexican descent. And the labels that each group had used for the other were well known: *comprado* ("bought") or *vendido* ("sold") and *manito* (contraction of the diminutive *hermanito*, "little brother," which meant "soft" or the opposite of *macho*) were used by Mexicans for the Spanish, while *surumato* (a person from the south, with a degree of disdain implied) was used by the Spanish for Mexicans. There was general agreement, moreover, that Spanish and Mexican people were culturally different. Examples of language came readily to mind: *cuarto de dormir* (Hispano Spanish) rather than *recámara* (Mexican

Spanish) for "bedroom," *cabello* rather than *pelo* for "hair," *medias* rather than *calcetines* for "socks," and *calzones* rather than *pantalones* for "trousers" (in Mexico, *calzones* means women's panties). When asked to slice up the *col* ("cabbage"), the Mexican-descent daughter-in-law, who had never heard the word, to avoid seeming stupid asked where it was rather than what it was while visiting in El Cerrito. For her, cabbage was *repollo*.

Gradually and in small numbers, then, first-generation villagers from El Cerrito had migrated to Pueblo during the 1940s and '50s. From the beginning they settled in a random pattern, especially in the affordable neighborhoods on the east side. At first, despite their scattered pattern, they formed a socially cohesive subsystem, but as families grew, the intensity of their social interactions declined—to the point that in the 1980s the one-time villagers and their descendants saw each other only on special occasions and only because they were related. At first they also revisited El Cerrito with some frequency in order to maintain their property and to see relatives, but as more and more villagers left for Pueblo and as property in El Cerrito was sold, their interest in El Cerrito waned and the revisiting for many became very occasional or ended altogether. By the 1980s most first-generation villagers in Pueblo had severed their ties with El Cerrito. Their children and their grandchildren had largely been assimilated into Pueblo's majority population. Besides the switch from Spanish to English, there was something symbolic about the change in names by which El Cerrito was known: "La Placita" suggested a small, special village full of people; "The Ranch" suggested only open grazing land and cattle.

THE CHANGING HISPANO URBAN HIERARCHY

Urbanization is generally recognized to be the process whereby relatively large numbers of people come to live in close proximity to engage in economic activities that are not usually tied to the land. Within the Homeland, Santa Fe was clearly the first Hispano urban center. It could even be argued that Santa Fe began as an urban center. By 1790, Santa Fe was attracting Hispanos from surrounding rural villages. And by 1850, 3,883 Hispanos, who represented 80.1 percent of the total 4,846, put

Santa Fe at the top of the Hispano urban hierarchy. By 1850 Sante Fe's power to attract also found 310 nonmilitary Anglos and 159 Mexican Americans living together in small clusters in what constituted a mild form of residential segregation.[11] By mid-century, moreover, Santa Fe's Anglos, although relatively few in number, were fairly much in control; a detailed analysis of Santa Fe in 1860, for example, shows that Anglos, who represented only 18.5 percent of the gainful workers that year, dominated the occupational structure, owned most of the wealth, and held most of the positions of authority.[12] Perhaps because of the Anglo-generated activity, or more likely through sheer inertia, Santa Fe's Hispano population continued to grow, keeping it at the top of the Hispano urban hierarchy down to 1900 (Fig. 9.2).

Santa Fe in 1900 had two distinct parts: the city proper, where 83.9 percent of the people lived, and the city's periphery, which contained the remaining 16.1 percent.[13] Santa Fe's periphery was almost purely Hispano; of 1,074 people, the only non-Hispanos were thirteen Anglos. The city itself, on the other hand, was ethnically diverse. Besides its 3,732 Hispanos, Santa Fe contained 1,355 Anglos, whose residences, as in 1850, were perceptibly clustered; forty-eight Mexican Americans, whose residences were now thoroughly integrated with those of the Hispanos; and 467 Indians, all of whom boarded at either the Indian Industrial School (305) or the Saint Catherine School

[11] Oakah L. Jones, Jr., "Spanish Civil Communities and Settlers in Frontier New Mexico, 1790–1810," in *Hispanic-American Essays in Honor of Max Leon Moorhead*, ed. William S. Coker, 49; Population Schedules of the Seventh Census [1850], Microcopy no. 432, 1963, roll 468: 632–750. Because census marshals listed households seriatim (in consecutive order) in the schedules, ethnic residential clusters can easily be identified. By "small" clusters and "mild" segregation, what is meant is groups of half a dozen to perhaps 50 or more Anglos that were interspersed with the Hispano population. As noted in chapter 5, the Anglo clusters correlated areally with the Hispano elite. Of the 963 non-Hispanos in Santa Fe in 1850, all 462 military Anglos lived in one cluster, and the only other Santa Fe population component, thirty-two nomad Indians, lived in given Hispano households.

[12] Bailey, "Stratification and Ethnic Differentiation," 62, 74, 94, 104, 105, 115, 116. Bailey noted that by 1870 Hispanos had made slight gains in all three areas.

[13] In 1900, Santa Fe was carved into four precincts, and within each was a ward of the city: Upper Santa Fe Precinct 3 and Ward 1; Lower Santa Fe Precinct 4 and Ward 2; Lower Santa Fe Precinct 17 and Ward 3; and Upper Santa Fe Precinct 18 and Ward 4. The wards, of course, constituted the city proper; Population Schedules of the Twelfth Census [1900], roll 1002, EDs 119–20, 126–27.

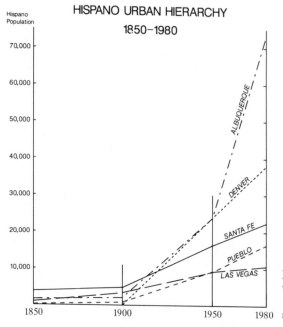

Fig. 9.2 The Hispano
urban hierarchy,
1850–1980. Sources:
see text.

(162). In greater Santa Fe, then, 4,793 Hispanos accounted for 71.8 percent of the total 6,676 population. Santa Fe in 1900 led the Hispano urban hierarchy with Las Vegas a distant second.

Las Vegas in 1900 was actually two communities, Old Las Vegas and East (New) Las Vegas. Old Las Vegas had grown as New Mexico's gateway settlement on the Santa Fe Trail. As early as 1850 one of its three or four clusters of Anglos included four merchants and the sheriff at the plaza.[14] East Las Vegas began a mile to the east as an adjunct community established on undeveloped land by the AT&SF in 1879. Separated by the Gallinas River, the two communities by 1900 were about equal in size but otherwise fundamentally different. Plaza-centered Old Las Vegas (3,254) was 82.9 percent Hispano (2,699). Its 502

[14] Old Las Vegas was enumerated in four precincts (5 South Las Vegas; 9 Upper Las Vegas; 26 Las Vegas, which included the plaza area; and 64 Central Las Vegas). East Las Vegas was one precinct: 29 East Las Vegas; Population Schedules of the Twelfth Census [1900], roll 1002, EDs 101, 104, and 113. One of the merchants was Missouri-born Levi J. "Keithley," as the census enumerator spelled it. The sheriff was North Carolina–born A. J. Donaldson; Population Schedules of the Seventh Census [1850], roll 469: 1. Las Vegas in 1850 had eighty-five nonmilitary Anglos (chapter 5).

Anglos lived in many residential clusters, the largest of which was at the plaza, while its forty-six Mexican Americans were residentially integrated with the Hispanos. On the other hand, East Las Vegas (3,574), now a major railroad center and wool entrepôt, was 82.6 percent Anglo. Its 620 Hispanos and two Mexican Americans were also clustered, mostly in one large segregated quarter which was clearly the creation of Anglo discrimination.[15] With 3,319 Hispanos, who accounted for 48.6 percent of the total 6,828, greater Las Vegas in 1900 was New Mexico's second leading Hispano community. Trailing in third position was Albuquerque.

Greater Albuquerque resembled greater Las Vegas in 1900. Both had plaza-centered, heavily Hispano old towns next to depot-centered, heavily Anglo new towns. In Old Albuquerque, moreover, where Anglos and Hispanos were congenial, Anglos were only mildly clustered, while Mexican Americans were residentially integrated, whereas in New Albuquerque, where Anglo intolerance and discrimination was open and overt, Hispanos and Mexican Americans lived together in a strongly clustered pattern.[16] But there the resemblances ended. Demographically, Old Albuquerque had not grown, while New Albuquerque had soared. Old Albuquerque had only 1,191 people, of whom 77.8 percent (927) were Hispanos, while New Albuquerque had a whopping 6,238 people, of whom 17.6 percent (1,097) were Hispanos. The sum of the two Hispano populations, only 2,024 of a total 7,429 (27.2 percent), left Albuquerque some distance behind Santa Fe and Las Vegas in the Homeland's Hispano urban hierarchy.

[15] Anglo-Hispano rivalry and ill feeling ran strong between East and Old Las Vegas about 1900. One example was the Anglo editor of the East Las Vegas *Optic*, who, in the 1880s, opposed consolidation of the two communities "because the east side, 'full of activity and enterprise,' should be governed 'by American only.' " The complicated story of why East and Old Las Vegas failed to consolidate until 1968 is a theme in Lynn Perrigo, *Gateway to Glorieta: A History of Las Vegas, New Mexico*, 68, 80–81, 88, 193.

[16] Old Albuquerque was enumerated as one precinct (13), and New Albuquerque as two precincts (12 and 26); Population Schedules of the Twelfth Census [1900], roll 999, EDs 9, 10, 18. Lehmann skillfully contrasted prerailroad Old Albuquerque's few Anglos, who were married to and had strong bonds with the local Hispanos, with New Albuquerque's newcomer Anglos of the 1880s, whose arrogance and intolerance on at least one occasion (in 1885) prompted a number of Hispanos to move from New Albuquerque to Old Albuquerque (p. 182); Terry Jon Lehmann, "Santa Fe and Albuquerque, 1870–1900: Contrast and Conflict in the Development of Two Southwestern Towns" (Ph.D. diss. [history] Indiana University, 1974), 180, 185–87, 278, 281.

Only four other places in the Homeland appear to have had more than 1,000 Hispanos in 1900: Ranchos de Taos (1,386), Taos (1,123), Española (1,112), and Ocate (1,066) (Map 9.3).[17] All four were dominantly Hispano, Hispano percentages ranging from 91.2 percent and 91.7 percent at Española and Taos to 96.9 percent and 98.5 percent at Ocate and Ranchos de Taos. Significant Anglo populations that residentially were clustered among the Hispanos existed only at Taos (100) and Española (106). What all these facts accurately portray is a Homeland in 1900 that was still a land of small villages, and in these small villages Hispano proportions generally increased as the village sizes decreased. Santa Fe, Las Vegas, and Albuquerque were the region's giants, the major points of Hispano-Anglo interaction, the foci of large Anglo wholesaling networks and banking, and, except for Santa Fe, which was New Mexico's seat of political and religious power, the major nodes of railroad transportation. Santa Fe, Las Vegas, and Albuquerque in 1900 were the substantial anchors in three corners of a recently reconstituted triangular Homeland core. And because the Homeland's demographic center point coincided exactly with Santa Fe, this core was literally the heart of the Homeland.

Albuquerque, in total population (7,429) the largest of New Mexico's urban places, was quite tiny compared to Denver and Pueblo, which by 1900 had populations of 133,859 and 28,157, respectively. Yet by 1900 neither Denver, with twenty-three Hispanos, nor Pueblo, with 147 Hispanos (in the city proper), had attracted the requisite number to be included in the Homeland. After 1900 this changed. The 1950 census is the first published census to contain data that can be used to estimate the sizes of Hispano populations in urban centers. In 1950, white persons of Spanish surname (WPSS) were enumerated in the five heavily Hispanic southwestern states, and the following totals were given for the native-born WPSS element, which in New Mexico and Colorado would have been largely Hispano: Denver (23,969), Albuquerque (23,740), Santa Fe (16,344),

---

[17] Population Schedules of the Twelfth Census [1900], roll 1001, ED 75, precinct 8 (Ocate, Mora County); roll 1001, ED 82, precinct 7 (part of Española, Rio Arriba County); roll 1002, ED 123, precinct 16 (part of Española, Santa Fe County); roll 1003, ED 152, precinct 1 (Taos, Taos County); roll 1003, ED 154, precinct 3 (Ranchos de Taos, Taos County). Because the census enumerators did not specify places within these precincts, small village populations may have been included in the totals.

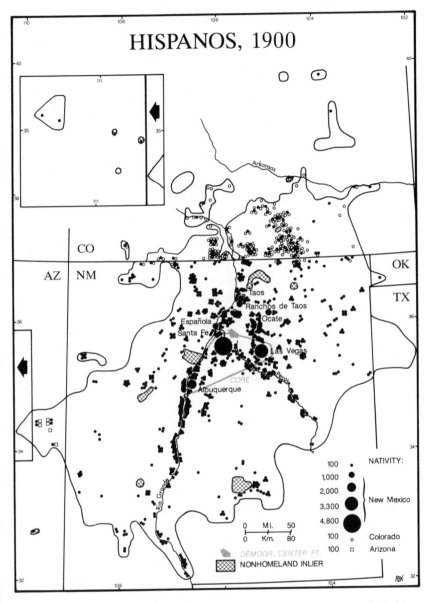

Map 9.2 Hispano numbers in 1900. By 1900 the Homeland core included Las Vegas. Most Hispanos lived within 150 miles of Santa Fe, the region's demographic center point. The Homeland and its thirteen outliers were a minimum 10 percent Hispano per census precinct. Source: Population Schedules of the Twelfth Census [1900].

and Pueblo (9,196). No figure was given for Las Vegas, apparently because its total population was under the 10,000 minimum needed for inclusion, yet in 1950 10,018 WPSS were listed as "urban" in San Miguel County, suggesting that the Hispano element in Las Vegas was about the same size as that in Pueblo.[18] Denver and Pueblo by 1950 had grown to become top-ranking communities in the Hispano urban hierarchy.

The remarkable growth of the Hispano community in Denver has received little scholarly attention. Two master's theses in social work at the University of Denver give some notion of what had happened by 1940. Based on welfare registrations, Denver's Spanish-speaking community, which included Hispanos and Mexican Americans, in 1940 was estimated to be twenty thousand. As determined from sampling the employment and welfare records, the majority, because they were New Mexico– and Colorado-born, were Hispanos. These Hispanos had come north to work in the sugar beet fields in the summers, and because of lenient welfare regulations, they began to stay over the winters in places like Denver where they could receive aid. Two-thirds of the total Spanish-speaking population in Denver in 1940 lived in only five census tracts, all in the central city of Denver. This was the part of Denver where rents were lowest and where much of the housing was classified as substandard.[19]

By 1980, Denver had 38,007 Hispanos, a number so large that it was included in the Homeland even though Hispanos

---

[18] Population Schedules of the Twelfth Census [1900], roll 128, EDs 93–108, wards 1–8 (Pueblo); and rolls 117–19 and 122, wards 1–16 (Denver). U.S. Bureau of the Census, 1950, Persons of Spanish Surname, 44, table 7; 64, table 9.

[19] Milan W. Gadd, "Significant Problems of Spanish-Speaking Persons and a Study of Their Registrations in the Denver Office of the Colorado State Employment Service" (master's thesis [social work], University of Denver, 1941); 11–14, 32, 90–91; and Ora Gjerde Ethell, "A Study of Fifty Spanish-Speaking and Mexican Families in Denver County Granted Aid to Dependent Children from April to October 1936 and Receiving Grants Continuously to June 1942" (master's thesis [social work], University of Denver, 1943), 42–43, 77–80. Gadd sampled 485 Spanish-speaking people registered with the Denver office of the Colorado State Employment Service in 1939; of them, 82.5 percent were born in New Mexico (208) and Colorado (192). Only 10.5 percent (51) were born in Mexico. Because it is unlikely that many Mexican-born would have registered for employment, these figures probably do not represent the size of the Mexican element. In her sample of fifty families on welfare between 1936 and 1942, Ethell found that 48 percent of the fathers and 68 percent of the mothers were New Mexico– and Colorado-born. The five heavily Spanish-speaking census tracts were 12, 16, 17, 22, and 24, as determined in 1939 by the Denver Housing Authority.

represented only 7.7 percent of the city's population. Denver was second to Albuquerque (73,708) in the Hispano urban hierarchy in 1980. Following Denver were Santa Fe (22,368), Pueblo (16,407), Las Vegas (10,678), Las Cruces (5,308), and Grants (4,809) (Map 9.3).[20] The Homeland's core in 1980 included Albuquerque, the contiguous region's most powerful economic center, and Santa Fe, the region's seat of religious and political control. Las Vegas since 1900 had slipped in importance and was now an oversized county seat in a poor and relatively stagnant rural area. Albuquerque's phenomenal rise since 1900 had pulled the Homeland's demographic center point southwest to about Bernalillo, located only fifteen miles north of the metropolis.

CONCENTRATION

The obvious outcome of urbanization in the Homeland is that Hispanos came to be concentrated geographically. Villages emptied out and urban centers grew; a rural Homeland whose Hispanos were spread thinly was transformed to an urban Homeland whose Hispanos were agglomerated. This concentration happened gradually and selectively before about 1940, when pull factors were foremost, then suddenly and in wholesale fashion after about 1940, when push factors also took hold. During the 1950s the majority of Hispanos came to live in communities that were larger than twenty-five hundred people, the Bureau of the Census's size criterion for urban. This significant transition when the majority of Hispanos became urban happened at the beginning of the decade in Colorado and in about the middle of the decade in New Mexico.[21]

[20] Figures for Hispanos are the sums of codes 205, 206, and 207 as explained in table 1.5; U.S. Bureau of the Census, Census of Population and Housing, 1980, STF 4. Hispano populations in metropolitan Albuquerque and Denver exceeded one hundred thousand and fifty thousand, respectively. Hispano percentages were as follows: Albuquerque, 22.2 percent; Denver, 7.7 percent; Santa Fe, 45.7 percent; Pueblo, 16.1 percent; Las Vegas, 74.6 percent; Las Cruces, 11.9 percent; Grants, 42.0 percent. In Map 9.3, eleven urban places with Hispano populations of about three thousand are also shown.

[21] The urban percentages of white persons of Spanish surname who were native-born of native parentage were as follows: Colorado—1950, 48.6 percent; 1960, 68.4 percent; New Mexico—1950, 40.5 percent; 1960, 58.2 percent. U.S. Bureau of the Census, 1950, Persons of Spanish Surname, p. 21, table 5, and U.S. Bureau of the Census, Census of Population, 1960: Subject Reports, Persons of Spanish Surname. Final Report PC(2)–1B, p. 2, table 1.

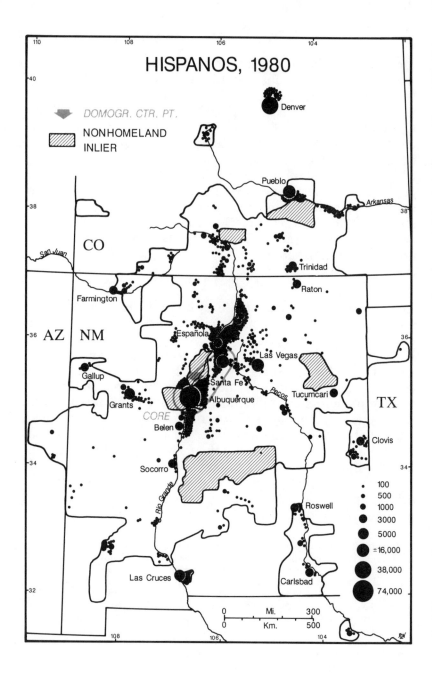

HISPANOS, 1980

In the emerging urban centers the interplay between Hispanos and Anglos, also between these two groups and Mexican Americans, produced degrees of residential segregation. Being played out, as it were, was the geography of dominance and subordination. In the *Hispano*-created urban centers of Santa Fe, Old Las Vegas, and Old Albuquerque, Anglos, who had rapidly ascended to positions of dominance, *chose* to live in mildly segregated quarters. Mexican Americans in Santa Fe, apparently because of their social and economic position, in 1850 also lived in the Anglo clusters, yet by 1900, presumably because they and the Hispanos were now equals, in Santa Fe (and elsewhere) they were thoroughly integrated with the Hispanos. On the other hand, in the *Anglo*-created urban centers of East Las Vegas, New Albuquerque, and Pueblo, Hispanos and Mexican Americans, who in 1900 had subordinate status, lived together in strongly clustered districts, a sharply segregated situation which was *forced* on them. The turn of the century may have marked the high point in sharp residential segregation. That first-generation El Cerrito villagers were living throughout Pueblo in the 1980s confirms its eventual demise. Yet precisely what happened after the turn of the century can be documented only as the census schedules are released and studied.

By 1980 the consequences of urbanization for Hispanos were far-reaching. Incomes, also standards of living, had risen. So had levels of education, the number of working mothers, and the number of mixed marriages. Meanwhile, the percentage of Hispanos with Spanish surnames had decreased, as had the percentage that was fluent in Spanish. Ties with the Roman Catholic church had weakened. The status of men in 1980 was based more on earnings and achievements and less on age and filial deference. Urban Hispano families faced problems of truancy, delinquency, and divorce. By 1980, then, Hispanos had become more like Anglos. Urbanization had brought much

---

Map 9.3 (*opposite*) Hispano numbers in 1980. Hispanos are those who identified themselves as Spanish (205), Spanish American (206), or Hispanic/Hispano(a) (207). With the exception of Denver (7.7 percent Hispano), the Homeland is a minimum 10 percent Hispano per CCD. Four distant Homeland outliers are omitted. Source: U.S. Department of the Census, Population Division, Census of Population and Housing, 1980, STF 4.

that was good, but at the same time it had undermined many of the subculture's fundamental and binding values. By accelerating Hispano assimilation, urbanization had hastened the decline of that remarkable geographical entity—the Homeland.

CHAPTER 10

✛　　✛　　✛

THE HOMELAND

WHILE GROWING UP in California, Tony Lucero remembers accompanying his parents, Juan A. and Josefita Lucero, to one of the "New Mexico clubs" where people from New Mexico gathered to reminisce about their villages back home. He also remembers how his father, as if speaking to a goose that was honking in the sky, would say, "*Grulla, grulla. A tu tierra, grulla. Porque esta no es tuya.*" The *dicho* (saying) means, "Goose, goose. Return to your home. Because this is not your land." Tony's father was expressing the hope that the Lucero family, like the migrating goose, would one day return home. What had happened was that in 1951, soon after the Forest Service denied Juan Lucero a permit to graze his cattle on the one-time common lands of Placitas—where Tony's grandfather had raised sheep and his great grandfather had raised goats—the family moved to California. They found employment at a dairy near Elk Grove and later moved to Davis, both near Sacramento. But the ties to small Placitas were maintained. Juan and Josefita visited annually. In 1975, Tony's own nuclear family moved back permanently, and in 1985 so did a married sister.[1] All of this is an example of the little-understood New Mexico–California connection. It is also an example of the degree of attachment felt by Hispanos for New Mexico, a mentality that is embodied in the concept of a Hispano Homeland.

---

[1] Born in Placitas in 1940, Tony Lucero is the youngest of fourteen children. Of the ten children that survive, eight live in California. Placitas is located some twenty miles northeast of Albuquerque; Lucero interview with author, Albuquerque, April 28, 1989.

ENVIRONMENTAL ADJUSTMENT

The concept of a "homeland," although abstract and elusive, has at least three basic elements: a people, a place, and identity with place. The people must have lived in a place long enough to have adjusted to its natural environment and to have left their impress in the form of a cultural landscape. And from their interactions with the natural and cultural totality of the place they must have developed an identity with the land— emotional feelings of attachment, desires to possess, even compulsions to defend. Hispanos developed such a level of consciousness about their land. Consider first adjustment to the environment.

The natural environment that Hispanos became bonded to is largely semiarid, meaning that it receives an average of only ten to twenty inches of precipitation annually. Dry conditions explain the relatively sparse vegetation cover. It is also a highland with elevations that reach from 4,500 feet above sea level some twenty miles downstream from Socorro to over 8,000 feet at villages like Truchas. High elevations in New Mexico mean rugged land and cold temperatures. Following the rising contours are basically two biotic life zones: the "Upper Sonoran" (4,500–6,500 feet), with its junipers and piñon pines, and the "Transition" zone (6,500–8,000 feet), with its ponderosa pines. Hispanos of course differentiate between the lower and warmer Rio Abajo, essentially a long swath of gently sloping Rio Grande floodplain where water and arable land are plentiful, and the higher and colder Rio Arriba, where for long stretches the Rio Grande is deeply entrenched and in its tributary valleys arable floodplain is not always plentiful.

That the Homeland is semiarid and sparsely vegetated seems not to have elicited much reaction from Spanish and Mexican chroniclers of New Mexico. Both Spain and New Spain, after all, were basically dry places. That the Rio Arriba part of the Homeland is high and cold, however, did evoke reaction. From Francisco de Coronado to Antonio Barreiro, cold winters, especially in northern New Mexico, were the climatic element that most frequently prompted comment. The cold temperatures, it was understood, were the result of high altitude; neither Tejanos nor Californios, who lived at about the same latitude as New Mexico but on lowlands near coasts, experienced such harsh winters. Significantly, Hispanos who lived in the Rio Arriba apparently perceived their rugged terrain to be preferable. In her ethnography of Hot Springs (now Montezuma), a small village set at the foot of the snow-capped Sangre de Cristo Mountains a half-dozen miles northwest of Las Vegas, Helen Zunser noted in the 1930s that Spanish Americans "spoke of low flat land with derision."[2]

In adjusting to their natural environment, Hispanos encountered no major problems. To be sure, the severe winters in the Rio Arriba forced them to construct livestock shelters in addition to open corrals. While traveling through the Taos area in the dead of winter in 1846–47, George F. Ruxton was able to stable his mules in warm "sheds," where he fed them corn and corn shucks. And in the high Rio Arriba, where the growing season is short, wheat, a cold-weather grain, sometimes replaced corn. This probably explains why wheat tortillas are preferred today in the Rio Arriba, while corn tortillas are preferred in the Rio Abajo. But in response to rainfall that is scant and unreliable, Hispanos irrigated their crops, much as they had in Spain and New Spain. Lacking timber at elevations below sixty-five hundred feet, they constructed buildings with adobe brick, much as they had in Spain and New Spain. And when low-elevation pastures dried up in summer months, they drove their animals to lusher forage at higher elevations, an old Spanish practice known as transhumance.[3]

Besides water, what is precious in New Mexico is the limited amount of arable floodplain. To apportion this floodplain so that everyone had access to water, Hispanos employed longlots, an ingenious adjustment to a scarce resource that Alvar W. Carlson postulated was invented independently in New Mexico in the mid-1700s. Stretching between irrigation

[2] Yi-Fu Tuan and Cyril E. Everard, "New Mexico's Climate: The Appreciation of a Resource," *Natural Resources Journal* 4 (1964–65): 270–71; Helen Zunser, "A New Mexican Village," *Journal of American Folk-Lore* 48 (1935): 143.

[3] George Frederick Ruxton, *Wild Life in the Rocky Mountains*, 86, 91. According to Josiah Gregg, the feeding of livestock in the winter in New Mexico was "almost entirely unknown"; *Commerce of the Prairies*, ed. Max L. Moorhead, 114. According to Marc Simmons, who is writing a book on agriculture in New Mexico, Hispanos grew both winter wheat and spring wheat in the Rio Arriba; Simmons interview with author, Albuquerque, April 27, 1989. Regarding irrigation, adobe brick, and transhumance in Spain, see George M. Foster, *Culture and Conquest: America's Spanish Heritage*, Viking Fund Publications in Anthropology, no. 27, Wenner-Gren Foundation for Anthropological Research, 38, 56, 62, 70.

ditches and rivers, long-lots are ribbonlike fields that are fed water at the ditch end and drain by gravity across the floodplain to the river end (Map 10.1). In New Mexico, where Roman legal tradition has heirs inheriting land equally, long-lots are known to be subdivided into the narrowest strips, yet all heirs still have access to irrigation water. At the same time, then, long-lots are equitable and efficient, and they accommodate population growth. And where long-lots back up against rivers, Hispanos are careful not to disturb the trees that line the river banks. Louis B. Sporleder reported that along the Cucharas River at La Plaza de los Leones (Walsenburg), flooding happened only after Anglos came along in the 1870s and cut down this riparian vegetation.[4]

Destroying the riparian vegetation points up a contrast between how Anglos and Hispanos went about adjusting to the same environment. The difference is characterized in the Harvard University "Values Study" as Anglo "mastery-over-nature" as opposed to Hispano "subjugation-to-nature."[5] Subjugation means literally "to bring under the yoke of." Assuming that this is an apt characterization, Hispanos were more under the yoke of nature in the Rio Arriba than in the Rio Abajo. Rugged terrain, constricted floodplains, rigorous winters, and a short growing season were simply greater challenges for *arribeños* than for *rivajeños*. Not surprisingly, at the time of the American takeover the Rio Abajo was the more highly cultivated and the more productive of the two subregions. When writing of agriculture in 1844, Josiah Gregg characterized the Rio Abajo as containing "the principal wealth of New Mexico."[6] But to say that Hispanos were "subjugated" by nature is

---

[4] Alvar W. Carlson, "Long-Lots in the Rio Arriba," *Annals of the Association of American Geographers* 65 (1975): 53 (Carlson is drawn on heavily in this paragraph); Louis B. Sporleder, "La Plaza de los Leones," *Colorado Magazine* 10 (1933): 29.

[5] Florence Rockwood Kluckhohn and Fred L. Strodtbeck, *Variations in Value Orientations*, 13, 179.

[6] *Rivajeños*, Haley pointed out, is a contraction of *río bajeños*, a term for New Mexicans who lived downstream from Albuquerque; J. Evetts Haley, "The Comanchero Trade," *Southwestern Historical Quarterly* 38 (1934–35): 162. During the Mexican era, California was polarized between *abajeños* (southerners) and *arribeños* (northerners), which suggests that California was also divided into subregions; Leonard Pitt, *The Decline of the Californios: A Social History of the Spanish-Speaking Californians, 1846–1890*, 7. On the comparative wealth of the Rio Abajo, see Alvin R. Sunseri, "Agricultural Techniques in New Mexico at the Time of the Anglo-American Conquest," *Agricultural History* 47 (1973): 331–32; and Gregg, *Commerce of the Prairies*, 104, n. 9. In 1848, Donaciano Vigil correctly observed that the "principal wealth" of

perhaps overstating the case. The Hispanos' cultural baggage, after all, had prepared them for the dry environment, and they had coped successfully with the high and cold Rio Arriba. Indeed, their excessive overstocking of the Puerco basin is an example of actual environmental exploitation.

THE LANDSCAPE IMPRESS

As Hispanos adjusted to their environment, they stamped it with their cultural impress. There are hundreds of examples of the Hispano impress, and although none are apparently unique, several make the Hispano Homeland distinctive. Long-lots are a case in point. Besides Hispanos, Tejanos employed long-lots at San Antonio in 1731 and along the lower Rio Grande in the 1760s. Noting that there is no precedent for long-lots in Iberia or in New Spain, Terry G. Jordan postulated that long-lots at San Antonio were invented independently and that those along the lower Rio Grande diffused from French Louisiana.[7] Jordan reported that Stephen F. Austin employed long-lots in his colony in the Mexican era and that there are examples of the use of long-lots in Texas after the Mexican era. But in Texas long-lots are not commonplace. By contrast, in New Mexico they are ubiquitous. They dominate the cadastral pattern into which riverine properties are divided. In a relative way they make the landscape of the Homeland distinctive.

Villages are a second reason why, in a relative sense, the Hispano impress is distinctive. During most of their experience most Hispanos have lived in villages. In California and in Texas, Spanish-speaking people also lived in villages. But in those two parts of the Borderlands, especially in California during the Mexican era, land grants awarded to individuals for purposes of stock raising were, on a per capita basis, many times greater than those in New Mexico.[8] In California and Texas a greater percentage of people lived in dispersed ranchsteads. Thus, New Mexico, which was by far the most populous part of the Borderlands in Spanish and Mexican times,

---

New Mexico was in its livestock, not its agriculture; George Archibald McCall, *New Mexico in 1850: A Military View*, ed. Robert W. Frazer, 39.

[7] Terry G. Jordan, "Antecedents of the Long-Lot in Texas," *Annals of the Association of American Geographers* 64 (1974): 70–74, 76, 82, 84, 86.

[8] Pitt, *Decline of the Californios*, 11.

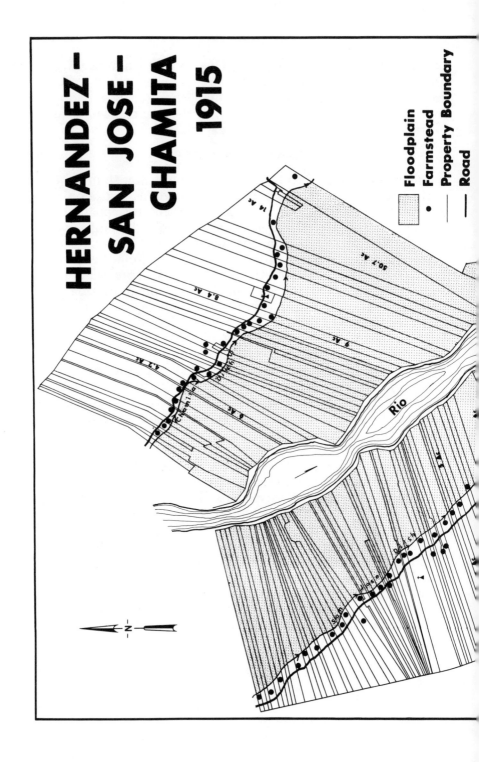

HERNANDEZ – SAN JOSE – CHAMITA 1915

Floodplain
Farmstead
Property Boundary
Road

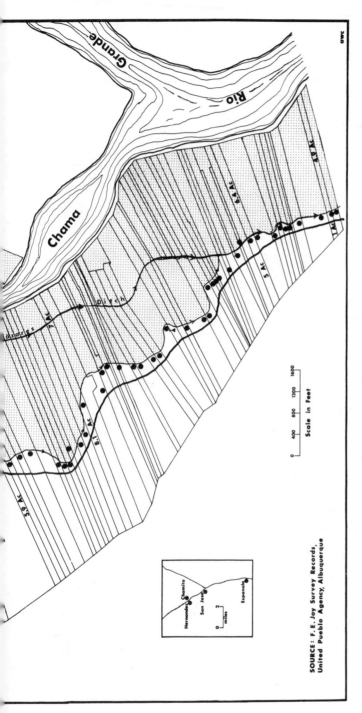

Map 10.1 Long-lots in the lower Chama Valley, Rio Arriba County, New Mexico, 1915. These long-lots are slices of floodplain and upland. Most farmsteads are located on upland just above the irrigation ditches. The three churches are foci of the three communities (see inset). This map was compiled by Alvar W. Carlson from surveys of Hispano claims within Pueblo Indian grants conducted in 1915 under Francis E. Joy of the General Land Office. It appears in Alvar W. Carlson, *The Spanish-American Homeland: Four Centuries in New Mexico's Río Arriba*, 44. Courtesy of the author and The Johns Hopkins University Press.

also had the highest proportion of people living in villages. In recent decades urbanization has of course siphoned off many one-time villagers. Yet New Mexico's "plazas" survive. Sprawling affairs of remarkably low density, with houses dispersed in linear fashion along the high sides of irrigation ditches or at intervals along roads, these loose agglomerations of people dominate the landscape of the Homeland. Indeed, in the American West, only Mormons, with roots in community-minded New England, live in rural villages to the same degree.

Log structures are a third example of the distinctive landscape impress. The Hispanos' habitat extends well above sixty-five hundred feet into a ponderosa pine life zone, and although adobe brick is the most common building material, even at high elevations, Hispanos also build with logs. Only in East Texas in the southwestern Borderlands did Spaniards also have available to them a pine forest resource, but their small numbers precluded much use of it. In New Mexico, however, Hispanos commonly build houses, barns, outbuildings, and even structures to house gristmills of notched and interlocked horizontally laid logs (Fig. 10.1). There appears to be little doubt that the technology for log construction was introduced by Spaniards instead of Anglos, for it was employed in New Mexico as early as the middle of the eighteenth century. And if John J. Winberry is correct that log construction techniques were taken to Mexico's Central Plateau by German miners in 1536, then this technology could conceivably have been introduced with Juan de Oñate.[9]

It is certain that the dome-shaped, outdoor, adobe ovens known as *hornos* were introduced with Oñate. *Hornos* are

[9] Gritzner correlated ecological life zones with building material availability and noted the Hispanos' universal preference for adobe; Charles Gritzner, "Construction Materials in a Folk Housing Tradition: Considerations Governing their Selection in New Mexico," *Pioneer America* 6 (1974): 26, 28, 29. John J. Winberry noted that shake roofing was used by Spaniards at Nacogdoches in 1767 and that such roofing was traditionally associated with corner-timbered log construction; "*Tejamanil*: The Origin of the Shake Roof in Mexico," *Proceedings of the Association of American Geographers* 7 (1975): 289, 292. In "Log Housing in New Mexico," *Pioneer America* 3 (1971): 54–62, Gritzner argued for the introduction of log construction from Mexico. He noted that the housing for a Santa Fe gristmill was constructed of horizontally laid notched logs in 1756; Charles F. Gritzner, "Hispano Gristmills in New Mexico," *Annals of the Association of American Geographers* 64 (1974): 518, 519. John J. Winberry, "The Log House in Mexico," *Annals of the Association of American Geographers* 64 (1974): 54, 62–64.

Fig. 10.1 The Córdova gristmill near Vadito, Taos County, New Mexico,
1967. When Gritzner took the photograph, the mill was approximately one hundred years old and was the only mill that was still
fully functional and located at its original site. Source: Charles F.
Gritzner, "Hispano Gristmills in New Mexico," *Annals of the
Association of American Geographers* 64 (1974): 514–24. Courtesy of the author and the *Annals*.

associated with wheat culture. They are found in Spain and in
New Mexico and Argentina—the relatively cold opposite ends
of Spain's New World empire where wheat is grown. According
to Marc Simmons, *hornos* are uncharacteristic of central Mexico, where corn is the favored grain. After their introduction
to New Mexico, *hornos* and the paraphernalia associated with
wheat culture, such as the metal sickle and milling technology, apparently diffused rather quickly among the Pueblo Indians.[10] In Spanish and Pueblo villages, then, *hornos* became the

[10] Florence Hawley Ellis found the remains of five hornos at San Gabriel del Yungue,
Oñate's capital after the winter of 1600–1601. Ellis was chief archeologist in the
excavation of San Gabriel between 1959–62. Florence Hawley Ellis, "The Long Lost
'City' of San Gabriel del Yungue, Second Oldest European Settlement in the United
States," in *When Cultures Meet, Remembering San Gabriel del Yunge Oweenge*, ed.
Herman Agoyo and Lynnwood Brown, 30. In a letter to the author dated February 6,
1983, Marc Simmons observed that the photograph shown in Michener's *Iberia* of the
family in Spain grouped around its *horno* could have been taken in New Mexico; also,

Fig. 10.2 In 1980 only two adobe *hornos* remained in El Cerrito. This one belonged to Albinita Quintana. By the end of the decade, because of disuse and erosion, both *hornos* had collapsed. Photograph RLN, May 17, 1980.

standard oven for baking wheat (and corn) products. They are commonplace today (Fig. 10.2). Given their scarcity in Mexico, California, and Texas, *hornos* are an item of material culture that sets the Homeland apart.

The impress of religion is also distinctive. Every Homeland village has its Roman Catholic church, centrally positioned with steeple and cross dominating the skyline. Villages with Penitente chapters have their moradas. In Chimayo the Santuario de Chimayo, which dates from 1816, annually draws thousands of pilgrims who seek to be cured by ingesting the *tierra bendita* or healing mud. Along rural roads and in the countryside are a variety of religious shrines. Also dotting the Homeland are scores of religious place names. Many, like San Miguel and San Jose, commemorate village patron saints, while others,

Marc Simmons, interview with author, Albuquerque, April 27, 1989, and letter to author, July 3, 1989. Foster noted that in Spain the sickle is used to harvest grain crops, whereas the scythe, which knocks grain from the heads, is used to harvest forage crops; *Culture and Conquest*, 55.

like Santa Fe (Holy Faith) and Santa Cruz (Holy Cross), are simply religious terms.[11] Except for the moradas and the Santuario de Chimayo, in a religious sense what differentiates the Homeland from other sections of the Borderlands is the sheer quantity of all these things.

PLACE IDENTITY

Ordinary Hispanos know intimately every bump on the landscape and every turn in the road in their own *patria chica*, meaning their native village and its adjacent area. And like Spaniards in Spain, ordinary Hispanos have an intense love for their community of birth. Pride in their natal place is fierce, and loyalty to it is unshakable, as in Spain. "To be Spanish American," wrote Margaret Mead in her study of New Mexico, "is to be of a village." In New Mexico, noted Olen E. Leonard and Charles P. Loomis, the individual is identified by his village of birth as much as by his family name.[12] What is known about the place identity of ordinary Hispanos, then, is their strong attachment to and identity with their own *patria chica*. Village prototypes in Spain explain why. A paucity of information, however, requires much conjecture when coming to grips with place identity beyond the *patria chica*.

Fray Angélico Chávez identified several images that were the basis for a sense of place beyond the *patria chica* in the Spanish period. Until 1771, New Mexico was called "the Kingdom and Provinces of New Mexico." By "Kingdom" what was meant was Santa Fe, the other Spanish communities, and the Pueblo villages that were staffed with resident friars. Chávez noted that the people themselves referred to their land as "the Kingdom" and hardly ever as "New Mexico." He also noted that the *Villa* of Santa Fe, because of its size and importance, was usually called simply *La Villa*, its inhabitants *Villeros*. Before 1771, at which time the *Provincias Internas* were cre-

---

[11] Stephen F. de Borhegyi documented the connection between earth eating (geophagy) at Chimayo and in the town of Esquipulas in southeastern Guatemala in Stephen F. de Borhegyi and E. Boyd, *El Santuario de Chimayo*, 2–23. The religious naming of towns is described in Fray Angélico Chávez, "Saints' Names in New Mexico Geography," *El Palacio* 56 (1949): 323–35; and Fray Angélico Chávez, "New Mexico Religious Place-Names Other Than Those of Saints," *El Palacio* 57 (1950): 23–26.

[12] Foster, *Culture and Conquest* 34–35; Margaret Mead, ed., *Cultural Patterns and Technical Change*, 152; Olen Leonard and C. P. Loomis, *Culture of a Contemporary Rural Community: El Cerrito, New Mexico*, Rural Life Studies, no. 1: 8.

ated and all of New Mexico became a "province," the term "provinces" referred to the unsettled areas around the periphery of the kingdom where the unchristianized Pueblo and nomad Indians lived. That this periphery was perceived to be dangerous country is confirmed by an eighteenth-century Spanish policy of establishing outposts, such as Ojo Caliente, Abiquiu, Las Trampas, Belen, Tome, and Sabinal, to serve as buffers against the nomad peoples. Indeed, in 1812, Pedro Bautista Pino conceived of all of New Mexico as one giant buffer between the settled parts of New Spain to the south and the warlike nomad Indians to the north.[13]

For the Mexican period David J. Weber likened geographical levels of the Hispanos' sense of place to widening circles of increasingly weaker loyalty. The innermost circle where loyalties were strongest was, of course, the *patria chica*. At the next level were four *partidos* or districts, whose head communities were Santa Fe, Santa Cruz, Albuquerque, and (until 1824) Paso del Norte. Then came the Rio Arriba and the Rio Abajo, subregions bifurcated by the so-called Rio del Norte, which Antonio Barreiro referred to in 1832 as the "Nile" and "the soul of the territory." The next level was New Mexico itself, which in the Mexican era was officially a "territory" (1824–36), then a "department" (1836–46). Finally, there was an awareness of Mexico as a nation. Antonio Barreiro noted that in 1832 New Mexicans celebrated *el diez y seis de Septiembre*, yet loyalties to distant Mexico seem to have been less strong than they were to the home province, which was also the case in California. Beyond the cordon of outposts that surrounded New Mexico were, of course, the *Indios bárbaros* in a dangerous frontier that Lansing B. Bloom said commenced just south of Socorro and as late as 1843 was being referred to as *la tierra afuera*, the land outside.[14]

[13] Fray Angélico Chávez, "The 'Kingdom of New Mexico,' " *New Mexico Magazine* 31, no. 8 (August 1953): 17, 58–59; no. 9 (September 1953): 17, 42–43; Pedro Bautista Pino, *Exposición . . .* , in *Three New Mexico Chronicles: The* Exposición *of Don Pedro Bautista Pino 1812; The* Ojeada *of Lic. Antonio Barreiro 1832; and the* Additions *by Don José Augustín de Escudero, 1849,* The Quivira Society Publications, vol. 11, trans. and ed. H. Bailey Carroll and J. Villasana Haggard, 71.

[14] David J. Weber's comments as a panel participant in a session organized by Clark S. Knowlton and entitled "The Spanish Americans: Independent Cultural Groupings or Mexican American Subculture?" (Western Social Science Association, Fort Worth, Texas, April 27, 1985); Hubert Howe Bancroft, *The Works of Hubert Howe Bancroft,* vol. 17, *History of Arizona and New Mexico, 1530–1888,* 311–12; Lansing Bartlett

The American takeover brought many changes in the Hispanos' sense of place. In her *No Separate Refuge*, Sarah
Deutsch analyzed one of them. About 1870, Hispano men
began to leave their villages to work seasonally for Anglos.
Anglo pull was always strongest to the north, especially to the
coal mines and sugar beet fields of Colorado. Entire families
eventually joined the migrant circuit, and many remained permanently. What evolved, to use Deutsch's terms, were "networks of kin" that found thousands of Hispanos interacting
between a northern New Mexico "village heartland" and "outposts" in Colorado—all in one giant "regional community."
Probably no contemporary Hispano used these terms to de-
scribe the phenomenon, yet for the thousands who engaged in
the seasonal pulsations out of New Mexico or who relocated
permanently to coal mining camps and beet field *colonias*,
there was a heightened awareness of the larger region beyond
the *patria chica*. Wages earned in Colorado, moreover, flowed
back to the villages, an affirmation of loyalty to the *patria
chica*, and perhaps, as Deutsch argued, a Hispanic strategy to
preserve a threatened culture.[15] In the 1930s the "regional
community" collapsed, thus ending Colorado's function as a
"separate refuge."

But what of the idea of a Homeland? Santa Fe–born Reverend
Jerome Martínez uses the evocative expression La Tierra Santa,
"The Holy Land," when referring to his land.[16] The common
term for referring to the Homeland, however, is *patria*, which
means fatherland. *Patria* embodies the aggregate of the hundreds of *patrias chicas* which ordinary Hispanos know intimately and for which they have sentimental and enduring

Bloom, "New Mexico under Mexican Administration, 1821–1846," *Old Santa Fe* 1
(1913–14): 12, 34, 157–58; Antonio Barreiro, *Ojeada . . .*, in "Barreiro's Ojeada Sobre
Nuevo-Mexico," trans. and ed. Lansing B. Bloom, *New Mexico Historical Review* 3
(1928): 79. Gregg noted that the common term for the Rio Grande among New
Mexicans in the Mexican era was the Rio del Norte; *Commerce of the Prairies*, 101.
Mexican-born Antonio Barreiro was president of the "grand commission" that put on
the celebration; Barreiro, *Ojeada . . .*, 73; David J. Weber, *The Mexican Frontier,
1821–1846: The American Southwest under Mexico*, Histories of the American Frontier, 255–72; Pitt, *Decline of the Californios*, 4, 6, 7, 25, 53, 174.
   [15] Sarah Deutsch, *No Separate Refuge: Culture, Class, and Gender on an Anglo-
Hispanic Frontier in the American Southwest, 1880–1940*, 101, 108, 116, 126, 155,
163, 164.
   [16] The Reverend Jerome Martínez, pastor at El Rito when interviewed at Ojo
Caliente, October 20, 1979, is today (1991) pastor at Santa María de la Paz Church in
Santa Fe.

feelings of attachment. The idea of a Homeland, then, is the totality of the *patrias chicas*. It is manifested in the mentality of a Tony Lucero, who chooses to leave California and return to his village of Placitas. It embraces a level of territorial consciousness or place identity that is uncommon in mainstream American society. The term *patria* is the closest Spanish-language equivalent for the "Homeland" idea.

HOMELAND MORPHOLOGY

Hispanos for the most part acted alone as they adjusted to their environment, stamped it with their impress, and created a sense of place. The areal growth and relative decline of the Homeland and its internal morphology, on the other hand, were products of interplay with non-Hispanos. Take, for example, areal growth. First, Spaniards encroached on the Pueblo Indians and created a missionary frontier whose outer boundary by 1680 was marked by Pueblo villages containing conventos. Santa Fe, the only authorized Spanish community, was an enclave in this Pueblo realm. Next, Hispanos reoccupied the area, founded new settlements, and by 1790 had transformed the old Pueblo realm to their own colonist province, the expansion of which all the while had been effectively contained by nomad Indians. The Pueblo villages were now enclaves in a Hispano realm. Finally, relatively peaceful times allowed Hispano sheepmen to expand in every direction, pushing the region's outer limits to about their greatest areal extent by 1900. Anglos blunted this expansion. Because areal gains and losses around the periphery of the region, except in Colorado, were relatively minor in the twentieth century, locational stability was reached about 1900 (Map 10.2).

In the interplay that brought about the relative decline in Hispano dominance, Anglos played the lead role. Anglo traders and trappers arrived after 1821, then came soldiers in 1846, and by 1850 modest numbers of each were found in the larger Hispano communities. The erosion of Hispano dominance had begun. After 1850 the number and variety of Anglo intruders increased, especially in the periphery of the Homeland, where, by 1900, Anglos were a majority. The interior half of the region in 1900 was still overwhelmingly Hispano, however. After 1900, Hispanos were increasingly pulled by Anglo economic opportunity from the interior to the periphery of their region,

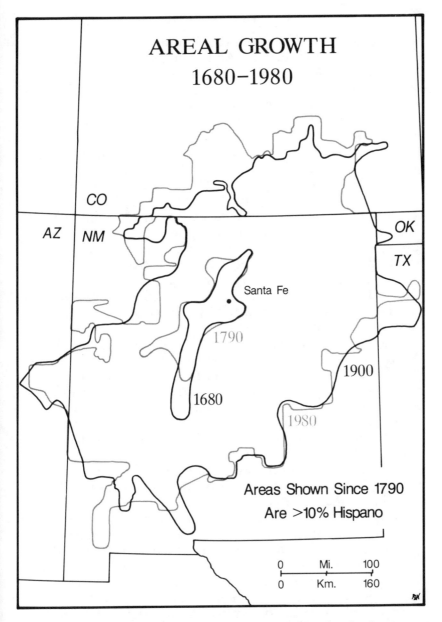

Map 10.2 Hispano areal growth, 1680–1980. Except in Colorado, the Homeland reached its greatest areal extent in 1900, at which time it
was the size of Utah. Omitted are all Homeland outliers and non-
Homeland inliers. Source: Compiled from maps in earlier chapters.

which to a degree evened out their numbers and reduced their percentages in the interior. And after the Great Depression, out of desperation, Hispanos left their villages and relocated in urban centers, which reduced the population in the countryside, created the present-day pattern of agglomerations, and further lowered Hispano percentages. Anglo intrusion meanwhile continued to be massive. By 1980 the exceptionally high Hispano percentages of 1900 were everywhere eroded except in the small Chimayo CCD (Map 10.3).

From all this interplay came a Homeland morphology, with the labels Stronghold, Inland, and Outland. The Stronghold (greater than 90 percent Hispano) existed by 1790, grew areally to about 1900, but had all but disappeared by 1980. The Inland (50–90 percent Hispano) consisted of discontinuous islands in 1850 which were considerably larger in 1900 and had coalesced to replace the Stronghold by 1980. The relatively short-lived Outland (10–50 percent Hispano) rose and fell between 1870 and 1930. Little more than rigidly defined gradations of Hispano dominance, these three zones portray the geographical outcomes of formative colonization, contiguous expansion, Anglo intrusion, and peripheral attraction (Fig. 10.3). As expanding and contracting areal entities, they call attention to the dynamic nature of the Homeland. As zones of internal gradation, they underscore the nonuniformity of the Homeland's surface. The Stronghold label, moreover, correctly suggests the image of a folk fortress, while the Inland and Outland labels usefully identify directions of movement.

In the United States the subculture whose morphology most closely parallels that of the Hispanos is probably that of the Louisiana French. In both cases Latin-derived folk societies were overrun by the dominant Anglo society, and in both cases the same morphological divisions were created: a zone where the folk society exceeded 90 percent of the population and was very much in political control, a zone where the folk society had been intruded upon yet still constituted the majority population (50–90 percent) and shared in political control, and a zone where the folk society had been pulled by Anglos to the region's periphery and was a minority population (10–50 percent) with little if any political control. One difference between Hispanos and the Louisiana French is that the Louisiana French moved through their evolutionary sequence a cen-

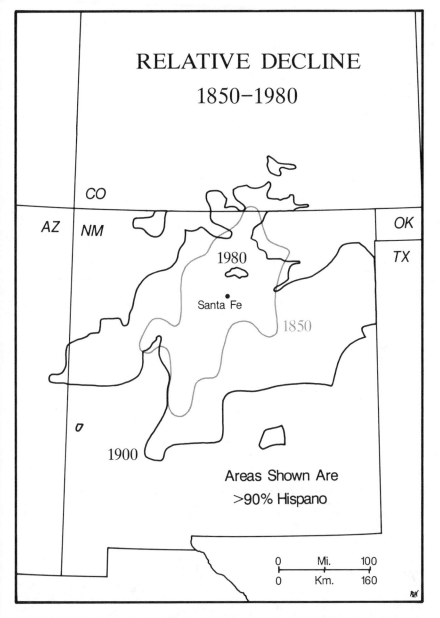

RELATIVE DECLINE
1850–1980

CO

AZ   NM   OK

                                                     TX

              1980

            Santa Fe

                        1850

      1900

            Areas Shown Are
            >90% Hispano

      0   Mi.   100
      0   Km.   160

Map 10.3 Hispano relative decline, 1850–1980. In 1900 an area the size of
         Tennessee was a minimum 90 percent Hispano, yet by 1980 only
         the Chimayo CCD exceeded 90 percent. Omitted in 1850 and 1900
         are small discontinuous inliers where Hispano percentages are less
         than 90 percent. Source: Compiled from maps in earlier chapters.

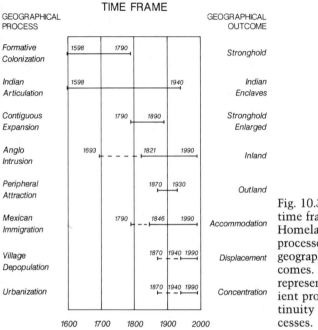

TIME FRAME

GEOGRAPHICAL
PROCESS

GEOGRAPHICAL
OUTCOME

Formative Colonization	1598 — 1790	Stronghold
Indian Articulation	1598 — 1940	Indian Enclaves
Contiguous Expansion	1790 — 1890	Stronghold Enlarged
Anglo Intrusion	1693 - - - 1821 — 1990	Inland
Peripheral Attraction	1870 — 1930	Outland
Mexican Immigration	1790 - - 1846 — 1990	Accommodation
Village Depopulation	1870 — 1940 - 1990	Displacement
Urbanization	1870 — 1940 - 1990	Concentration

1600   1700   1800   1900   2000

Fig. 10.3 Approximate time frames of eight Homeland-shaping processes and their geographical outcomes. Dashed lines represent either incipient processes or continuity between processes.

tury before Hispanos. In 1820, for example, the Louisiana French Stronghold equivalent (greater than 90 percent) was already much eroded, by 1860 small Saint James Parish was its sole remnant, and by 1900 it no longer existed.[17]

THE HEYDAY

In 1900 the Hispano Homeland was in its heyday. Spread over parts of five states, its 85,000 square miles made it as large as Utah. Of its 220,000 people, two-thirds were Hispanos. At its exact demographic center was Santa Fe, its largest Hispano community, its political and religious focus, the point within 150 miles of which 90 percent of all Hispanos lived. The interior half of the Homeland (42,315 square miles), an area the size of Tennessee, was a minimum 90 percent Hispano and averaged an incredibly high 97.1 percent. Indeed, twenty-nine

[17] Lawrence Ernest Estaville, Jr., "The Louisiana French Culture Region: Geographic Morphologies in the Nineteenth Century," (Ph.D. diss. [geography], University of Oklahoma, 1984) 1: 229, 232, 301, 316; 2: 366, 373.

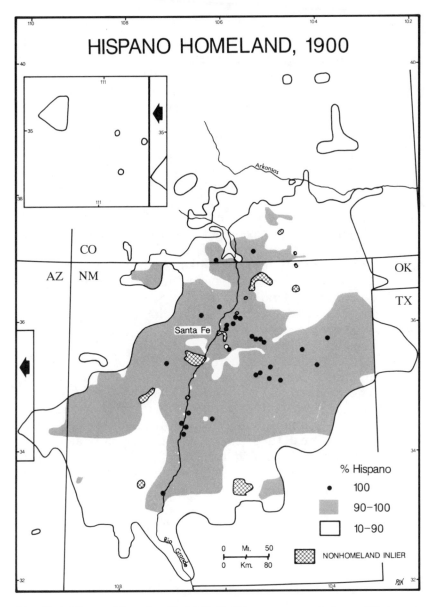

Map 10.4 Hispano Homeland in 1900. Half its area was a minimum 90 percent
Hispano, and 29 census precincts were 100 percent Hispano. Santa
Fe was the region's focus. Source: Population Schedules of the
Twelfth Census [1900].

census precincts, each containing at least one village, were 100 percent Hispano (Map 10.4).[18] Rarely in America has so large an area had such uniformly high percentages so recently. Given the Homeland's circular shape, its capital-city focus, its Hispano plurality, and its concentrated population, few parts of America would have made more ideal states, were geopolitical boundaries to have been redrawn.

Thus, like an island on the land, much of the Homeland in 1900 stood tall and flat, so uniformly high were its Hispano proportions. Its edges were like steep cliffs, so few Hispanos lived off the island. But then came the torrential shower of Anglos, falling on and all around the island. The lofty plateau with its high Hispano percentages was eroded to but one small butte. And as Anglos pulled Hispanos off the island, the steep cliffs became severely eroded banks. Such is the Homeland today: less majestic, but still an island that stands apart. Anglos eroding a Hispano island bring to mind Spaniards storming up the cliffs at Acoma to defeat the Pueblos on that particular island. History repeats itself.

The geographical outcome of four centuries of Hispano activity in the Borderlands, then, is the stuff of a Homeland: environmental adjustment, a landscape impress, a sense of place. The geographical outcome of Hispano interplay with non-Hispanos is the stuff of some cultural regions: gradations of dominance or a morphology which in this instance shows clearly the decline of the Hispano. And the legacy of all of this is a truly remarkable geographical entity, a distinctive part of America, the Homeland of the only surviving Spanish colonial subculture.

[18] Richard L. Nostrand, "The Hispano Homeland in 1900," *Annals of the Association of American Geographers* 70 (1980): 382, 384, 392, 393.

APPENDIX

⌖ ⌖ ⌖

SPANISH ANCESTRY DATA IN THE 1980 CENSUS

IN 1980, for the first time, the Bureau of the Census gathered data on one's ancestry or ethnicity regardless of the number of generations that person was removed from his or her country of origin. Question 14 in the long form, which was administered to some 19 percent of the population, asked "What is this person's ancestry"? By ancestry, the instructions explained, what was meant was "the nationality group, the lineage, or the country in which the person or the person's parents or ancestors were born before their arrival in the United States."[1] Those who were of more than one origin were to self-identify their multiple ancestry (for example, German-Irish). In the published results, wherein data were given for areas no smaller than states, 13,500,133 people responded that at least part of their ancestry was "Spanish," as this was coded by the bureau. Of the twenty-one "Spanish" ancestry groups reported in the census, "Mexican" (7,692,619), "Spanish/Hispanic" (2,686,680), "Puerto Rican" (1,443,862), and "Cuban" (597,702) were the largest. The rest (1,079,270) were primarily individual countries such as "Dominican" or "Colombian."[2] It looked like within the "Spanish/Hispanic" ancestry group some reliable data on Hispanos might finally be available.

But there were problems. That Hispanos identified themselves as "Spanish/Hispanic" was clear: New Mexico (21.6) and Colorado (5.3) led the nation in the percentage in each state that claimed this identity. But that many non-Hispanos also identified themselves as "Spanish/Hispanic" was just as clear: the number who self-identified as "Spanish/Hispanic" in California (539,285), for example, was nearly twice that in New Mexico (281,189). My inquiries about the Spanish/Hispanic ancestry group at the Ethnic and Spanish Statistics

---

[1] U.S. Bureau of the Census, "Your Guide to Census '80," Form D–4: 11.

[2] U.S. Bureau of the Census, *Census of Population: Ancestry of the Population by State, 1980*, Supplementary Report PC80-S1–10: 14, table 2.

Branch of the Population Division of the Bureau of the Census revealed that all "Spanish Categories" were assigned codes 200–43, and that three of them were combined to form "Spanish/Hispanic": 205 (Spanish), 206 (Spanish American), and 207 (Hispanic or Hispano[a]). Were I to want these more detailed data for units smaller than states, a special computer-generated tabulation would have to be run. Because the cost of such a tabulation for all codes for all states was prohibitive, my compromise was to purchase a breakdown of Spanish-category codes 200–12 by Census County Divisions (CCD) and by Incorporated Places and some Census Designated Places (CDP) for only the fifteen western states.[3]

Responses to codes 200–12 in New Mexico and Colorado are given in Table A.1. Following the categories employed by the bureau (that is, 200–204, "Spaniard"; 205–207, "Spanish/Hispanic"; 208, a part of "Other Spanish n.e.c." [not elsewhere classified]; and 209–12, "Mexican"), the relative strength of the Spanish/Hispanic category is obvious. What is not obvious is the high degree to which these Spanish/Hispanic responses were for a single ancestry. Tables in the published census distinguish between single- and multiancestry responses. In New Mexico and Colorado, 88.5 and 75.7 percent, respectively, of the responses to codes 205, 206, and 207 were for a single ancestry. By contrast, in Texas and especially California, where large numbers identified themselves to be Spanish/Hispanic, the percentages of single-ancestry response were only 63.5 percent and 50.8 percent, respectively.[4] Those in Texas or California who reported "Mexican" as a primary ancestry and "Spanish" or "Hispanic" as a secondary ancestry, or vice versa, for example, explain at least part of the sizable Spanish/Hispanic responses in those states.

The relative importance of codes 205, 206, and 207 for the fifteen states is shown in Table A.2. In all states the largest numbers reported "Spanish" (205), and in all states except California and Texas, "Spanish American" (206) was second, followed by "Hispanic/Hispano(a)" (207). In New Mexico and Colorado, 26.4 and 23.7 percent, respectively, identified themselves as "Spanish American" (206). Signifi-

[3] U.S. Bureau of the Census, *Ancestry of the Population*, 28, 31, table 3. Codes 200–43 are listed in U.S. Bureau of the Census, Data User Service Division, Census of Population and Housing, 1980, Summary Tape File (STF) 4 Technical Documentation, Classified Ancestry Code List, Codes 001–999, V–7-D–103 and V–7-D–104. The citation for the special tabulation is U.S. Bureau of the Census, Population Division, Census of Population and Housing, 1980, Summary Tape File (STF) 4 (data for long-form question 14 for fifteen states). An award of $4,600 from the University Research Council, Norman Campus, enabled me to purchase this special tabulation.

[4] U.S. Bureau of the Census, *Ancestry of the Population*, 46, 49, 50, table 3*a*; 64, 67, 68, table 3*b*.

Table A.1 Responses to Spanish Categories 200–12[a] (and estimates for codes 213–43)[b], New Mexico and Colorado, 1980

Code		New Mexico	Percent	Colorado	Percent
200	Spaniard/Spain	1,860		1,933	
201	Balearic/Canary/Majorca	52		34	
202	Basque (Spanish)	83	0.46	168	0.66
203	Catalan(a)/Catalonian	11		1	
204	Gallego(a)/Galician	48		23	
205	Spanish	189,618		111,173	
206	Spanish American	75,737	64.10	37,297	47.82
207	Hispanic/Hispano(a)	21,379		8,693	
208	Californio	23	} 0.01	55 }	0.02
209	Mexican/Mexico	106,483		114,396	
210	Mexican American	44,257	34.52	42,891	49.00
211	(Parts of Mexico)	18		7	
212	Chicano(a)	3,646		3,757	
213–43	Puerto Rican/Cuban/ parts of Middle-South America	4,126 }	0.92	8,218 }	2.50
	Total	447,341	100.01	328,646	100.00

Sources: See text.
[a] Persons reporting at least one ancestry group in U.S. Bureau of the Census, Population Division, Census of Population and Housing, 1980, Summary Tape File (STF) 4 (data for long-form question 14 for fifteen states).
[b] Persons reporting at least one ancestry group exclusive of the "Spaniard," "Spanish/Hispanic," and "Mexican" ancestry categories in U.S. Bureau of the Census, Ancestry of the Population, table 3, pp. 28 and 31.

cantly, the percentage reporting code 206 decreased in every direction away from New Mexico and Colorado. What this spatial gradient suggests is that "Spanish American" (206) everywhere identified basically, perhaps almost exclusively, Hispanos, whereas away from New Mexico and Colorado, "Spanish" (205) and "Hispanic/Hispano(a)" (207) began to identify mainly non-Hispanos.

Lacking data that specifically and reliably identified Hispanos, I chose the following procedure to estimate the total Hispano population. First, the high levels of single-ancestry responses in New Mexico and Colorado persuaded me that codes 205, 206, and 207 should all be included as counts of Hispanos in that core part of the Hispano region. This yielded 433,897 Hispanos (Table A.2). Second, the decreases in the percentages of those who reported themselves to be Spanish Americans (206) away from New Mexico and Colorado persuaded me that of the three codes, data for 206 were the most reliable for identifying Hispanos outside New Mexico and Colorado. I as-

Table A.2   Spanish/Hispanic Responses, Fifteen States, 1980[a]

| | 205 | | 206 | | 207 | | |
State	Spanish	Percent	Spanish American	Percent	Hispanic/ Hispano(a)	Percent	Total
Arizona	40,379	82.4	5,018	10.2	3,582	7.3	48,979
California	481,101	88.4	28,398	5.2	34,880	6.4	544,379
Colorado	111,173	70.7	37,297	23.7	8,693	5.5	157,163
Idaho	7,832	86.6	783	8.7	428	4.7	9,043
Kansas	9,320	85.8	1,020	9.4	521	4.8	10,861
Montana	3,202	90.3	254	7.2	89	2.5	3,545
Nebraska	5,763	89.5	468	7.3	207	3.2	6,438
Nevada	14,788	90.5	1,170	7.2	389	2.4	16,347
New Mexico	189,618	66.1	75,737	26.4	21,397	7.5	286,734
Oklahoma	12,624	86.0	1,541	10.5	513	3.5	14,678
Oregon	18,975	90.8	1,131	5.4	786	3.8	20,892
Texas	190,136	83.8	14,977	6.6	21,696	9.6	226,809
Utah	18,848	79.4	3,997	16.8	897	3.8	23,742
Washington	29,278	90.6	1,536	4.8	1,519	4.7	32,333
Wyoming	9,991	81.0	2,087	16.9	263	2.1	12,341
Total	1,143,028	80.8	172,414	12.4	95,842	6.8	1,414,284

SOURCE: U.S. Bureau of the Census, Population Division, Census of Population and Housing, 1980, Summary Tape File (STF) 4 (data for long-form question 14 for fifteen states).
[a] Persons reporting at least one ancestry group.

sumed that if a quarter of all Hispanos identified with Spanish American (206) in New Mexico and Colorado, then the same proportion would likely prevail in the other thirteen states to which Hispanos had moved. Therefore, I multiplied counts for 206 by four to determine the total Hispano population outside New Mexico and Colorado, which yielded a total 249,520. The sum of these two figures, 693,417, not only ignores any Hispanos not in the fifteen states, but is only a crude estimate within the fifteen states.

My procedure for mapping the Homeland in 1980 was much more conservative. I assumed that codes 205, 206, and 207 represented Hispanos in New Mexico and Colorado. After all, members of this subculture had for decades been concentrated there, and those who self-identified as Spanish, Spanish American, or Hispanic/Hispano(a) were giving by and large single-ancestry responses. However, I chose to limit the area where codes 205, 206, and 207 were still valid at the line that represented a Hispano minimum of 10 percent per CCD. This seemingly arbitrarily chosen criterion was justified in delimiting the Hispano Homeland in 1900, and for consistency I employed it once again. I made only one notable exception: the Denver CCD, although only 7.7 percent Hispano, had 38,007 Hispanos, who were counted. Thus regionalized, the Homeland embraced much of New Mexico and southern Colorado, with minor extensions into Arizona and Texas, plus three distant tiny outliers in Wyoming, Utah, and Kansas. The number of Hispanos living within the Homeland was 364,545.

BIBLIOGRAPHY

MANUSCRIPT MATERIALS

Census of Santa Fe, 1841. Mexican Archives of New Mexico. State Records Center and Archives, Santa Fe.

[Clergymen of] "Archdiocese of Santa Fe." Undated typescript. Chancery Office, Archdiocese of Santa Fe, Albuquerque.

Gibson, Charles E., Jr. Interview no. 18 (1934). Civil Works Administration Pioneer Interviews, Pamphlet 349, Alamosa, Conejos, and Costilla counties. Documentary Resources Department, Colorado Historical Society, Denver.

Hope Decree, 1933. State Engineer Office, Santa Fe.

"Parishes in the Archdiocese of Santa Fe." Undated typescript. Chancery Office, Archdiocese of Santa Fe, Albuquerque.

Plat of the San Miguel del Bado Grant, Tracts 1, 3–10, surveyed by Wendell V. Hall, December 9, 1902–February 8, 1903, approved by Court of Private Land Claims, June 14, 1904. Bureau of Land Management, Santa Fe.

Private Land Claims Docket No. 119, San Miguel del Bado Grant, January 6, 1910. General Land Office Record of Patents. Bureau of Land Management, Santa Fe.

Santa Fe Baptisms. Archives of the Archdiocese of Santa Fe. State Records Center and Archives, Santa Fe.

Santa Fe Marriages. Archives of the Archdiocese of Santa Fe. State Records Center and Archives, Santa Fe.

Saint Louis College/University students from New Mexico, 1831–1853. Comp. Catherine Weidle. Pius XII Library, Saint Louis University, Saint Louis, ca. 1987.

U.S. Bureau of the Census, Data User Services Division. Census of Population and Housing, 1980: Summary Tape File 4 Technical Documentation, Classified Ancestry Code List, Codes 001–999. Washington, D.C., 1980, 1981.

———, Population Division. Census of Population and Housing,

1980, Summary Tape File 4 (data for long-form question 14 for fifteen states). Washington, D.C., 1986. In possession of the author.

INTERVIEWS AND PERSONAL CORRESPONDENCE

Aragón, Candido, and Mary (Barela) Aragón, residents, Pueblo, Colorado. Interview, July 7, 1988.

Aragón, Luis Roberto, and Linda (Quintana) Aragón, residents, El Cerrito. Interview, July 4, 1988.

Atencio, Olivama J., postmistress, Chamisal, New Mexico. Interview, August 15, 1980.

Candelaria, Juanita, Senior Citizens' Center, Manzano, New Mexico. Interview, August 14, 1980.

Conway, John R., pastor, Saint Alice Church, Mountainair, New Mexico. Interview, October 22, 1979.

Flores, Tobias, treasurer, San Miguel del Bado Grant Commission, Villanueva, New Mexico. Interview, May 17, 1980.

Hammond, Robert, visiting pastor, Immaculate Conception Church, Muleshoe, Texas. Interview, August 22, 1969.

Huertado, Locario, president, San Miguel del Bado Grant Commission, San Miguel, New Mexico. Interview, April 26, 1980.

Lanstra, John (Jack), and Heidi Lanstra, residents, El Cerrito, New Mexico. Thirteen interviews between March 28 and December 7, 1980.

Leonard, Olen E., U.S. Department of Agriculture, retired, Tucson. Personal correspondence, August 25, 1980.

Loomis, Charles P., professor emeritus of sociology, Michigan State University, retired, Las Cruces. Personal correspondence, August 12, 1980, and December 27, 1980.

Lovato, Mel, resident, San Luis, New Mexico. Interview, August 17, 1980.

Lucero, George, Lucero's Grocery, Chamisal, New Mexico. Interview, October 16, 1979.

Lucero, Tony, real estate (agent-owner), Placitas, New Mexico. Interview, Albuquerque, April 28, 1989.

Martínez, Jerome, pastor, Saint John's Church, El Rito, New Mexico. Interview, Ojo Caliente, October 20, 1979.

Meyer, Howard, pastor, Immaculate Conception Church, Cuba, New Mexico. Interview, October 27, 1979.

Miera, Theresa, principal, Peñasco Elementary School, Peñasco, New Mexico. Interview, August 16, 1980.

Perrigo, Lynn I., professor emeritus of history, New Mexico Highlands University, Las Vegas. Personal correspondence, April 4, 1980, and November 12, 1984.

Quintana, Abran, and Margarita (Margie Trujillo) Quintana, residents, El Cerrito, New Mexico. Four interviews between March 29 and August 12, 1980.

Quintana, Eduardo E., and Jesucita (Gutiérrez) Quintana, residents, Pueblo, Colorado. Interview, July 8, 1988.

Quintana, Elvira (Corrales), resident, Rocky Ford, Colorado. Interview, July 9, 1988.

Quintana, Florencio, and Agneda (González) Quintana, residents, El Cerrito, New Mexico. Eight interviews between March 29 and December 7, 1980.

Quintana, Florencio, and Helen (C. de Baca) Quintana, residents, Pueblo, Colorado. Interview, El Cerrito, New Mexico, July 3, 1988.

Quintana, Rick, and Repita (Chacón) Quintana, residents, El Cerrito. Interview, July 5, 1988.

Sánchez, George I., professor, Latin American Education, University of Texas, Austin. Personal correspondence, September 29, 1969.

Sena, Joe, and Mary (Quintana) Sena, residents, Pueblo, Colorado. Interview, July 8, 1988.

Simmons, Marc, historian, Cerrillos, New Mexico. Interview, Albuquerque, April 27, 1989.

———. Personal correspondence, February 6, 1983, and July 3, 1989.

Spencer, Joseph E., professor, Department of Geography, University of California, Los Angeles. Interview, August 27, 1969.

Tapia, Abel, and Josie (Martínez) Tapia, residents, Pueblo, Colorado. Interview, July 8, 1988.

Taylor, Rafelita Lovato, resident, Cuba, New Mexico. Interview, August 17, 1980.

Torres, Annabelle, store owner in Peñasco, resident of Rodarte, New Mexico. Interview, August 16, 1980.

Torres, Macario, and Rose (Sandovál) Torres, residents, Pueblo, Colorado. Interview, July 6, 1988.

Vogt, Evon Z., professor, Department of Sociology, Harvard University. Interview, University of Massachusetts, Amherst, October 29, 1970.

THESES AND PAPERS

Andrews, John Philip. "History of Rural Spanish Settlement and Land Use in the Upper Culebra Basin of the San Luis Valley, Costilla County, Colorado." Master's thesis (geography), University of Colorado, 1972.

Bailey, David Thomas. "Stratification and Ethnic Differentiation in Santa Fe, 1860 and 1870." Ph.D. diss. (sociology), University of Texas, Austin, 1975.

Baydo, Gerald Robert. "Cattle Ranching in Territorial New Mexico." Ph.D. diss. (history), University of New Mexico, 1970.

Bloom, Maude Elizabeth McFie. "A History of Mesilla Valley." Bachelor's thesis, New Mexico College of Agriculture and Mechanic Arts, Mesilla Park, 1903.

Charles, Ralph. "Development of the Partido System in the New Mexico Sheep Industry." Master's thesis (economics), University of New Mexico, 1940.

Ebright, Malcolm. "The Tecolote Land Grant." Paper read at the Historical Society of New Mexico Annual Conference, Montezuma, New Mexico, June 7, 1986.

Estaville, Lawrence Ernest, Jr. "The Louisiana French Culture Region: Geographic Morphologies in the Nineteenth Century." 2 vols. Ph.D. diss. (geography), University of Oklahoma, 1984.

Ethell, Ora Gjerde. "A Study of Fifty Spanish-Speaking and Mexican Families in Denver County Granted Aid to Dependent Children from April to October 1936 and Receiving Grants Continuously to June 1942." Master's thesis (social work), University of Denver, 1943.

Foster, H. Mannie. "History of Mormon Settlements in Mexico and New Mexico." Master's thesis (history), University of New Mexico, 1937.

Gadd, Milan W. "Significant Problems of Spanish-Speaking Persons and a Study of Their Registrations in the Denver Office of the Colorado State Employment Service." Master's thesis (social work), University of Denver, 1941.

Hernández, Andrés S. "This They Said (a Report of Interviews with Old-Time Residents of Las Vegas and San Miguel County, New Mexico)." Seminar paper, New Mexico Highlands University, Las Vegas, June 1, 1955.

Howard, Donald S. "A Study of the Mexican, Mexican-American and Spanish-American Population in Pueblo, Colorado, 1929–1930." Master's thesis (sociology), University of Denver, 1930.

Hurt, Wesley Robert, Jr. "Manzano: A Study of Community Disorganization." Master's thesis (sociology), University of New Mexico, 1941.

Kluckhohn, Florence Rockwood. "Los Atarqueños: A Study of Patterns and Configurations in a New Mexico Village." 2 vols. Ph.D. diss. (sociology), Radcliffe College, 1941.

Lehmann, Terry Jon. "Santa Fe and Albuquerque 1870–1900: Contrast and Conflict in the Development of Two Southwestern Towns." Ph.D. diss. (history), Indiana University, 1974.

McConville, J. Lawrence. "A History of Population in the El Paso–Cuidad Juarez Area." Master's thesis (Latin American studies), University of New Mexico, 1966.

Morton, Dorothy Virginia. "A History of Quay County, New Mexico." Master's thesis (history), University of Colorado, 1938.

Reese, Linda. "Anglo Intrusion to Hispanic Roswell: Frontier Articulation in Nineteenth-Century New Mexico." Paper read at Eleventh Comparative Frontier Symposium, University of Oklahoma, Norman, April 5, 1985.

Rubright, Lynnell. "A Sequent Occupance of the Espanola Valley, New Mexico." Master's thesis (geography), University of Colorado, 1967.

Sandoval, T. Joe. "A Study of Some Aspects of the Spanish-Speaking Population in Selected Communities in Wyoming." Master's thesis (education), University of Wyoming, 1946.

Trindell, Roger Thomas. "Sequent Occupance of Pueblo, Colorado." Master's thesis (geography), University of Colorado, 1960.

Weber, David J. Participant in panel, "The Spanish Americans: Independent Cultural Groupings or Mexican American Subculture?" organized by Clark S. Knowlton. Western Social Science Association, Fort Worth, Texas, April 27, 1985.

Winnie, William W., Jr. "The Hispanic People of New Mexico." Master's thesis, University of Florida, 1955.

GOVERNMENT PUBLICATIONS

Abel, Annie Heloise, ed. The Official Correspondence of James S. Calhoun while Indian Agent at Santa Fé and Superintendent of Indian Affairs in New Mexico. Washington, D.C.: Government Printing Office, 1915.

Carleton, James Henry. "Diary of an Excursion to the Ruins of Abó, Quarra, and Gran Quivira, in New Mexico, under the Command of Major James Henry Carleton, U.S.A." Ninth Annual Report of the Board of Regents of the Smithsonian Institution. Washington, D.C.: A. O. P. Nicholson, Public Printer, 1855.

Leonard, Olen, and C. P. Loomis. Culture of a Contemporary Rural Community: El Cerrito, New Mexico. Rural Life Studies, no. 1. Washington, D.C.: Department of Agriculture, Bureau of Agricultural Economics, 1941.

Rusinow, Irving. A Camera Report on El Cerrito, a Typical Spanish-American Community in New Mexico. Miscellaneous Publication no. 479. Washington, D.C.: Department of Agriculture, Bureau of Agricultural Economics, 1942.

U.S. Bureau of the Census. Census of Population: American Indian Areas and Alaska Native Villages, 1980. Supplementary Report no. PC80-S1–13. Washington, D.C.: Government Printing Office, 1984.

———. *Census of Population: Ancestry of the Population by State, 1980.* Supplementary Report no. PC80-S1-10. Washington, D.C.: Government Printing Office, 1983.

———. *Census of Population, 1960: Subject Reports, Persons of Spanish Surname.* Final Report no. PC(2)-1B. Washington, D.C.: Government Printing Office, 1963.

———. "Persons of Spanish Surname." In *Census of Population, 1950,* vol. 4, *Special Reports,* part 3, chapter C. Washington, D.C.: Government Printing Office, 1953.

———. Population Schedules of the Ninth Census [1870]. Microcopy no. M-593. Washington, D.C.: National Archives Microfilm Publications, 1965.

———. Population Schedules of the Seventh Census [1850]. Microcopy no. 432. Washington, D.C.: National Archives Microfilm Publications, n.d.

———. Population Schedules of the Tenth Census [1880]. Microcopy no. T-9. Washington, D.C.: Bureau of the Census Microfilm Lab, n.d.

———. Population Schedules of the Thirteenth Census [1910]. Microcopy no. T-624. Washington, D.C.: National Archives Microfilm Publications, n.d.

———. Population Schedules of the Twelfth Census [1900]. Microcopy no. T-623. Washington, D.C.: National Archives Microfilm Publications, n.d.

———. *Population of the United States in 1860; Compiled from the Original Returns of the Eighth Census. . . .* Washington, D.C.: Government Printing Office, 1864.

———. *Population of the United States . . . Compiled from the Original Returns of the Ninth Census . . . , 1870.* Washington, D.C.: Government Printing Office, 1872.

———. "Your Guide to Census '80." Form D-4. Washington, D.C.: Government Printing Office, 1979.

U.S. Department of Agriculture, Soil Conservation Service. *Population of the Upper Rio Grande Watershed.* Regional Bulletin no. 43, Conservation Economics Series no. 16. Albuquerque: Southwest Region, 1937.

———. *A Report on the Cuba Valley.* Regional Bulletin no. 36, Conservation Economics Series no. 9. Albuquerque: Southwest Region, 1937.

———. *The Spanish-American Villages,* vol. 2, *Tewa Basin Study, 1935.* Albuquerque: Economic Surveys Division, Southwest Region, 1939. Reprinted in *Hispanic Villages of Northern New Mexico,* ed. Marta Weigle, 29–212. Santa Fe: The Lightning Tree, 1975.

———. *Village Dependence on Migratory Labor in the Upper Rio*

Grande Area. Regional Bulletin no. 47, Conservation Economics Series no. 20. Albuquerque: Southwest Region, 1937.

U.S. Geological Survey. *Twelfth Annual Report to the Secretary of the Interior, 1890–'91,* part 2, "Irrigation." Washington, D.C.: Government Printing Office, 1891.

———. Villanueva Quadrangle, 15-minute series, 1960.

BOOKS AND PAMPHLETS

Abert, J. W. *Abert's New Mexico Report, 1846–'47.* 1848. Reprint. Albuquerque: Horn & Wallace, Publishers, 1962.

Bancroft, Hubert Howe. *The Works of Hubert Howe Bancroft,* vol. 17, *History of Arizona and New Mexico, 1530–1888.* San Francisco: The History Company, 1889.

———. *The Works of Hubert Howe Bancroft,* vol. 19, *History of California,* vol. 2, *1801–1824.* San Francisco: The History Company, 1886.

———. *The Works of Hubert Howe Bancroft,* vol. 22, *History of California,* vol. 5, *1846–1848.* San Francisco: The History Company, 1886.

Barreiro, Antonio. *Ojeada.* . . . Puebla, Mexico, 1832. Reprinted in "Barreiro's Ojeada Sobre Nuevo-Mexico," trans. and ed. Lansing B. Bloom, *New Mexico Historical Review* 3 (1928): 73–96, 145–78.

Baxter, John O. *Las Carneradas: Sheep Trade in New Mexico 1700–1860.* Albuquerque: University of New Mexico Press, 1987.

Bieber, Ralph P., ed. *Southern Trails to California in 1849.* The Southwest Historical Series, vol. 5. Glendale, Calif.: Arthur H. Clark Company, 1937.

Bolton, Herbert E. *The Spanish Borderlands: A Chronicle of Old Florida and the Southwest.* Chronicles of America Series, vol. 23. New Haven: Yale University Press, 1921.

Bowden, J. J. *Private Land Claims in the Southwest.* 6 vols. Houston: privately published, 1969.

Brown, Ralph H. *Historical Geography of the United States.* New York: Harcourt, Brace and World, 1948.

Bunting, Bainbridge. *Taos Adobes: Spanish Colonial and Territorial Architecture of the Taos Valley.* Santa Fe: Museum of New Mexico Press, 1964.

Callon, Milton W. *Las Vegas, New Mexico, the Town That Wouldn't Gamble.* Las Vegas, N.M.: Las Vegas Publishing Company, 1962.

Campa, Arthur L. *A Bibliography of Spanish Folk-Lore in New Mexico.* University of New Mexico Bulletin, Language Series, vol. 2, no. 3, whole no. 176:1–28. Albuquerque: University of New Mexico, 1930.

————. *Spanish Folk-Poetry in New Mexico*. Albuquerque: University of New Mexico Press, 1946.

————. *The Spanish Folksong in the Southwest*. University of New Mexico Bulletin, Modern Language Series, vol. 4, no. 1, whole no. 232:1–67. Albuquerque: University of New Mexico Press, 1933.

Carlson, Alvar W. *The Spanish-American Homeland: Four Centuries in New Mexico's Río Arriba*. Baltimore: The Johns Hopkins University Press, 1990.

Carlson, Paul H. *Texas Woollybacks: The Range Sheep and Goat Industry*. College Station: Texas A&M University Press, 1982.

Chávez, Fray Angélico. *La Conquistadora: The Autobiography of an Ancient Statue*. Paterson, N.J.: Saint Anthony Guild Press, 1954.

————. *Origins of New Mexico Families in the Spanish Colonial Period*. Santa Fe: The Historical Society of New Mexico, 1954.

Cobos, Rubén. *A Dictionary of New Mexico and Southern Colorado Spanish*. Santa Fe: Museum of New Mexico Press, 1983.

Corwin, Arthur F., ed. *Immigrants—and Immigrants: Perspectives on Mexican Labor Migration to the United States*. Westport, Conn.: Greenwood Press, 1978.

Craver, Rebecca McDowell. *The Impact of Intimacy: Mexican-Anglo Intermarriage in New Mexico, 1821–1846*. Southwestern Studies Monograph no. 66. El Paso: Texas Western Press, 1982.

Davis, W. W. H. *El Gringo: New Mexico and Her People*. 1857. Reprint. Lincoln: University of Nebraska Press, 1982.

de Borhegyi, Stephen F., and E. Boyd. *El Santuario de Chimayo*. 1956. Reprint. Santa Fe: Ancient City Press, 1987.

De León, Arnoldo. *The Tejano Community, 1836–1900*. Albuquerque: University of New Mexico Press, 1982.

Deutsch, Sarah. *No Separate Refuge: Culture, Class, and Gender on an Anglo-Hispanic Frontier in the American Southwest, 1880–1940*. New York: Oxford University Press, 1987.

Ducker, James H. *Men of the Steel Rails: Workers on the Atchison, Topeka & Santa Fe Railroad, 1869–1900*. Lincoln: University of Nebraska Press, 1983.

Edmonson, Munro S. *Los Manitos: A Study of Institutional Values*. New Orleans: Middle American Research Institute, Tulane University, 1957.

Elliott, J. H. *Imperial Spain, 1469–1716*. New York: St. Martin's Press, 1963.

Escudero, José Augustín de. *Additions*. Mexico City, 1849. Reprinted in *Three New Mexico Chronicles: The* Exposición *of Don Pedro Bautista Pino 1812;* The Ojeada *of Lic. Antonio Barreiro 1832; and the* Additions *by Don José Augustín de Escudero, 1849*, trans.

and ed. H. Bailey Carroll and J. Villasana Haggard. The Quivira Society Publications, vol. 11. Albuquerque: The Quivira Society, 1942.

Espinosa, Aurelio M. *The Folklore of Spain in the American Southwest: Traditional Spanish Folk Literature in Northern New Mexico and Southern Colorado*, ed. J. Manuel Espinosa. Norman: University of Oklahoma Press, 1985.

———. *Los Comanches: A Spanish Heroic Play of the Year Seventeen Hundred and Eighty*. University of New Mexico Bulletin, Language Series, vol. 1, no. 1, whole no. 45:1–46. Albuquerque: University of New Mexico, 1907.

———. *The Spanish Language in New Mexico and Southern Colorado*. Historical Society of New Mexico, no. 16. Santa Fe: New Mexican Printing Company, 1911.

———. *Studies in New Mexican Spanish*. University of New Mexico Bulletin, Language Series, vol. 1, no. 2, whole no. 53:47–162. Albuquerque: University of New Mexico, 1909.

Espinosa, José E. *Saints in the Valleys: Christian Sacred Images in the History, Life, and Folk Art of Spanish New Mexico*. Albuquerque: University of New Mexico Press, 1960.

Fergusson, Erna. *New Mexico: A Pageant of Three Peoples*. New York: Alfred A. Knopf, 1951.

Floyd, Ethel L., and R. T. Floyd, eds. *Torrance County History*. Estancia, N.M.: Torrance County Historical Society, 1979.

Foster, George M. *Culture and Conquest: America's Spanish Heritage*. Wenner-Gren Foundation for Anthropological Research, Viking Fund Publications in Anthropology, no. 27. Chicago: Quadrangle Books, 1960.

Gámio, Manuel. *Mexican Immigration to the United States: A Study of Human Migration and Adjustment*. Chicago: University of Chicago Press, 1930.

Garrard, Lewis H. *Wah-To-Yah and the Taos Trail*. 1850. Reprint. Palo Alto: American West Publishing Company, 1968.

González, Nancie L. *The Spanish-Americans of New Mexico: A Heritage of Pride*. Albuquerque: University of New Mexico Press, 1969.

Grebler, Leo. *Mexican Immigration to the United States: The Record and Its Implications*. Mexican-American Study Project, Advance Report no. 2. Los Angeles: Division of Research, Graduate School of Business Administration, University of California, Los Angeles, 1966.

———; Joan W. Moore; and Ralph C. Guzmán. *The Mexican-American People: The Nation's Second Largest Minority*. New York: Free Press, 1970.

Gregg, Josiah. *Commerce of the Prairies*, ed. Max L. Moorhead. 1844. Reprint. Norman: University of Oklahoma Press, 1954.

Hackett, Charles Wilson. *Revolt of the Pueblo Indians of New Mexico and Otermín's Attempted Reconquest, 1680–1682*. Coronado Cuarto Centennial Publications, 1540–1940, ed. George P. Hammond, vols. 8, 9. Albuquerque: University of New Mexico Press, 1942.

Hafen, LeRoy R., and Ann W. Hafen. *Old Spanish Trail: Santa Fé to Los Angeles*. The Far West and the Rockies Historical Series, 1820–1875, vol. 1. Glendale, Calif.: Arthur H. Clark Company, 1954.

Hall, G. Emlen. *Four Leagues of Pecos: A Legal History of the Pecos Grant, 1800–1933*. New Mexico Land Grant Series. Albuquerque: University of New Mexico Press, 1984.

Hammond, George P. *Don Juan de Oñate and the Founding of New Mexico*. Historical Society of New Mexico Publications in History, vol. 2. Santa Fe: El Palacio Press, 1927.

———, and Agapito Rey, eds. *Don Juan de Oñate, Colonizer of New Mexico, 1595–1628*. Coronado Cuarto Centennial Publications, 1540–1940, vols. 5, 6, ed. George P. Hammond. Albuquerque: University of New Mexico Press, 1953.

Harper, Allan G.; Andrew R. Córdova; and Kalervo Oberg. *Man and Resources in the Middle Rio Grande Valley*. Inter-American Studies, vol. 2. Albuquerque: University of New Mexico Press, 1943.

Hertzog, Peter. *The Gringo & Greaser*. Western Americana Series, no. 6. Santa Fe: The Press of the Territorian, 1964.

Horgan, Paul. *Lamy of Santa Fe: His Life and Times*. New York: Farrar, Straus and Giroux, 1975.

Hughes, Anne E. *The Beginnings of Spanish Settlement in the El Paso District*. University of California Publications in History, vol. 1, no. 3:295–392. Berkeley: University of California Press, 1914.

Jaffe, A. J.; Ruth M. Cullen; and Thomas D. Boswell. *The Changing Demography of Spanish Americans*. New York: Academic Press, 1980.

Johansen, Sigurd. *Rural Social Organization in a Spanish-American Culture Area*. University of New Mexico Publications in Social Sciences and Philosophy, no. 1. Albuquerque: University of New Mexico Press, 1948.

Jones, Oakah L., Jr. *Los Paisanos: Spanish Settlers on the Northern Frontier of New Spain*. Norman: University of Oklahoma Press, 1979.

Kercheville, F. M., and George E. McSpadden. *A Preliminary Glossary of New Mexican Spanish, together with Some Semantic and Philological Facts of the Spanish Spoken in Chilili, New Mexico.* University of New Mexico Bulletin, Language Series, vol. 5, no. 3, whole no. 247:1–102. Albuquerque: University of New Mexico Press, 1934.

Kessell, John L. *The Missions of New Mexico since 1776.* Albuquerque: University of New Mexico Press, 1980.

Kluckhohn, Florence Rockwood, and Fred L. Strodtbeck. *Variations in Value Orientations.* Evanston, Ill.: Row, Peterson, 1961.

Kubler, George. *The Religious Architecture of New Mexico in the Colonial Period and since the American Occupation.* Albuquerque: University of New Mexico Press, 1940.

———. *Santos: An Exhibition of the Religious Folk Art of New Mexico.* Fort Worth: Amon Carter Museum of Western Art, 1964.

Lecompte, Janet. *Pueblo, Hardscrabble, Greenhorn: The Upper Arkansas, 1832–1856.* Norman: University of Oklahoma Press, 1978.

Leonard, Olen E. *The Role of the Land Grant in the Social Organization and Social Processes of a Spanish-American Village in New Mexico.* [1943]. Reprint. Albuquerque: Calvin Horn Publisher, 1970.

Lovell, Emily Kalled. *A Personalized History of Otero County, New Mexico.* Alamogordo: Star Publishing Company, 1963.

Lummis, Charles F. *The Land of Poco Tiempo.* 1893. Reprint. Albuquerque: University of New Mexico Press, 1966.

Mayer, Vincente V., Jr., ed. *Utah: A Hispanic History.* Salt Lake City: American West Center, University of Utah, 1975.

Mays, Buddy, and Marc Simmons. *People of the Sun: Some Out-of-Fashion Southwesterners.* Albuquerque: University of New Mexico Press, 1979.

McCall, George Archibald. *New Mexico in 1850: A Military View,* ed. with intro. by Robert W. Frazer. [1850]. Reprint. Norman: University of Oklahoma Press, 1968.

McCarty, John L. *Maverick Town: The Story of Old Tascosa.* Norman: University of Oklahoma Press, 1946.

McWilliams, Carey. *North from Mexico: The Spanish-Speaking People of the United States.* The People of America Series. Philadelphia: J. B. Lippincott Company, 1949.

Mead, Margaret, ed. *Cultural Patterns and Technical Change.* New York: New American Library, 1955.

Meinig, D. W. *Southwest: Three Peoples in Geographical Change, 1600–1970.* New York: Oxford University Press, 1971.

Moorhead, Max L.. *The Apache Frontier: Jacobo Ugarte and Spanish-*

Indian Relations in Northern New Spain, 1769–1791. The Civilization of the American Indian Series, vol. 90. Norman: University of Oklahoma Press, 1968.

———. *New Mexico's Royal Road: Trade and Travel on the Chihuahua Trail*. Norman: University of Oklahoma Press, 1958.

———. *The Presidio: Bastion of the Spanish Borderlands*. Norman: University of Oklahoma Press, 1975.

Pearson, Jim Berry. *The Maxwell Land Grant*. Norman: University of Oklahoma Press, 1961.

Perrigo, Lynn. *Gateway to Glorieta: A History of Las Vegas, New Mexico*. Boulder, Colo.: Pruett Publishing Company, 1982.

Pike, Zebulon Montgomery. *The Journals of Zebulon Montgomery Pike, with Letters and Related Documents*, ed. and annot. Donald Jackson. 2 vols. Norman: University of Oklahoma Press, 1966.

Pino, Pedro Bautista. *Exposición. . . .* Cádiz, 1812. Reprinted in *Three New Mexico Chronicles: The* Exposición *of Don Pedro Bautista Pino, 1812;* The Ojeada *of Lic. Antonio Barreiro, 1832; and the* Additions *by Don José Augustín de Escudero, 1849.* The Quivira Society Publications, vol. 11, trans. and ed. H. Bailey Carroll and J. Villasana Haggard. Albuquerque: The Quivira Society, 1942.

Pitt, Leonard. *The Decline of the Californios: A Social History of the Spanish-Speaking Californians, 1846–1890*. Berkeley: University of California Press, 1966.

Rael, Juan B. *Cuestos Españoles de Colorado y Nuevo México (Spanish Folk Tales from Colorado and New Mexico): Spanish Language Originals with English Summaries*. 2 vols. Santa Fe: Museum of New Mexico Press, 1977.

———. *The New Mexican* Alabado *with Transcription of Music by Eleanor Hague*. Stanford University Publications, University Series, Language and Literature, vol. 9, no. 3:169–322. Stanford: Stanford University Press, 1951.

Reeve, Frank D. *History of New Mexico*, 2 vols. New York: Lewis Historical Publishing Company, 1961.

Rittenhouse, Jack D. *Cabezon: A New Mexico Ghost Town*. Santa Fe: Stagecoach Press, 1965.

Robb, John Donald. *Hispanic Folk Music of New Mexico and the Southwest: A Self-Portrait of a People*. Norman: University of Oklahoma Press, 1980.

Rodriguez, Sylvia. "The Hispano Homeland Debate." Stanford Center for Chicano Research Working Paper no. 17: 1–22. Stanford University, 1986.

Ruxton, George Frederick. *Wild Life in the Rocky Mountains*. 1848. Reprint. New York: MacMillan, 1916.

Salpointe, John Baptist. *John Baptist Salpointe: Soldier of the Cross,* ed. Odie B. Faulk. 1898. Reprint. Tucson: Diocese of Tucson, 1966.

Semple, Ellen Churchill. *Influences of Geographic Environment.* New York: Henry Holt, 1911.

Sheridan, Tom. *The Bitter River: A Brief Historical Survey of the Middle Pecos River Basin.* Boulder: Western Interstate Commission for Higher Education, 1975.

Shinkle, James D. *"Missouri Plaza," First Settled Community in Chaves County.* Roswell: Hall-Poorbaugh, 1972.

Simmons, Marc. *Albuquerque: A Narrative History.* Albuquerque: University of New Mexico Press, 1982.

Spears, Beverley. *American Adobes: Rural Houses of Northern New Mexico.* Albuquerque: University of New Mexico Press, 1986.

Spicer, Edward H. *Cycles of Conquest: The Impact of Spain, Mexico, and the United States on the Indians of the Southwest, 1533–1960.* Tucson: University of Arizona Press, 1962.

Stanley, F. [Crocchiola]. *The Las Vegas (New Mexico) Story.* Denver: World Press, 1951.

———. *The Manzano, New Mexico, Story.* Pantex, Tex.: privately published, 1962.

———. *The San Miguel del Bado, New Mexico, Story.* Pep, Tex.: privately published, 1964.

Steinel, Alvin T. *History of Agriculture in Colorado . . . 1858 to 1926.* Fort Collins, Colo.: State Agricultural College, 1926.

Stone, Wilbur Fisk, ed. *History of Colorado.* 4 vols. Chicago: S. J. Clarke Publishing Company, 1918.

Swadesh, Frances Leon. *Los Primeros Pobladores: Hispanic Americans of the Ute Frontier.* Notre Dame: University of Notre Dame Press, 1974.

Taylor, Morris F. *Pioneers of the Picketwire.* Pueblo: O'Brien Printing, 1964.

Thomas, Alfred Barnaby, trans. and ed. *Forgotten Frontiers: A Study of the Spanish Indian Policy of Don Juan Bautista de Anza, Governor of New Mexico, 1777–1787.* Norman: University of Oklahoma Press, 1932.

Thompson, Goldianne; William H. Halley; and Simon Herzstein. *History of Clayton and Union County, New Mexico.* Denver: Monitor Publishing Company, 1962.

Tobias, Henry J. *A History of the Jews in New Mexico.* Albuquerque: University of New Mexico Press, 1990.

Vickery, Joyce Carter. *Defending Eden: New Mexican Pioneers in Southern California, 1830–1890.* Riverside: Department of History, University of California and the Riverside Museum Press, 1977.

Weber, David J. *The Mexican Frontier, 1821–1846: The American Southwest under Mexico.* Histories of the American Frontier. Albuquerque: University of New Mexico Press, 1982.

————. *The Taos Trappers: The Fur Trade in the Far Southwest, 1540–1846.* Norman: University of Oklahoma Press, 1971.

Weigle, Marta. *Brothers of Light, Brothers of Blood: The Pentitentes of the Southwest.* Albuquerque: University of New Mexico Press, 1976.

Westphall, Victor. *Mercedes Reales: Hispanic Land Grants of the Upper Rio Grande Region.* New Mexico Land Grant Series. Albuquerque: University of New Mexico Press, 1983.

Wilder, Mitchell A., and Edgar Breitenbach. *Santos: The Religious Folk Art of New Mexico.* Colorado Springs: Taylor Museum, 1943.

Woods, Richard D., and Grace Álvarez-Altman. *Spanish Surnames in the Southwestern United States: A Dictionary.* Boston: G. K. Hall, 1978.

ARTICLES, CHAPTERS, AND SERIES

Albrecht, Dorothy E. "John Lorenzo Hubbell, Navajo Indian Trader." *Journal of Arizona History* 4 (1963): 33–40.

Allison, W. H. H. "Santa Fe as It Appeared during the Winter of the Years 1837 and 1838 . . . as Narrated by the Late Colonel Francisco Perea." *Old Santa Fe* 2 (October 1914): 170–183.

Alvis, Berry Newton. "History of Union County, New Mexico." *New Mexico Historical Review* 22 (1947): 247–73.

Anderson, H. Allen. "The Encomienda in New Mexico, 1598–1680." *New Mexico Historical Review* 60 (1985): 353–77.

Anderson, Lillie Gerhardt. "A New Mexico Pioneer of the 1880's." *New Mexico Historical Review* 29 (1954): 245–58.

Archambeau, Ernest R. "The First Federal Census in the Panhandle— 1880." *Panhandle-Plains Historical Review* 23 (1950): 22–132.

Archibald, Robert. "Acculturation and Assimilation in Colonial New Mexico." *New Mexico Historical Review* 53 (1978): 205–17.

Armijo, Antonio. "Armijo's Journal of 1829–30: The Beginning of Trade between New Mexico and California." Intro. and notes by LeRoy R. Hafen. Trans. Arthur Campa. *Colorado Magazine* 27 (1950): 120–31.

Arneson, Edwin P. "The Early Art of Terrestrial Measurement and Its Practice in Texas." *Southwestern Historical Quarterly* 29 (1925–26): 79–97.

Baca, Luis. "The Guadalupita Colony of Trinidad." *Colorado Magazine* 21 (1944): 22–27.

Baldwin, P. M. "A Short History of the Mesilla Valley." *New Mexico Historical Review* 13 (1938): 314–24.

Baldwin, Stuart J. "A Reconsideration of the Dating of a Seventeenth-Century New Mexican Document." *New Mexico Historical Review* 59 (1984): 411–13.

Barker, Ruth Laughlin. "Where Americans Are 'Anglos.' " *North American Review* 228 (1929): 568–73.

Beerman, Eric. "The Death of an Old Conquistador: New Light on Juan de Oñate." *New Mexico Historical Review* 54 (1979): 305–19.

Bernal, Louis E. "Los Vallejos and San Pablo." *Colorado Magazine* 22 (1945): 178–79.

Blaut, J. M., and Antonio Ríos-Bustamante. "Commentary on Nostrand's 'Hispanos' and their 'Homeland.' " *Annals of the Association of American Geographers* 74 (1984): 157–64.

Bloom, John P. "New Mexico Viewed by Anglo-Americans, 1846–1849." *New Mexico Historical Review* 34 (1959): 165–98.

———. "Note on the Population of New Mexico, 1846–1849." *New Mexico Historical Review* 34 (1959): 200–202.

Bloom, Lansing B. "A Glimpse of New Mexico in 1620." *New Mexico Historical Review* 3 (1928): 357–80.

———. "New Mexico under Mexican Administration, 1821–1846." *Old Santa Fe* 1 (1913–14): 3–49, 131–75, 235–87, 347–68.

———. "When Was Santa Fe Founded?" *New Mexico Historical Review* 4 (1929): 188–94.

———. "The 'Peñalosa' Map." *New Mexico Hitorical Review* 9 (1934): facing 113, 228–29.

———, trans. "A Trade-Invoice of 1638." *New Mexico Historical Review* 10 (1935): 242–48.

———, ed. "Alburquerque and Galisteo Certificate of Their Founding, 1706." *New Mexico Historical Review* 10 (1935): 48–50.

———. "The Vargas Encomienda." *New Mexico Historical Review* 14 (1939): 366–417.

———. "Notes and Comments." *New Mexico Historical Review* 17 (1942): 279.

Bolton, Herbert E. "French Intrusions into New Mexico, 1749–1752." In *The Pacific Ocean in History*, ed. H. Morse Stephens and Herbert E. Bolton, 389–407. New York: MacMillan, 1917.

Boswell, Thomas D., and Timothy C. Jones. "A Regionalization of Mexican Americans in the United States." *Geographical Review* 70 (1980): 88–98.

Bourke, John G. "Notes on the Language and Folk-Usage of the Rio Grande Valley." *Journal of American Folk-Lore* 9 (1896): 81–116.

Boyd, E. "The Literature of Santos." *Southwest Review* 35 (1950): 128–40.

———. "Penitentes in California." *El Palacio* 57 (1950): 372–73.

———. "The Plaza of San Miguel del Vado." *El Palacio* 77 (1971): 17–27.

———. "Troubles at Ojo Caliente, a Frontier Post." *El Palacio* 64 (1957): 347–60.

Boyd-Bowman, Peter. "Patterns of Spanish Emigration to the Indies until 1600." *Hispanic American Historical Review* 56 (1976): 580–604.

Bryan, Kirk. "Historic Evidence on Changes in the Channel of Rio Puerco, a Tributary of the Rio Grande in New Mexico." *Journal of Geology* 36 (1928): 265–82.

Buechley, Robert W. "Characteristic Name Sets of Spanish Populations." *Names* 15 (1967): 63–69.

Burnett, Hugh, and Evelyn Burnett. "Madrid Plaza." *Colorado Magazine* 42 (1965): 224–37.

Cabeza de Baca, Fabiola. "Puerto de Luna." *New Mexico Magazine* 36 (October 1958): 20, 42–43.

Campa, Arthur L. "Chile in New Mexico." *New Mexico Business Review* 3 (1934): 61–63.

———. "Protest Folk Poetry in the Spanish Southwest." *Colorado Quarterly* 20 (1971–72): 355–63.

Carlson, Alvar W. "El Rancho and Vadito: Spanish Settlements on Indian Land Grants." *El Palacio* 85 (1979): 28–39.

———. "Long-Lots in the Rio Arriba." *Annals of the Association of American Geographers* 65 (1975): 48–57.

———. "New Mexico's Sheep Industry, 1850–1900: Its Role in the History of the Territory." *New Mexico Historical Review* 44 (1969): 25–49.

———. "Seasonal Farm Labor in the San Luis Valley." *Annals of the Association of American Geographers* 63 (1973): 97–108.

———. "Spanish-American Acquisition of Cropland within the Northern Pueblo Indian Grants, New Mexico." *Ethnohistory* 22 (1975): 95–110.

Carter, Harvey L. "Kit Carson." In *The Mountain Men and the Fur Trade of the Far West: Biographical Sketches of the Participants by Scholars of the Subject and with Introductions by the Editor*, ed. LeRoy R. Hafen, vol. 6, pp. 103–31. Glendale: Arthur H. Clark, 1968.

Chávez, Fray Angélico. "Early Settlements in the Mora Valley." *El Palacio* 62 (1955): 318–23.

———. "The 'Kingdom of New Mexico.' " *New Mexico Magazine* 31, no. 8 (August 1953): 17, 58–59; 31, no. 9 (September 1953): 17, 42–43.

———. "Neo-Mexicanisms in New Mexico Place Names." *El Palacio* 57 (1950): 67–79.

————. "New Mexico Religious Place-Names other than Those of Saints." *El Palacio* 57 (1950): 23–26.

————. "New Names in New Mexico, 1920–1850." *El Palacio* 64 (1957): 291–318.

————. "The Pentitentes of New Mexico." *New Mexico Historical Review* 29 (1954): 97–123.

————. "Rejoinder" [to Nostrand's "Hispano Cultural Distinctiveness: A Reply"]. *Annals of the Association of American Geographers* 74 (1984): 170–71.

————. "Saints' Names in New Mexico Geography." *El Palacio* 56 (1949): 323–35.

————. "Santa Fe Church and Convent Sites in the Seventeenth and Eighteenth Centuries." *New Mexico Historical Review* 24 (1949): 85–93.

Cheetham, Francis T. "The Early Settlements of Southern Colorado." *Colorado Magazine* 5 (1928): 1–8.

Chipman, Donald. "The Oñate-Moctezuma-Zaldívar Families of Northern New Spain." *New Mexico Historical Review* 52 (1977): 297–310.

Cornish, Beatrice Quijada. "The Ancestry and Family of Juan de Oñate." In *The Pacific Ocean in History*, ed. H. Morse Stephens and Herbert E. Bolton, 452–64. New York: MacMillan, 1917.

de Borhegyi, Stephen F. "The Evolution of a Landscape" [Chimayo]. *Landscape* 4 (Summer 1954): 24–30.

Denevan, William M. "Livestock Numbers in Nineteenth-Century New Mexico, and the Problem of Gullying in the Southwest." *Annals of the Association of American Geographers* 57 (1967): 691–703.

Denhardt, Robert. "Mexican Demography." *Pacific Historical Review* 7 (1938): 147–59.

Dozier, Edward P. "The Pueblo Indians of the Southwest: A Survey of the Anthropological Literature and a Review of Theory, Method, and Results." *Current Anthropology* 5 (1964): 79–97.

Dunham, Harold H. "Ceran St. Vrain." In *The Mountain Men and the Fur Trade of the Far West: Biographical Sketches of the Participants by Scholars of the Subject and with Introductiôns by the Editor*, ed. LeRoy R. Hafen, vol. 5: 297–316. Glendale: Arthur H. Clark, 1968.

————. "Charles Bent." In *The Mountain Men and the Fur Trade of the Far West: Biographical Sketches of the Participants by Scholars of the Subject and with Introductions by the Editor*, ed. LeRoy R. Hafen, vol. 2: 27–48. Glendale: Arthur H. Clark, 1965.

————. "Manuel Alvarez." In *The Mountain Men and the Fur Trade of the Far West: Biographical Sketches of the Participants by Scholars of the Subject and with Introductions by the Editor*, ed. LeRoy R. Hafen, vol 1: 181–97. Glendale: Arthur H. Clark, 1965.

Ellis, Florence Hawley. "The Long Lost 'City' of San Gabriel del Yungue, Second Oldest European Settlement in the United States." In *When Cultures Meet: Remembering San Gabriel del Yunge Oweenge*, ed. Herman Agoyo and Lynnwood Brown, 10–38. Santa Fe: Sunstone Press, 1987.

Espinosa, Aurelio M. "Pentitentes, Los Hermanos." In *The Catholic Encyclopedia* 11:635–36. New York: The Encyclopedia Press, Inc., 1913.

———. "Speech Mixture in New Mexico: The Influence of the English Language on New Mexican Spanish." In *The Pacific Ocean in History*, ed. H. Morse Stephens and Herbert E. Bolton, 408–28. New York: Macmillan Company, 1917.

Espinosa, Aurelio M., and J. Manuel Espinosa. "The Texans: A New Mexican Spanish Folk Play of the Middle Nineteenth Century." *New Mexico Quarterly Review* 13 (1943): 299–308.

Espinosa, J. Manuel. "The Recapture of Santa Fé, New Mexico, by the Spaniards—December 29–30, 1693." *Hispanic American Historical Review* 19 (1939): 443–63.

Fergusson, Erna. "New Mexico's Mexicans." *Century Magazine* 116 (1928): 437–44.

Fierman, Floyd S. "Jewish Pioneering in the Southwest: A Record of the Freudenthal-Lesinsky-Solomon Families." *Arizona and the West* 2 (1960): 54–72.

———, ed. "Nathan Bibo's Reminiscences of Early New Mexico." *El Palacio* 68 (1961): 231–57.

Folmer, Henri. "Contraband Trade between Louisiana and New Mexico in the Eighteenth Century." *New Mexico Historical Review* 16 (1941): 249–74.

———. "The Mallet Expedition of 1739 through Nebraska, Kansas and Colorado to Santa Fe." *Colorado Magazine* 16 (1939): 161–73.

Frisbie, Parker. "Illegal Migration from Mexico to the United States: A Longitudinal Analysis." *International Migration Review* 9 (1975): 3–14.

González, William H., and Genaro M. Padilla. "Monticello: The Hispanic Cultural Gateway to Utah." *Utah Historical Quarterly* 52 (1984): 9–28.

Greenleaf, Richard E. "Atrisco and Las Ciruelas, 1722–1769." *New Mexico Historical Review* 42 (1967): 4–25.

———. "The Founding of Albuquerque, 1706: An Historical-Legal Problem." *New Mexico Historical Review* 39 (1964): 1–15.

Greenwood, N. H. "Sol Barth: A Jewish Settler on the Arizona Frontier." *Journal of Arizona History* 14 (1973): 363–78.

Greer, Richard R. "Origins of the Foreign-born Population of New Mexico during the Territorial Period." *New Mexico Historical Review* 17 (1942): 281–87.

Greever, William S. "Railway Development in the Southwest." *New Mexico Historical Review* 32 (1957): 151–203.

Gritzner, Charles F. "Construction Materials in a Folk Housing Tradition: Considerations Governing Their Selection in New Mexico." *Pioneer America* 6 (1974): 25–39.

———. "Hispano Gristmills in New Mexico." *Annals of the Association of American Geographers* 64 (1974): 514–24.

———. "Log Housing in New Mexico." *Pioneer America* 3 (1971): 54–62.

Gutiérrez, Ramón A. "Honor Ideology, Marriage Negotiation, and Class-Gender Domination in New Mexico, 1690–1846." *Latin American Perspectives*, issue 44, vol. 12, no. 1 (1985): 81–104.

Hafen, LeRoy R. "Mexican Land Grants in Colorado." *Colorado Magazine* 4 (1927): 81–93.

Haley, J. Evetts. "The Comanchero Trade." *Southwestern Historical Quarterly* 38 (1934–35): 157–76.

Hammond, George P. "The Date of Oñate's Return from New Mexico." *El Palacio* 64 (1957): 142–44.

Haskett, Bert. "History of the Sheep Industry in Arizona." *Arizona Historical Review* 7 (July 1936): 3–49.

Hill, Joseph J. "The Old Spanish Trail." *Hispanic American Historical Review* 4 (1921): 444–73.

Hillerman, Tony. "Las Trampas." *New Mexico Quarterly* 37 (1967–68): 20–32.

Hoffmeister, Harold. "The Consolidated Ute Indian Reservation." *Geographical Review* 35 (1945): 601–23.

Jaehn, Thomas. "Charles Blumner: Pioneer, Civil Servant, and Merchant." *New Mexico Historical Review* 61 (1986): 319–27.

Jenkins, Myra Ellen. "Spanish Land Grants in the Tewa Area." *New Mexico Historical Review* 47 (1972): 113–34.

———. "Taos Pueblo and Its Neighbors, 1540–1847. *New Mexico Historical Review* 41 (1966): 85–114.

———. "The Baltasar Baca 'Grant': History of an Encroachment." *El Palacio* 68 (1961): 47–64, 87–105.

Jones, Oakah L., Jr. "Pueblo Indian Auxiliaries in New Mexico, 1763–1821." *New Mexico Historical Review* 37 (1962): 81–109.

———. "Spanish Civil Communities and Settlers in Frontier New Mexico, 1790–1810." In *Hispanic-American Essays in Honor of*

Max Leon Moorhead, ed. William S. Coker, 37–60. Pensacola: Perdido Bay Press, 1979.

Jordan, Terry G. "Antecedents of the Long-Lot in Texas." *Annals of the Association of American Geographers* 64 (1974): 70–86.

Kajencki, Francis C. "Alexander Grzelachowski: Pioneer Merchant of Puerto de Luna, New Mexico." *Arizona and the West* 26 (1984): 243–60.

Kelley, Wilfrid D. "Settlement of the Middle Rio Grande Valley." *Journal of Geography* 54 (1955): 387–99.

Knowlton, Clark S. "Causes of Land Loss among the Spanish Americans in Northern New Mexico." *Rocky Mountain Social Science Journal* 1, no. 2 (April 1964): 201–11.

———. "Patron-Peon Pattern among the Spanish Americans of New Mexico." *Social Forces* 41 (1962–63): 12–17.

———. "The Town of Las Vegas Community Land Grant: An Anglo-American Coup D'Etat." *Journal of the West* 19 (July 1980): 12–21.

Kutsche, Paul. "Introduction: Atomism, Factionalism, and Flexibility." In *The Survival of Spanish American Villages,* ed. Paul Kutsche, 7–19. Colorado College Studies No. 15. Colorado Springs: Colorado College, 1979.

Lacy, James M. "New Mexican Women in Early American Writings." *New Mexico Historical Review* 34 (1959): 41–51.

Lawrence, Eleanor. "Mexican Trade between Santa Fe and Los Angeles, 1830–1848." *California Historical Society Quarterly* 10 (1931): 27–39.

Loomis, Charles P. "El Cerrito, New Mexico: A Changing Village." *New Mexico Historical Review* 33 (1958): 53–75.

———. "Systemic Linkage of El Cerrito." *Rural Sociology* 24 (1959): 54–57.

———. "Wartime Migration from the Rural Spanish Speaking Villages of New Mexico." *Rural Sociology* 7 (1942): 384–95.

Loomis, Charles, and Glen Grisham. "The New Mexican Experiment in Village Rehabilitation." *Applied Anthropology* 2, no. 3 (April–June, 1943): 12–37.

Loomis, Charles P., and Nellie H. Loomis. "Skilled Spanish-American War-Industry Workers from New Mexico." *Applied Anthropology* 2, no. 1 (October–November–December 1942): 33–36.

López, Larry. "The Founding of San Francisco on the Rio Puerco: A Document." *New Mexico Historical Review* 55 (1980): 71–78.

Marino, C. C. "The Seboyetanos and the Navahos." *New Mexico Historical Review* 29 (1954): 8–27.

Marshall, C. E. "The Birth of the Mestizo in New Spain." *Hispanic American Historical Review* 19 (1939): 161–84.

Marshall, Thomas Maitland. "St. Vrain's Expedition to the Gila in 1826." *Southwestern Historical Quarterly* 19 (1915–16): 251–60.

McCourt, Purnee A. "The Conejos Land Grant of Southern Colorado." *Colorado Magazine* 52 (1975): 34–51.

McDonald, Jerry N. "La Jicarilla." *Journal of Cultural Geography* 2 (1982): 40–57.

Meinig, D. W. "The Mormon Culture Region: Strategies and Patterns in the Geography of the American West, 1847–1964." *Annals of the Association of American Geographers* 55 (1965): 191–220.

———. "Rejoinder" [to Nostrand's "Hispano Cultural Distinctiveness: A Reply"]. *Annals of the Association of American Geographers* 74 (1984): 171.

Metzgar, Joseph V. "The Ethnic Sensitivity of Spanish New Mexicans: A Survey and Analysis." *New Mexico Historical Review* 49 (1974): 49–73.

Miller, Robert Ryal, trans. and ed. "New Mexico in Mid-Eighteenth Century: A Report Based on Governor Vélez Capuchín's [sic] Inspection." *Southwestern Historical Quarterly* 79 (1975–76): 166–81.

Moorhead, Max L. "The Presidio Supply Problem of New Mexico in the Eighteenth Century." *New Mexico Historical Review* 36 (1961): 210–29.

———. "Rebuilding the Presidio of Santa Fe, 1789–1791." *New Mexico Historical Review* 49 (1974): 123–42.

Morgan, Paul, and Vince Mayer. "The Spanish-Speaking Population of Utah: From 1900 to 1935." In *Working Papers toward a History of the Spanish-Speaking People of Utah*, 6–62. Salt Lake City: Mexican-American Documentation Project, American West Center, University of Utah, 1973.

Murphy, Lawrence R. "The Beaubien and Miranda Land Grant 1841–1846." *New Mexico Historical Review* 42 (1967): 27–47.

———. "Charles H. Beaubien." In *The Mountain Men and the Fur Trade of the Far West: Biographical Sketches of the Participants by Scholars of the Subject and with Introductions by the Editor*, ed. LeRoy R. Hafen, vol. 6: 23–35. Glendale: Arthur H. Clark, 1968.

———. "Rayado: Pioneer Settlement in Northeastern New Mexico, 1848–1857." *New Mexico Historical Review* 46 (1971): 37–56.

Noggle, Burl. "Anglo Observers of the Southwest Borderlands, 1825–1890: The Rise of a Concept." *Arizona and the West* 1 (1959): 105–31.

Nostrand, Richard L. "The Hispanic-American Borderland: Delimitation of an American Culture Region." *Annals of the Association of American Geographers* 60 (1970): 638–61.

———. "The Hispano Homeland in 1900." *Annals of the Association of American Geographers* 70 (1980): 382–96.

———. " 'Mexican American' and 'Chicano': Emerging Terms for a People Coming of Age." *Pacific Historical Review* 42 (1973): 389–406.

———. "Mexican Americans circa 1850." *Annals of the Association of American Geographers* 65 (1975): 378–90.

Nuttall, Zelia. "Royal Ordinances Concerning the Laying Out of New Towns." *Hispanic American Historical Review* 5 (1922): 249–54.

Oberg, Kalervo. "Cultural Factors and Land-Use Planning in Cuba Valley, New Mexico." *Rural Sociology* 5 (1940): 438–48.

Ornstein, Jacob. "The Archaic and the Modern in the Spanish of New Mexico." *Hispania* 34 (1951): 137–41.

Parish, William J. "The German Jew and the Commercial Revolution in Territorial New Mexico 1850–1900." *New Mexico Historical Review* 35 (1960): 1–29, 129–50.

Parkhill, Forbes. "Colorado's First Survey." *Colorado Magazine* 33 (1956): 177–80.

Paul, Rodman W. "The Spanish-Americans in the Southwest, 1848–1900." In *The Frontier Challenge: Responses to the Trans-Mississippi West*, ed. John G. Clark, 31–56. Lawrence: Regents Press of Kansas, 1971.

Powell, Philip Wayne. "Presidios and Towns on the Silver Frontier of New Spain, 1550–1580." *Hispanic American Historical Review* 24 (1944): 179–200.

Romero, José Ynocencio (as told to Ernest R. Archambeau). "Spanish Sheepmen on the Canadian at Old Tascosa." *Panhandle-Plains Historical Review* 19 (1946): 45–72.

Samora, Julian, and Richard F. Larson. "Rural Families in an Urban Setting: A Study in Persistence and Change." *Journal of Human Relations* 9 (1960–61): 494–503.

Sandoval, David A. "Who is Riding the Burro Now? A Bibliographic Critique of Scholarship on the New Mexican Trader." In *The Santa Fe Trail: New Perspectives*. Essays in Colorado History no. 6: 75–92. Denver: Colorado Historical Society, 1987.

Sauer, Carl O. "The Personality of Mexico." *Geographical Review* 31 (1941): 353–64.

Scholes, France V. "Civil Government and Society in New Mexico in the Seventeenth Century." *New Mexico Historical Review* 10 (1935): 71–111.

———. "Correction." *New Mexico Historical Review* 19 (1944): 243–46.

———. "Documents for the History of the New Mexican Missions

in the Seventeenth Century." *New Mexico Historical Review* 4 (1929): 45–58.

Scholes, France V., and Lansing B. Bloom. "Friar Personnel and Mission Chronology, 1598–1629." *New Mexico Historical Review* 19 (1944): 319–36; 20 (1945): 58–82.

Servín, Manuel Patricio. "California's Hispanic Heritage: A View into the Spanish Myth." In *New Spain's Far Northern Frontier: Essays on Spain in the American West, 1540–1821*, ed. David J. Weber, 117–33. Albuquerque: University of New Mexico Press, 1979.

Simmons, Marc. "The Chacón Economic Report of 1803." *New Mexico Historical Review* 60 (1985): 81–89.

———. "New Mexico's Spanish Exiles." *New Mexico Historical Review* 59 (1984): 67–79.

———. "On the Trail of the Comancheros." *New Mexico Magazine* 39 (May 1961): 30–33, 39.

———. "Rejoinder" [to Nostrand's "Hispano Cultural Distinctiveness: A Reply"]. *Annals of the Association of American Geographers* 74 (1984): 169–70.

———. "Settlement Patterns and Village Plans in Colonial New Mexico." *Journal of the West* 8 (1969): 7–21.

———. "Spanish Irrigation Practices in New Mexico." *New Mexico Historical Review* 47 (1972): 135–50.

Smith, Emilia Gallegos. "Reminiscences of Early San Luis." *Colorado Magazine* 24 (1947): 24–25.

Sporleder, Louis B. "A Day and a Night on Spoon River." *Colorado Magazine* 9 (1932): 102–15.

———. "La Plaza de los Leones." *Colorado Magazine* 10 (1933): 28–38.

Strout, Clevy Lloyd. "The Resettlement of Santa Fe, 1695: The Newly Found Muster Roll." *New Mexico Historical Review* 53 (1978): 260–70.

Sunseri, Alvin R. "Agricultural Tehniques in New Mexico at the Time of the Anglo-American Conquest." *Agricultural History* 47 (1973): 329–37.

Swadesh, Frances Leon. "Structure of Hispanic-Indian Relations in New Mexico." In *The Survival of Spanish American Villages*, ed. Paul Kutsche, 53–61. Colorado College Studies, no. 15. Colorado Springs: Colorado College, 1979.

Taylor, Paul S. "Mexican Labor in the United States: Valley of the South Platte, Colorado." University of California Publications in Economics, vol. 6, no. 2: 95–235. Berkeley: University of California Press, 1929.

Tjarks, Alicia V. "Demographic, Ethnic and Occupational Structure of New Mexico, 1790." *Americas: A Quarterly Review of Inter-American Cultural History* 35 (1978–79): 45–88.

Trulio, Beverly. "Anglo-American Attitudes toward New Mexican Women." *Journal of the West* 12 (1973): 229–39.

Tuan, Yi-Fu, and Cyril E. Everard. "New Mexico's Climate: The Appreciation of a Resource." *Natural Resources Journal* 4 (1964–65): 268–308.

Twitchell, Ralph E. "Spanish Colonization in New Mexico in the Oñate and De Vargas Periods." *Publication of the Historical Society of New Mexico* 22 (1919): 1–39.

van Diest, Edmond C. "Early History of Costilla County." *Colorado Magazine* 5 (1928): 140–43.

Van Hook, Joseph O. "Mexican Land Grants in the Arkansas Valley." *Southwestern Historical Quarterly* 40 (1936–37): 58–75.

Velásquez, Melitón. "Guadalupe Colony Was Founded 1854." *Colorado Magazine* 34 (1957): 264–67.

Warner, J. J. "Los Angeles County from September 8th, 1771, to January, 1847." In *An Historical Sketch of Los Angeles County California,* ed. J. J. Warner, Benjamin Hayes, J. P. Widney, 9–39. 1876. Reprint. Los Angeles: O. W. Smith, Publisher, 1936.

Weber, David J. "American Westward Expansion and the Breakdown of Relations between Pobladores and '*Indios Bárbaros*' on Mexico's Far Northern Frontier, 1821–1846." *New Mexico Historical Review* 56 (1981): 221–38.

———. "Stereotyping of Mexico's Far Northern Frontier." In *An Awakened Minority: The Mexican-Americans,* ed. Manuel P. Servín, 18–26. 2d ed. Beverly Hills: Glencoe Press, 1974.

Whelan, Harold A. "Eden in Jurupa Valley: The Story of Agua Mansa." *Southern California Quarterly* 55 (1973): 413–29.

Widdison, Jerold Gwayn. "Historical Geography of the Middle Rio Puerco Valley, New Mexico." *New Mexico Historical Review* 34 (1959): 248–84.

Wilson, John P. "How the Settlers Farmed: Hispanic Villages and Irrigation Systems in Early Sierra County, 1850–1900." *New Mexico Historical Review* 63 (1988): 333–56.

Winberry, John J. "The Log House in Mexico." *Annals of the Association of American Geographers* 64 (1974): 54–69.

———. "*Tejamanil:* The Origin of the Shake Roof in Mexico." *Proceedings of the Association of American Geographers* 7 (1975): 288–93.

Winnie, William W., Jr. "The Spanish Surname Criterion for Identifying Hispanos in the Southwestern United States: A Preliminary Evaluation." *Social Forces* 38 (1959–60): 363–66.

Zunser, Helen. "A New Mexican Village." *Journal of American Folk-Lore* 48 (1935): 125–78.

INDEX

A&P (Atlantic and Pacific Railroad):
116–17
Abajeños, of California: 216n.6
Abbot, Horace C.: 140
Abert, James William: 107
Abiquiu, N.M.: 41, 46, 84; as colonist
springboard, 96; *genízaros* of, 44, 135;
as Pueblo village 55n.12; as Spanish
buffer area, 224; as trail town, 87;
U.S. troops in, 105, 106n
Abiquiu Indian agency: 65, 84n.22
Abo (mission): 51n.5
Abreu (Peñasco farmhand): 189n.29
Abuelo Cebolla, N.M.: 70
Acoma (Pueblo village): 36, 55, 59,
108n.13, 232; mission at, 53n.5
ACP (Agricultural Conservation Pro-
gram): 150
Adelino, N.M.: *see* Los Ranchos de
Tome
Adobe brick: 215, 220 & n
Agencies, Indian: 65
Agricultural Conservation Program
(ACP): 150
Agua Azul, N.M. (plaza): 95
Agua Mansa: *see* San Salvador, Calif.
Aguilar, Colo.: 143
Alamillo, N.M. (settlement): 92, 93n
Alamogordo, N.M.: 95
Alamo Reservation: 68n.31
Alamosa, Colo.: Hispanos of, 143; rail-
road from, 116
Alamosa Creek: 95
Alarí (Alarid), Juan Bautista: 99
Alaríe (N.M. immigrant): 45n.39
Alário, Nepomuceno: 139n.9
Alaska, state of: 169n
Albert, N.M.: *see* Tequesquite (plaza)
Albuquerque, N.M.: 47; Anglos of, 107,

119, 205 & n.16, 206, 211; as colonist
springboard, 88, 96; founding of, 42;
Hispanos of, 43, 205 & n.16, 206, 209
& n.20, 211; Indian schools of, 65;
Jewish merchants of, 112; Mexican
Americans of, 205; Mexicans of, 163,
165, 167; New Albuquerque and, 143
(*see also* New Albuquerque, N.M.);
as *partido* center, 224; population
patterns in, 46n.40, 205 & n.16; rail-
road to, 116; U.S. troops in, 105; *see
also* Los Ranchos de Albuquerque;
New Albuquerque, N.M.
Alcaldías: 45, 46n.40
Álvarez, Manuel: 101 & n
Alvis, Barry Newton: 81n.17
Americanos: see Anglo(s)
Amish, agricultural mastery of: 181n
Analla, N.M. (plaza): 95
Andalucía: 27 & n.2
Andrews, John Philip: 84n.22
Anglo(s): 22; defined, 99; in depopulated Hispano villages, 190; His-
pano(s) and, 7, 10, 15, 82, 206, 211,
216, 226 (*see also* Anglo(s), westward
thrust of); as Hispano colleagues, 80;
as Hispano employers, 97, 131n, 137,
139–55, 163, 167, 193, 225; Hispano
friction with, 81–82, 96, 205n.15; as
Hispano neighbors, 85, 86, 92 (*see
also* San Juan, Ariz.; Trinidad, Colo.);
as Hispano spouses, 101–103 & n.8,
108n.12, 112, 116, 117, 118, 129, 147,
158, 188n.28, 193 & n, 195; Hispano
view of, 107; in Louisiana, 228–30;
as Mexican employers, 161, 162–67;
as railroaders, 116; Utes armed by,
63; westward thrust of, 4–6, 96, 98–
130, 226–28, 232; *see also* blacks, as

263

Anglos; Jews; military, U.S.; Mormons
Anián, Strait of: 36
Animas Valley: 65, 67n.30
Anton Chico, N.M.: 77
Anza, Juan Bautista de: 70, 71n.2
Apache County, Hispanos of: 92n
Apaches: 49 & n, 62; Hispano-enslaved, 64 & n.26; Hispano spouses of, 67; New Mexico vs., 70; raids of, 51, 63 & n.25; reservations for, 65; see also Jicarilla Apaches; Mescalero Apaches; Navajos
Apishapa River: 85
Apodaca, Colo.: 85
Arabela, N.M. (plaza): 95
Aragón, Candido: 192, 198n.9
Aragón, Cirilio: 192
Aragón, Linda Quintana: 178n.13, 198n.9
Aragón, Luis: 192 & n, 198n.9
Aragón, Luis Roberto: 177n.13
Aragón, Mary Barela: 198n.9
Aragón, Teodoro: 192
Aragón family: 192 & n, 197
Arapahoe County (Colo.): 131n
Archibeque, Jean: see L'Archeveque, Jean
Archuleta County (Colo.): 65, 67n.30
Argentina, hornos of: 221
Arizona, state of: Hispanos of, 22, 91, 95, 142, 144, 145; Mexican Americans to New Mexico from, 157, 162 & n.11; Mexican immigrants to, 6, 164, 165; Mexicans of, 167n; mines of, 175; Mormons of, 114; settlement of, 4
Arkansas River: 85, 193, 196; Hispanos on, 79–80, 137, 139n.9 (see also Pueblo [Colo.], Hispanos of)
Arkansas Valley: 86; sugar beets of, 147, 162
Armijo, Antonio: 132 & n.3, 134 & n.5, 135n.5
Armijo, Jesús: 135n.5
Armijo, Juan: 135n.5
Armijo family: 196
Arneson, Edwin P.: 32n.12
Arribeños: 216 & n.6
Arroyo Hondo, N.M.: 76; settlement of, 71, 82
Arroyo Seco, N.M.: 82
AT&SF (Atchison, Topeka, and Santa Fe Railroad): 79, 101, 116–17 & n.22, 119, 204; Hispano employees of, 140

& n.11, 181; railroad towns of (see East Las Vegas, N.M.; New Albuquerque, N.M.; New San Marcial, N.M.; New Socorro, N.M.)
Atarque, N.M.: 91
Atchison, Topeka, and Santa Fe: see AT&SF
Atencio, Olivama J.: 188n.28
Atencio family: 86
Athapaskan (lang.): 62
Atlantic and Pacific Railroad: see A&P
Atrisco, N.M.: 42 & n.32; see also Los Ranchos de Atrisco
Austin, Stephen F.: 217
Austrians, as Homeland coal miners: 117
Aztecs: 46n.40; conquest of, 26, 27

Baca, Felipe: 85, 86 & n.26
Baca, Manuel: 135
Badito, Colo.: 137n.8
Bailey, David Thomas: 194n, 203n.12
Bancroft, Hubert Howe: 45n.37, 53n.5, 57n.15, 134n.5
Bandini, Juan: 135
Barela, Colo.: see San Francisco (plaza)
Barker, Ruth Laughlin: 16
Barranco, N.M. (settlement): 87
Barreiro, Antonio: 14, 15, 58n.16, 76n.10, 103n.8, 214, 224, 225n.14
Barth, Solomon: 91–92
Bayard, N.M.: 127
Beach, Charles: 98
Beaubien, Charles: 80n, 82, 101–103, 139n.9
Beaubien, Luz: 80n
Beaubien, Narciso: 139n.9
Beaver, overtrapping of: 101
Beaver County (Okla.): 81n.19
Beaver River: 81
Becknell, William: 100, 101
Beerman, Eric: 26n
Belen, N.M.: 127, 161; as colonist springboard, 96; founding of, 43 & n.33; genízaros of, 44; as Pueblo village, 55n.12; as Spanish buffer area, 224
Belen Valley: 43, 92, 93, 95
Benavides, Alonso: 53n.5
Benedict XIV, Pope: 11n.13
Bennett, Colo.: 131n
Bent, Charles: 101
Bernal, N.M.: 77
Bernalillo, N.M.: 42n.32, 209; founding of, 42

Bernalillo County: 185n.21
Bessemer (Pueblo [Colo.] community): 196, 198
Bibo, Nathan: 110n.15
Blacks, Homeland: 36, 118; as "Anglos," 99; as coal miners, 117 & n.22; see also Hispanos, black
Blacksmiths, Pennsylvania-born: 112
Blanco, N.M. (plaza): 88
Blende (Pueblo [Colo.] district): 198
Bloom, John P.: 108n.12
Bloom, Lansing B.: 34, 42n.32, 224
Bloomfield, N.M.: 88; as Mormon village, 114
Bluewater, N.M.: as Mormon village, 114; school segregation in, 116; see Agua Azul (plaza)
Bluewater, N.M.: see Agua Azul (plaza)
Blumner, Carlota: 108n.12
Blumner, Charles: 108n.12
Blumner, Feliciana: 108n.12
Bolton, Herbert E.: 4n.2
Borderlands: 3, 4 & n.2, 6; see also Homeland
Borhegyi, Stephen F. de: 223n.11
Bosque Redondo, Indians of: 113
Boswell, Thomas D.: 129
Bourgade, Peter: 62
Bourke, John G.: 12
Bowden, J. J.: 77n.12, 124
Boyd, E.: 72n.5, 77n.11
Brazoso, Colo. (settlement): 84n.24
Brazos River: 81
Brighton, Colo.: 164n.13
Brown, John: 193n
Bryan, Kirk: 183n.18
Buechley, Robert W.: 8, 9n.10
Bueyeros, N.M. (plaza): 80
Buffalo, Hispano use of: 64
Bultos: 11
Burma, John: 176n
Burnett, Evelyn: 87n.29
Burnett, Hugh: 87n.29

Cabezon, N.M.: 90–91n.33, 183n.17
Cachupín (N.M. governor): 43n.34, 45n.38
Cajon Pass: 132
Calhoun, James S.: 108n.13
California, Gulf of: 32
California, state of: Anglo "invasion" of, 4–6; Hispano sheep trailed to, 76; Hispanos of, 134–36, 153–54 (see also San Salvador); Hispano traders in, 132–35; Mexican Americans to New

Mexico from, 157, 158, 162 & n.11; Mexican immigrants to 6, 164–65, 168, 216n.6; Mexico and, 224; "New Mexico clubs" of, 213; Penitentes in, 13n.16; real-estate boom in, 4–6; settlement of, 4; Spanish surnames of, 9n.10; U.S. acquisition of, 6; villages of, 217; see also Californios; San Salvador; Spanish Trail
Californios: 4, 17, 19, 20, 22, 23; climate of, 214; dissolution of, 6; Hispano trade with, 132–35; of Manzano, N.M., 186; as "Spanish-Americans," 16
Calzones: as troublesome noun, 164, 202
Camino Alto: 41
Camino Real: 100
Campa, Arthur L.: 19
Canada, idiom of French: 8n.8
Canadian River: 81n.18; Hispano plazas on, 80
Canadian Valley: 81
Candelaria, Eleno: 185n.25
Candelaria, Juan: 91
Candelaria, Juanita: 99n.1, 187n.25
Cañada, La, N.M.: see Santa Cruz Valley
Cañada Alamosa, N.M.: 95
Cañada Bonita (Ute community): 67n.30
Cañon, Colo. (settlement): 84n.24
Cañoncito Reservation: 68n.31
Cañon City, Colo.: 142
Cañones, N.M. (settlement): 87
Cañon Largo: 87
Cape Girardeau College: 139n.9
Capulin District: 85
Caravans, Hispano trading: 45 & n.38, 70–71, 79 & n.14; on Spanish Trail, 132 & n.3, 134 & n.5, 135 n.6
Carlsbad, N.M.: 153; Mexicans to, 163, 165
Carlson, Alvar W.: 215
Carnero, Colo. (settlement): 85n.25
Carnero Creek: 85
Carpenters, Kentucky-born: 112
Carroll, H. Bailey: 93n
Carson, Christopher ("Kit"): 80n, 101
Carson National Forest: 190
Catholicism: see Roman Catholic Church
Cattlemen, Anglo: 112–14, 118
CCC (Civilian Conservation Corps): 150
Cebolla: 70n

Cebolla Valley: 70
Cebolleta (Navajo mission): 64n.28
Cebolleta, N.M.: 91; Anglos of, 107; as colonist springboard, 96; Franciscan mission at, 88 & n.32; U.S. troops in, 105
Center, Colo.: 148
Central Americans, assimilation of U.S.–resident: 130
CF&I (Colorado Fuel and Iron): 195, 200
Chama, Colo. (plaza): 82
Chama Valley: 41, 84, 87
Chamisal, N.M.: 189; Anglos of, 188 & n.28; colonists from, 80; population patterns in, 181; survival of, 187–88
Chamita, N.M.: 84n.22; founding of, 41
Chaperito, N.M.: 79
Charette, Juan R.: 122
Chaves, Julián: 134 & n.5, 135n.5
Chaves County, Hispanos of: 145
Chávez, Fray Angélico: 11, 12, 64n.26, 100n.4, 103n.8, 223
Cheetham, Francis T.: 76
Cheyenne, Wyo.: 150
Cheyennes: 49
Chicago, Ill.: 164
Chicanos: 19, 154, 165 & n.17; see also Spanish-Americans
Chichimecas: see nomad Indians
Chico Springs, N.M. (plaza): 80
Chihuahua, Mex.: annual fair of, 44; emigrants to New Mexico from, 158, 161; Missouri wagons to, 100
Chihuahua, state of: surnames of, 9n.10
Children, abduction of Indian/Hispano: 63–64 & n.26, 68; see also genízaros
Chili, Hispano affinity for: 13 & n.18
Chimayo, N.M.: 41, 44; miraculous mud of, 222, 223n.11
Chinese: in Arizona, 142; of New Mexico, 98
Chipman, Donald: 26n
Chisum, John S.: 113
Christopher, S.: 112n.16
Cia (Pueblo village): 108n.13
Cimarron, N.M.: 80
Cimarron Indian agency: 65
Cinco de Mayo: 13, 14n.18
Ciudad Juárez, Mex.: see Paso del Norte
Civil Conservation Corps (CCC): 150
Clapham, N.M. (plaza): 81
Clayton, N.M.: Hispanos of, 143; as railhead, 80

Cleveland, N.M.: see San Antonio, N.M.
Clothing, Anglo influence on Hispano: 123 & n.26
Clovis, N.M.: 153; Mexicans to, 163
Coal: 117 & n.22, 118, 119, 143, 163, 194, 225
Cochiti (Pueblo village): 108n.13; Hispanos in, 60
Coconino County (Ariz.): 162n.11
Colchas, Hispano trade in: 132
Colfax County: 113
Colorado, state of: Hispanos of, 20, 84–88, 96 & n, 131, 140, 143, 144 & n, 145, 147, 148, 153, 162–63, 175, 209, 225, 226 (see also Pueblo [Colo.]); Indians of, 61, 65; Mexicans of, 6, 162–63, 164–67 & n; plazas of, 82–84; sugar beets of, 147, 148, 162–63, 173, 196, 208, 225; see also Conejos Grant; Del Norte; Denver; Pueblo (Colo.); Trinidad; Walsenburg
Colorado Fuel and Iron (CF&I): 195, 200
Colorado Plateau: 91
Colorado River: 87
Comancheros: 137–39
Comanches: 137; Anglo trade with, 100; Hispano-enslaved, 64; Hispanos vs., 10; Hispano trade with (see Comancheros); vs. Jicarilla Apaches, 62; New Mexico vs., 70; raids by, 63 & n.25
Comanches, Los (play): 10
Comisión Honorífica, Pueblo-based: 163, 164n.13
Commerce, Colo.: 153
Comprados, Hispanos as: 196, 201
Concho, Ariz., Hispanos at, 91, 92n.; as Mormon village, 114
Conejos, Colo.: 84 & n.23
Conejos Grant: 84, 85
Conejos River: 84 & n.23, 85n.24
Conklin, Joseph P.: 122 & n
Conquistadora, La: 13
Consolidated Ute Indian Reservation: 67n.33
Contradero, N.M. (settlement): 92
Conventos: 50–51 & nn.4, 5, 226
Conway, John R.: 185, 187n.25
Coolidge, N.M. (Mormon village): 114
Copper: Colorado, 193; of Homeland, 118
Copper Hill Mining Camp: 189n.29
Coraque, N.M. (plaza): 88

Cordova, N.M. (plaza): 41; *see also* Pueblo Quemado
Corn, Mexican: 221
Cornelio Vigil–Cerán St. Vrain Grant: 72n.4, 86
Coronado, Francisco de: 50n.2, 214
Corrumpa Creek: 81
Cortés, Hernán: 26
Corwin, Arthur F.: 164n.13
Costilla, N.M.: 82
Cotton, Tex.: 173
Coyote, N.M.: 137
Craver, Rebecca McDowell: 103n.8
Creoles, as New Mexico colonists: 4, 28–29 & nn.5, 6, 35; *see also* Oñate, Juan de
Cuarac: *see* Querac
Cuba, N.M.: *see* Nacimiento, N.M.
Cubans: assimilation of U.S.–resident, 129; Hispanos and, 8
Cubero, N.M.: 91; as colonist springboard, 96; settlement of, 88 & n.32
Cucharas, Colo. (plaza): 86
Cucharas River: 216
Cucharas Valley: 86
Cuchillo (Negro), N.M.: 95
Cuchillo Negro Creek: 95
Culebra Creek: 82; Hispano settlement along, 85
Cullen, Ruth M.: 129
Curas, in New Mexico: 57 & n.15, 62

Dacotas: 49
Dallas–Fort Worth, Tex.: 163
D&RG (Denver and Rio Grande Railroad): 116; Hispano employees of, 140, 148
Davis, W. W. H.: 76n.10
Day laborers, Hispano: 75
Décima: 10
Deerfield, Kan.: 153
Deer Trail, Colo.: 131n
Delinquency, among urban Hispanos: 211
Del Norte, Colo.: 85 & n.25; Hispanos of, 143, 148
Deming, N.M.: 116, 117
Denevan, William M.: 183n.18
Denver. Colo.: Hispanos near, 131; Hispanos of, 119, 153, 206, 208–209 & n.20; Mexican Americans of, 208 & n.19; Mexicans of, 163, 165
Denver and Fort Worth Railroad: 80
Denver and Rio Grande Railroad: *see* D&RG

Derry, N.M.: 93n
Desertion, from Oñate forces: 29
Deus, Peter: 196n.4
Deutsch, Sarah: 225
Dirty Barry (El Cerrito hippie): 177
Discrimination: *see* segregation
Divorce, urban Hispanos and: 211
Dogpatch (Pueblo [Colo.] district): 198
Domestics, Hispanos as Anglo: 194n
Donaldson, A. J.: 204n
Don Fernando de Taos Grant: 42, 56n
Doña Ana, N.M.: 105n, 159 n.8; establishment of, 92; Mexican-born of, 159
Doña Ana County: 162n.11
Dozier, Edward P.: 50n.2
Drought: 150, 154; missions closed by, 51; in Puerco Valley, 183n.18
Durango, Colo.: 143
Durango, Mex.: 159, 161

East Carbon, Utah: 153
East Dale (Mormon village): 114
East Las Vegas, N.M.: 204–205; Anglos of, 119, 211; black laborers of, 117 n.22; Hispanos of, 143, 211; Mexican Americans of, 211; railroad yards at, 116
Eastside (Pueblo [Colo.] district): 198
Eastwood Heights (Pueblo [Colo.] district): 198
Ebright, Malcolm: 77n.12
Edmonson, Munro S.: 13, 14n.18
El Cerrito, N.M.: 73, 76, 77n.12, 140, 170n.2, 184, 190, 192; Anglos of, 177 & nn.11, 13; clan antagonisms in, 155; depopulation of, 169–81 & n; founding of, 71 & n.3, 77; Hispanos to Pueblo [Colo.] from, 175, 192, 196–202; houses of, 124; language patterns in, 122–23; New Deal relief agencies in, 150; stockmen of, 170–71, 174, 179–81
Elephant Butte Reservoir: 148n.18
El Gusano, N.M.: 77
Ellis, Florence Hawley: 221n
El Llanito, N.M.: 84
El Moro, Colo.: 135n.5
El Oro Cebolla, N.M.: 70
El Paso, Tex.: 38n.22, 105n, AT&SF to, 116; Mexican labor recruited in, 163
El Pueblo, N.M.: 175n.9; establishment of, 77
El Rito, N.M.: 84n.22
Elsberg and Amberg (Santa Fe firm): 110n.15

Embudo, N.M.: 41; colonists from, 80
Encinal (Navajo mission): 64n.28, 88
Encomiendas: 34–35, 36
English (lang.), Hispanos and: 122–23, 130
English (nationals), as Homeland coal miners: 117
Ensenada, N.M. (settlement): 87
Entrañosa, N.M.: 77
Escudero, José Augustín de: 93n
Española, N.M.: citizens of, 206; railroad to, 116
Española Valley: 39–41
Espinosa, Aurelio M.: 8, 10, 16n.23
Espinosa, Hipólito: 134 & n.5, 135
Esquipulas, Guat.: 223
Estancias: 34–35, 36, 44
Ethell, Ora Gjerde: 208n.19
Ethnic islands: 24n.30

Faherty, William Barnaby: 139n.9
Fairview, N.M. (Mormon village): 114
Farmers: Anglo, 114, 118; Hispano, 75–76 & n.10
Farmington, N.M.: 153
Farm Security Administration/Rehabilitation (FSA/FSR): 150
Febre (Febro), L.: 100n.4
Fences, of New Mexico: 107
Fergusson, Erna: 99
Fisher, Robert: 193n
Fitzpatrick, Thomas: 193, 194n
Florence, John: 119
Flores, Tobias: 177n.12
Floyd, Ethel L.: 187n.25
Floyd, R. T.: 187n.25
Folklore, Hispano: 9–10
Fort Cass: 139n.9
Fort Davis division: 153
Fort Marcy: 105, 110
Fort Stanton: 93
Fort Sumner: 65, 113
Fort Worth, Tex.: see Dallas–Fort Worth, Tex.
Foster, George M.: 222n
Fountain Creek: 193, 198
France, Mexico vs.: 14
Franciscans: 11, 45, 53–55, 57, 88; abuses of, 53–55; crafts taught by, 53; Hopi souls abandoned by, 54n.9; nomad Indian rejection of, 64 & n.28; return to New Mexico of, 62; in San Gabriel, N.M., 34n; withdrawal of, 57 & n.15; see also Third Order of Saint Francis

Frazer, Robert W.: 105n
Frémont, John C.: 193
Fresadas, Hispano trade in: 132
Frisbie, Parker: 164n.14
Fry (Manzano resident): 98
FSA (Farm Security Administration): 150
FSR (Farm Security Rehabilitation): 150
Fuentes, Antonio: 162n.10
Furs: see hides

Gadd, Milan W.: 208n.19
Gadsden Purchase: 6, 159n.8
Galisteo, N.M.: 38, 39, 55
Gallegos, N.M. (plaza): 80–81
Gallegos, Epifanio: 183n.17
Gallejos, Frank: 197n
Gallina, N.M.: 135n.5; and Spanish Trail, 137
Gallinas, N.M.: 79
Gallinas River: 204; Hispano settlement along, 79
Gallup, N.M.: Hispanos of, 143; Mexicans to, 163; railroad yards at, 116
Gantt, John: 139n.9
Garcia, N.M. (plaza): 81
Garcia family: 91
Gardiner, N.M.: 117n.22
Garland, Utah: 148
Garrard, Lewis H.: 107
Gauthier, José: 185 & n.23
Genízaros: 44, 55n.12, 63–64 & n.26, 68; as California migrants, 135; of San Miguel del Vado, 77
Geophagy: 223n.11
Gerhardt, Frederick: 140
German-Russians, as Colorado stoop labor: 162–63
Germans, as Homeland coal miners: 117
Gervacio Nolán Grant: 86
Gibson, Charles E., Jr.: 85n.25
Gila River: 95; Hispano sheep to, 137
Gila Valley: 95 & n.40
Gilbert, Albert: 109n.14
Gilcrease Institute: 39
Gladel division: 153
Glenn (trader/trapper): 101
Goat Hill (Pueblo [Colo.] district): 195, 196n.4, 198
Gold: in California, 4, 6, 136; Colorado, 193; of Homeland, 118
Goodnight, Charles: 113
Gordejuela, Don Juan de: 29n.6
Graham County (Ariz.): 162n.11

Grant County: cattle raising in, 113; Mexican-born of, 162n.11
Grants, N.M.: 209 & n.20
Gray Creek, Colo.: *see* San Lorenzo (plaza)
Great Depression: Hispanos after, 228; Hispanos during, 150, 154, 173, 225; Peñasco during, 189
Great Western Sugar Company: 163
Grebler, Leo: 176n
Greenleaf, Richard E.: 42
Gregg, Josiah: 13, 63n.25, 101, 107 & n.10, 215n.3, 216, 225n.14
Gritzner, Charles: 220n
Grolé, Jacques: 99
Grove, The (Pueblo [Colo.] district): 198
Grzelachowski, Alexander: 98
Guadalupe, Colo.: *see* Conejos, Colo.
Guadalupe Hidalgo, Treaty of: 124
Guadalupita Grant: 80
Gullying, in Puerco Valley: 183 & n.18
Gurulé, Jacques: *see* Grolé, Jacques
Gutiérrez, Ramón A.: 14

Haciendas: 44
Hafen, LeRoy R.: 84n.22, 134
Haggard, J. Villasana: 93n
Haley, J. Evetts: 216n.6
Hall, Wendell V.: 171n.4
Hammond, George P.: 28–29n.5
Hammond, Robert: 3
Hardscrabble, Colo.: 193, 194n
Hastings, Colo.: 143
Head, Lafayette: 84n.23
Heber, Ariz. (Mormon village): 114
Hermanes Plaza, Colo.: 86n.27
Hernández, Andrés S.: 79n.15
Hernández, Juan: 176n
Hides: Hispano clothing from, 64; Hispano trade in, 44, 45n.37, 71, 80
Hillerman, Tony: 41n.30
Hippies, of El Cerrito: 177
Hispanidad, New Mexico Hispanos and: 7
Hispano(s): 4, 7, 19–25; accomplishments of, 47; Anglo view of, 106n; assimilation of, 16, 24, 98–130, 211–12 (*see also* Anglo[s], Hispano[s] and); black, 45; Borderlands clout of, 19–23; ethnicity of, 14–19, 45; expansionism of, 70–97 (*see also* nomad Indians, Hispano encroachment on; Pueblo Indians, Hispano encroachment on); language of, 7–8 & n.9; legacy of, 217–23; Mexican heritage of, 15, 16–19, 24 & n.29; Mexican immigrants and, 7; nature of, 7–15, 24–25; origin of, 3; and pride of place, 223–26; as Roman Catholics, 129; surnames of, 8 & n.10, 9 & n.11, 38, 39 & n.28, 45n.39, 103n.8, 130; and Tejanos/Californios contrasted, 7; *see also* Comancheros; Homeland
Homeland (concept): 214
Homeland, Hispano: 49 & n, 213–32; Anglos in, 98–130 (*see also* Anglo[s], Hispano[s] and; Inland, Hispano); boundaries of, 8n.9; California-born Hispanos return to, 137; decline of, 212, 226; enlargement of, 97 (*see also* Hispano[s], expansionism of); environment of, 214–17 (*see also* Rio Abajo; Rio Arriba); heart of (*see* Inland, Hispano); heyday of, 230–32; Hispano migrations from, 23; Hispano signature on, 217–23; outlying areas of, 131–36, 137, 139–45, 147–55 (*see also* Outland, Hispano); population patterns of, 47 & n.42, 61–62 & n.22, 105 & n, 107–108 & n.12, 118–19, 124–27 & n.28, 143–44, 157–62, 165–67 & n; Spanish-speaking migrants to (*see* Mexicans); today, 232; transformation of, 209 (*see also* Anglo[s], westward thrust of; urbanization, Hispanos and); *see also* Arizona; Colorado; Inland, Hispano; Mexico; New Mexico; Outland, Hispano; Stronghold, Hispano
Homesteaders, Hispanos victimized by: 173
Hondo, N.M. (plaza): 95
Hope Decree: 171n.4
Hopi (mission): 53n.5
Hopis: 32, 36, 50 & n.2, 51, 108n.13; exempted from tribute, 53n.5; as generous hosts, 54; missionaries rejected by, 46, 54 & n.9
Hornos: 220–22
Horses: California wild, 132n.2; as Hispano gift to Indians, 64
Hot Springs, N.M.: 215
Hovey, Juan: 122n
Hovey, Oliver P.: 122n
Hovey, O. P.: 119, 122n
Howard, Donald S.: 196n.5
Hubbell, J. Felipe: 119, 122 & n
Hubbell, John Lorenzo: 92n
Huerfano River: 86
Huertado, Locario: 177n.12

Hurt, Wesley Robert, Jr.: 185n.22, 186n
Hymns, Hispano: 10

Iberia (Michener): 221n
Idaho, state of: 150
Ignacio Subagency: 67n.30
Ilfeld brothers: 110 & n.15
Illinois, state of: Anglos to New Mexico from, 103n.8; Mexican immigrants to, 164
Indian Industrial School (Santa Fe): 203
Indians: 49–69; of Arizona, 142; of Bosque Redondo, 113; christianization of, 32, 39, 53 & n.5, 58, 62; of Colorado, 61n; Mexican, 36, 45 (*see also* Aztecs; Tarascans; Tlaxcalans); Hispanos married to, 49; of New Mexico Territory, 4, 60n.21; nomad (*see* nomad Indians); Oñate and, 29 & n.5, 31; Pueblo (*see* Pueblo Indians); as Pueblo (Colo.) brides, 193 & 194n; "ration," 65; of Rayado, 80n; of Santa Ana River area, 135; of Santa Fe, 203; as Spanish slaves, 45n.37; *see also* nomad Indians; Pueblo Indians
Indies, Laws of the: 32
Inland, Hispano: 98, 118, 127, 168, 228; defined, 108, 127; Mexican Americans of, 162n.10; parameters of, 127; Stronghold to, 119
Irish, as Homeland laborers: 117
Iron, Colorado: 194, 195, 196; *see also* steel mills
Isleta (del Sur) (Pueblo village): 37 & n.21, 55, 108n.13; clergy in, 59 & n.18, 62
Isleta, N.M.: 116
Italians: as Homeland coal miners, 117; as Homeland immigrants, 118

Jacals: 71
Jaehn, Thomas: 108n.12
Jaffe, A. J.: 129
Jalisco, Mex.: 159
Japanese of Arizona, 142; as Colorado stoop labor, 162–63
Jáquez, José María: 84
Jarales, N.M.: 95
Jaraloso Canyon: 91
Jaramillo, Juan C.: 185 & n.23
Jemez (Pueblo village): 108n.13; mission at, 50n.4, 51n.5, 59 & n.18, 62
Jenkins, Myra Ellen: 56n.13, 88n.32
Jews, as New Mexico merchants: 110–12

Jicarilla, N.M.: 137n.8
Jicarilla Apache Reservation: 65, 68 & n.31
Jicarilla Apaches: Comanches vs., 62; Franciscans rejected by, 64n.28; habitat of, 63n.24
Johansen, Sigurd: 159n.9
Johnson and Koch (Santa Fe firm): 110n.15
Jones, Oakah L., Jr.: 29n.5, 37n.21, 39n.28, 75
Jordan, Terry G.: 217
Jornada del Muerto: 31
Juanita, Colo. (plaza): 88

Kansas, state of: Hispanos of, 153; Mexicans of, 167n; Oñate in, 32
Keithl["e"]y, L. J.: 101 & n, 204n
Kentucky, commonwealth of: 103n.8, 112
Kercheville, F. M.: 8
Kidnapping, of Indian/Hispano children: 63–64 & no.26, 68 (see also *genízaros*)
Kinkead, Mathew: 193n
Kiowas, Hispano-enslaved: 64
Knowlton, Clark S.: 224n.14
Kubler, George: 47, 93n
Kusz, Charles L., Jr.: 98
Kutsche, Paul: 190n.32

Labadía (Labadíe), Domingo: 100 & n.4
Labadíe (N.M. immigrant): 45n.39
Labadíe, Lorenzo R.: 122 & n
La Bajada: 37
Labor, Hispano: *see* day laborers; pastores; *peones*
La Cuesta, N.M.: as El Cerrito schoolhouse, 179n.15; founding of, 77
Lacy, James: 107n.10
La Fraqua, N.M. (plaza): 88
La Garita, N.M.: 197 & n
La Garita Creek: 85
Laguna (Pueblo village): 88 & n.32; 108 n.13
La Jara, N.M.: Mormons of, 114; and Spanish Trail, 137
La Jolla, N.M.: 41; colonists from, 80
La Joya, N.M.: 93n; Hispano reoccupation of, 92
La Junta, Colo. (plaza): 85
Lake County (Colo.): 153
LaLande, Baptiste: 100
La Liendre, N.M.: 79 & n.15
La Loma (*rancho*): 72n.5, 85

La Luz, N.M. (plaza): 95
Lamy, Jean Baptiste: 11, 12, 58, 59, 109
Landavazo family: 91, 92
Land grants: 124, 139, 153, 155; in California, 217; to Hispano settlers, 71–72 & n.4; for Hispano stockmen, 77; in Texas, 217; see also San Miguel del Vado Grant
Lanes, The (Pueblo [Colo.] district): 198
Lanstra, Heidi: 177n.11, 178n.13
Lanstra, Jack: 177n.11, 178n.13
Lantis, David William: 85n.25
La Parida, N.M. (settlement): 92, 93n
La Placita, N.M.: 93; see also El Cerrito, N.M.
La Placita de los Trujillos: see San Salvador, Calif.
La Plaza de los Leones, Colo.: 71, 72, 86; see also Walsenburg, Colo.
La Posta, Colo. (Ute community): 67n.30
La Puente, N.M. (settlement): 87
L'Archeveque, Jean: 99
Largo (plaza): 88
Larson, Richard F.: 197n
La Salle, Robert Cavelier Sieur de: 99
Las Animas, Colo.: 143
Las Animas County (Colo.): coal of, 117n.21; Indians of, 49n
Las Animas Grant: see Cornelio Vigil–Cerán St. Vrain Grant
Las Cruces, N.M.: 92; Hispanos of, 209 & n.20; Mexicans of, 159, 163, 165
Las Garritas, Colo. (settlement): 85n.25
Las Mulas, N.M.: 77
Las Palomas, N.M.: see Rio Palomas
Las Trampas, N.M.: 44, 46; colonists from, 80; founding of, 41; as Spanish buffer area, 224
Las Vegas, N.M.: Anglos of, 79n.14, 107–108, 119, 204–205, 206, 211; as colonist port, 77–79 & nn.13, 14, 15, 80, 96; founding of, 79 & n.13; Hispanos of, 204–205, 206, 208, 209 & n.20, 211; Jewish merchants of, 110–12; Mexican Americans of, 205; municipal divisions of, 204n; population patterns in, 204–205; railroad to, 79, 116 (see also East Las Vegas, N.M.); as trail town, 80, 101, 204; U.S. troops in, 105, 106n; see also East Las Vegas, N.M.
Lavalley, Colo.: see San Francisco (plaza)
La Ventana, N.M.: 181

Lead, Colorado: 193
Leadville, Colo.: 153
Lebanese, of Peñasco: 189
Lecompte, Janet: 193n
Ledoux, N.M.: see San Jose Cebolla
Lehmann, Terry Jon: 205n.16
Leonard, Olen E.: 76, 109n.14, 122, 171n.4, 173–74n.6, 174n.7, 179n.15, 223; in El Cerrito, 170n.2
Leutis (Pueblo village): 108n.13
Limestone, Colorado: 194
Limon, Colo.: 131n
Lincoln, N.M.: see La Placita, N.M.
Lincoln County (Colo.): 131n
Lincoln County (N.M.): 145
Literature, Hispano folk: 9–10 & n.12
Little Colorado River: 91
Lobato, Paulita: 80n, 139n.9
Logs, Hispano structures of: 220 & n
Lombard Village (Pueblo [Colo.] district): 198
Long-lots: 215–16, 217
Longmont, Colo.: 164n.13
Loomis, Charles P.: 76, 122, 173–74n.6, 197n, 223; in El Cerrito, 170n.2
Lordsburg, N.M.: 117n.21
Los Angeles, Calif.: 132, 154
Los Angeles County (Calif.): 135
Los Baros, Colo. (plaza): 85
Los Cerros, N.M. (village): 88
Los Luceros, N.M.: see Soledad, N.M.
Los Lunas, N.M.: 112n.16; founding of, 43 & n.33
Los Ojos, N.M. (settlement): 87
Los Pinos, N.M. (plaza): 88
Los Pinos, N.M.: 144n
Los Quelites, N.M.: 43, 88
Los Ranchos de Albuquerque: 43
Los Ranchos de Atrisco: 43
Los Ranchos de Tome: 43
Los Sauces, Colo. (plaza): 84
Los Vigiles, N.M.: 79
Louisiana, state of: French of, 228–30; long-lots of, 217
Lovato, Mel: 184n.19
Loving, Oliver: 113
Lower Eastside (Pueblo [Colo.] district): 198
Lower San Francisco Plaza, N.M.: 95
Lucero, George: 188n.28
Lucero, Josefita: 213
Lucero, José J.: 187 & n.26, 188, 189n.29
Lucero, Juan A.: 213
Lucero, Tony: 213 & n, 226

Lugo family: 135
Luis Lopez, N.M. (settlement): 93n; founding of, 92
Lumbering, in Homeland: 98, 118
Lumberton, N.M.: 144n
Luna, N.M. (Mormon village): 114

Llano Estacado: 81

McKenzie, Henry P.: 119, 122n
McKnight-James (trader/trappers): 101
McSpadden, George E.: 8n.9
McWilliams, Carey: 157n.2
Mad John (El Cerrito hippie): 177
Madrid, Colo.: 85, 87n.29
Maes, N.M.: 79
Maize, Pueblo tribute in: 35n.14
Mallet, Paul: 99
Mallet, Pierre: 99
Manassa, Colo. (Mormon village): 114
Manila (P.I.), trade between California and: 132
Manito, Hispanos as: 201
Mantas, Pueblo Indian: 35n.14, 45n.37
Manuelitas, N.M.: 79
Manzanares family: 155
Manzano, N.M.: Anglo influence in, 98, 129, 186; as colonist springboard, 96; decline of, 184–87; depopulation of, 181; establishment of, 93, 98, 99n.1
Manzano Mountains: 93, 98, 184, 186
Marmaduke, Mr.: 123n.26
Martinez, Colo. (plaza): 85
Martínez, Antonio José: 57n.15
Martínez, Jerome: 225 & n.16
Martínez, Roger: 189n.31
Maryland, state of: 103n.8
Maxwell, Lucien B.: 80n
Mazeta, Colo. (settlement): 84n.24
Mead, Margaret: 155n.25, 223
Meinig, D. W.: 47
Menard, Pierre: 80n
Mendinueta (N.M. governor): 43n.34
Mesa, The (Pueblo [Colo.] district): 198
Mesa lands, loss of El Cerrito: 171
Mescalero Apache Reservation: 68 & n.31
Mescalero Apaches: 62; reservation for, 65, 68 & n.31
Mesilla, Mex.: 159n.8
Mesilla, N.M.: 93; Mexican-born of, 159
Mesilla Valley: 93; Hispanos of, 96; Mexican-born of, 159 & n.8
Mesitas, Colo.: 84n.23

Mestizaje: 45, 69
Mestizos: 29n.7, 46n.40; as Hispanos, 24, 45; Indians and, 57n.14; of New Mexico, 4, 14, 29n.5, 35; Spaniards and, 57n.14
Metzgar, George W.: 119, 122 & n
Metzgar, Joseph V.: 17n.24
Mexican Americans: 19; assimilation of, 129; of Borderlands, 4; first, 6; Hispano marriage to, 196; Hispanos distinguished from, 13; see also Chicanos
Mexicanidad: 7
Mexican Independence Day: 3, 14n.18; Hispanos and, 13
Mexicanos: 17n.25; and mexicanos de México contrasted, 17
Mexican Revolution: 6, 7
Mexicans: of Arizona, 142; Hispano conflict with, 147, 163–64, 201; Hispano marriage with, 156, 158, 161, 167–68, 185, 201; Hispanos and, 156–68; as illegal aliens, 164 & n.14; "Northern" (see Hispano[s]); see also Mexican Americans; Mexico
Mexican War: 6
Mexico: emigrants to Homeland from, 6, 157–68; German miners in, 220; Hispano sheep trailed to, 76; independence of, 4, 100 (see also Mexican Independence Day); log construction in, 220; New Mexico and, 15, 224; post–Mexican War losses of, 6; see also California; Chihuahua; Durango, Mex.; New Mexico; Sonora; Texas
México (Mexico City), Mex.: Tenochtitlán becomes, 27
Meyer, Howard: 184n.20
Michener, James: 221n
Miera, N.M. (plaza): 81
Miera, Theresa: 189n.31
Mignon, Jean: 100n.4
Military, New Mexico "invaded" by U.S.: 105–108
Mimbres, N.M.: 95
Mimbres River: 95
Mines: Arizona, 175; Hispanos as workers in, 117, 140, 143, 150; of Homeland, 118; Mexican workers in Colorado, 163; see also coal; copper; gold; iron; lead; quartz; silver
Miñon, Juan: see Mignon, Jean
Miscegenation, New World: 4; see also mestizos; mulattos; Pueblo Indians, Hispano intermarriage with

Missionaries: indifference toward Pueblos of, 57–59; Mormon, 114; Roman Catholic, 32, 35, 36, 46, 50–55 (see also Franciscans; missions)

Missions: 50–53 & n.5, 55, 88 & n.32; layout of Homeland, 50; secularization of, 55n.10; see also conventos; Franciscans; missionaries

Missouri, state of: Anglos to New Mexico from, 103n.8; trade between New Mexico and, 100, 137

Missouri River: 100

Moctezuma II: 26, 27

Mogote, Colo.: 84n.23

Montana, state of: 150

Monte Vista, Colo.: 148

Montezuma, N.M.: see Hot Springs, N.M.

Monticello, Utah: 148

Moorhead, Max L.: 101n

Mora, N.M.: 80, 81, 96

Mora County: cattle-raising in, 113; Indians of, 49n

Moradas: 222, 223

Mora Valley: 80

Morfi (priest): 43n.34, 46n.40

Mormons: 114–16; as Hispano employers, 148; Hispanos and, 91, 92, 116; as missionaries, 114; as Pueblo (Colo.) brides, 194n; as village folk, 220

Moses, N.M. (plaza): 81

Mosquero, N.M. (plaza): 80

Mountainair, N.M.: 186, 187

Mud, ingestion of miraculous: 222, 223n.11

Mulattos: 36; as Hispanos, 45 (see also Hispano[s], black); as New Mexico colonists, 4, 28, 29 & n.5

Muleshoe, Tex.: 3 & n

Murphy, Lawrence R.: 105n

Mutiny, in Oñate forces: 29

Nacimiento, N.M. (village): 43, 88, 91

Nacogdoches, Tex.: 220n; Tejanos of, 17

Nuhuatl (lang.): 57

Nambe (Pueblo village): 108n.13; Hispano infiltration of, 55

National Youth Administration (NYA): 150

Navajo, N.M. (Mormon Village): 116n

Navajo County: 92n

Navajo Reservation: 68n.31; see also Navajos, on reservations

Navajos: 49 & n, 62–63; Colorado, 67n.30; Franciscans and, 64n.28, 88 & n.32; Hispanos and, 64, 67, 88; missionaries among, 114 (see also Navajos, Franciscans and); raids by, 63 & n.25, 88, 185 & n.22; on reservations, 65, 67–68 & n.31 (see also Navajo Reservation)

Nevada, state of: 150

New Albuquerque, N.M.: Anglos of, 119, 211; black laborers of, 117n.22; blossoming of, 205; Hispanos of, 143, 211; Mexican Americans of, 211; railroad yards at, 116

New Deal: Hispano migrant labor and, 150; welfare programs of, 173

New Las Vegas: see East Las Vegas, N.M.

New Mexico, state of: Anglos of (see Homeland, Anglos of); boundaries of Spanish, 36; conquest of, 157; French traders into, 99–100 & n.4; Hispanos of (see Hispano[s]; Homeland); importance to Spain of, 46–47; Indians of, 4 (see also nomad Indians; Pueblo Indians); Mexican suzerainty over, 15, 224; "penitente-ism" of, 12; peoples of, 4; settlement of, 3, 4, 6, 16, 45–46, 157 (see also Hispano[s]; Homeland); Spanish reconquest of, 54, 68, 157; Spanish suzerainty over, 14, 224; trade between Mexico and, 44–45; U.S. acquisition of, 6, 16, 225 (see also Guadalupe Hidalgo, Treaty of); see also Abiquiu; Albuquerque; Belen; Borderlands; Cebolleta; Chamisal; El Cerrito; Hispano[s]; Homeland; Las Vegas, N.M.; Las Trampas; Manzano; nomad Indians; Oñate, Juan de; Peñasco; Pueblo Indians; Raton; Rio Abajo; Rio Arriba; Rio Grande; Roswell; San Juan; San Luis; San Miguel; Santa Cruz; Santa Fe; Socorro; Taos

New San Marcial, N.M.: Hispanos of, 143; railroad yards at, 116

New Socorro, N.M.: Hispanos of, 143; railroad at, 116

New Spain: population patterns in, 47 & n.42; Spaniards born in (see creoles); Spanish immigration to, 26–27 & n.2; see also Mexico; New Mexico

New York, state of: 103n.8

Nieto, Okla. (plaza): 81

Nine Mile Bottom: 86

Nomad Indians: 4, 24, 27, 41, 49 & n, 62–69, 224; Hispano intermarriage with, 65, 67, 68; Hispanos and, 63–64 & n.28, 87, 92, 108, 226; lore of, 64; pacification of, 65, 69, 76, 96; *ranchos* attacked by, 44; of Red River area, 82; Taos attacked by, 42; today, 67–68, 69; trade goods of, 44; *see also* Apaches; Cheyennes; Comanches; Dacotas; *genízaros*; Kiowas; Navajos; Pawnees; Pueblo Indians; Utes
Nostrand, Richard L.: 123, 198
Nueva Vizcaya, Mex.: 38
Nuevo León, Mex.: 159
Nutritas, N.M. (settlement): 87
NYA (National Youth Administration): 150

Ocate, N.M.: 206
Ohio, state of: 103n.8
Ojito, N.M.: 187–88n.27, 188n.28
Ojo Caliente, N.M.: 41, 44, 46, 84 & n.22; as Spanish buffer area, 224
Ojo Caliente Valley: 41
Ojo Sarco, N.M.: 189n.31
Okeh: *see* San Juan, N.M.
Oklahoma, state of: Hispano herdsmen into, 81; Hispanos of, 22, 82n.20, 144, 145
Old Las Vegas: *see* Las Vegas, N.M.
Oñate, Cristóbal de: 26
Oñate, Juan de: 7, 50, 220, 221n; background of, 26, 29n.5; death of, 26n; New Mexican campaign of, 27–32, 34; party led by, 27–31, 53; resignation of, 32 & n; self-flagellation of, 11
Open range, New Mexican: 113
Optic, East Las Vegas (N.M.): 205n.15
Orange County (Calif.): 135
Ornstein, Jacob: 8n.9
Oso, Colo. (plaza): 86n.27
Otero County: Hispanos of, 145; Mexican-born of, 162n.11
Our Lady of Guadalupe: 13
Outland, Hispano: 145–47, 153, 154–55, 163, 228; Hispanos of, 168; Mexican Americans of, 162n.10

Pagosa Springs, Colo.: 153
Palo Duro Canyon: 81
Paraje: *see* La Parida
Parish, William J.: 110
Park View, N.M.: *see* Los Ojos

Partidos: 73 & n.6, 224
Paso del Norte, Mex.: 35, 45n.39, 46; as bone of contention, 38; as *partido* center, 224; priests at, 46n.40
Pastores: 81
Patria, Homeland as: 225–26
Patrias chicas: see villages, Hispano
Patrones: 73
Pawnees, Hispano-enslaved: 64
Pecos (Indians): 32, 77
Pecos (Pueblo village): 51n.5; Hispano encroachment on, 56n.13
Pecos, N.M.: 55
Pecos, Tex.: 153, 165
Pecos River: 170; Hispano settlement on, 77
Pecos Valley: 71, 113, 171, 181; Hispanos in, 95
Pecos Valley Bosque Redondo Reservation: 65
Peninsulares: Hispanos as, 45, 46n.40; as New Mexico colonists, 4, 28–29 & nn.5, 6, 35
Penitentes: 11–13 & nn.16, 17, 222; Lamy vs., 109; of San Luis, 184; today, 13; see also *santos*
Penjamo Village (Pueblo [Colo.] district): 198
Pennsylvania, commonwealth of: Amish of, 181n; Anglos to New Mexico from, 103n.8, 112
Peñasco, N.M.: Anglos of, 189; colonists from, 80; flourishing of, 188–90; founding of, 41; population patterns of, 181; *see also* Copper Hill Mining Camp
Peones: 73
Peralta, Pedro de: 32, 34n
Perea, Francisco: 123n.26
Perrigo, Lynn I.: 77n.12, 79n.15, 176n
Petaca, N.M.: 84
Picacho, N.M. (plaza): 95
Picuris (Pueblo village): 55, 108n.13; mission at, 51n.5, 59
Piedra Pintada, Colo. (settlement): 85n.25
Piedra River: 88
Pike, Zebulon: 100, 123n.26
Pino, Justo Pastor: 156
Pino, Nicolás de Jesús: 156, 158
Pino, Pedro Bautista: 55n.12, 93n, 156, 224
Piro (Indians): 54
Piro (lang.): 50n.2
Placitas: 35, 80, 81

Placitas, N.M.: 213 & n
Plaza de Missouri, La: *see* San Jose, N.M., Lincoln-Chaves County border (plaza)
Plaza Rota, N.M.: 84n.22
Plazas: 44, 72 & n.5, 80–95, 220; see also *placitas*
Poblazon, N.M. (village): 88
Pochos, Hispanos as: 163, 164n.13
Poetry, Hispano protest: 10
Pojoaque (Pueblo village): 108n.13; Hispano infiltration of, 55
Pojoaque, N.M.: 55
Poles, as Homeland coal miners: 117
Portales, N.M.: 153
Portugal, Oñate soldiers from: 29nn.5, 6
Post offices, Hispano village: 73
Presidio(s): 37; of Santa Fe, 38–39 & n.27
Priests, circuit-riding: 73; see also Franciscans
Protestants, Anglo: 112; see also Mormons
Provincias Internas: 223
Pryor, N.M.: 117n.22
Pueblo, Colo.: 143; Anglos of, 193 & n, 194n, 211; barrios of, 195, 196; El Cerrito natives to, 175, 192, 196–202; founding of, 193; Hispanos of, 119, 142, 153, 192–202, 206, 208, 209 & n.20, 211; Mexican Americans of, 196, 198, 211; Mexicans of, 163, 164 & n.13, 165; minority districts of, 198 (*see also* Pueblo [Colo.], barrios of); railroad to, 117n.22; see also Salt Creek Village
Pueblo Indians: 4, 37, 50–62, 108n.13, 224; christianized, 39, 53 & n.5, 58, 62; crafts of, 54; decline of, 19, 38, 55–57 & n.14, 59; defection to Anglos of, 59; distribution of, 36; Franciscans and, 45; Hispano enslavement of, 64n.26; Hispano intermarriage with, 49 & n.1, 57 & n.14, 62 & n.23, 68–69; Hispanos as seen by, 14; Hispanos and, 42, 46 & n.40, 48, 55–57, 59–60, 68, 69; language of, 50 & n.2, 58n.16; native religion of, 53–54; nomad Indian attacks on, 59, 63; Oñate and, 31, 32; as original Mexicans, 15; on reservations, 69; of Rio Grande Valley, 34n; Spanish vs., 226, 232; today, 62, 68, 69; trade goods of, 45n.37; tribute ex-

acted from, 53 & n.5; U.S. Congress and, 59 & n.19; villages of, 37, 38, 50, 54, 55 & n.12, 56–57, 58 & n.16, 59 & nn.18, 19, 60–62, 223, 226; wheat cultivated by, 221; see also Acoma; encomiendas: Galisteo; Hopis; Lagunas; Pecos (Indians); Piro (Indians); Southern Tiwa; Taos Indians; Tewas; Zuñis
Pueblo Quemado: 41 & n.30
Pueblo Revolt: 9n.10, 35, 36n.17, 37, 38, 51, 54, 63; missionary casualties of, 36n.17, 54n.7
Pueblo Viejo, Ariz.: 95 & n.40; Hispanos of, 145; as Mormon town, 114
Puela (word): 8 & n.9
Puerco River: *see* Rio Puerco
Puerco Valley: 43, 181; erosion in, 183 & n.18; overstocking of, 217; settlement of, 46, 88
Puerta del Cajon, La, Calif.: 134
Puertecito, N.M.: 77
Puerto de Luna East (West), N.M.: 95
Puerto Ricans: assimilation of continental, 129; Hispanos and, 8
Punta de Agua Creek: 81
Purcell, James: 100
Purgatoire River: 85, 86

Quartz, mining of: 118, 143
Querac (mission): 51n.5
Querétaro, Mex.: 159
Questa, N.M.: *see* San Antonio, N.M.
Quintana, Agneda: 169 & n
Quintana, Anastacio: 192n
Quintana, Eduardo E.: 198n.9
Quintana, Eliodoro: 197n
Quintana, Elvira Corrales: 198n.9
Quintana, Estefanita: 192 & n
Quintana, Felipa: 192n
Quintana, Florencio: 169 & n, 178, 198, 200nn.9, 10
Quintana, Helen Baca: 200nn.9, 10
Quintana, Jesucita Gutiérrez: 198n.9
Quintana, Linda: *see* Aragón, Linda Quintana
Quintana, Perfecto: 198n.9
Quintana, Repita Chacón: 200n.9
Quintana, Rick: 200n.9
Quintana family: 155, 192, 196, 197

Rael, Juan B.: 10
Railroads: through Colorado, 196; Hispano employees of, 116, 143, 150, 171; through Homeland, 116–18 (*see*

also East Las Vegas, N.M.; New Albuquerque, N.M.); Mexican-born employees of, 161; *see also* AT&SF (Atchison, Topeka, and Santa Fe Railroad); D&RG (Denver and Rio Grande Railroad)
Ramah, N.M. (Mormon village): 68n, 114, 116n
Ramírez, Francisco P.: 16
Ranch, The: *see* El Cerrito, N.M.
Ranchers: *see* stockmen
Ranchos: 43–44, 72 & n.5
Ranchos de los Mestas, N.M. (settlement): 183
Ranchos de Taos, N.M.: 206
Rascón, Gertrudis: 156
Rascón, José María: 156
Rascón, María Juana: 156
Raton, N.M.: Anglos of, 119; coal of, 117, 143; Colorado-born Hispanos of, 144n; railroad yards at, 116
Raton Pass: 85, 100, 117; railroad through, 116, 117n.22
Rawlins, Wyo.: 150
Rayado, N.M.: context of founding of, 193n; founding of, 80 & n; U.S. troops in, 105 & n
Raza, La: 19
Read, Alexander: 119, 122n
Red River: 81; Hispano settlements on, 82
Reeve, Frank D.: 98–99n.1
Reid, Hugo: 13n.16
Reservations, Indian: 65, 67–68 & n.31, 69; *see also* Indians, "ration"
Retablos: 11
Ribera: *see* San Miguel (N.M.), railroad to
Rincon, N.M.: 116
Rincones, Colo.: 84 & n.23
Rio Abajo: 37, 42, 43, 103, 224; Hispano villages of, 73; nature of, 214, 216; settlement of, 46; see also *rivajeños*
Rio Arriba: 37, 42, 103, 140, 148, 224; crops of, 215 & n.3; Hispanos of, 215; nature of, 214, 215, 216, 217; villages of, 62n.23; see also *arribeños*
Rio Arriba County: 49n
Rio Arriba Pueblo grants: 59
Rio Bonito: 95; Hispano settlements on, 93
Río Bravo del Norte: *see* Rio Grande
Río Conchos: 31
Rio Conejos: *see* Conejos River

Rio de las Animas Perdidas en Purgatorio, El: *see* Purgatoire River
Rio del Norte: *see* Rio Grande
Rio Grande: 3, 36; Hispano settlements along, 37–43, 46, 47, 92, 93n; Oñate to, 31; *see also* Española Valley; Rio Abajo; Rio Arriba
Rio Hondo: 93–95; irrigationists' drying up of, 95n.38
Rio Palomas, N.M. (settlement): 92, 93n
Rio Puerco: 183; capriciousness of, 90; settlements along, 43n.33; *see also* Puerco Valley
Rio San Antonio: 85n.24
Rivajeños: 216 & n.6
Riverside County (Calif.): 135
Robb, John David: 10
Robinson, James D.: 108n.12
Rociada, N.M.: 79
Rock Springs, Wyo.: 150n.19, 153
Rodríguez, Sylvia: 19n.27
Roman Catholic Church: Hispanos and, 211, 222–23; Indian converts to, 32, 39, 53 & n.5, 58, 62; in New Mexico, 109 (*see also* Franciscans; Lamy, Jean Baptiste); secular clergy of (see *curas*); *see also* missionaries; missions; Penitentes; priests
Roofs, Anglo influence on Hispano dwelling: 123–24
Rosa, N.M. (plaza): 88
Rosa, José Antonio Martínez de la: 135n.6
Roswell, N.M.: 95, 153; Mexicans of, 163, 165; railroad yards of, 117n.21
Rowland, John: 101n
Rowland, Thomas: 101 & n
Rowland-Workman party: 135 & n.6
Rubi, Lena: 92n
Rudulph, Eugenio: 119, 122n
Rudulph, Wilnor: 122n
Ruidoso, N.M. (plaza): 95
Rush Creek, Colo.: 131n
Ruxton, George Frederick: 123n.26, 215

Sabinal, N.M.: 92; founding of, 43 & n.33; *genízaros* of, 44; as Spanish buffer area, 224
Sabinoso, N.M. (plaza): 80
Sachs, Moses: 112n.16
Sacramento Mountains: 95
Sáenz, Josefa: 156
Sage, Rufus B.: 139n.9
Saguache, Colo.: 85 & n.25
Saguache Creek: 85

Saint Catherine School (Santa Fe): 59, 62, 203
Saint Charles Mesa: 198
Saint Charles River: 86
Saint James Parish (La.): 230
Saint Johns, Ariz.: 92n; see San Juan, Ariz.
Saint Louis College/University, Hispano students at: 137, 139n.9
Saints, Hispano place-names commemorating: 222
Saint Vrain, Cerán: 101–103
Salado: see Salt Creek Village
Salazar, Catalina de: 26 & n
Salazar, Juan de Frías: 28n
Saloons, Hispano village: 73
Salpointe, Jean Baptiste (John Baptist): 12–13, 59, 91n.35
Salt Creek Village, Colo.: 143, 195, 196 & n.4, 198
Salt Lake City, Utah: 148
Samora, Julian: 197n
San Acacio, Colo. (plaza): 82
San Antonio, N.M.: 85n.24, 93n; establishment of, 80, 82, 92
San Antonio, Tex.: layout of, 32n.12; long-lots of, 217; Mexican labor recruited in, 163
San Augustin, N.M.: 79
San Bernardino County (Calif.): 135
Sanborn, Colo.: 131n
Sánchez, George I.: 164n.13
Sánchez, Ramón: 189n.29
Sánchez, Robert: 62
San Cristobal, N.M.: 82
Sanders Division (Pueblo [Colo.] district): 198
Sandia (Pueblo village): 35, 108n.13; Hispanos in, 60
San Diego, Calif.: 132
Sandoval, David A.: 139n.9
San Elizario (garrison): 105n
San Felipe (Pueblo village): 108n.13
San Fernando, N.M. (village): 88
Sanford, Colo. (Mormon village): 114
San Francisco, Colo. (plaza): 82–84 & n.24, 86; establishment of, 95
San Francisco Bay: 154
San Francisco River: 95
San Gabriel, Calif.: 13n.16
San Gabriel, N.M.: abandonment of, 34 & n; convento of, 50n.4; as Oñate base, 31, 32
San Gabriel del Yungue: 221n
San Geronimo, N.M.: 79

Sangre de Cristo Grant: 82
Sangre de Cristo Mountains: 80, 86, 215
San Ignacio, N.M.: 79
San Ildefonso (Pueblo village): 108n.13; Catholic Church in, 50n.4, 59, 109n.14; Hispano infiltration of, 55
San Joaquin Valley: 154
San Jose, Ariz.: 95, 114
San Jose, Colo. (plaza): 84
San Jose, N.M., Lincoln-Chaves County border (plaza): 93–95 & n.38, 96
San Jose, N.M., San Miguel County (plaza): 77
San José Cebolla, N.M.: 70
San Juan (Pueblo village): 58n.16, 108n.13; Catholic clergy at, 53n.5, 59, 62, 109n.14; Hispano infiltration of, 41, 55, 60; as Oñate base, 31–32
San Juan, Ariz.: 91 & n.35, 92, 114, 145
San Juan, Colo.: 84
San Juan, N.M. (plaza): 95
San Juan County: 49n
San Juan River: 87, 132n.3; Hispano settlers on, 87–88
San Juan Valley: 87
San Lazaro, N.M.: 50–51n.4
San Lorenzo, Colo. (plaza): 85, 95
San Lorenzo, N.M. (plaza): 95
San Luis, Colo.: 82, 84 & n.22
San Luis, N.M.: 181–84, 190
San Luis Potosí, Mex.: 159
San Luis Valley: 84, 85; Hispano stoop labor in, 147, 148; Mormons of, 114
San Marcial, N.M. (settlement): 93n; establishment of, 92; see also New San Marcial, N.M.
San Mateo, N.M.: 88
San Miguel, Colo.: 85
San Miguel [del Vado], N.M.: 77 & n.11, 79; as colonist springboard, 96; community "offspring" of, 71, 77 & n.12; houses of, 123n.26; Las Vegas (N.M.) and, 79 & n.14; as Missouri Trail town, 101; as plaza community, 72 & n.5; railroad to, 79; roofs of, 123
San Miguel County (Colo.): Gladel division of, 153
San Miguel County (N.M.): 208; cattle raising in, 113; colonization of, 79 & n.15
San Miguel del Vado Grant: 124, 171 & n.4
San Miguel del Vado Grant Commission: 177n.12

San Pablo, Colo. (plaza): 82
San Patricio, N.M. (plaza): 95
San Pedro, Colo. (plaza): 82
San Rafael, Colo. (plaza): 84n.23
San Salvador, Calif.: 135–36 & n, 139, 154; Anglos of, 136
Santa Ana (Pueblo village): 108n.13
Santa Ana Grant: 59
Santa Ana River: 135
Santa Barbara, Calif.: 17
Santa Bárbara, Mex.: 27
Santa Barbara, N.M.: see Peñasco
Santa Clara (Pueblo mission): 108n.13; Hispano infiltration of, 55; mission at, 51–52n.5
Santa Cruz, N.M.: 41, 47; as colonist springboard, 96; establishment of, 39 & n.28; as partido center, 224; population patterns in, 46n.40; and Spanish Trail, 137
Santa Cruz Valley: 41
Santa Fe, Archdiocese of: 61–62 & n.22
Santa Fe, N.M.: 36 & n.17, 37, 223, 226; Anglos of, 99–100, 103 & n.8, 107, 108n.12, 110, 119–22, 132, 159, 203n.11, 206, 211; Catholic clergy in, 109 (see also Lamy, Jean Baptiste); as colonist springboard, 96; founding of, 32–34 & n; Galisteo occupation of, 38; at Hispano "core," 47; Hispanos of, 43 & n.33, 47, 202–204, 206, 209 & n.20, 211, 230; houses of, 123 & n.26; Indian majority of, 54 & n.8; Indian schools of, 59, 62, 65; Jewish merchants of, 110–12; Mexican Americans of, 203, 211; Mexicans of, 158, 159, 162, 165, 167; mission at, 50 & n.4; municipal divisions of, 203n.13; as partido center, 224; population patterns in, 46n.40, 202–204; presidio of, 45n.39; railroad to, 116; as trail town, 100–101, 132, 137
Santa Fe River: 32
Santa Fe Trail: 100–101, 204; Cimarron Division of, 117
Santa Gertrudis: see Mora, N.M.
Santa Rita, N.M.: 143
Santa Rosa, N.M.: 181
Santeros: 10; Benedict XIV vs., 11n.13
Santo Domingo (Pueblo village): 108n.13; mission at, 50, 59; Oñate in, 31
Santos: 10–11 & n.13, 12; see also bultos; retablos
Santuario de Chimayo: 222, 223

Sapello, N.M.: 79
Sarapes: 123 & n.26; Hispano trade in, 132
Sauer, Carl O.: 27n.3
Savoya, N.M. (Mormon village): 116n
Sawmills, Hispanos as workers in: 140, 142, 143
Scholes, France: 53n.5, 64
Schools: discrimination in, 116, 201; of El Cerrito, 122–23, 170, 171n.3, 174–75 & n.8, 179n.3; Hispano village, 73; nomad Indians in Hispano, 65; of Peñasco, 189–90; for Pueblo Indians, 59, 60–61; rancho, 72; of Santa Fe (see Indian Industrial School; Saint Catherine School); of Taos County, 189 & n.31
Scotsmen, as Homeland coal miners: 117
Scythe, and sickle contrasted: 222n
Segregation: in New Mexico communities, 205, 211; in New Mexico schools, 116, 201; in Pueblo (Colo.), 201, 211
Segundo, Colo.: see Los Baros (plaza)
Seligman, Simon: 110n.15
Seligman family: 110
Semple, Ellen Churchill: 24n.30
Sena, Joe: 200n.9
Sena, Mary Quintana: 200n.9
Sena, Néstor: 122, 170n.2
Sena, N.M.: see Puerticito, N.M.
Senecu (mission): 37 & n.21, 53n.5
Servietta (settlement): 84n.24
Servín, Manuel Patricio: 14
Seville (city), as New World embarcation point: 27
Seville, province of: 27n.2; Penitente rites in, 12
Sevilleta (settlement): see La Joya, N.M.
Sheep, Hispano: cattle vs., 81, 113–14; as currency, 73; as gift to Indians, 64; proliferation of, 75 & n.8; trailing of, 76, 80–82, 87, 91, 137
Sheepmen, Hispano: and Anglo cattlemen, 113–14
Shinkle, James D.: 95n.38
Shrines, Homeland: 222
Sickle, and scythe contrasted: 222n
Sierra County: cattle raising in, 113; Mexican-born of, 162n.11
Silk, Hispano trade in Chinese: 132
Silver: of Homeland, 118, 193; New World, 27

Silver City, N.M.: 153; Mexicans of, 163, 165
Silver Creek, Ariz.: 91, 114
Simmons, Marc: 24n.29, 43, 59n.19, 72n.5, 215n.3, 221–22n
Simpson, George: 193n
Sixteenth of September celebration: 15
Slaves, Hispano trade in: 44–45 & n.37
Smith (Peñasco merchant): 189n.29
Smith, Emilia Gallegos: 84n.22
Socorro (del Sur) (Pueblo village): 37 & n.21, 108n.13; mission at, 51n.5
Socorro, N.M.: Anglos of, 107; as borderland, 8n.9, 162; as colonist springboard, 96; Hispano reoccupation of, 92, 93n; houses of, 123; U.S. troops in, 105; see also New Socorro, N.M.
Socorro County: cattle raising in, 113; Mexican-born of, 162n.11
Socorro Valley: 92, 96
Soil Conservation Service, U.S.: 183
Soledad, N.M.: 41
Solomon, Isador E.: 95n.40
Solomonville, Ariz.: see Pueblo Viejo
Sonoma, Calif.: 132
Sonora, Mex.: 159, 161
Sotelo, Juan de: 29n.6
South Americans, assimilation of U.S.–resident: 130
Southern Pacific Railroad: 116
Southern Tiwa: 54
Southern Ute Reservation: 65, 67n.30, 68n.31; Hispano encroachment on, 88
South Platte River: 137, 139n.9
South Platte Valley: 147, 162
Spain: emigrants to Homeland from, 157, 158, 162; hornos of, 221 & n; natives of, 4; pride of place in, 223
Spanish (lang.), of Homeland: 57
Spanish-Americans, Hispanos as: 16 & nn.22, 23, 17–19, 23
Spanish Trail: 137; opening of, 132
Spencer, Joseph E.: 17
Spicer, Edward H.: 55 nn.10, 12
Spiegelberg, Elias: 110 & n.15
Spiegelberg, Levi: 110 & n.15
Spiegelberg, Solomon Jacob: 110 & n.15
Sporleder, Louis B.: 76, 86n.27, 216
Springer, N.M.: 80
Springerville, Ariz.: 91, 114
Squatters' rights, Hispano assertion of: 59–60
Staab family: 110 & n.15
Steel mills, Homeland: 143, 173, 194, 195, 196; see also iron

Stockmen, Hispano: 75–76, 170–71, 174, 179–81; expansionism of, 71–72, 76–97; see also cattlemen, Anglo; sheepmen, Hispano
Stronghold, Hispano: 96–97, 119, 168, 228; Anglicization of, 127; blacks of, 117; defined, 108; into Inland, 98, 119; Mexican Americans of, 162n.10; today, 129
Sugar beets: of Colorado, 147, 148, 162–63, 173, 196, 208, 225; of Utah, 148
Superstitions, Hispano: 9–10
Surumatos, Mexicans as: 163, 164n.13, 201
Swadesh, Frances Leon: 16n.22, 67n.30, 84n.23, 85n.25, 87
Syrians, of Manzano: 186

Tabet, Tenos: 98, 186
Tafoya (Chihuahua governor): 9n.10
Tajique (mission): 53n.5
Tamaulipas, Mex.: 161
Tano (lang.): 50n.2
Taos (Pueblo village): 55, 56n.13, 108n.13; durability of, 59; mission at, 51n.5
Taos, N.M.: 44, 55, 56n.13; Anglos of, 101, 103 & n.8, 108, 206; Apache mission near, 64n.28; community "offspring" of, 71; as expansionist base, 80, 82, 96; Hispano community of, 42, 206; as Indian village, 41–42 (see also Taos [Pueblo village]); Martínez ministry in, 57n.15; as plaza community, 72 & n.5; rebellion in, 139n.9; stockmen from, 81; as trapper headquarters, 101–103, U.S. troops in, 105, 106n; see also Don Fernando de Taos Grant; Ranchos de Taos; Taos (Pueblo village); Taos Indians
Taos Indians: 42, 82
Tapia, Abel: 200n.9
Tapia, Josie Martínez: 200n.9
Tapia family: 196
Tarascans: 27
Tascosa, Tex.: 81
Taylor, Carl C.: 170n.2
Taylor, Rafelita Lovato: 184n.19
Taylor, Paul S.: 164n.13
Teachers, Anglo: 112; see also schools
Tecolote, N.M.: 77 & n.12
Tejanos: 4, 17, 19, 20, 22, 23; climate of, 214; dissolution of, 6; Hispanos

vs., 10; revolt of, 6; as "Spanish-Americans," 16; use of long-lots by, 217

Tejanos, Los (play): 10

Tennessee, state of: 103n.8

Tenochtitlán: *see* México (Mexico City)

Tequesquite, Colo. (plaza): 86n.27

Tequesquite, N.M. (plaza): 80

Tesuque (Pueblo village): 108n.13; Hispano infiltration of, 55

Tewa (lang.): 31, 50n.2

Tewar, Hispano incursions among: 55

Texas, state of: Anglo "invasion" of, 4, 6; cattle to New Mexico from, 113; Hispanos in, 22, 81–82 & n.20, 144, 145, 153, 173; independence of, 6; Mexican Americans to New Mexico from, 157, 158, 162 & n.11; Mexicans of, 6, 164, 165, 167n, 168; settlement of, 4; U.S. annexation of, 6; villages of, 217; *see also* San Antonio; Tejanos

Third Order of Saint Francis: 11–12; *see also* Franciscans

Tierra Amarilla, N.M.: *see* Abiquiu Indian agency; Nutritas (settlement)

Tierra Amarilla Grant: 87

Tierra bendita: 222, 223n.11

Tijeras, Colo. (plaza): 85

Tijera Town: *see* San Luis, N.M.

Tinnie, N.M.: *see* Analla (plaza)

Tiwa (lang.): 50n.2

Tjarks, Alicia V.: 46n.40

Tlaxcalans, of Santa Fe: 54n.8

Tolosa, Isabel de: 26

Tome, N.M.: founding of, 43 & n.33; Mexican-born residents of, 158; as Spanish buffer area, 224; *see also* Los Ranchos de Tome

Torreónes: 72

Torres, Annabelle: 189n.31

Torres, Audry: 197n

Torres, Macario: 200nn.9, 10

Torres, Rose Sandoval: 200nn. 9, 10

Torres family: 196

Tortillas: 215

Trade, Homeland: Anglo domination of, 79n.14; between Hispanos and nomad Indians, 44; New Mexican/Mexican, 44–45, 70–71, 79n.14; *see also* caravans, Hispano trading; Santa Fe Trail; Spanish Trail

Tramperos Creek: 81

Transhumance: 215

Trappers: 101–103, 106

Trementina, N.M. (plaza): 80

Trinchera, Colo. (plaza): 86

Trinchera Pass: 80

Trinidad, Colo.: Anglos of, 114, 119; as bicultural community, 85; black laborers of, 117n.22; clergy in, 109n.14; coal of, 117; as colonist springboard, 96; founding of, 86; Hispanos of, 143, 150n.19; as trail town, 80

Trovadores, Hispano: 10

Truchas, N.M.: 44, 46, 214; founding of, 41 & n.30

Trujillo, Atanacio: 84n.23

Trujillo, Lorenzo: 135n.6

Trujillo, Mose: 197n

Trujillo, N.M.: 79, 88

Trulio, Beverly: 107n.10

Tucumcari, N.M.: 3n

Tulare Basin: 154

Tule, Ariz.: 91

Tulles, John R.: 93n, 108n.12, 184, 185n.21

Union County: 81n.17

United States, Mexican War gains of: 6

Urbanization, Hispanos and: 191–212, 220, 228

Utah, state of: Hispanos of, 148, 153; Mexicans of, 167; railroad through, 148; Spanish Trail through, 132 & n.3; sugar beets of, 148

Ute Creek: 81

Ute Mountain Reservation: 67n.30, 68n.31

Utes: 63; Colorado, 68; Hispano-enslaved, 64; Hispano spouses of, 65, 67n.30; raids of, 63; on reservations, 65, 68 & n.31 (*see also* Ute Mountain Reservation)

Vaca, Manuel: 135n.6

Vacaville, Calif.: 135

Valdez, N.M.: *see* San Antonio, N.M.

Vallecitos, N.M.: 84 & n.23

Vallejos family: 86, 96

Valverde, N.M. (settlement): 92, 93n

Vargas, Diego de: 34n, 35 & n.14, 38

Velarde, N.M.: *see* La Jolla, N.M.

Velásquez, Melitón: 84n.23

Vendido, Hispanos as: 201

Vera Cruz, Mex.: 159

Vermont, state of: 103n.8

Vernon, Ariz.: 91 & n.34

Vigil, Colo. (plaza): 85

Vigil, Donaciano: 216n.6

Vigil, Francisco Estev.: 135n.6
Vigil and St. Vrain Grant: 72n.4
Vigil family: 196
Villages, Hispano: 73–75, 77–81, 85, 88–97, 217–20; depopulation of, 169–91; "offspring," 71; social strata of, 73; see also *plazas*; Pueblo Indians, villages of
Villagra, Gaspar Pérez de: 11
Villanueva, N.M.: *see* La Cuesta, N.M.
Villarreal, Guadalupe Salas: 164n.13
Villas, Hispano: *see* Albuquerque, N.M.; Santa Cruz, N.M.; Santa Fe, N.M.
Virginia, commonwealth of: 103n.8
Vogt, Evon Z.: 13

Walsenburg, Colo.: 71, 216; coal of, 117; Hispanos of, 143, 145, 150n.19; *see also* La Plaza de los Leones
Walsen Mines, blacks of: 117n.22
Warner, J. J.: 132n.2
Weber, David J.: 101n, 224 & n.14
Weidle, Catherine: 139n.9
Weigle, Marta: 11, 12
Welshmen, as Homeland coal miners: 117
Weston, Colo.: *see* La Junta (plaza)
Westphall, Victor: 124
Westside (Pueblo [Colo.] district): 198
Wheat, as Hispano crop: 215 & n.3, 221–22
Whelan, Harold A.: 136n
White Oaks, N.M.: 143
Widdison, Jerold Gwayn: 91n.33, 183n.18
Wilder, Mitchell A.: 11n.13
Williams, Ariz.: 142, 143

Wilson, Frank E.: 176n
Wilson, John P.: 93n
Winberry, John J.: 220 & n
Wine, of Paso del Norte: 44, 45
Wingate, N.M. (Mormon village): 114
Winnie, William W., Jr.: 9n.10, 154
Winslow, Ariz.: 116, 143
Women: Anglo affinity for Hispano, 107 & n.10; Hispano village, 73; New Spain and Spanish, 29n.7
Work Projects Administration (WPA): 150
World War I, Mexican northward migration after: 164
World War II: Hispanos after, 150n.21; Hispanos during, 150–51, 153–54, 175 & n.9
WPA (Work Projects Administration): 150
Wyoming, state of: Hispanos of, 148–49 & n.19, 153; Mexicans of, 167n

Ysleta: *see* Isleta (del Sur) (Pueblo village)
Yuman (lang.): 64
Yungue: *see* San Gabriel, N.M.

Zacatecas, Mex.: 26, 27; emigrants to New Mexico from, 159, 161
Zapato, N.M.: 114
Zia (Pueblo village): 59
Zunser, Helen: 215
Zuñi (Pueblo village): 32, 36, 46, 108n.13; mission at, 53n.5
Zuñis: 50 & n.2, 51, 63; exempted from tribute, 53n.5; missionaries among, 114
Zurumate (Mexican hacienda): 164n.13